EIGHTH EDITION

Lab Manual and Workbook for Physical Anthropology

Diane L. France

Colorado State University

CENGAGE
Learning·

Australia • Brazil • Mexico • Singapore • United Kingdom • United States

Lab Manual and Workbook for Physical Anthropology, **Eighth Edition**
Diane L. France

Product Director: Marta Lee-Perriard

Product Manager: Elizabeth Beiting-Lipps

Content Developer/CDM: Melissa Sacco, Lumina Datamatics, Inc.

Product Assistant: Allison Balchunas

Marketing Manager: Eric Wagner

Media Developer: Trudy Brown

Content Project Manager: Rita Jaramillo

Art Director: Michael Cook

Manufacturing Planner: Judy Inouye

Production Service/Compositor: Lori Hazzard, MPS Limited

IP Analyst: Jennifer Bowes

IP Project Manager: Reba Frederics

Copy Editor: Heather McElwain

Text Designer: Diane Beasley

Cover Designer: Michael Cook

Cover Image: iStockPhoto.com/Alan Phillips; Pasieka/Science Photo Library/Getty Images

Unless otherwise noted, all photos and art are owned by Diane France.

For product information and technology assistance, contact us at **Cengage Learning Customer & Sales Support, 1-800-354-9706.**

For permission to use material from this text or product, submit all requests online at **www.cengage.com/permissions.** Further permissions questions can be e-mailed to **permissionrequest@cengage.com.**

Library of Congress Control Number: 2016961092

Student Edition:
ISBN: 978-1-305-25904-1

Cengage Learning
20 Channel Center Street
Boston, MA 02210
USA

Cengage Learning is a leading provider of customized learning solutions with employees residing in nearly 40 different countries and sales in more than 125 countries around the world. Find your local representative at **www.cengage.com**

Cengage Learning products are represented in Canada by Nelson Education, Ltd.

To learn more about Cengage Learning Solutions, visit **www.cengage.com**

Purchase any of our products at your local college store or at our preferred online store **www.cengagebrain.com**

Printed in the United States of America
Print Number: 05   Print Year: 2020

Brief Contents

Contents

Preface

My goal in writing this text is, and always has been, to provide a foundation of information about physical anthropology and to encourage independent thinking and research. When it is so easy to obtain information (true or not) from the Internet with a few keystrokes, it is more important than ever to have the tools to evaluate whether that information has come from a reliable source, and not just from an opinion page. Education in any discipline and at any level should always stress the importance of critical thinking, and to that end, I expect students to think critically about everything in this book.

The cover of this book reflects the increasing role of genetics in the study of evolution, the relationships of extant primates, and the understanding of humans in general. Current knowledge about the role of genetics in interpreting our world, as well as the research into actually modeling our world through gene therapy and genetically modified organisms (GMOs), is woven through the chapters.

Physical anthropology is a fascinating discipline. It encompasses information about humans and their place in nature more completely than any other field. Within this subject, we explore human biology, how humans have evolved, and how and why we know that we are still evolving. We study our primate cousins in their natural (and unfortunately shrinking) environments, and we compare ourselves to other primate and nonprimate animals. Within the field of physical anthropology, it is possible to explore (and celebrate) the differences and similarities of all modern humans. We examine the human skeleton to discover the wide range of natural variation and learn how to provide clues about the identity of unidentified remains in the medicolegal system. How could anyone not be interested in such a vast and exciting field?

NEW TO THIS EDITION

The eighth edition has been completely updated to reflect recent research. Illustrations and photographs have been improved throughout, and more have been added, and for the first time, the chapters have been professionally edited. Specific changes made for the eighth edition include the following:

- Real-world controversies and concerns, such as GMOs, the role of gene therapy in medicine, and the presence of Neanderthal genes in modern populations, are present in many chapters.

- Chapters 1 and 2 include up-to-date information about some of the contributions of the Human Genome Project to the understanding of human genetics. After delving into the basics as well as current research, students are asked to evaluate whether society should accept GMOs and whether it is beneficial or even ethical to actually manipulate a person's DNA. Evolution in general, and human evolution in particular, are introduced.

- Chapter 3 still explores human osteology with the addition of side identification and some tips on what bone fragments can tell us about the individual and the bone. More photographs and drawings with labels are particularly useful in those laboratories without adequate osteological material.

- Chapter 4 includes more detail about the growth and development of dentition and bone, with added photographs and updated drawings. The chicken bone exercise gives students the chance to dissect a fried chicken leg, an exercise designed to let them investigate the morphology and mechanics of something very familiar to them, while learning about muscles and bone.

- Chapter 5 explores the theory and practice of species identification and classification and adds the advances in genetics to the concept of species in primates.

- Chapter 6 discusses biomechanical properties of morphological differences in primates and in quadrupedal mammals, leading to later chapters about how primates move and live. This chapter, as well as the following two explore the physical and social characteristics of primates and provide background for the primate fossil record.

- Chapters 7 and 8 still investigate living primate morphology and behavior, with updated photographs.

- Chapters 9 through 12 probe the primate fossil record from before the Paleocene era to more recent prehistory. More illustrations and charts facilitate comparisons between the species, and very recent discoveries have been included. Questions and exercises promote discussion about what these fossil discoveries really mean about how humans and our primate cousins evolved. Recent discoveries of Neanderthal DNA in some modern humans shed a fascinating light on our current variability.

- The remaining chapters further explore modern humans. How do bones respond to disease, genetic conditions, trauma, and intentional modification? How do we use the differences between human populations, age-related changes, and sexual dimorphism to help us determine who an individual was and what happened to that individual at about the time of death? Forensic anthropology is a hot topic today and is covered in some detail in the final chapter.

ACKNOWLEDGMENTS

As with previous editions of this book, many individuals reviewed the seventh edition and suggested changes and additions for the eighth edition. It was apparent that the reviewers thoroughly read the seventh edition, for their suggestions were very helpful. Also, the book has been heavily edited and corrected as per their suggestions.

I also thank the following for generously providing photographs and illustrations: A. Blackstone; Jayne Bellavia; Kathryn Born; Wayne Bryant; the Human Genome Project and developers of genome.gov; M. Y. Iscan; Demris Lee generously provided a valuable section on DNA identification; J. R. Napier; National Museum of Health and Medicine; National Museums of Kenya Casting Program; National Museum of Natural History and the Smithsonian Institution; D. Pilbeam; Plenum Press; W. Sacco; Joseph Henry Press; Shane Walker; D. Ubelaker; Tim White; and Jay Villemarette from Skulls Unlimited provided photographs and access to skeletal materials in his wonderful museum in Oklahoma City.

David Hunt from the Smithsonian Institution was very generous with his time in helping to find subjects for photography for this and previous editions. I also thank Franklin Damann and Brian Spatola from the National Museum of Health and Medicine for providing access to specimens for photography. I also thank them for their help in obtaining what I needed for this book.

I thank all of the people who worked on this book from Cengage Learning and Lumina Datamatics, Inc., including, but not limited to, Elizabeth Beiting-Lipps, Melissa Sacco, Lori Hazzard, Rita Jaramillo, Heather McElwain, and Julia Giannotti.

As always, my husband Art Abplanalp, Jr., was patient and kind through many long days and nights of research, writing, and editing. He is wonderful.

A NOTE ABOUT THE FOSSIL CAST PHOTOGRAPHS

Many of the illustrations of fossil primates and hominins in this book are photographs of casts. The National Museums of Kenya Casting Program, the University of Pennsylvania Casting Program, the Wenner-Gren Foundation, and the Institute of Human Origins manufactured these casts directly from the original fossils. It is important to understand that these casting programs are assuming all of the risk to the original fossils. It is equally important to understand that a mold made directly from an original specimen will yield the most accurate casts and therefore the most useful casts for instruction.

Money received from the sale of casts produced by the National Museums of Kenya funds research and supports those individuals who are working in the museum. Without that support, the research into our past will suffer greatly. I encourage instructors to purchase casts from those institutions that make molds directly from the originals.

The Scientific Method

1. What is the scientific method?

2. How does the scientific method differ from the belief in intentional causality?

3. Is science just another belief system?

4. How do you set up a scientific experiment?

There are basically two philosophies in understanding the universe and everything in it, although some people combine bits of these philosophies to describe their own belief systems. Those philosophies can be described as "intentional causality" and "natural causality."

Intentional causality (*teleology*) is the belief that everything in the universe is here for a reason and that reason existed before the event or object or individual existed. The modern form of that assertion is contained within the beliefs of intelligent design, which states that the universe and all contained within it are under the intelligent direction of a higher power and that an undirected process such as natural selection cannot explain the final design of living beings or the reason they exist in the first place. In this philosophical model, all change in the world is directed to an end designated by a higher power.

The scientific method (the philosophy followed in this book) does not assume that change is a means to an end or that the end result is designated by a higher power. It is a *process* of testing hypotheses and theories with certain assumptions as a background. Science assumes that there is a *natural* causality and that events, living organisms, and so on, do not appear without something preceding them (also there because of natural causality). Natural causality assumes that change is not directed to a final form or purpose. For every effect there was, and is, a natural (not a supernatural) cause.

Further, there is an assumption in science of *uniformitarianism,* or that the same natural processes operate now as they have in the past, and that the same laws of, for example, physics and chemistry apply everywhere and have for all time. Therefore, hypotheses can be tested because the basic laws that govern them exist everywhere and throughout time.

The scientific method also assumes a high level of *transparency* in reports and publications. This is necessary for the process of testing because if researchers do not know the methods and materials used in an experiment they cannot test the results and conclusions.

EXPERIMENTAL DESIGN: HYPOTHESES AND THEORIES

How many times have you heard "The theory of evolution is just that . . . a *theory*"? This at least implies that it is probably not true, that it is based on false logic, cannot be proven, or perhaps cannot even be adequately described or tested. In fact, a theory is a specific, important step in the scientific method, but it is not the first step.

Before an idea can be said to be a theory, it has to start out as a hypothesis and as a part of the design of an experiment. A hypothesis must be stated in a way in which it can be tested, and it must be stated in such a way that it has the possibility of being proven incorrect. Hypotheses are not stated as a question, but as a statement with an explanation following it (it states what the experimenter thinks will occur). Hypotheses are usually written in the "if–then form" such as "*if* I add fertilizer to one set of geraniums, *then* they will grow bigger than the geraniums to which no fertilizer is added."

A theory is a hypothesis that has been repeatedly tested and the tests have failed to disprove the hypothesis underlying that theory. However, even after a hypothesis has been tested to reach the theory stage, a theory is still testable. A theory is generally recognized as the simplest, most parsimonious explanation (sometimes described as Occam's razor) for a phenomenon, a class of phenomena, or the underlying reality that explains phenomena. It is based on observations that have been tested. These observations are things that you and everyone with normal senses can see or measure with or without aids, and something that can be documented.

If a theory that explains a phenomenon has been observed for a long enough period of time and has not been disproved, it is usually called a "law" or a fact. For example, gravity is explained by the fact (repeatedly tested) that objects with mass attract one another. This is a very simple explanation that can be tested and can be observed. Because this idea has reached the point in scientific testing that it is no longer a hypothesis, it is a theory. In fact, the theories concerning gravity have been tested so many times under so many different controlled conditions that instead of saying that it is the theory of gravity, most people refer to it as the law of gravity. It is generally recognized as a fact. We all understand that gravity exists and affects our lives in countless ways (from how much we weigh to how much fuel rockets must use to escape the Earth's attraction).

When designing an experiment that will test the hypothesis, it is important to set up a simple hypothesis based on few variables because it can be more easily tested and is potentially falsifiable. (Naturally, if the hypothesis is tested by experimental design and *not* falsified, it does not always mean that the hypothesis is true!) **Independent variables** are the subject of the hypothesis, the experiment, and the variables, and are not controlled. The **dependent variables** are those that can be controlled in the experimental design. Experiments are designed to test cause and effect, so a dependent variable is changed to record the effect of the change on an independent variable. When conducting a scientific study, only one variable at a time should be tested. This is only practical—if you change too many variables in one experiment, you don't know which variable is the explanation for the end result.

Independent variables: The subject of the hypothesis and are not controlled.

Dependent variables: Those that can be controlled in the experiment.

EVOLUTION AND SCIENCE

This book discusses evolution on two levels: evolution on a small scale, as can be observed by everyone in everyday life, and evolution as a series of hypotheses and theories used to describe the changes in organisms (in this book we discuss primates) over time.

Evolution on a small scale is simply a change in gene or allele frequencies from one generation to the next. As we shall discuss in the first two chapters of this book, when organisms multiply through the combination of separate genes from two parents, the offspring have frequencies of alleles that differ from the parents. Farmers take advantage of this when they take a cow that produces a high yield of milk and breed that cow more frequently than a cow that produces less milk. Over a few generations of directed breeding, the farmer's herd as a whole likely produces more milk. This change in gene frequency favoring high milk production over generations is evolutionary change.

The other, larger aspect of evolution discussed in this book concerns how humans and our primate relatives came to be who we are today. This part of evolution contains hypotheses and theories about specifically which fossil led to other fossils. Those theories are based, in large part, on the principle of uniformitarianism (as discussed earlier); that is, the same basic laws in nature that occurred 20 million years ago occur today. Some of the evidence for the theories of evolution include where the fossil was discovered in the world. What other fossils have come from that geologic layer and geographical location? Are there associated floral, faunal, or artifacts that might give clues about its age? What is the morphology of the fossil? How is that morphology similar to modern animals, and what does that tell us about how that animal moved or what it ate?

When researchers at the National Museums of Kenya discover a new fossil, they cannot "test" it by modifying a dependent variable to observe the changes in the independent variable. It is still part of the scientific method, however, because of its transparency and the ability of other researchers to observe the scientific evidence and challenge the conclusions.

Science is a method of critical thinking and testing. To that end, please critically evaluate everything in this book. Do not accept any of this on faith.

The scientific publication should fulfill one of the primary assumptions of the scientific method: transparency.

THE SCIENTIFIC PUBLICATION

A few different types of papers are published in scientific journals. Some publications report the results of a scientific experiment, and those papers closely follow the format and content of the experiment (as shown in Table I.1). Other publications may describe an instructive forensic case, an interesting new fossil hominin find, or a new technique in genetic identification, but they usually still describe research related to the topic, the description of the discovery or finding, and the author's conclusions. In these scientific reports, and indeed in any scientific experiment, accurate description is vital! In fact, in many reports and publications, a *diagnosis* of, for example, a pathological condition in a skeleton is less important than a precise *description* of the condition. Why? It comes back to the scientific method—it is important to provide enough information so that other researchers are able to take that information and test it, and perhaps develop an alternative diagnosis.

As stated earlier, the publication that reports on the results of a scientific experiment closely follows the format of the scientific inquiry.

TABLE I.1 Comparisons between the Scientific Method and the Scientific Publication	
Scientific Method	**Scientific Publication**
1. Ask a question.	1. Abstract and Introduction
2. Do background research: Has this question (or one like it) already been researched?	2. Background
3. Construct your hypothesis.	3. State the hypothesis (usually stated in the abstract, but can be stated at this point).
4. Test your hypothesis with an experiment.	4. Materials and Methods
5. Analyze your data and come up with results.	5. State your results.
6. Draw a conclusion about the hypothesis.	6. Draw a conclusion about the hypothesis.
7. Communicate your results and conclusion.	7. Publications and talks communicate your results.

The outline of a scientific publication is as follows:

- **Abstract**: A short synopsis of the question and a brief summary of the results.
- **Introduction:** A basic description of the problem and a statement of the hypothesis.
- **Background:** A history of studies related to the hypothesis and the results of those studies.
- **Materials and Methods:** What did you observe or measure (bones, teeth, fossils, primates, and so on), and how did you measure or observe your subjects?
- **Results**: What were the outcomes of the measurements, observations, statistical tests, and so on?
- **Discussion**: Were you able to falsify your hypothesis? What are your conclusions about the results? In what way(s) would you want to change your research design, materials, methods, and so on, to retest the same or modified hypothesis?
- **References:** List previous work or personal correspondence incorporated in your research.

EXERCISE I.1 **NAME** _____ **SECTION** _____ **DATE** _____

1. Jean-Baptiste Lamarck (1744–1829), a French scientist who believed in evolution, is known for Lamarckism, or inheritance through acquired characteristics. He argued that environmental influences could put pressure on animals, making them use some characteristics more and some less, and that the changes acquired by the parents would be passed to the next generations. A common example of this theory is that giraffes could actually grow longer necks by straining to get to higher and higher branches for food, and that the offspring of these longer-necked giraffes would have longer necks at birth.

    a. Is this argument at the level of a hypothesis or is it a theory? Why?

    b. How would you set up an experiment to test Lamarck's beliefs?

    c. What would be your dependent variables?

    d. What would be your independent variable?

2. Design an experiment to test which company sells the best tomato seeds (the first thing you must do is to define "best"). Be specific when answering the following questions:

    a. What is your hypothesis?

    b. What are your dependent variables?

    c. What is your independent variable?

3. Is anecdotal evidence the same as scientific evidence? Why or why not?

CHAPTER 1

Cellular Genetics

OBJECTIVES

1. What is DNA (deoxyribonucleic acid)?

2. How can we use DNA to show evolutionary relationships between species (discussed in more detail in Chapter 2)?

3. How can DNA be used to solve a crime?

4. Are scientists about to create a genetically engineered human?

The study of genetics is growing and changing at a dizzying speed, particularly after the completion in 2003 of the **Human Genome Project** (HGP), which mapped over 20,000 genes of humans. Scientists are now mapping the genomes of humans in various parts of the world, and are using knowledge about what genes or combinations of genes actually do in the body to research medical advances against disease and genetic conditions. Spin-off projects from the HGP are mapping the DNA of Neanderthals to see how they might be related to modern people (more about that in Chapter 12), and of microbes in the human body to research how they influence our biology and even behavior. To explore this project further, visit http://web.ornl.gov/sci/techresources/Human_Genome/index.shtml.

But before we delve into the incredible advances in genetics, we must first explore the structures of the cell that incorporate DNA into their structure and function.

CELL BIOLOGY

Although DNA is important in all living organisms, we are primarily interested in cells with a nucleus, which include most of the cells of a multicelled (**eukaryotic**) organism. In contrast, single-celled

FIGURE 1.1 Structures of a typical cell.

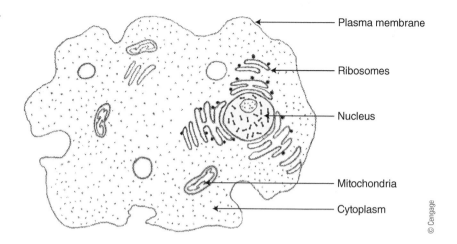

Plasma membrane

Ribosomes

Nucleus

Mitochondria

Cytoplasm

© Cengage

(**prokaryotic**) organisms are those without a discrete nucleus (for example, bacteria). Although we will be primarily interested in structures and events and within the nucleus of the cell, some features of the cell and the organelles (small structures within the cell with specific functions) are also important. These include the following (see Figure 1.1):

- **Plasma membrane:** The outer surface of the cell that protects the cell from the extracellular environment, and that is selectively permeable so as to allow some materials into the cell but keep others out.

- **Cytoplasm:** The fluid within the cell.

- **Mitochondria:** Organelles responsible for the manufacture of energy within the cell. Different cell types have different numbers of mitochondria, depending upon their function. They are located outside of the nucleus, and, interestingly for our discussions, they have their own genome (mitochondrial DNA). As we shall see, nuclear DNA is contributed by the parents to the offspring, but mitochondrial DNA is only contributed by the mother.

- **Ribosomes:** Organelles made up of ribosomal RNA (ribonucleic acid) responsible for the translation of the DNA code within the nucleus into specific proteins. As will be discussed when we explore protein synthesis, **messenger RNA** (mRNA) is transcribed from a section of DNA within the nucleus and it takes that protein code to the ribosomes. **Transfer RNA** (tRNA) recognizes that code and transfers appropriate amino acids to the appropriate location on the mRNA chain.

Messenger RNA: RNA molecules that take information from the DNA within the nucleus to ribosomes outside of the nucleus.

Transfer RNA: RNA molecules that recognize the DNA code on messenger RNA and transfer amino acids to the appropriate location on the mRNA chain.

WITHIN THE NUCLEUS

The nucleus contains **chromosomes**, each of which consists of a series of DNA molecules strung together in long spirals of double strands (called a double helix, which might be visualized as sort of a spiral staircase) (see Figure 1.2a-e). Each strand (or **chromatid**) of DNA is composed of smaller molecules (**nucleotides**), each of which is made of one of four chemical bases: **adenine (A), guanine (G), cytosine (C),** or **thymine (T)** held together with a sugar (deoxyribose) and a phosphate compound (see Figures 1.2e and 1.3). A single strand of DNA is held to the other strand in the double helix by hydrogen bonds (like rungs in a ladder), but note in the diagrams that the molecular shape of the bases are such that adenine can only bind to thymine and cytosine can only bind to guanine. They can be connected in no other way within the nucleus (we will discuss an exception to this rule when the code is carried outside of the nucleus, but within the nucleus, A binds with T and C binds with G).

There are two types of chromosomes in a normal cell: **Autosomes** are the chromosomes that carry DNA, which codes for all genetically determined characteristics except for the determination of the sex of the individual. **Sex chromosomes** (X and Y) determine the sex of the individual (although the presence or absence of only the Y chromosome actually determines sex).

Chromosome number varies by species. Most cells in a fruit fly have 8 chromosomes; there are 40 chromosomes in a house mouse, 24 in a tomato, and so on. Every normal human cell that contains a nucleus (except for sperm and ova, which will be explained later) contains 46 chromosomes, which carry all of the genetic information for that cell and for the organism. These 46 chromosomes consist of 23 pairs; one of each pair is from the mother and one from the father. These are termed **homologous chromosomes**, meaning that they each carry genetic information for the same trait at the same location (although they can carry different information for that trait). DNA codes on chromosomes that carry information for the same trait are called alleles. For example, a particular location (**locus**) on each homologous chromosome codes for the condition of earlobe attachment, but one chromosome may carry the genetic code for attached earlobes, and the other chromosome may carry the code for free earlobes. Also, information for a single trait may be carried on multiple chromosomes. We will discuss this further when we talk about specific genetic traits.

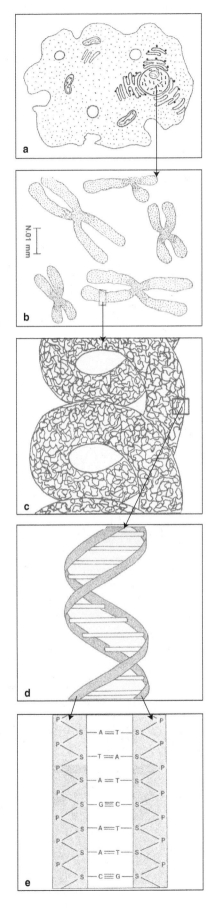

FIGURE 1.2 (a) A generalized cell. Arrow from nucleus: (b) chromosomes; (c) close-up of chromosome; (d) coiled DNA strand; (e) close-up of single DNA strand showing the base, sugar, and phosphate components of a nucleotide.

Strand 1   Strand 2

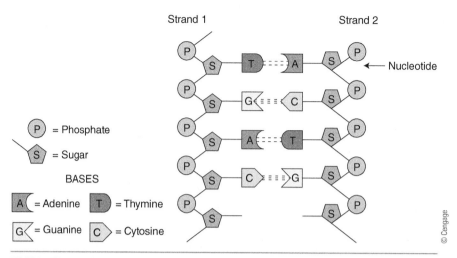

FIGURE 1.3 Nucleotides in a DNA double helix.

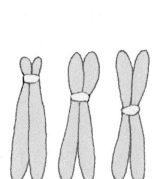

FIGURE 1.4 Positions of a centromere.

Telocentric (left): Centromere at extreme end.

Acrocentric (middle): Centromere off center.

Metacentric (right): Centromere in center.

FIGURE 1.5 Normal human male karyotype. *Courtesy: National Human Genome Research Institute*

We can look microscopically at the individual chromosomes and match them with their homologues with a **karyotype** (several sites online allow you to create a karyotype). A karyotype is the summary of the chromosomes within a nucleus and is often viewed as an image with the paired chromosomes lined up according to the position of the **centromere** (the place where two sister chromatids are joined together; see Figure 1.4) and by size (though to truly be able to recognize the homologues so that they may be paired, a dye is often used to create banding patterns within the chromosomes).

Notice on the karyotype shown in Figure 1.5 that there are 22 pairs of autosomes and two sex chromosomes. In this illustration

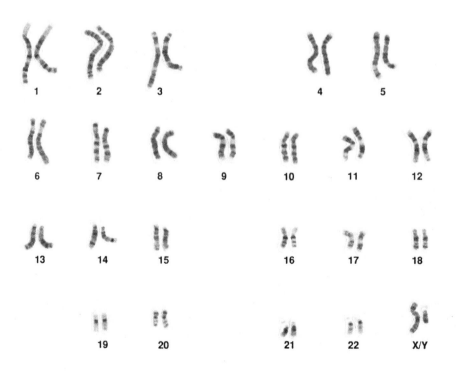

there is one X and one Y chromosome, so this karyotype is from a normal male. Karyotyping can also assist in demonstrating abnormal genetic sequences, as we will discuss.

NUCLEAR DNA REPLICATION

DNA often has to make copies of itself in whole (during cell replication) or in part (in making proteins outside of the nucleus). The specific processes of cell division and protein synthesis will be discussed later, but this is an appropriate location to explore the basic process common to all DNA replication. When DNA replicates or when a portion of DNA code is needed for protein synthesis, the hydrogen bonds binding the two strands of DNA are broken by an **enzyme** (**polymerase** and other enzymes control different portions of the replication sequence), and the strands essentially "unzip." These hydrogen bonds are shown as double or triple lines in Figure 1.3. The bases (A, T, C, G) on the single DNA strand attract the bases on free nucleotides within the fluid of the nucleus. Those free nucleotides attach themselves to the appropriate loci of the original (now unzipped) DNA chain (see Figure 1.6). Just as in the original DNA chains, adenine can only attach itself to thymine, and cytosine can only attach itself to guanine. Each original single strand of DNA has now paired with a new strand of DNA (these are called **chromatids**), and there are twice as many DNA strands in the nucleus. At this point in humans, there are now copies of 46 chromosomes, or 92 chromatids. The cell can now divide, with each new cell receiving one of the two copies. As will be discussed later, this process is important in many practical applications involving DNA (such as DNA typing).

Enzyme: A protein that accelerates a specific chemical reaction in a living system.

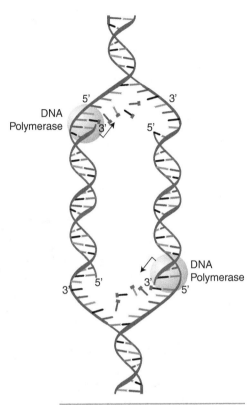

FIGURE 1.6 DNA replication. *Courtesy: National Human Genome Research Institute*

TERMINOLOGY

Allele: Alternative forms of a gene. For example, if the genotype of an individual is Pp for the trait of PTC tasting (see page 38 in Chapter 2), it contains two alleles determining this trait: P and p, one allele for PTC tasting, one for nontasting.

Autosomes: Chromosomes that carry DNA for all characteristics except for the sex of the individual.

Bases: Part of a nucleotide held together with a sugar and a phosphate compound. The bases make up the DNA and RNA chains. DNA bases are adenine, guanine, cytosine, and thymine. RNA bases are adenine, guanine, cytosine, and uracil.

Centromere: Where two sister chromatids are joined.

Chromatid: One of two identical copies of DNA comprising a replicated chromosome.

Codominant alleles: Alleles that, when paired in an organism, are both expressed.

continues

Cytoplasm: The fluid within the cell.

Dominant allele: An allele that is phenotypically expressed in the heterozygote and that prevents the expression of the recessive allele (that is, masks recessive alleles phenotypically). A dominant allele is written in uppercase letters.

Enzyme: Protein that acts as a catalyst for chemical reactions.

Eukaryote: An organism whose cells contain organelles and a nucleus enclosed by a membrane.

Gene: That section of DNA that defines the specific code for a series of amino acids making up a protein or a part of a protein.

Gene pool: The total complement of genes in a population.

Genome: A complete set of chromosomes (and genes).

Genotype: All of the genetic information contained in an organism.

Heterozygote: An organism with unlike members of any given pair or series of alleles at a particular locus. Consequently, this individual produces more than one type of gamete (for example, Aa or Bb).

Homologous chromosomes: Carry genetic information for the same trait at the same location.

Homozygote: An organism whose chromosomes carry identical members of a given pair of alleles. The gametes are, therefore, all alike with respect to this locus. For example, a gamete with the genotypes AA or BB or aa carries only one type of allele for each locus.

Karyotype: The summary of the chromosomes within a nucleus often viewed as an image.

Meiosis: A process of cell replication and division that produces gametes, each with half of the complement of DNA.

Mitochondria: Organelles within the cytoplasm responsible for manufacturing energy within the cell.

Mitosis: Process of cell replication and division in which two "daughter" cells are produced with a full complement of genetic information.

Nucleotide: The molecules that make up strands of nucleic acids like DNA (deoxyribonucleic acid). They are attached to the bases adenine, thymine, cytosine, and guanine (and uracil in RNA).

Phenotype: Characteristic (or combination of characteristics) of an individual visually observed or discernible by other means; for example, tallness in garden peas or color blindness or blood type in humans. Individuals of the same phenotype appear alike but they may have different genotypes.

Plasma membrane: Outer surface of the cell.

Polymerase: An enzyme that assembles long chains of nucleic acids. DNA polymerase assembles strands of DNA.

Prokaryote: A single-celled organism (for example, bacteria).

Recessive allele: An allele that is not expressed when paired with a dominant allele. A recessive allele is written in lowercase letters.

Ribosomes: Organelles made of ribosomal RNA (ribonucleic acid) responsible for protein synthesis.

Sex chromosomes: Determine the sex of the individual.

Trait: A distinguishing characteristic or quality of a phenotype (for example, hair color, blood type, eye color, and so on).

MITOSIS

When a cell divides, the DNA must make full copies of itself so that each new cell receives a full complement of the genetic code.

Mitosis is a process of cell replication and division in which two daughter cells, each with a full complement (46 chromosomes in 23 pairs in humans) of genetic information, are produced from a parent cell with a full complement of genetic information as described in the preceding section on "Nuclear DNA Replication." If there are no mutations, the cells from this division carry genetic information identical to that of the parent cell. Most of the cells in the body replicate throughout life by this process. Because of this process, bones grow in a developing child and skin heals itself after a cut.

We will not be concerned with describing in detail the different phases of mitosis (interphase, prophase, metaphase, anaphase, and telophase) or meiosis in this book, as the individual phases are not as important in this level of discussion as is the knowledge of the outcome.

As cell division proceeds, the chromatids line up along the "equator" of the nucleus, and then separate as cell division occurs. As the cell divides, the chromatids move away from each other, each to a different resultant cell, which now contains 46 chromosomes, still in 23 pairs. For a schematic diagram, see Figure 1.7a.

REMEMBER: In mitosis the cells resulting from cell division carry exactly the same genetic information as the parent cell (as long as there are no mutations).

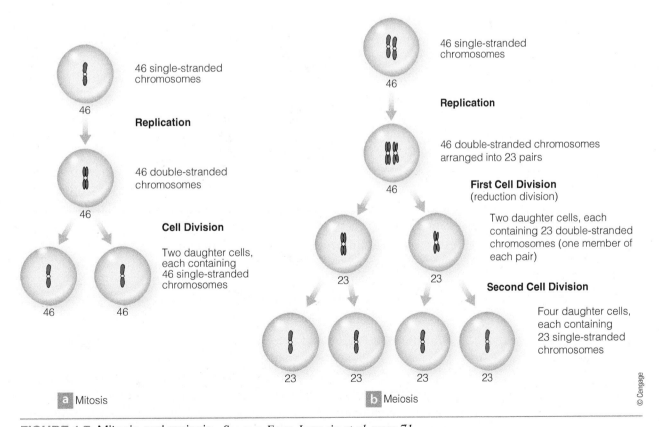

FIGURE 1.7 Mitosis and meiosis. *Source: From Jurmain et al. page 71*

MEIOSIS

Gamete: Sex cells (sperm or ova) that contain half of the number of chromosomes of the adult of that species.

Certain cells participate in the reproduction of the individual by a process of **meiosis,** which creates sex cells, called **gametes** (sperm or ova). Meiosis is the method by which sexually reproducing organisms transfer genetic information through generations; it is therefore important in our discussions of evolution.

The first cell division in meiosis undergoes chromosomal duplication in a manner different from that in mitosis, but it still results in twice the number of chromosomes of a normal cell. After duplication, each set of paired homologous chromosomes (each with two chromatids) lines up along the equator of the nucleus (this is the point in time at which crossing over or recombination can occur, a process that will be discussed in the following section). As the cell undergoes the first division, each member of a paired homologue segregates (separates) into its own daughter cell. After the first division, then, each daughter cell contains one of the homologous chromosomes, but each of these has two chromatids. Each of the daughter cells, in addition, contains only half of the genetic information that had been contained in the parent cell; hence, this first division is also called reduction division.

The two daughter cells next undergo a second mitosis-like division in which the two chromatids of each of the 23 chromosomes separate into two daughter cells. At the end of this division, each of four gametes, or sex cells, contains one copy of one chromosome from the original pair. In other words, each still contains half of the genetic information originally contained within the parent cell, and contains only one copy of each of 23 chromosomes (see Figure 1.7b).

This sequence in meiosis is typical of spermatogenesis, in that for each meiotic cell division, four sperm are formed. During the first division of oogenesis in the female, however, only one viable, functional cell is produced, and that cell in turn produces only one viable, functional cell after the second division. The other nonviable cells are called polar bodies and give up their cytoplasm (future nutrition for the fertilized zygote) to the one viable cell. The end result of oogenesis, then, is one gamete, the egg, which still has only half of the genetic information of the parent cell (as in spermatogenesis), but which is very much larger than a sperm cell. After fertilization, the nucleus of the egg contains half of its genetic information for any trait (except for sex-linked traits) from the father and half from the mother. Each half is in the form of one of the homologous chromosomes.

REMEMBER: In meiosis each daughter cell carries half of the genetic information of the parent cell.

Why must gametes contain only half of the genetic information of a regular body cell? During fertilization of the egg by the sperm, the sperm injects its nuclear genetic information into the egg. If the gametes contained a full complement of DNA, then the resulting cell would contain a "double dose" of DNA, which in most cases is lethal.

CONSIDER THIS

Sometimes chromosomes fail to separate appropriately during meiosis and that causes problems due to an abnormal number of chromosomes in the fetus. This **nondisjunction** can result in only one of a pair of chromosomes (called **monosomy**) or three chromosomes (**trisomy**):

- Trisomy 21 (sometimes called Down syndrome) is caused when the fetus receives three copies of chromosome 21.

- Monosomy X (Turner's syndrome) occurs in females with only one X chromosome. Most females with monosomy X die before birth, but if they survive, they are sterile and usually have skeletal deformities and heart and kidney problems.

- Trisomy X occurs in females with an extra X chromosome, though they often appear relatively normal. Males who inherit an extra X chromosome (Klinefelter's syndrome) sometimes show some breast development and reduced testicular development by puberty. They exhibit reduced fertility and sometimes mental retardation.

- Trisomy 13 (Patau syndrome) have an extra chromosome 13, which causes severe skeletal and organ problems. They have profound mental retardation and usually die at a relatively early age.

NAME _____ SECTION _____ DATE _____

Cells and Chromosomes

1. The following sequence of bases is found on one strand of DNA. What is the sequence of bases of the other DNA strand?

   A A C G T T C C G

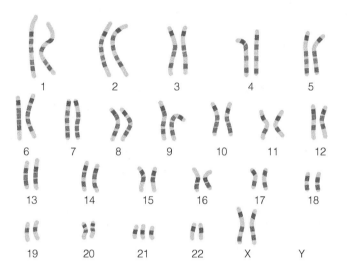

FIGURE 1.8 Karyotype for Question 2.
Courtesy: National Human Genome Research Institute

2. Figure 1.5 illustrates the karyotype of a normal human male. In Figure 1.8, identify the autosomes and the sex chromosomes.

   a. Is this a male or a female?

   b. This is an abnormal genetic sequence. What is abnormal about it?

   c. Can you diagnose the syndrome?

FIGURE 1.9 Karyotype for Question 3.
Courtesy: National Human Genome
Research Institute

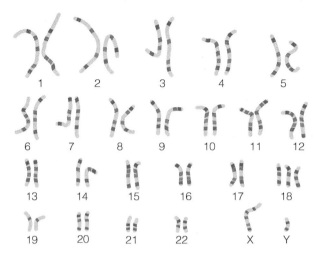

3. Figure 1.9 is also an abnormal karyotype.

   a. Is this a male or a female?

   b. What is abnormal about this sequence?

   c. Research this abnormality on the Internet and identify the syndrome as well as its consequences.

PROTEIN SYNTHESIS

The DNA in the nucleus of the cell is responsible for more than cell replication in mitosis and gamete formation in meiosis. It is also responsible for providing the blueprint for protein synthesis, which actually occurs outside the cell in small organelles called **ribosomes**. Proteins can be typical structural proteins, enzymes, and hormones, and all are made of smaller molecules called amino acids. These amino acids are defined by three bases, or triplets (remember, the bases are adenine, guanine, cytosine, and thymine). Because this synthesis occurs outside of the nucleus, there has to be a way to get the codes from the nucleus to the ribosomes, and that is the job of the messenger RNA (mRNA) (see Figure 1.10). The nuclear DNA unzips (in a way similar to mitosis though it is called transcription because it "transcribes" the codes), and the bases of the mRNA join with the particular segment of the DNA strand that codes for the prescribed amino acid. The mRNA consists of the bases adenine, guanine, cytosine, and *uracil* (uracil binds with adenine in place of thymine). The strands of mRNA are able to pass through the nuclear wall and translate the "message" from the nuclear DNA to the ribosome. Only a very small percentage of the DNA in the nucleus

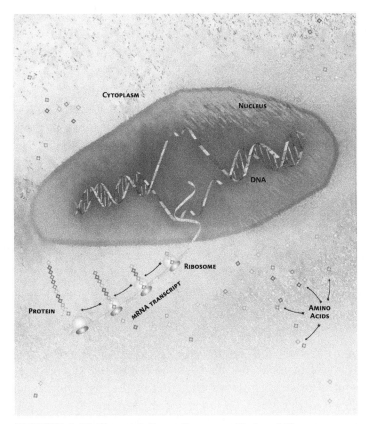

FIGURE 1.10 Transcription. *Courtesy: National Human Genome Research Institute*

Introns: A section of the DNA or RNA molecule that interrupts the code for genes.

codes for proteins or parts of proteins (these areas are called exons in the DNA and in the RNA molecules). There are areas on the DNA strand that do not code for proteins (called **introns**), and if the mRNA strand "reads" an intron, it will snip it out before leaving the nucleus (Strachan and Read 2004). A different RNA—transfer RNA (tRNA)—actually builds the proteins in amino acid blocks. Of the 20 amino acids that exist, 12 are produced by the human body, but 8 (called "essential" amino acids) cannot be manufactured by the body. Those amino acids must be obtained from food (this is why vegetarians must be careful to augment their diet with foods that contain those essential amino acids that would readily be supplied in a diet that contains meat).

Specific proteins are created from specific amino acids, and those amino acids are produced according to the code on the DNA strand (and ultimately on the different RNA strands). The codes for each amino acid consist of three bases (called **triplets** on the DNA chain and **codons** on the mRNA chains); however, for some amino acids, several base triplet codes can code for one amino acid. Likewise, although it has been thought that a specific codon would code for only one amino acid, new research suggests that under certain circumstances a codon may actually be able to code for more than one amino acid (Turanov et al. 2009).

In addition to encoding for proteins, parts of the DNA strand may code for the starting and ending point for coding specific base sequences, and for regulating the expression of other genes elsewhere in the DNA sequence, in other areas of our bodies, or at different times of our lives. Likewise, only a portion of the RNA in a cell is directly involved in the production of proteins (other RNA molecules are involved in diverse functions in the cells). DNA codes and the proteins produced are extremely conservative, such that the basic sequences for protein synthesis and regulatory genes are basically the same from bacteria to humans (Turanov et al. 2009), which is an important consideration in the analysis of evolutionary relationships, as we will discuss in Chapter 2.

SOURCES OF VARIABILITY

Variability can be at the level of the nucleotides and also at the level of the chromosomes. Before and during the first division of meiosis, several events can occur that can alter the genetic configuration of the gametes and, therefore, potentially alter the evolutionary outcome in a population. Most mutations are deleterious or even lethal, but many are neutral or seemingly neutral (that is, they will not immediately alter the selective advantages of the individual). For example, a point mutation occurring during meiosis changes the genetic code in the sperm or egg. If that mutation changes a base to another base in an area responsible for protein synthesis, and if the resulting code no longer results in a protein required by the body, then that mutation may be lethal or deleterious. But if that mutation changes the base code from ACA to ACG (guanine is substituted for adenine), the resultant amino acid, cysteine, is the same (see Table 1.1, Amino Acids List), so the mutation may have no natural selection advantage or disadvantage. Mutations that appear to be neutral under one set of environmental circumstances, however, may prove to be beneficial or maladaptive under others. Hence, if an environmental change occurs, a neutral mutation is subjected to different selective pressures and may consequently confer advantage or disadvantage to its carrier.

TABLE 1.1 Amino Acids List

DNA Triplets	mRNA Codons	Amino Acid	
ACA, ACG	UGU, UGC	Cysteine	
AAT, AAC	UUA, UUG	Leucine	
AAA, AAG	UUU, UUC	Phenylalanine	Essential
AGA, AGG, AGT, AGC	UCU, UCC, UCA, UCG	Serine	
ACC	UGG	Tryptophan	Essential
ATA, ATG	UAU, UAC	Tyrosine	
CGA, CGG, CGT, CGC	GCU, GCC, GCA, GCG	Alanine	
CTA, CTG	GAU, GAC	Aspartic acid	
CTT, CTC	GAA, GAG	Glutamic acid	
CCA, CCG, CCT, CCC	GGU, GGC, GGA, GGG	Glycine	
CAA, CAG, CAT, CAC	GUU, GUC, GUA, GUG	Valine	Essential
GCA, GCG, GCT, GCC	CGU, CGC, CGA, CGG	Arginine	
GTT, GTC	CAA, CAG	Glutamine	
GTA, GTG	CAU, CAC	Histidine	Essential
GGA, GGG, GGT, GGC	CCU, CCC, CCA, CCG	Proline	
GAA, GAG, GAT, GAC	CUU, CUC, CUA, CUG	Leucine	Essential
TTA, TTG	AAU, AAC	Asparagine	
TAA, TAG, TAT	AUU, AUG, AUA	Isoleucine	Essential
TTT, TTC	AAA, AAG	Lysine	Essential
TAC	AUG	Methionine	Essential (usually a start codon)
TCT, TCC	AGA, AGG	Arginine	
TCA, TCG	AGU, AGC	Serine	
TGA, TGG, TGT, TGC	ACU, ACC, ACA, ACG	Threonine	Essential
ATT, ATC, ACT	UAA, UAG, UGA	Terminating triplets	

FIGURE 1.11 Recombination at crossover.

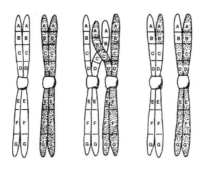

Chromosome-Level Variation

During the first division, paired homologous chromosomes may exchange genetic material. This exchange, recombination or crossing over, occurs when the chromosomes are arranged in pairs and after they have duplicated themselves (when there are four DNA strands). Before cell division, the "sister" molecules may exchange sections of DNA (see Figure 1.11). In addition to recombination, chromosomes can be changed by the deletion, duplication, insertion, or other changes of sections of chromosomes (see Figure 1.12). This may alter the specific information carried on a chromosome for a particular trait and can greatly increase the variation of information carried in the gametes. We will talk about recombinant DNA in which sections of DNA are purposely placed in the chromosome in the laboratory shortly.

Mitochondrial DNA

Mitochondrial DNA (see Figure 1.1) is found outside the nucleus of the cell in its own structures (*mitochondria;* singular: *mitochondrium*). The mitochondrial DNA takes the nutrients we eat and produces energy for the cell. The mitochondrial DNA does not divide during meiosis and is not carried by the sperm to the egg during reproduction (only nuclear DNA is injected into the egg). Because of this, all mitochondrial DNA passed from generation to generation is the DNA from the female (even the mitochondrial DNA in the son's cells), and that mtDNA is an exact copy (barring mutations) from the mother. This form of DNA has become important in discussions about evolution and in the investigation of identity in modern forensic cases. It will also be discussed shortly.

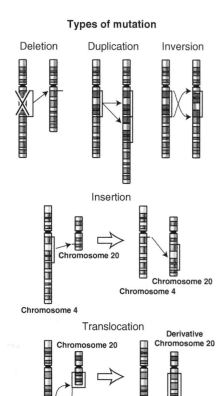

Types of mutation

Deletion   Duplication   Inversion

Insertion

Chromosome 20

Chromosome 20
Chromosome 4

Chromosome 4

Translocation

Chromosome 20   Derivative Chromosome 20

Derivative Chromosome 4

Chromosome 4

FIGURE 1.12 Types of mutation at the chromosome level.
Courtesy: National Human Genome Research Institute

DNA Replication and Protein Synthesis

1. If a point mutation occurred so that adenine was changed to thymine in the amino acid triplet code CTA, what would the resulting amino acid be?

2. If a point mutation occurred so that the second thymine was changed to cytosine in the amino acid triplet code TTT, what would the resulting amino acid be?

3. There are over 17,000 base pairs on chromosome 17 that code for a type of human collagen (COL1A1) found in many tissues, including bone (Bardai et al. 2016; International Human Genome Sequencing Consortium; map can be seen on University of California Santa Cruz genome browser, https://genome.ucsc.edu). If there are significant changes to the normal code for this collagen, it may result in problems with skeletal development and other tissues. Part of the protein sequence for this code is:

   CAGGGCCAGGGGGTCCCTCAGCTCCAGCCTGAGCTCCAGCCTCTCCAT

Fill out the following table containing 10 of those allele codes:

DNA	Complementary DNA Triplet Code	mRNA Code	tRNA Code	Amino Acid
CAG	_____	_____	_____	_____
GGC	_____	_____	_____	_____
GGG	_____	_____	_____	_____
GTC	_____	_____	_____	_____
CCT	_____	_____	_____	_____
CTC	_____	_____	_____	_____
CAG	_____	_____	_____	_____
GAG	_____	_____	_____	_____
CAT	_____	_____	_____	_____
TGC	_____	_____	_____	_____

DNA TESTING AND TYPING

DNA is found in body fluids such as blood, saliva, urine, and semen, soft tissues, bone, teeth, nails, hair roots (nuclear DNA), and hair shafts (mitochondrial DNA; see Figure 1.13). The nuclear human genome consists of approximately three billion base pairs, and, other than identical twins, is unique between individuals. Actually, less than 1 percent of the genome is unique in individuals around the globe, but that is enough to identify any individual with an astounding degree of accuracy. Its uses in forensics are often reported in the news, as it is utilized to identify human remains and trace evidence to perpetrators at crime scenes, although high temperature, humidity, and bacterial activity can degrade the quality of the DNA. DNA has been used in the medical arena for years, tracing mutated genes in families with genetic diseases, and now that the Human Genome Project has mapped the entire human genome, the loci of genes controlling other diseases and genetic conditions continues.

So how does the technology work?

The polymerase chain reaction (PCR), invented by Kary Mullis in 1986, revolutionized DNA analysis. Three main steps occur in PCR analysis: (1) denaturation, in which the two strands of the double helix are separated so that each strand can be used as a template for synthesis of a new strand; (2) annealing, in which primers (short segments of synthetic DNA) bind to the template DNA strands; and (3) extension, in which nucleotides or bases are added to the growing strand of newly synthesized DNA. The three steps are repeated until millions of copies of that section of DNA are created, such that PCR can be used on specimens that were once considered too small or degraded for DNA analysis. A process called "touch DNA" uses

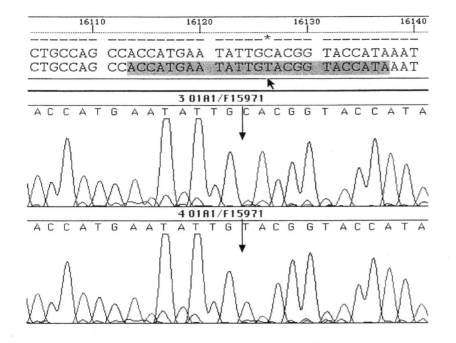

FIGURE 1.13 Mitochondrial DNA sequence analysis. Notice that one allele in the sample (highlighted) is different from the reference sample above it. The reference sample contains a cytosine base at the same location as the thymine base below. *Source: Courtesy of Demris Lee*

FIGURE 1.14 Adding DNA to the gel strip.

The gel used in electrophoresis is either a gelatin made from seaweed, or a compound also used to make soft contact lenses.

FIGURE 1.15 Electrophoresis starting.

FIGURE 1.16 Variable number of tandem repeats (VNTR) samples from four individuals.

the PCR process so that only a few cells are needed to be able to synthesize enough DNA for typing.

Throughout the human genome, stretches of DNA sequences are repeated over and over. These repetitive sequences are commonly known as variable number of tandem repeats (VNTR). These can be divided into two categories: long tandem repeats (LTRs) or short tandem repeats (STRs). These are distinguished according to the number of base pairs that repeat in a series. LTRs have a large number of repeating base pairs (usually more than seven), while STRs have between three and seven repeating units. If several of these analyses are performed simultaneously for different stretches of DNA sequences, the power to discriminate between individuals can exceed the world's population. See Figures 1.14 and 1.15 for two steps of the process for DNA testing.

In Figure 1.16, a particular DNA sequence of base pairs was repeated three times in Individual 1, four times in Individual 2, and so forth. This segment of DNA is, therefore, of different lengths in these different individuals. When the segment is labeled with a radioactive substance and submitted to electrophoresis (in which the gel is subjected to an electric charge), bands develop on the gel strip. The molecules of DNA will move a distance across that electrically charged gel according to their size (molecules in general will move a distance determined by characteristics other than their size). The largest DNA segment is at the top of the strip, and the shortest at the bottom.

In Figure 1.17, an unknown sample (U) from four different DNA locations is compared with two known individuals. Note that there are two bands for each sample, denoting one DNA segment

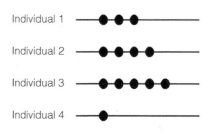

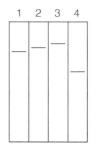

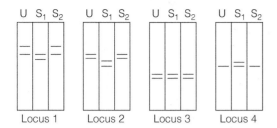

Locus 1   Locus 2   Locus 3   Locus 4

FIGURE 1.17 Unknown "U" compared with two samples.

length from the mother and one from the father. In the event that there is only one band, the segment lengths from the mother and father are the same. In this example, S_2 matches the unknown sample and cannot be excluded from further consideration.

Mitochondrial DNA Typing

The mitochondrial genome is a circular double-stranded molecule consisting of approximately 16,500 base pairs. Most of the differences between individuals are found in the control region, which is the region in the DNA strand that controls the actions of the rest of that region. Instead of two copies, as with nuclear DNA, there are hundreds to thousands of copies of mitochondrial DNA per cell. This is advantageous for typing highly degraded samples (see Figure 1.13 for an example of how a base pair can differ in the sequence of DNA). In fact, even samples as old and degraded as Neanderthal bones have been typed using mitochondrial DNA (more about exciting discoveries in Chapter 12). As was stated previously, mitochondrial DNA is maternally inherited, so assuming mutations have not occurred, all maternal relatives will have the identical mitochondrial DNA sequence. Also, as the mutation rate in mtDNA is greater than nuclear DNA, it can be used to trace inheritance through the female line and can track ancestry for many generations. Mitochondrial DNA is being used to identify the genetic relationship between even distant species.

Similarly, Y chromosomes are only inherited by males in a family. These, too, have the potential to be typed.

The Present and Future of DNA Typing

There is no doubt that DNA typing is a powerful investigative tool, but at present there is a tendency to overstate its power. Note that to use DNA typing, a reference sample must first be obtained. There is no benefit in typing an unknown fragment of tissue or blood stain if there is no person with whom to compare the sample (except to hold the unknown sample until there is a reference). There is at present no mass DNA reference collection, as there is for fingerprints, for example, although since 1994 all states in the United States are required to send DNA samples from many violent criminals after they have been convicted of a crime. The database CODIS (Combined DNA Index System) is searched when unknown DNA is recovered from a crime scene, and if no match is immediately made, it is stored for future comparisons.

DNA "fingerprinting" is increasingly being used to identify the victims of mass fatality incidents, such as victims of a plane crash; the victims of the 9/11 terrorist acts in Washington, DC, New York City, and Pennsylvania; and victims of other terrorist acts or natural disasters. A decision was made early in the recovery process in New York City after 9/11 to take DNA samples from all remains recovered from "Ground Zero" and to have them analyzed to compare to family members or to objects known to have been used only by the victim (such as a toothbrush, chewing gum, and so on). As was stated previously, we must remember that DNA typing is not useful in all situations (for example, if the remains are badly burned in a plane crash, thereby destroying the DNA). In these situations, family members often demand the "best technology" (that is, DNA typing) for their deceased relatives even when that technology is not practical or possible. In those situations it is sometimes difficult to convince the public that the "low-tech" means of identification such as those discussed in Chapter 15 are the most appropriate.

Significant contributions to the discussion of DNA were made by Demris A. Lee.

CONSIDER THIS

In 1918, after being held captive by the Bolsheviks in the Ipatiev House in Yekaterinburg, Russia, the seven members of the Czar Nicholas II family and four members of his entourage (including his doctor and a maid) were taken to the basement of that farmer's house and killed. In 1991, the Russian government ordered the exhumation of the family members and entourage of the Russian royal family of Czar Nicholas II from a grave outside of Yekaterinburg, where the remains of all but two of the family were finally discovered. The questions before the experts were the following: Are these the remains of the Russian royal family and entourage, and, because two were missing, what members of the family were represented by the remains? No antemortem (before-death) dental records or radiographs (X-rays) were available, so the most promising way to identify the skeletons was through comparison of the DNA, but to whom?

The czar's wife, Czarina Alexandra, was related to Prince Philip, the husband of England's Queen Elizabeth II, in that Prince Philip's maternal grandmother was the czarina's sister. By testing, the researchers discovered that the mitochondrial DNA from the czar's wife and daughters was a match to the DNA from Prince Philip.

Genetically Modified Humans?

We will discuss other genetically modified organisms (GMOs) in Chapter 2 because some of the concern about them involves natural selection, but it is appropriate to start the discussion here when considering modification of genomes.

Consider this example: Over 35 million people around the world are infected with the human immunodeficiency virus (HIV) and many develop acquired immunodeficiency syndrome (AIDS). A gene (CCR_5) that is present in most human beings' genes codes for a protein that allows the virus to attach itself to the body's T cells, part of the body's immune system (actually, more than just this gene plays a part in the HIV story). A very small percentage (less than 1 percent) of the world's population has a mutation that eliminates that gene, and most of them are naturally immune to HIV.

One option for curing the disease is to take stem cells from the bone marrow of a person resistant to the virus and inject them into the infected patient with the hope that the donor's stem cells will repopulate the patient's body with resistant cells. This has actually been successful in one patient, but because patients' immune systems are so compromised by the disease, they can die from fighting the donor's cells before the stem cells have a chance to work. Also, there are so few people with the mutation that this treatment is impractical.

But what if the patient's own stem cells could be genetically modified to eliminate the gene and then inject those cells back into the patient? The patient would not reject his own cells, but you would have to be able to snip out only the offending gene without affecting nearby genes—a very precise target! Various methods are being researched to do just that. Researchers discovered that bacteria have an enzyme (Cas9) that snips out a section of DNA from the genetic code of viruses that try to invade them. Using that enzyme with CRISPR (clustered regularly interspaced short palindromic repeats) technology, it is possible to target only small snippets of DNA and remove them (Kaminski et al. 2016). CRISPR and other technology are being studied to not only remove "malware" in the DNA (or RNA, depending on the situation) but also to insert sections of desirable DNA into the genome of humans, other animals, and plants, and this will be discussed in the next chapter.

At the time of writing this chapter (November 2016), no one has yet claimed to have genetically modified a *viable* human embryo, but Chinese researchers have claimed to modify the genome of a nonviable human embryo, which was destroyed after it was altered (Kang et al. 2016). The attempts to modify the genome for the CCR_5 gene have not always been successful, but the advances in gene modification are fascinating.

EXERCISE 1.3 NAME _____ SECTION _____ DATE _____

DNA Typing

You are asked to analyze a complex case using the evidence provided in Questions 1 through 3.

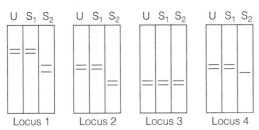

FIGURE 1.18

1. In Figure 1.18, blood samples are taken from a gate (U), an injured woman (S_1), and her former husband (S_2). The woman claimed that she was attacked by her former husband. The man had a cut on his hand, which he explained as a cut from a broken water glass. Is the unknown sample from her wound, from her former husband, or from an unknown third person?

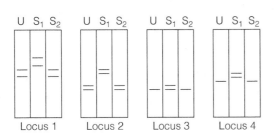

FIGURE 1.19

2. From the same case a second blood sample was collected from a stain on the floor of the former husband's home (see Figure 1.19). Is this stain from the woman, her former husband, or an unknown third person?

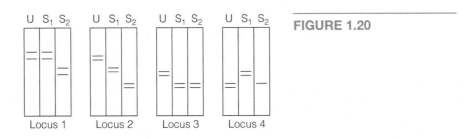

FIGURE 1.20

3. Again from the same case a third blood sample was collected from a knife in the alley two blocks from the woman's home (see Figure 1.20). Is this stain from the woman, her former husband, or an unknown third person?

4. What do these tests tell you about the case?

5. Refer to page 22 about identifying the remains of the Russian royal family. What kind of DNA was used to identify the czar's family's remains? Why was it possible?

6. Would it have been possible to identify which of the czar's daughters was which by using mitochondrial DNA? Why or why not?

TALKING POINTS

- Now that the Human Genome Project has successfully mapped the human genome, there are debates about what to do with the information that now can be obtained about a person's DNA.

  What is your opinion about the following scenarios and why (most of these have actually been suggested by lawmakers and/or insurance companies)?

  - Individuals *convicted* of a felony (homicide, rape, and so on) should have their DNA on file to link them to past and future criminal activity.

  - Individuals *arrested* for a felony should have their DNA on file to link them to past and future criminal activity.

  - Everyone should have their genome mapped:

    - So that health or life insurance companies can analyze the risk of insuring that individual.

    - For identification purposes in mass fatality incidents (plane crashes, and so on).

  - Because the technology is available to perform DNA typing for identification purposes in a mass fatality incident, every element (bodies or body parts, skeletons or skeletal elements and fragments) should be typed, regardless of the cost.

    - Should the families of the victims decide how much money should be spent to identify everyone in a mass fatality incident, or should the medical examiner make that decision? At what point do you draw the line on the amount of money being spent (Thousands? Tens of thousands? Hundreds of thousands?—The costs can easily reach these points in a large disaster).

  - Should we attempt to modify the genome of humans (or other animals or plants)?

    - Under what circumstances should geneticists be allowed to modify a human embryo? How bad should the disease or condition be before embryos should be modified?

    - It is theoretically possible to modify an embryo for sex or even eye color. Should this be permitted?

CHAPTER 2

Population Genetics

OBJECTIVES

1. How does your genetic code express itself in your physical characteristics?

2. How do genetic counselors use these physical characteristics to advise their clients about the genetics of children they may have?

3. How can we determine that evolution is occurring in a population?

4. What are genetically modified organisms (GMOs) and why are some people concerned about them?

5. How can DNA show us the details about evolution?

In this chapter, we will explore genetics at the individual and population levels and discuss how evolution operates. You will explore your own genetic code for certain traits based on how those traits are visibly expressed, and you will learn how to trace the genes and gene frequencies through several generations. We will also discuss the basics of GMOs and explore how GMOs could be beneficial and/or potentially detrimental.

CONSIDER THIS

GREGOR MENDEL

Gregor Mendel was an Augustine monk born in 1822 in Moravia (the southeastern part of the Czech Republic) who was interested in the inheritance patterns of traits in plants and animals. In his time, one of the widely accepted theories of evolution was that offspring inherited characteristics that their parents acquired throughout their lives (championed by Jean-Baptiste Lamarck).

Another theory stated that characteristics of the parents would be blended in the offspring. Mendel's most famous experiments involved pollinating pea plants with, for example, gray and round peas with plants with white and wrinkled peas to determine whether or not the resulting "daughter" peas were a blend of the colors and smoothness of the parent generation. Mendel discovered no blending, but instead, a certain percentage of the offspring had wrinkled peas and a certain percentage had round peas. Through experimentation and mathematical calculations, he developed his principles concerning segregation and independent assortment—the principles we use today and will study in this chapter. Even though his work did not become well known until after his death, he is considered an important figure in modern genetics. For more information, research the many important works about Mendel.

TERMINOLOGY

Allele: Alternative forms of a gene. For example, if the genotype of an individual is Pp for the trait of PTC tasting (see page 38), it contains two alleles determining this trait: P and p, one allele for PTC tasting, and one for nontasting.

Autosomes: Chromosomes that carry DNA for all characteristics except for the sex of the individual.

Chromatid: One of two identical copies of DNA comprising a replicated chromosome.

Codominant alleles: Alleles that are both expressed when paired in an organism.

Dominant allele: An allele that is phenotypically expressed in the heterozygote and that prevents the expression of the recessive allele (that is, masks recessive alleles phenotypically). A dominant allele is written in uppercase letters.

Gene: That section of DNA that defines the specific code for a series of amino acids making up a protein or a part of a protein.

Gene pool: The total complement of genes in a population.

Genome: A complete set of chromosomes (and genes).

Genotype: All of the genetic information contained in an organism; the genetic constitution (gene makeup) of an organism.

Heterozygote: An organism with unlike members of any given pair or series of alleles at a particular locus. Consequently, this individual produces more than one type of gamete (for example, Aa or Bb).

Homologous chromosomes: Carry genetic information for the same trait at the same location.

Homozygote: An organism whose chromosomes carry identical members of a given pair of alleles. The gametes are, therefore, all alike with respect to this locus. For example, a gamete with the genotypes AA or BB or aa carries only one type of allele for each locus.

Phenotype: Characteristic (or combination of characteristics) of an individual visually observed or discernible by other means; for example, tallness in garden peas or color blindness or blood type in humans. Individuals of the same phenotype appear alike but may not have offspring of the same phenotype because the offspring may have different genotypes.

Principle of independent assortment: Paired chromosomes and the alleles on those chromosomes separate into gametes independently of one another. For example, the way in which the genetic information on chromosome #1 separates into gametes has no influence on how the genetic information on chromosome #3 separates into gametes.

Principle of segregation: During meiosis, paired chromosomes (and therefore alleles) separate into different gametes.

Recessive allele: An allele that is not expressed when paired with a dominant allele. A recessive allele is written in lowercase letters.

Sex chromosomes: Determine the sex of the individual.

Trait: A distinguishing characteristic or quality of a phenotype (that is, hair color, blood type, eye color, and so on).

PRINCIPLES OF INHERITANCE

We return to the discussion of gamete production in meiosis to understand how traits are passed from one generation to the next. The key to understanding the principles of inheritance resides in remembering Gregor Mendel's **principle of segregation** and the **principle of independent assortment**. Remember that during meiosis, or the formation of gametes (sex cells), the number of chromosomes in a cell is reduced from 46 to 23 (see Chapter 1). Each pair of chromosomes thus separates, and one chromosome goes to one gamete while the other goes to the other gamete. With the separation of chromosomes, the alleles on those chromosomes also separate.

This is essentially Mendel's principle of segregation, that during meiosis the alleles separate. The principle of independent assortment states that the members of different pairs of alleles assort independently into gametes. Obviously, these principles are true *only* if the alleles in question are on separate chromosomes. Alleles on the same chromosome are not usually independent and, with the exception of some mutations, will stay together during meiosis. As long as a trait isn't lethal or severely deleterious it can "ride along" on the same chromosome with other traits that are beneficial in natural selection. For this reason, it is not valid to suggest that every trait has to have *some* natural selective advantage!

We will assume that all alleles in the following examples and exercises are able to sort independently.

Suppose an individual possessed the two alleles Rr for the trait earwax type (we will explore the specific traits later). In the production of sex cells, these two alleles segregate and go into two different gametes:

 These are the gametes, or sex cells.

PTC (phenylthiocarbamide or phenylthiourea) A bitter synthetic chemical that some people (but not all) can taste.

If you wanted to determine the genetics of an individual for two different traits, earwax type and phenylthiocarbamide (PTC) tasting, for example, we could say that his genotype is RrPp. The alleles would separate into gametes as follows:

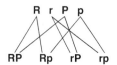

These are the gametes.

This second example uses the principle of independent assortment; that is, regardless of how the alleles for earwax type segregate, the alleles for PTC tasting will segregate independently, so that every combination possible will occur in different gametes.

CONSIDER THIS

WHY DO WE USE UPPERCASE AND LOWERCASE LETTERS FOR ALLELES?

Answer: To keep track of the alleles under discussion, we must follow certain conventions in terminology. Any symbol can be used to designate the alleles, but the letters A, B, C, and so on, or the first letters of the traits being discussed (for example, "P" for PTC tasting) are common. The alleles determining the same trait are written together (PpTt), and the dominant form of the allele is written first. Capital letters designate the dominant form of the allele, and small letters are used for the recessive forms.

SAMPLE PROBLEMS

1. An individual with a genotype Aa would create what kinds of gametes?

2. An individual with a genotype AaBb would create what kinds of gametes?

3. An individual with a genotype AaBbCc would create what kinds of gametes?

Answers:

1. The gametes would be

2. The gametes would be

3. The gametes would be

Simple Punnett Square:

	A	a
A	AA	Aa
a	Aa	aa

After you have determined the gametes possible for each individual in your mating pair, it is easy to figure out the results of matings between individuals because you simply put the different gametes into all of the possible combinations. One of the easiest ways to do this is by using the Punnett square.

A second method sometimes used to predict the gamete combinations:

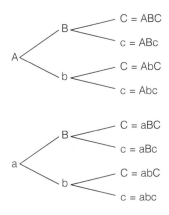

C = ABC
c = ABc
C = AbC
c = Abc
C = aBC
c = aBc
C = abC
c = abc

Example:

What are the possible outcomes of a mating between individuals AaBb and AaBb? *Hint:* Put the gametes along the top and side of the square and then cross-multiply.

Answer:

The **genotypes** for this cross are:

	AB	Ab	aB	ab
AB	AABB	AABb	AaBB	AaBb
Ab	AABb	AAbb	AaBb	Aabb
aB	AaBB	AaBb	aaBB	aaBb
ab	AaBb	Aabb	aaBb	aabb

The results in this case are shown here:

AABB (1)
AaBB (2)
AABb (2)   There are nine different genotypes for a cross
AaBb (4)   between individuals who are heterozygous for
AAbb (1)   two traits.
Aabb (2)
aaBB (1)
aaBb (2)
aabb (1)

What are the **phenotypes** for the preceding cross?

AB (both traits dominant) = 9

Ab = 3

ab (both traits recessive) = 1

Any time you cross two individuals who are heterozygous for two traits, the phenotype ratio will be 9:3:3:1. If you cross two individuals who are heterozygous for three traits, the phenotype ratio will be 27:9:9:9:3:3:3:1 (try it!).

SURVEY OF SOME GENETIC TRAITS

Most phenotypic traits are the results of a combination of effects of heredity and the environment. For example, skin color in an individual is determined to a large extent by genetic and ancestral background but is also affected by the sun and even by diet. A small number of traits have been used traditionally to demonstrate simple Mendelian genetic patterns, although many of these are now known to be affected by much more complex hereditary patterns than once thought. Traits such as tongue rolling and folding (also called "tongue gymnastics"), interlocking fingers and thumbs, and the presence or absence of the palmaris longus tendon are not completely understood but are likely not simply determined by a single allele.

For our exercises, we will assume that the following are inherited as simple Mendelian traits:

1. **Sickle-cell anemia (S, s)** is a condition in which the red blood cells are sickle-shaped (like a "C") instead of disc-shaped. Hemoglobin is a protein molecule in red blood cells that contains iron and transports oxygen and carbon dioxide in the blood. In sickle-cell anemia, the hemoglobin and the shape of the red blood cells are abnormal, which causes problems because the cells cannot deliver sufficient oxygen to the tissues and because the abnormal shape of the cells causes them to get stuck in blood vessels, which causes pain. They can cause a stroke by prohibiting blood flow in areas of the brain, and, in general, the victim suffers from hypoxia (insufficient oxygen). Those individuals with the genotype heterozygous for the sickle trait carry the trait but do not show classic sickle-cell anemia (although under certain conditions, the red blood cells can become sickle-shaped). Those individuals carrying both recessive alleles will show the trait.

Although sickle-cell anemia is a terrible disease, there is an interesting benefit to being heterozygous for the trait. Malaria is caused by a parasitic organism (*Plasmodium falciparum*),

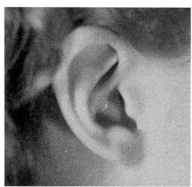

FIGURE 2.1 Attached earlobe (recessive).

which is transmitted by mosquitoes. When a mosquito carrying the parasite bites a human, the parasite is injected into the human bloodstream and into the red blood cells. The parasite consumes the hemoglobin in a normal red blood cell and ultimately kills the cell. If enough of these red blood cells are destroyed, the victim can die. As we have already discussed, a person with the homozygous genotype for sickle-cell anemia can die of the disease, but if a person who is heterozygous for the sickle-cell trait is injected with the *P. falciparum* parasite, the red blood cells attacked by the parasite become sickle-shaped and cannot support the parasite. Those sickled red blood cells are taken out of the body's circulation. Therefore, people who are heterozygous for the trait are protected against malaria. This is a *balanced polymorphism,* the gene for which is located on chromosome 11.

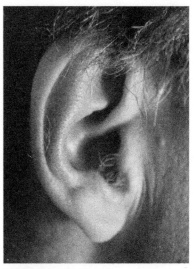

FIGURE 2.2 Free-hanging earlobes (dominant).

2. **Earwax type (R, r):** There are two basic types of earwax: wet and dry. The dry type is frequent in East Asians, while wet earwax is more frequent in other populations around the world. Yoshiura et al. (2006) have demonstrated that the dry earwax occurs with a homozygous recessive state of a gene on chromosome 16 (locus 16q12.1). This trait does seem to be inherited as a simple Mendelian trait.

3. **The ability to taste PTC (phenylthiocarbamide or phenylthiourea) (P, p):** This bitter-tasting, synthetic chemical is believed to be an approximation of a naturally occurring substance that is present in plants such as turnips, kale, and Brussels sprouts. Individuals who can taste the chemical are therefore more likely to reject large amounts of those foods and to be less subject to goiter, which is caused by substances contained in these foods (Kitchin et al. 1959). Kim et al. (2003) found a small area on chromosome 7 that accounts for much of the variation in PTC tasting. It is inherited as a dominant. Though this region has been discovered to directly influence PTC tasting, it is unlikely inherited as a simple Mendelian trait. Mangold et al. (2008) have found a connection between the inability to taste PTC and nicotine dependence in some individuals.

4. **Earlobes (E, e):** Attached earlobes are characterized by the attachment of the lower part of the lobe to the skin of the head (see Figure 2.1), whereas free-hanging lobes are not attached (Figure 2.2). The attached earlobe is inherited as a recessive.

5. **Darwin's tubercle (D, d):** This is a projection on the helix of the ear, or a pointed thickening of the cartilage of the ear (see Figure 2.3). The size of the projection varies, and it may be seen only on one of the ears. This trait is inherited as a dominant.

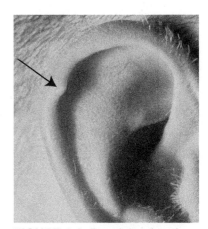

FIGURE 2.3 Darwin's tubercle (dominant).

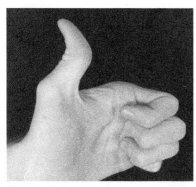

FIGURE 2.4 Hitchhiker's thumb (recessive).

FIGURE 2.5 Hair whorl direction.

6. **Hitchhiker's thumb (T, t):** If, in the hitchhiker's position (Figure 2.4), one can bend the thumb back at an angle of 50 degrees or greater, one has inherited the trait as a recessive.

7. **Hair whorl (H, h):** Observe this trait while standing behind and above an individual: a hair pattern that whorls clockwise is dominant, whereas a counterclockwise whorl is inherited as a recessive (see Figure 2.5). Interestingly, Klar (2003) found a connection between handedness and hair whorl rotation and believes that it is caused by a gene at a single locus. He found that left-handers and ambidextrous people displayed a random pattern of hair whorl rotation, while right-handers showed clockwise hair whorl as a dominant.

8. **Palmaris longus tendon (A, a):** Place your fingertips under the table edge and move to lift the table with your fingertips. If two flexor tendons arise at the wrist, this is inherited as a recessive. If there is a third (palmaris longus) tendon in the middle, it is inherited as a dominant (although it is actually the less frequent genotype).

9. **Tongue rolling (B, b):** For years, it was reported that ability to roll the edges of one's tongue upward was inherited as a dominant, although Martin (1975) disputes that the trait is genetically determined at all.

Incomplete Dominance

Thalassemia is one instance in which the recessive allele in a heterozygote is not completely overshadowed by the dominant allele, and has an effect on the individual. Thalassemia minor is the heterozygote condition in which an individual has a lower red blood cell count with some anemia, but the significant anemia in thalassemia is found in the homozygote condition.

EXERCISE 2.1   NAME _____   SECTION _____   DATE _____

Gamete Formation

Show your work.

1. What are the gametes that can be produced by the following individuals?

    a. AABB

    b. AaBB

    c. AABBcc

    d. AAbbCc

2. What are the possible genotypes of the offspring from a mating of the following individuals?

    a. EE x ee

    b. Ee x Ee

    c. AaBb x AAbb

EXERCISE 2.2   NAME _____   SECTION _____   DATE _____

Phenotype Summary

Survey a sample of about 30 to 50 individuals for one or more of the traits listed. Fill in the following chart; the information will be used in later exercises.

Summary of Genetic Data for Sample

Trait	N	Number Dominant Phenotype	Number Recessive Phenotype	% Dom	% Rec	Yourself Dom/Rec	Letters to Be Used in Exercise
Earwax type	___	_____	_____	_____	_____	_____	R, r
PTC taste	___	_____	_____	_____	_____	_____	P, p
Earlobes	___	_____	_____	_____	_____	_____	E, e
Darwin's tubercle	___	_____	_____	_____	_____	_____	D, d
Hitchhiker's thumb	___	_____	_____	_____	_____	_____	T, t
Hair whorl	___	_____	_____	_____	_____	_____	H, h
Palmaris longus	___	_____	_____	_____	_____	_____	A, a
Tongue rolling	___	_____	_____	_____	_____	_____	B, b

EXERCISE 2.3 NAME _____ SECTION _____ DATE _____

Genotype Formations

1. What are the possible genotypes for each of the phenotypes tested in the survey?

2. Investigate the relationship between handedness and hair whorl direction described by Klar (2003) and defined on page 40. Do you see a correlation?

3. What are the genotype possibilities for those individuals in your survey who have hitchhiker's thumb?

4. What are the genotype possibilities for those individuals in your survey whose hair whorls in a clockwise direction?

5. What percentage of the offspring from a mating of two individuals, each heterozygous for earlobes and PTC tasting, will be able to taste PTC and have free-hanging earlobes?

6. What percentage of the offspring from the preceding mating will not be able to taste PTC but will have attached earlobes?

7. What percentage of the offspring from the preceding mating will be heterozygous for both traits?

PEDIGREE ANALYSIS

When a researcher comes across a subject who phenotypically shows a trait that the researcher knows to be dominant, as we have seen, the subject can genetically be either homozygous dominant or heterozygous for that trait. With the advances in gene mapping, it is possible to determine the complete genotype of an individual for any given trait. It is also sometimes possible to determine a person's genotype by researching the phenotypes of that person's biological family. By reconstructing the "family tree" for the expression of phenotypes of a trait, we can, to an extent, even predict the expression of that trait in descendants.

The steps for determining whether a trait is dominant or recessive and for determining the genotypes in a family are:

1. In the case of dominant inheritance, the individual who exhibits a trait must have at least one parent who also shows it.

2. If only one parent shows the trait, the individual in question must be heterozygous for it. Because of the rule of dominant inheritance, an individual who exhibits the dominant trait will have at least one parent who also shows it (assuming there are no mutations).

3. If an individual showing a recessive trait has two parents neither of whom shows the trait, both parents must be carriers of one recessive and one dominant allele (that is, heterozygous).

The recessive traits are, therefore, not found in every generation. *Note:* A recessive condition with a substantial gene frequency will sometimes mimic a dominant trait in a pedigree chart. In the following exercises, however, assume the typical situation just described.

Symbols used in pedigree analysis:

	Exhibits Trait	Unaffected
Male	■	□
Female	●	○
Unknown	▲	△
Twins	●●	○○
Deceased	■	□

SAMPLE PROBLEMS

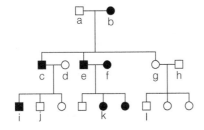

FIGURE 2.6 Case A pedigree chart.

1. Is this trait inherited as a dominant or a recessive?

2. What are the probable genotypes of individuals a and b?

a.

b.

3. If individual **a** had married an individual of the same genotype as himself, how many of the children from this mating would show the trait (what percentage)?

Answers:

1. In the case of dominant inheritance, any individual who shows the trait must have at least one parent who shows the trait. Notice that this is true in this problem; therefore, the trait is inherited as a dominant.

   a. homozygous recessive

   b. heterozygous

2. None of the children would show the trait.

SEX LINKAGE

Sex-linked traits: Occur on the chromosomes that determine the sex of the individual.

Genes are said to be **sex-linked traits** when the genes that influence them are located on the X or Y chromosome. A female receives two X chromosomes from her parents, while a male receives an X chromosome from his mother and a Y from his father. Remember that during meiosis, the paired chromosomes segregate so that each gamete receives half of each paired chromosome, and those chromosomes may exchange genetic information before separating (described on page 24). This is also true in the paired X chromosomes of the females, but because the Y chromosome carries few of the loci of the X chromosomes, it can only exchange information at its ends. For this reason, most of the Y chromosome is passed directly from fathers to sons.

Because the Y chromosome carries few of the loci of the X chromosome, most of the sex-linked genes are carried on the X chromosome. For most traits, therefore, a female with two X chromosomes will carry a pair of alleles for a trait, while a male,

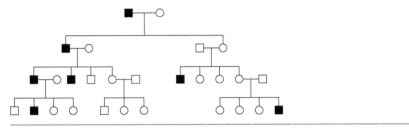

FIGURE 2.7 Pedigree chart for sex-linked trait.

who has an XY configuration, will carry only one allele of a trait. Hence, the male has a greater chance of phenotypically showing a sex-linked trait. Males are referred to as being **hemizygous** for X-linked traits, and in this situation, recessive alleles behave as dominants in males.

Hemizygous: Usually refers to males in sex-linked traits because most of these traits are contained on the X chromosome and have no corresponding locus on the Y chromosome.

Notice in the pedigree chart in Figure 2.7 that no women in the family group expressed the trait shown. However, females can show sex-linked traits if the father is affected, and the mother carries the trait on at least one of her X chromosomes.

Defective color vision, or color-blindness, is a sex-linked trait, as is hemophilia, or "bleeder's disease." More than 1,500 other conditions and diseases are now known to be sex linked. A red–green color-blind man has a single recessive allele on his X chromosome. The Y chromosome carries no locus for this trait, so whatever allele form is carried by the X chromosome will determine the man's phenotype. If this man has children with a woman who is homozygous dominant (that is, normal), all of the daughters will be carriers of the trait but will be phenotypically normal. The sons will all be normal and will not carry the trait.

SAMPLE PROBLEMS

Why will all of the sons of a marriage between a red–green color-blind man and a woman who is homozygous dominant for the trait (that is, normal) be normal?

Answer:
The homozygous normal woman can give only a normal allele to any offspring, sons or daughters. The Y chromosome passed by the father to the sons carries *no* allele for the trait, so the mother's normal allele passed to the son will be expressed.

EXERCISE 2.4   NAME _____   SECTION _____   DATE _____

Pedigree Exercises

1. Clark and Cindy have two grown sons and two infant daughters. On a separate sheet of paper, draw the pedigree chart for this family.

2. Clark and Cindy were formerly married to Margaret and John, respectively. Clark and Margaret had one daughter, now deceased. Cindy and John had one son. Combine this pedigree chart with the previous one for Clark and Cindy.

3. Jack and Betty are married, and they have two sons and one daughter. Jack's mother is deceased, but his father is still living. Betty's parents are both still alive. Jack's mother showed trait A, but his father does not. Jack and one of his sons show trait A, but the other son and daughter are free of the trait. No one on Betty's side of the family shows the trait. The trait is inherited as a recessive. Determine the genotypes of each member of the extended family.

4. In Case A (page 47), what are the genotypes of individuals c through l?

   c.   e.   g.   i.   k.
   d.   f.   h.   j.   l.

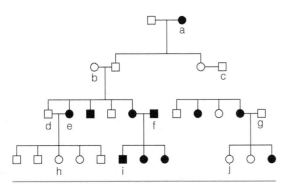

FIGURE 2.8 Case B pedigree chart.

5. Is the trait indicated in Case B (see Figure 2.8) dominant or recessive? Is it a sex-linked trait?

6. What are the possible genotypes of individuals a through j?

a.   c.   e.   g.   i.

b.   d.   f.   h.   j.

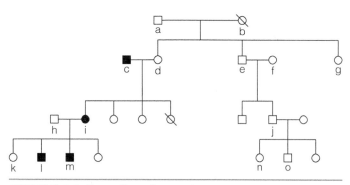

FIGURE 2.9 Case C pedigree chart.

7. Is the trait in Case C (see Figure 2.9) dominant or recessive? Is it inherited as a sex-linked trait?

8. What are the possible genotypes of individuals a through o?

a.   c.   e.   g.   i.   k.   m.   o.

b.   d.   f.   h.   j.   l.   n.

BLOOD TYPING

The ABO blood group system is one of the best understood multiple allele systems. All of the ABO blood types are determined by two genetically determined proteins called **antigens,** the A antigen and the B antigen. These proteins occur on the surface of the red blood cells. An individual's blood may contain one, both, or neither of these antigens, giving rise to the four blood groups: A, B, AB, and O, as shown in Table 2.1.

Antigens: (as used in this book) Proteins that occur on the blood cells of the individual.

TABLE 2.1 Blood Groups

Phenotype	Genotype
A	AA or AO
B	BB or BO
AB	AB
O	OO

© Cengage

As you can surmise from Table 2.1, the A and the B alleles are dominant to the O allele, while the A and B alleles are codominant with one another. How do we know? If the A or B allele is paired with O, only the A or B is displayed phenotypically. Because the AB genotype is displayed phenotypically as AB blood type, the two alleles are codominant.

Individuals with blood group A have the A antigen on the red blood cells, those with group B have the B antigen, those with AB blood type have both the A and B antigens, and those with genotype OO have neither blood group antigen. **Antibodies** destroy antigens, resulting in the destroyed red blood cells clumping together, or **agglutinating,** so in this case, the anti-A antibodies cause agglutination of the A and the AB blood types, as both have the A antigen on the red blood cells.

Likewise, the anti-B antibodies will cause agglutination of the B and the AB blood types. Neither anti-A nor anti-B antibodies will cause agglutination of type O blood, as neither antigen is present on those red blood cells.

Table 2.2 should make these combinations easier to understand.

Antibodies: Proteins produced by the body in response to, and in an attempt to neutralize, a foreign antigen.

Agglutination: Clumping of red blood cells as a result of the destruction of blood antigens by antibodies.

TABLE 2.2 Blood Group Phenotypes and Genotypes

Blood Group	Contains Antigens	Can Donate to	Can Receive
A	A	A or AB	A or O
B	B	B or AB	B or O
AB	A or B	AB	A, B, AB or O
O	Neither	A, B, or O	O

© Cengage

Blood group O, as can be seen in Table 2.2, contains neither antigen, so is commonly referred to as the "universal donor" because the host antibodies can find nothing against which to react. Conversely, individuals with blood group AB will create antibodies against neither antigen (because it contains both antigens on its blood cells and would not make antibodies against its own type). Because of this, type AB is commonly referred to as the "universal recipient."

The distribution of blood groups varies in different areas of the world and among different groups. Europeans most commonly have either blood group A or O (about 40 percent each), about 15 percent have type B blood, and about 5 percent show type AB blood. The highest frequency of type A blood occurs in the Blackfoot Native Americans of North America and the Lapps in northern Scandinavia. The lowest frequency of type A blood occurs in Central and South American natives. In most of the world, the frequency of type A blood is about 10 percent to 35 percent. The highest frequency of type B blood occurs in central Asia, and it is virtually absent among American Indians and Australian Aborigines. In most of the world, the frequency of type B blood is about 5 percent to 25 percent (Mourant 1954; Mourant et al. 1958).

SAMPLE PROBLEMS

A man has been taken to trial in a paternity suit by a woman who claims that he is the father of her son. The man claims innocence. At the trial, the expert witness disclosed the blood types of all three, as follows:

> Woman: Type A
>
> Man: Type B
>
> Child: Type O

Could the man be the father of the child?

Answer:

First, list the possible genotypes of each of the previous blood types, as follows:

> Woman: Genotypes AA or AO
>
> Man: Genotypes BB or BO
>
> Child: Genotype OO

If the woman possessed genotype AO, and if the man had BO, then the cross could look like this:

	B	O
A	AB	AO
O	BO	OO

Because 25 percent of the offspring are likely to be genotype OO, or blood type O, then the man *could* be the father. However, any other man with blood types B, A, or O (though not AB: why?) could be the father, so this case cannot be decided on this evidence alone.

EXERCISE 2.5   NAME _____   SECTION _____   DATE _____

Blood-Type Genetics

1. You have been testing blood samples to determine blood type and have found that sample one agglutinates with anti-A serum, but you haven't tested it against any other serum.

    a. What is (are) the possible blood type(s)?

    b. What antigen(s) is (are) present?

    c. What are the possible genotypes?

2. A different blood sample agglutinates with anti-A and anti-B serum.

    a. What is (are) the possible blood type(s)?

    b. What antigen(s) is (are) present?

    c. What are the possible genotypes?

3. If a baby has blood type AB, and the mother has blood type A, what genotypes could the father be?

4. Should a person with blood type A accept an offer of a blood transfusion from someone with blood type O? Why or why not?

5. Should a person with blood type O accept an offer of a blood transfusion from someone with blood type A? Why or why not?

EVOLUTION AND THE HARDY–WEINBERG FORMULA

As you have learned, evolution occurs when allele frequency changes from one generation to the next in a population. Even though the specific sequence of the evolutionary process in humans contains theory, the general processes of evolution can be documented every day in, for instance, the success of farmers to select for greater milk production in cattle and, unfortunately, in the increased success of bacteria to resist the effects of many of our antibiotics. Even more direct evidence for evolution resides in our genomes and in the genomes of every plant and animal. The genomes of humans are being compared to those of chimpanzees and gorillas, for example, and researchers are finding that some alleles have changed and some alleles have degraded to the point that they are "fossils" of the previous DNA. A notable example was reported in 2004 (Stedman et al. 2004), in which researchers discovered that the alleles coding for a particular muscle protein for chewing mutated after the lineage leading to humans and chimpanzees diverged. You will see in later chapters that chimpanzees, gorillas, and some of the hominid fossils in the late Miocene epoch (over 2 million years ago) had very large muscles that require a large area of muscle attachment on the cranium. Mutations in two of the alleles for that protein, including an increase in brain/cranial size meant that fossils in the human line no longer had large muscles for chewing and no longer needed that muscle attachment crest.

Now let's look at factors that produce and redistribute variation in a population in the course of evolution:

- **Mutation:** An actual alteration in genetic material either at the level of the base or at the level of the chromosome. This is the creative force in evolution and is the only way to produce new variation in a population.

- **Gene flow:** A movement of genes from one population to another; also termed *migration* (although that can imply that individuals are migrating, when in fact only the genes may remain in the new area).

- **Genetic drift** (random genetic drift): An effect of sampling error and random fluctuations in gene frequency based simply on a variation from a statistically expected outcome. This is a function of population size in that a shift in gene frequencies will have a proportionately greater effect in a small mating population than in a large mating population. If the traits involved in genetic drift have a selective advantage or disadvantage, the change in frequencies can be due to natural selection (described as follows) and not to genetic drift.

- **Founder effect:** A newly isolated sample from the original population soon diverges genetically from the parent

Evolution: Occurs when allele frequency changes from one generation to the next in a population.

Mutation, gene flow, genetic drift, and founder effect: These act to produce variation in a population. Natural selection acts on that variation.

population. For example, if 10 people from a normal population started a new population on a deserted island, and if all of those individuals had attached earlobes, the new population and all of the offspring would be very unlike the original population.

All of the preceding forces act to produce variation in a population, while the following act on that variation:

- **Natural selection:** If there is variation in a population, some of these variations may influence reproductive success (numbers of offspring successfully raised to have offspring of their own). Natural selection may, then, be defined as *differential net reproductive success.* The unit of natural selection is the individual; the unit of evolution is the population. The individuals best adapted to an environment will be the ones who survive to pass their genetic information to the next generation, while those who are not so adapted will not be selected and will not pass their genes to the next generation. Adaptation is, therefore, a shift in gene frequencies due to selection. **Artificial selection** is the *intentional* selection of two parents with desirable traits.

All of these factors in a particular environment define situations in which gene frequencies change in a population from generation to generation (that is, the population is evolving). If a population wasn't evolving, we could define that the population was in genetic equilibrium, and we could describe it in terms of a mathematical model, the **Hardy–Weinberg equilibrium formula.** Naturally, it would be very complicated to look at every trait possible in a population to see if the gene frequency was in equilibrium, so the simplest way to proceed is to look at one trait at a time. If that trait is determined by two alleles in simple Mendelian inheritance, the equation contains two allele frequencies, p and q (which might, for example, stand for H and $h,$ the alleles that control hair whorl direction). These two alleles are the only determinants of the trait, so the frequencies are represented by $p + q = 1$ (or $p + q = 100$ percent of the population). If we looked at all of the possible genotypes that represent hair whorl, we see the following:

$$HH + Hh + hh = 1$$

In the Hardy–Weinberg formula, this would be represented by the general **binomial** ("two names") equation:

$$p^2 + 2pq + q^2 = 1$$

P (or p) denotes the dominant allele, q denotes the recessive, and the preceding general equation reflects the potential outcomes of

Hardy–Weinberg equilibrium formula: A mathematical model in which genetic equilibrium is defined.

In a two-allele system, the formula for allele frequencies is

$$p^2 + 2pq + q^2 = 1$$

The genotype frequencies are represented by p^2, pq, and q^2.

p is the frequency of the dominant allele; q is the frequency of the recessive allele.

REMINDER: A binomial formula always equals 1 (100 percent)! This is an important fact for calculating the allele and genotype frequencies.

crosses between the dominant and recessive forms of the allele
(remember the Punnett square).

Remember in the following discussions:

$p^2 = pp = p \times p$

p = the frequency of the dominant allele

q = the frequency of the recessive allele

Convention uses p and q to denote the frequencies of the dominant and recessive alleles, and this
convention will be followed in this book.

In our studies so far, we have used both the two-allele traits (or
those traits determined by two alleles such as attached earlobes,
PTC tasting, and so on) and the three-allele traits, such as the ABO
blood-grouping system. We could look at more traits than this, but
of course the equation becomes more complicated.

SAMPLE PROBLEMS

We have stated earlier that people who exhibit clockwise hair whorls inherit the trait as a dominant
(HH or Hh), whereas people who exhibit counterclockwise whorls inherit the trait as a recessive (hh).
Suppose we have taken a survey from campus and have found that 75 of 100 students
(75 percent) have clockwise hair whorl patterns. Our genotypes are the following:

hh = 25 percent, or .25 (100 students minus the 75 students who have the dominant genotypes)

HH and Hh = 75 percent or .75

The first step in determining the frequencies of the genotypes (p^2, 2pq, q^2) in a population is to
calculate the allele frequencies (p, q). To do this, begin with the homozygous recessive genotype
frequency (the frequency of the homozygous recessive [qq] is known from the sample data collected, so calculations start with this number, and you always work from the known to the unknown in any mathematical problem).
The following loop is a reminder of the sequence to follow in calculating gene and genotype
frequencies:

Start with qq

1. In this method, you calculate the frequency of the homozygous recessive allele q first. We
   want the allele frequency, q, and we know the pp genotype frequency, q^2.

   Because $q = \sqrt{q^2}$, in this case, t = $\sqrt{.25}$, or .5. This, remember, describes the allele t in our
   formula, so we have determined the frequency of one allele.

2. Determine p (in this case, the frequency of H).

> Since p + q = 1,
> then 1 − .5 = p,
> so p = .5

3. Determine the observed genotype frequencies.

> We just plug these numbers into our formula:

	p^2	+	2pq	+	q^2	=	1
so	$(.5)^2$	+	2(.5)(.5)	+	$(.5)^2$	=	1
and	(.25)	+	(.50)	+	(.25)	=	1

> which corresponds to our genotypes

HH   Hh   hh

REMEMBER: The Hardy–Weinberg formula gives expected frequencies when the population is in genetic equilibrium. The real frequencies may vary. We can determine whether the population is in genetic equilibrium by testing whether the observed frequencies match the frequencies expected from the calculation of the Hardy–Weinberg formula.

Although we can observe whether or not the observed allele frequency is different from the expected allele frequency from one generation to the next, to test whether or not that difference is statistically significant enough *not* to have been the product of chance, we would use a chi-square (χ^2) test. In this chapter, we will simply look at the expected and observed frequencies.

As an example of the difference between observed and expected frequencies, the frequency of male to female students in a population (which can be a classroom) is expected to be 50 percent males and 50 percent females (although in reality there are slightly more females than males on Earth). If the observed frequency is significantly different from the expected frequency, the population is not in equilibrium, and the researcher can begin to question the forces at work that create that difference. That is, if that frequency is actually 45 percent males and 55 percent females, is that deviation caused by sampling error, or is the difference statistically significant and perhaps linked to a specific cause or event? In a real-life example, the expected frequency of males to females within a university program can be expected to be equal if it represents random sampling of the larger population. However, 30 years ago, many more males than females pursued a career in forensic anthropology, while about 10 years ago significantly more females than males were in forensic anthropology classes. It seems unlikely that the original male-to-female ratio was strictly due to chance, and it is equally unlikely that the shift in frequency is due to chance, but the exact reason for the shift is unknown.

EXERCISE 2.6   NAME _____   SECTION _____   DATE _____

Hardy–Weinberg and Evolution

1. If the frequency of the dominant allele (P) for PTC tasting is 50 percent in a population, what are the genotype frequencies for that trait in that population?

2. You have sampled 550 college students and found that 352 have Darwin's tubercle.

    a. What are the frequencies of alleles T and t?

    b. What are the genotype frequencies (TT, Tt, and tt)?

    c. If the *expected* allele frequencies are equal, what are the expected genotype frequencies?

    d. What does this tell you about the population?

3. Using the numbers obtained in your survey of individuals for the sample Mendelian traits (see page 40), what are the probable genotype frequencies of your sample for these traits?

POPULATIONS IN EQUILIBRIUM AND POPULATIONS EVOLVING

As a reminder, we have discussed various forces that work on gene frequencies in populations, including mutations, gene flow, genetic drift, founder effect, and natural selection. Let's take a closer look at some of these forces and how the allele frequencies can change from one generation to the next (thereby meeting our definition of evolution).

NATURAL SELECTION

Remember that natural selection can be defined as net differential reproductive success, which means that the "fittest" individuals are those who pass their genetic information to subsequent generations. Individuals who do not mate or who do not have offspring that successfully have offspring of their own are not "fit" in an evolutionary sense and are at a genetic dead-ends. Note that in this definition, the individual can live to a very old age and be able to run marathons, but if he does not pass his genes to the next generations, he is not "fit" in a natural selection sense. Conversely, if an individual has a fatal disease that kills him *after* he passes the genes to the next generation, he is still "fit" in a natural selection sense.

Sickle-cell anemia is a classic example of natural selection at work (see page 40). To understand the effects of natural selection on a disease, a more dramatic and tragic effect can be seen with classic (infant onset) Tay-Sachs disease. Infants who are homozygous recessive for this terrible disease show onset of physical and mental disabilities due to abnormalities in the nerve cells caused by insufficient activity of an enzyme (beta-hexosaminidase A) that acts to reduce fatty acids around nerve cells. Symptoms appear at about six months of age, and the infant usually dies by the age of four. The disease is caused by a mutation at a single locus on chromosome 15 (therefore, it is an autosomal mutation).

EXERCISE 2.7   NAME _____   SECTION _____   DATE _____

Evolving Populations

1. Tay-Sachs disease is actually very rare, but for this demonstration, assume that the frequency of the dominant and recessive alleles are equal in your population. Take 50 red beans (representing the dominant allele) and 50 black beans (representing the recessive allele) and put them into a can. Without looking, draw pairs of beans out of the can and place each pair together on the table.

   What are the genotype frequencies in your study population?

2. Because the homozygous recessive condition is fatal early enough in life that no offspring are possible from that genotype, remove all of the homozygous black bean pairs.

   What are the frequencies of dominant and recessive alleles after this step?

3. Put all of the remaining beans into the can and, again without looking, draw pairs of beans out of the can and place each pair together on the table (if you end up with a single bean at the end, place it back in the can if it is a red bean and remove it if it is a black bean).

   a. What are the genotype frequencies of this generation?

   b. What are the allele frequencies of this generation?

4. Repeat these steps for three to five generations. How do the genotype and allele frequencies change from generation to generation? This is natural selection (and evolution) in action.

ASSORTATIVE MATING

We don't have to use an example as dramatic as a fatal disease to demonstrate the effects of natural selection on a population. Assortative mating is a type of *intentional* selection in which individuals select mates because those mates have certain traits (or lack undesirable traits). Birds mate with other birds that know the correct song and avoid mates that do not know the correct songs (even within species). Humans also make selections of mates because of certain desirable traits. Even though this is intentional selection, those individuals with traits undesirable to potential mates do not have as great a chance to pass their genetic information to the next generations.

MIGRATION OR GENE FLOW (HYBRIDIZATION)

Migration has occurred for millions of years in millions of species. In a book such as this, we would naturally talk about genetic trait transfer between humans as individuals from one geographic region migrate and mate with individuals around the world. What would happen to genotypes and phenotypes if, for example, a group of individuals carrying the sickle-cell trait migrated from a malarial zone to an area in which there was no malaria? If the trait is a balanced polymorphism in a malarial zone (there is a selective advantage to the heterozygous state but disadvantages for individuals with either homozygous state), what are the genotypes with the selective advantage in the new nonmalarial zone? What then happens to the allele and genotype frequencies over generations in the new population?

REMEMBER: Evolution is said to be occurring when the allele frequencies change from generation to generation within a population.

CONSIDER THIS

DARWIN'S FINCHES

In 1835, the *Beagle,* the ship carrying Charles Darwin, arrived at the Galapagos Islands, a series of islands about 500 miles from the coast of Ecuador. Darwin was the ship's naturalist, and as such he collected plant and animal specimens from around the world. After he returned home to England (he didn't study the finches on the *Beagle*), he and colleagues noticed that the finches on these islands somewhat resembled the finches on the mainland, but they were noticeably different, and they exhibited much more variety, particularly in the size and shape of the beak and of the bird itself. Because competition for resources was low on the islands (thus natural selection pressures were lowered), the birds could take advantage of the different food sources, from cactus, various seeds, insects, and other resources. One species even pecks larger birds until they bleed and then drinks the blood!

The finches demonstrate several genetic features of interest to us, the most notable of which are adaptive radiation and natural selection resulting in evolution of the finches into different species. Adaptive radiation occurs when organisms come into an area with many empty ecological niches (the environment to which a species is adapted, including diet, habitat preference, activity pattern, and other features) or when an organism evolves a character or characters that allow it to prevail over another organism for its ecological niche. Natural selection pressure is nicely illustrated by research on finches conducted by Peter and Rosemary Grant on Daphne Major in the Galapagos Archipelago (see Figure 2.10). They have seen evolution (a change in gene frequency from one generation to the next) occurring by natural selection throughout the over 40 years that they have spent on the island, but the changes were more extreme in a severe drought that occurred in 1977. As the drought progressed, the birds with the larger beaks could break into the large, tough seedpods, while the birds with the smaller beaks couldn't survive. But in 1983, a strong El Nino brought heavy rain to the Galapagos, and the birds with the large beaks began dying while leaving the small-beaked birds to thrive. This is evolution in real time (Grant 1999; Grant and Grant 2014)!

Recently, the genomes of Darwin's finches were sequenced, which adds more information to their evolutionary history. Lamichhaney et al. (2015) reported that a section of DNA that includes the gene ALX1 controls beak shape across all of Darwin's finches, including the medium ground finch, which has undergone rapid evolution in response to a changing environment. In addition, mitochondrial DNA suggests that all of the finches arose from a common ancestor in the Galapagos in the past 1.5 million years. Also, they found that gene flow produced hybridization in many of the finch species. Other researchers suggest that all of Darwin's finches arose from one species of seed-eating ground finch that arrived from the mainland (see Figures 2.11 to 2.14).

For a great read about the Grants' research, see Jonathan Weiner's *The Beak of the Finch: A Story of Evolution in Our Time* (Vintage Press, 1995).

FIGURE 2.10 Daphne Major in the Galapagos Archipelago.

FIGURE 2.11 Cactus finch (eats cactus seeds and parts).

FIGURE 2.12 Medium ground finch (eats primarily seeds).

FIGURE 2.13 Small ground finch (eats primarily seeds).

FIGURE 2.14 Tree finch (eats primarily insects).

EXERCISE 2.8   NAME _____   SECTION _____   DATE _____

Gene Flow

Suppose 10 individuals who were all heterozygous for sickle-cell anemia migrated into a population of 30 individuals in which everyone was homozygous dominant for normal red blood cells. How would the gene frequencies of the next generation from random matings of the new population be different from the original population?

1. How many red beans (representing the dominant S allele) and how many black beans (representing the recessive s allele) should you put into the can?

2. Blindly draw pairs of beans out of the can, and place each pair together on the table.

   a. How many homozygous dominant genotypes do you have?

   b. How many homozygous recessive genotypes do you have?

   c. How many heterozygous genotypes do you have?

   Remove all homozygous recessive genotypes, as they will have sickle-cell anemia. With treatments today, many will survive to reproductive age and pass their genes to the next generation, so this is for demonstration purposes.

3. Repeat this experiment, and document the changes to the genotype and phenotype frequencies over generations.

MATHEMATICAL APPROACH TO GENOTYPE, PHENOTYPE, AND ALLELE FREQUENCY CHANGE

Example: Suppose that 10 individuals who were all homozygous for Darwin's tubercle migrated into a population of 100 individuals in which 36 individuals had no Darwin's tubercle. How would the allele frequencies of the next generation (from random matings) be different from the original population?

Answer: In the original population, 36 percent of the individuals were genotype dd, so the frequency for d = $\sqrt{.36}$ = .6; therefore, D = 1 − .6 = .4. The genotype frequencies for the original population would be

$$DD + 2Dd + dd = 1$$
$$(.4)^2 + 2(.4)(.6) + (.6)^2 = 1$$
$$.16 + .48 + .36 = 1$$

The number of individuals for each genotype is

$$DD = .16(100) = 16 = 16 \text{ percent}$$
$$Dd = .48(100) = 48 = 48 \text{ percent}$$
$$dd = .36(100) = 36 = 36 \text{ percent dd (already discovered)}$$

If the individuals who migrated into the population are all genotype DD (discovered from their past records), then the numbers for the new population are as follows:

$$DD = 16 + 10 = 26/110 = 24 \text{ percent}$$
$$Dd = 48 + 0 = 48/110 = 44 \text{ percent}$$
$$dd = 36 + 0 = 36/110 = 33 \text{ percent}$$

New allele frequencies are

$$d = \sqrt{.33} = .57$$
$$D = 1 − .57 = .43$$

DD, Dd = Darwin's tubercle

dd = no tubercle

GENETIC DRIFT AND FOUNDER EFFECT

Genetic drift and founder effect (a more dramatic form of genetic drift) are situations in which a very small sample of individuals (and therefore genes) are removed from a larger population and start new populations.

The fact that many species of plants and animals are becoming extinct (because of encroachment by humans on their habitat, global warming, or other human and nonhuman causes) is common knowledge. Unfortunately, many animals such as the gorilla and orangutan will almost certainly become extinct in the wild and will only live in zoos and wildlife centers. This is a disturbing fact in and of itself, but it is also of concern because of the diminished gene pool in these species.

The California condor is a success story about bringing a species back from the brink of extinction. In 1982, fewer than 25 were left in the wild (because of a combination of habitat encroachment, pesticides, poaching, and so on), and the problem was exacerbated because a mating pair only produced an egg every two years (see National Parks Conservation Association, at www.npca.org). In an attempt to save the species in the wild, condor eggs were gathered from cliff sites and other nesting sites and hatched by wildlife officials (sometimes the mating pair would lay another egg if the first egg was taken), and today, through the breeding programs, about 160 condors are alive in the wild.

Although this is a great success story, think of the limited gene pool in the population of condors today because the wild population dwindled to so few mating pairs. This is an example of founder effect, and with limited variation inherent in the genotypes for many traits comes a potential limit in the ways in which the population and individuals can react to changes in environment.

CONSIDER THIS

GENETICALLY MODIFIED ORGANISMS (GMOs)

The United Nations' Food and Agriculture Organization (www.fao.org) defines GMOs as "genetically engineered/modified organisms, and products thereof, . . . produced through techniques in which the genetic material has been altered in a way that does not occur naturally by mating and/or natural recombination."

A very early example of GMOs was driven by the need for pure insulin for diabetes patients. Before 1980, people who needed insulin would obtain it from the pancreas of cattle or pigs, which is actually very close to the structure of human insulin, but tons of pig pancreases would produce a small vial of insulin. However, like injecting type A blood into a person with type B blood will cause antibodies in the human body to attack the foreign blood antigens, some people would develop antibodies against the cow or pig insulin. In 1978, the genetic code for human insulin (on the 11th chromosome) inserted into weakened Escherichia coli (*E. coli*) bacteria caused that bacteria to manufacture human insulin. With a purification process, the insulin could be injected into the human body with no antibody reaction. As of 1987, the genes are being inserted into yeast, resulting in plenty of insulin for anyone who requires it. Is this a good use of genetic engineering?

But what about some of the other GMOs? Are they beneficial? Are they safe? What about cancer medicines that are genetically modified to treat *your* cancer by *only* going after the cancer and not your healthy cells? Would you accept treatment with that medication?

A genetically modified rice (called "golden rice") has been developed that contains a precursor to vitamin A that is turned into vitamin A in the body. Where people are dependent on rice, vitamin A deficiency can result in blindness and death, particularly among children and pregnant women. A high percentage of a person's vitamin A requirement can be satisfied with this rice.

Some other genetically modified plants have been and are being developed for increased production in a crowded world, as well as resistance to drought, insects, viruses, and herbicides. There is no doubt that we use too many pesticides, herbicides, and antibiotics on and in our food, and those chemicals can migrate into our water supplies and persist in the environment and in our food. With growing climate change, food production is being reduced even in a rapidly increasing world population. Would it be more efficient to build resistance to insects in the genetics of our food instead of using so many pesticides?

According to the World Health Organization, some of the primary concerns over GMOs are:

- Will the modified organisms (particularly food) cause allergic reactions in some people?
- Could the modified genes be transferred to cells in our body (particularly cells in our gastrointestinal tract)? What if those cells had been manufactured to increase resistance to antibiotics or even an increased resistance to the bacteria in our digestive system?
- Could the genes that are inserted into the GMOs be transferred to other crops?
- What are the risks to the environment?

What is the answer? Actually, it depends on what genes are being inserted into any organism. It depends upon the testing of the resulting organism for safety. It is no overstatement to say that millions of people will be affected by our collective opinions about this topic.

Research this topic thoroughly to formulate an opinion, but as this is science, rely on peer-reviewed journal articles for your information. Many biased websites, both pro- and anti-GMO, are not necessarily based on scientific research.

EXERCISE 2.9   NAME _____   SECTION _____   DATE _____

Population Genetics

1. Suppose that out of a population of 100 individuals, 25 could not taste PTC and the individuals in that population who could taste this chemical decided to marry only other individuals who could taste PTC. How would the genotype and allele frequencies change in the second generation?

    This is an example of what evolutionary force?

2. Suppose that a small island population of 100 individuals is visited by 25 sailors who decide to stay and raise families. Suppose also that 36 percent of the original population had a counter-clockwise hair whorl and all the sailors had a counterclockwise hair whorl. What will be the genotype and allele frequencies of the next generation?

    This is an example of what kind of evolutionary force?

3. Suppose that 35 percent of a population of 100 individuals has hitchhiker's thumb, which is inherited as a recessive. Suppose also that 10 individuals, 5 of whom have hitchhiker's thumb, decide to go deep-sea fishing and are stranded on a deserted island for at least a generation, and all stranded individuals mate. What are the genotype and allele frequencies of both new populations in the next generation?

    This is an example of what kind of evolutionary force?

4. What would you say to someone who says "bacteria are learning how to survive today's antibiotics"?

5. What is the genetic reason why farmers can increase milk production in their cows?

REEXAMINING THE ISSUES

In this chapter, we have learned:

- How genetic information from both parents is passed from generation to generation in the nuclear DNA and how that is important in understanding how allele frequencies can change in populations.

- That sources of genetic variability in populations are produced by mutation, gene flow, genetic drift, and founder effect, and that natural selection acts on that variability.

- How to determine whether or not a population is in stasis, and how to track changes in allele frequency in populations through time.

- That recent advances in genome research can tell us a great deal about who we are and how we are related to other primates.

CHAPTER 3

Human Osteology

OBJECTIVES

1. What is bone?

2. How do muscles attach to bone?

3. How do you figure out what bone you have if you only have a fragment?

Much of what physical anthropologists do involves bone morphology in some way. Current theories about fossil hominins start with comparisons of the fossils with modern bones. Human identification and even the differentiation between human and nonhuman bones involve skeletal clues. Likewise, understanding primate locomotion begins with a study of the biomechanics of the bones, joints, and muscle attachments. To build on our knowledge of these (and many more) interesting aspects of physical anthropology, we must have a foundation in skeletal anatomy.

INTRODUCTION

Bone is a living, dynamic tissue that responds to its environment. Many of the clues to learning about this environment, and therefore learning about the life of the individual, will be covered later in this book, but you can begin to learn about the functional interrelationships between the specific bones and muscles of the body in this chapter. During this laboratory period, you will learn terminology of the skeleton and dentition (see Figures 3.1 to 3.3), and the names of the bones and of major landmarks of the skeleton. Although this task requires some memorization, the landmarks discussed have functional significance and are easier to learn if you think of that function, particularly as you think of how your own body operates.

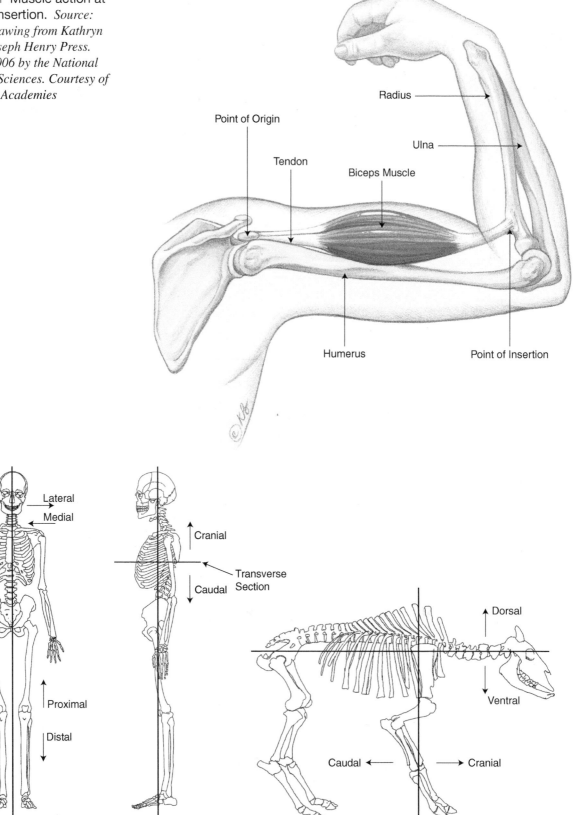

FIGURE 3.1 Muscle action at origin and insertion. *Source: Based on Drawing from Kathryn Born and Joseph Henry Press. Copyright 2006 by the National Academy of Sciences. Courtesy of the National Academies*

FIGURE 3.2 Planes of the body.

To a large extent, the form of the bone is determined by its function, and its function is limited by its form.

Some of the best clues for determining the function of a particular bone are also just common sense. For instance, in healthy bone, the area of **articulation** between two bones that are designed to move against each other will have a smooth surface. This surface will be separated from the articular surface of the other bone by a layer of cartilage, which is soft tissue able to withstand the movements and impacts of the bones.

The joints are held together by **ligaments** that sometimes completely envelop the joint capsule (as in the humeral head). Most movable joint capsules are filled with a slippery lubricant (somewhat like raw egg whites) called **synovial fluid** (*syn* means "together" and *ova* means "egg") that helps keep the joint and cartilage healthy and moving freely with little friction. If the cartilage or articular surface of the bone is damaged, or if there is insufficient synovial fluid, the bone may show areas in which the bones rub against each other and polish the surface of each bone (as described in later chapters), or the bone may break down altogether at those surfaces. If too much synovial fluid is produced in the joint capsule, a condition popularly known as "water" on the joint is produced, which results in swelling at the joint.

Two other kinds of joints occur in the body. **Synarthroses** (singular: **synarthrosis**) are joints in which the two bones are so tightly bound by cartilage that there is virtually no movement between them (such as in the sutures of the cranium). Later in this chapter, we will briefly discuss the spheno-occipital synchondrosis, which is a form of synarthrosis. These types of joints often disappear in adulthood, when the bones they join fuse. This information will become useful to us later in the determination of age.

The third type of joint is called an **amphiarthrosis** (plural: **amphiarthroses**), which is a joint in which some movement is allowed. The bones in these joints are held together by disks of fibrous cartilage, such as in the pubic symphysis and between vertebral bodies (the intervertebral disks). Another type of this joint is seen at the ankle, where the tibia and fibula articulate.

Although healthy bony surfaces are smooth at the areas of movement, they are generally not smooth at synarthroses or amphiarthroses. Also, the area of **origin of a muscle** or **insertion of a muscle** (or muscle **tendon**) or ligament on bone is rough and often raised (though not all rough areas are locations of muscle attachment). Generally, the larger and more powerful a muscle is, the more area of the bone it needs on which to anchor itself (see Figures 3.4a and 3.4b).

Muscle fibers can only actively contract and then relax. Therefore, when you flex (or bend) your lower arm to your shoulder, the anterior muscles of the arm are contracting, and the muscles of

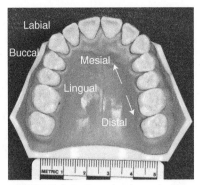

FIGURE 3.3 Terminology in the mouth.

Articulation: In osteology, this occurs when two or more bones are joined, whether or not they move at that point.

Ligament: Flexible fibrous tissue connecting the articular ends of bones (and sometimes making up a capsule that envelops them).

Synovial fluid: A slippery lubricant that fills most joint capsules.

Synarthrosis: A joint in which there is virtually no movement.

Amphiarthrosis: A joint in which there is some movement.

Origin of a muscle: Area of its attachment to bone that remains relatively fixed during the contraction of that muscle.

Insertion of a muscle: Area of attachment of a muscle to bone that usually moves through a greater range of motion when a muscle contracts.

Tendon: A band of dense fibrous tissue that forms the ends of muscles, particularly at the insertion, and attaches the muscle to the bone.

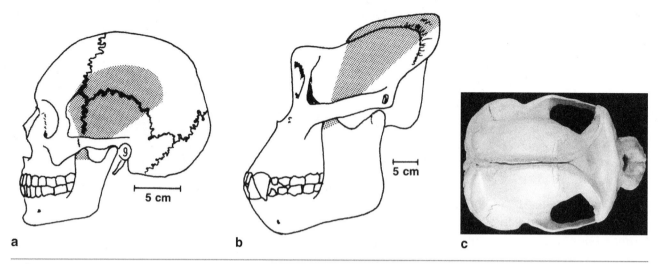

a   b   c

FIGURE 3.4 Origin of temporal muscle in modern humans and gorilla.

the posterior arm are passive. When you extend (or straighten) your arm against gravity, the posterior muscles of the arm are contracting, while the anterior muscles are passive. A general observation in gross anatomy, when describing the action of a muscle, is that the insertion of muscle is pulled toward the origin—that is, the point of origin remains fairly stationary, while the insertion moves. The muscle tendon at the insertion point must move through a greater angular range of motion than does the origin and must therefore be a smaller point on the bone (see Figure 3.1). If muscle fibers covered a large area, some fibers at the extreme edge of the insertion would stretch further during muscle contraction and might be strained or torn. The origin may be attached over a greater area of bone as it travels through a very limited range of motion, and the muscle fibers in general remain more parallel to the bone. The same force is acting on each end of the muscle, but because the insertion is typically smaller, more force per unit area is placed on the insertion than at the origin, both at the muscle tendon and at the bone. Because bone reacts to the amount of force applied by increasing both the density and the amount of roughening on the bone, the area of insertion will show more of the effects of a large muscle than will the origin.

These general rules can be used to decipher the significance of large crests or other areas of muscle attachment on bone. For example, the large sagittal crest on the male gorilla (see Figures 3.4b and 3.4c) is produced by a combination of a very large temporal muscle (one of the major chewing muscles) with a relatively small cranium. This temporal muscle becomes more powerful in the male gorilla as the gorilla matures (in part because the large teeth are developing) and gradually requires more bone on which to anchor itself. As the muscle becomes larger, it spreads out over the bone of its origin until it becomes so large that it literally runs out of cranium (see Figure 3.4c). The bone is then stimulated to produce more bone to provide this attachment area (a muscle does not anchor itself to another muscle) and will produce the crests you see in the sagittal region of the gorilla cranium.

The results of muscle origin and insertion need not be as spectacular as the sagittal crest in a gorilla to be useful to us as indicators of function. Even relatively small raised areas of muscle attachment can be useful in determining, even from small fragments, which bone we are holding, the side of the body and some features about the individual. Determining the occupation or lifestyle of an individual by analyzing these muscle attachments, although popular in television and movies, is not reliable.

After learning the morphology of human bones, it is also possible to identify most nonhuman bones because they are often very similar in shape, though they may differ in function. For example, the femur and humerus have very similar gross morphology in the human and bison (see Figures 3.5 and 3.6) even though the humerus performs different functions in the two animals.

INSTRUCTIONS FOR HANDLING BONE: Skeletal material is irreplaceable. Each skeleton is the only copy of a "book" of unique information. Treat it with the respect with which you would want your own skeleton to be treated.

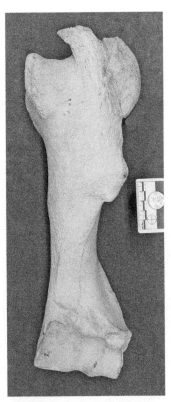

FIGURE 3.5 Bison humerus.

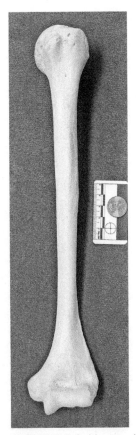

FIGURE 3.6 Human humerus.

EXERCISE 3.1   NAME _____   SECTION _____   DATE _____

Comparing Muscles, Cartilage, and Bone

This exercise will give you a chance to explore the relationship among muscles, cartilage, and bone, and will introduce the basics of growth and development in bone. It is intended to be a fun exercise that will no doubt influence the way you look at some of your food!

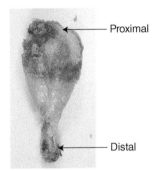

FIGURE 3.7
Chicken leg without skin.

FIGURE 3.8
Chicken leg with muscle being removed.

FIGURE 3.9
Chicken leg, bones separated.

FIGURE 3.10
Chicken leg with cartilage.

FIGURE 3.11
Chicken leg without soft tissue.

FIGURE 3.12
Proximal chicken leg.

FIGURE 3.13
Cut proximal chicken leg.

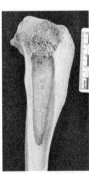

FIGURE 3.14
Cut deer tibia.

FIGURE 3.15
Deer tibia, close-up of trabeculae.

Safe food handling practices should be used during this exercise!

Materials:

- Chicken drumsticks, preferably cooked (it is safer to handle cooked meat). Each student should have a drumstick.
- Paper plates or paper towels, moist towelettes.
- Knife (does not have to be a sharp knife, and the class can share one or two knives).

At the beginning of this exercise, remove the skin from the drumstick very carefully (see Figure 3.7). If the meat (or muscle as we will call it from now on) begins to tear away, leave the skin on in that area.

Using blunt dissection (meaning just with your fingers—do not use a knife!), gently investigate the muscles (see Figure 3.8).

1. Are the muscles in layers, or are they side by side?

2. Are the muscles larger near the proximal end or near the distal end?

3. What do you notice about the characteristics of the muscles at each end (proximal and distal)?

   Carefully remove the top muscle (meaning the muscle nearest the surface). Describe it.

4. Is the muscle smooth? Slippery? Why do you think this is true?

5. Pull that muscle apart. Which way do the muscle fibers run (from proximal to distal or medial to lateral)? Given the earlier discussion about the function of a muscle, why do the muscle fibers run in this direction?

   Gently pull all of the muscles off of the drumstick, being careful to leave the cartilaginous ends (proximal and distal).

6. How many bones are there (see Figure 3.9)? Describe each of the bones (size and shape). You will be asked to determine which bones of the body you are studying at the end of this chapter.

7. As was described earlier, muscles originate and insert on bone. They cannot originate on other muscles. As you are pulling the muscles away from your drumstick, where are the muscles originating and inserting? Are they all originating on bone, or are some of them originating on cartilage? You will be asked to talk about this in more detail later in this book.

After you have cleaned the muscles from the bone, gently pry the proximal cartilage from the bone as completely and as neatly as possible (see Figures 3.10 and 3.11). Your goal is to remove the entire cartilage cap in one piece. If you are successful, there will still be some cartilage remaining on the bone, but it will be more or less interwoven into the bone itself (remember this when we talk about skeletal maturation and fracture patterns in bone). Set the cartilage cap aside.

Use your fingernail to scrape the bone near the midshaft. Can you remove a very thin, delicate layer of soft tissue? It is so delicate that it will not come off in a continuous layer. This is the periosteum, the thin soft tissue layer surrounding the bone. This will be discussed in more detail later, but it is important to know that the periosteum plays a large role in the development and continuing health of a bone.

Now concentrate on the bone itself. Notice the differences in external texture in different areas of the bone (also see Figures 3.12 and 3.16). In fact, texture differences throughout the bone are just as important as gross morphological differences for diagnosing whether or not what you are observing is actually bone, which bone of the skeleton you have, which part of that bone, the age of the individual, and often even the species represented.

Use your thumb and forefinger and try to pinch the bone at the proximal aspect, and then in the middle of the bone.

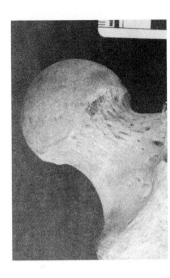

FIGURE 3.16 Human femoral neck.

The internal and external textures of bone are often as important in your diagnoses as the general shape of the bone itself!

8. Describe the differences in the "pinch" test at the proximal end and near the midshaft. You may have to use a pair of pliers to pinch the bone.

9. Carefully use the knife and split the proximal third of the bone in half along its long axis. Describe the morphological differences between the proximal end and the midshaft in the split bone.

    a. Do you see differences in the quantity of the soft, reddish-brown material in the proximal portion relative to the midshaft (see Figure 3.13)? This soft, fatty material is the bone marrow and is responsible for the production of red and white blood cells.

    b. Do you see differences in bone type between the proximal end and the midshaft? What are those differences? It may help to rinse the marrow off and out of the proximal end of the bone.

    The type of bone in any animal typically seen near articular surfaces is called trabecular, cancellous, or spongy bone (see Figures 3.14 and 3.15). Cortical or compact bone is typically seen in long bone shafts (though not exclusively) and is, as the name implies, very compact and dense bone.

10. Inspect the section of cartilage that you removed from the proximal aspect of the drumstick. If some bone residue is on the inner surface of the cartilage, gently scrape this off so that you are looking at a relatively clean cartilage surface. Hold the cartilage up to light, and look into its translucent center. What do you see? This feature will be discussed in more detail in Chapter 4, Growth and Development. Even though you are looking at a chicken drumstick, the elements you have described translate to mammalian (including human) bone, although the growth patterns in other animals can be quite different. As we proceed through the chapter, we will use these characteristics to understand the biomechanics of human bone and even to help us identify bone fragments.

As we explore growth and development and forensics, we will occasionally come back to the drumstick exercises. You may want to continue to play with your food by dissecting other meals that contain bones.

The entire chicken bone exercise includes additional elements of osteology, human versus nonhuman bone identification, growth and development, and fracture characteristics of fresh and dry bone.

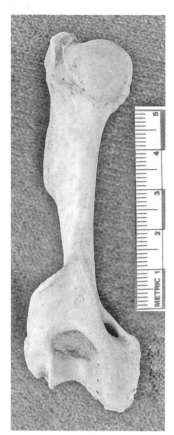

FIGURE 3.17 Common long bone.

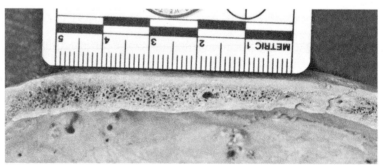

FIGURE 3.18 Cranial cross section.

The morphology and terminology of bone discussed to this point are typical of most of the bones (see Figure 3.17) of the body. The morphology seen and terminology used to discuss the cranium differ, however (see Figure 3.18), as do the patterns of growth and development (discussed in Chapter 4).

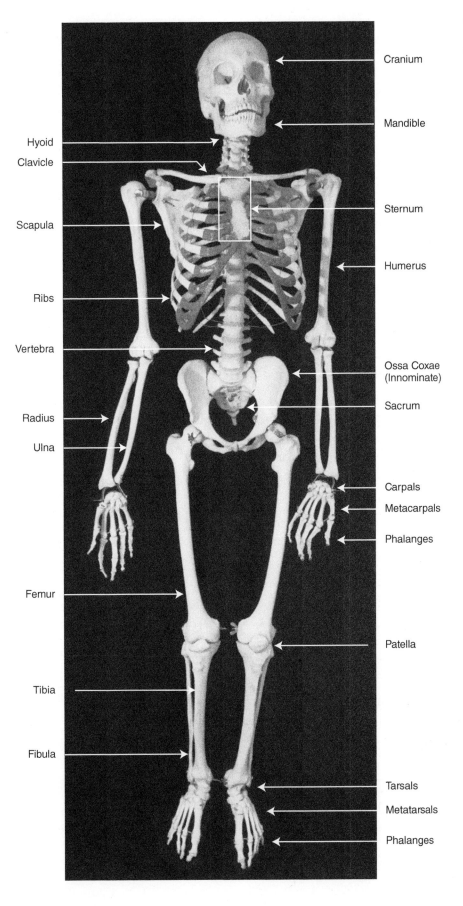

FIGURE 3.19 The human skeleton.

Cranium

Mandible

Hyoid

Clavicle

Sternum

Scapula

Humerus

Ribs

Vertebra

Ossa Coxae
(Innominate)

Sacrum

Radius

Ulna

Carpals

Metacarpals

Phalanges

Femur

Patella

Tibia

Fibula

Tarsals

Metatarsals

Phalanges

TERMINOLOGY

Anatomical position:	Body with arms by side, palms forward.
Anterior:	In front (similar to ventral).
Appendicular:	The limbs.
Axial:	The head and trunk.
Caudal:	Toward the tail.
Coronal plane:	Parallel to the coronal suture.
Cranial:	Toward the head.
Distal:	Away from trunk of body along a limb.
Dorsal:	In back (similar to posterior).
External:	Outside of.
Inferior:	Lower.
Internal:	Inside of.
Lateral:	Perpendicularly away from midsagittal plane.
Longitudinal:	Coursing or placed lengthwise.
Medial:	Perpendicularly toward the midsagittal plane.
Posterior:	Behind, to the back (similar to dorsal).
Pronation:	Rotation of the hand and forearm so that the palm faces dorsally or toward the body.
Proximal:	Toward the trunk of the body along a limb.
Sagittal section:	Any section of the body parallel to the sagittal suture of the cranium (refer to Figure 3.2) .
Superficial:	Near the surface.
Superior:	Above, top.
Supination:	Turning the palm of the hand anteriorly.
Transverse:	Any crosswise section.
Ventral:	In front (similar to anterior).
Vertex:	Top, highest point.
In mouth:	
Buccal:	Toward the cheek.
Distal:	At greatest distance from the anterior midline of the mouth.
Labial:	Toward the lips.
Lingual:	Toward the tongue.
Mesial:	Toward the anterior midline of the mouth.
Occlusal:	The chewing surface of the teeth.
Frankfort plane:	A standard plane of reference on the cranium in which the upper border of the external auditory meatus is on the same level as the lower border of the eye (also called the Frankfort horizontal).

FEATURES OF BONE

Feature (Plural):	Definition:
Cavity (cavities):	An open area.
Condyle (condyles):	Rounded process at the point of articulation with another bone.
Crest (crests):	A projecting ridge.
Diaphysis (diaphyses):	The shaft of bone and primary center of bone growth.
Epiphysis (epiphyses):	A process of bone initially attached to another piece of bone by cartilage and usually later consolidated with it by bone.
Fontanelle (fontanelles):	Membranous space between cranial bones in fetal life and infancy.
Foramen (foramina):	A hole or opening.
Fossa (fossae):	A pit, depression, or cavity.
Meatus (meatuses):	A canal.
Process (processes):	Any outgrowth or prominence of bone.
Sinus (sinuses):	Bone cavity lined with mucous membrane.
Suture (sutures):	Areas of articulation between cranial bones.
Torus (tori):	An elevation or prominence.
Tubercle (tubercles):	A small, knob-like projection on bone.
Tuberosity (tuberosities):	A large, rough eminence or projection on bone.

BONES OF THE SKULL

The skull, consisting of cranium and mandible, is a complex set of bones that protects and supports the functioning of the brain, eyes, ears, nose, and mouth. See Figures 3.20 through 3.32 for drawings of the skull bones.

Cranium The cranium articulates with the first cervical vertebra (the atlas) by means of the occipital condyles (see Figure 3.33). The **occipital condyles** lie on the anterolateral borders of the foramen magnum ("large hole"). The spinal cord passes through the **foramen magnum** on its way from the brain to the vertebral column.

The **nuchal** (neck) muscles are actually a group of muscles positioned on the neck. The posterior nuchal muscles have as their uppermost point of insertion a raised line on the posterior portion of the occipital bone, the **superior nuchal line** (also sometimes called the *superior nuchal crest* if it's large enough, particularly in other animals). One large anterior nuchal muscle, the *sternocleidomastoid* (or sternomastoid), inserts on a large, downward-projecting process of bone, the **mastoid process** (see Figure 3.33).

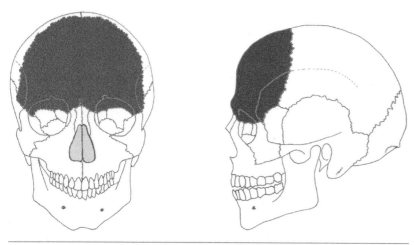

FIGURE 3.20 Frontal bone (single bone).

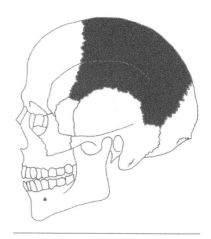

FIGURE 3.21 Parietal bone (paired).

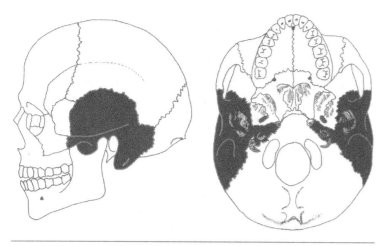

FIGURE 3.22 Temporal bone (paired).

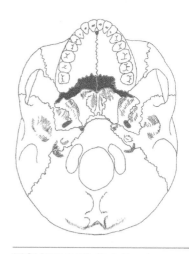

FIGURE 3.23 Palatine bone (paired).

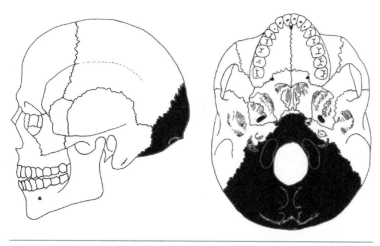

FIGURE 3.24 Occipital bone (single).

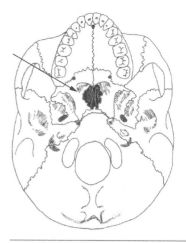

FIGURE 3.25 Vomer bone (single).

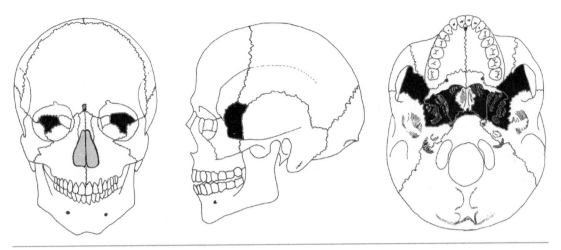

FIGURE 3.26 Sphenoid bone (single).

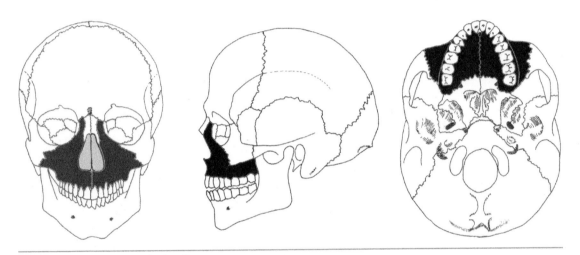

FIGURE 3.27 Maxilla (paired).

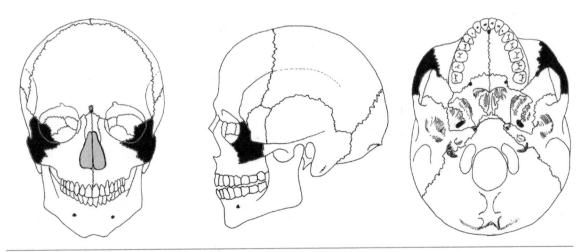

FIGURE 3.28 Zygomatic bone (paired).

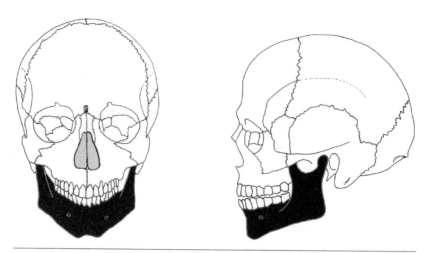

FIGURE 3.29 Mandible (single).

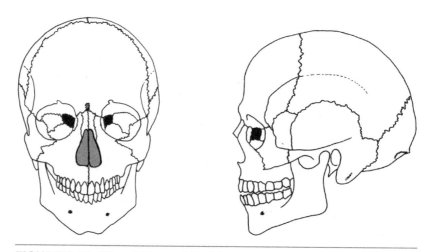

FIGURE 3.30 Ethmoid bone (single).

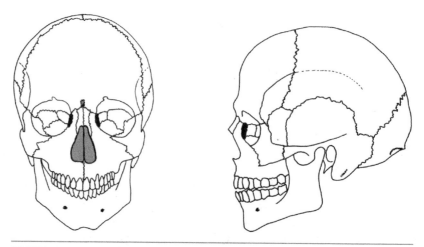

FIGURE 3.31 Lacrimal bone (paired).

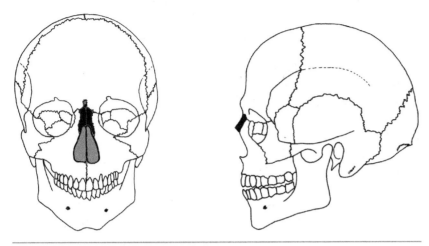

FIGURE 3.32 Nasal bone (paired).

Features of the skull
1. Metopic suture
2. Mental foramen
3. Mental eminence
4. Supraorbital torus (browridge)
5. Temporal line
6. Superior nuchal line
7. Mastoid process
8. External auditory meatus
9. Zygomatic arch
10. Ascending ramus
11. Gonial angle
12. Foramen ovalis
13. Occipital condyle(s)
14. Foramen magnum
15. Temporomandibular joint
16. Mandibular foramen
17. Coronoid process
18. Condyle
19. Sella turcica
20. Crista galli
21. Cribiform plate
22. External occipital protuberance

The temporal muscle, one of the major muscles of mastication (chewing), originates on the **temporal line** (see Figure 3.33), on the frontal and parietal bones of the skull.

Locate the **external auditory meatus** (external opening of the ear shown in Figure 3.33) and the **zygomatic arches** (which, along with the zygomatic [also called zygoma or malar] bone, form the bony prominence of the cheek and can be felt just below and lateral to the eye; see Figure 3.33). Another protrusion that can be felt through the skin is the **supraorbital torus** (as will be discussed in Chapter 15, this is a rounded ridge above the eyes that is usually more prominent in males than in females; see Figure 3.33). The **foramen ovale** is an opening on either side of the basilar portion of the occipital bone on the sphenoid bone (see Figure 3.33). This opening allows the passage of a small artery and one or two nerves (varies by individual).

The sagittal suture (see Figure 3.34) is a long straight suture "tying together" the two parietal bones, running anteroposteriorly along the top of the cranium. The coronal suture runs laterally from

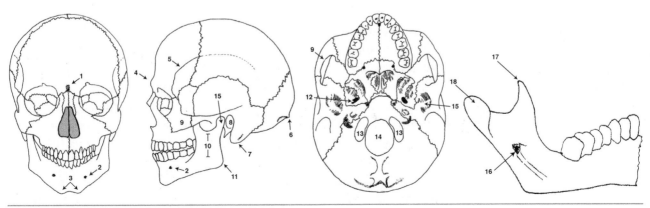

FIGURE 3.33 Features of the skull.

Sutures of the cranium

A. Sagittal

B. Coronal

C. Lambdoidal

D. Spheno-occipital synchondrosis (basilar suture)

E. Squamosal suture

F. Metopic suture (remnant)

G. Palatal suture

Most other sutures are named for the two bones joined by the suture (for example, zygomaxillary).

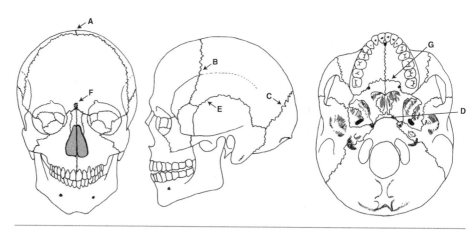

FIGURE 3.34 Sutures of the cranium.

the top of the cranium and ties together the frontal and two parietal bones. The lambdoidal suture ties together the occipital and two parietal bones on the posterior cranium. The squamosal suture is an area in which the squamosal section of the temporal bone is beveled and overlaps the parietal bone.

The spheno-occipital synchondrosis, sometimes called the basilar suture, is the point of articulation by synchondrosis (a joint in which the surfaces are connected by a growth of cartilage) of the basilar portion of the occipital bone with the body of the sphenoid bone. As early as mid-teens in males and about two years earlier in females (Schaefer et al., 2009), there is complete union of the two bones. Occasionally one sees a **metopic suture** dividing the frontal bone. The metopic suture is a remnant of a suture that is usually united and obliterated by the time a child reaches four years of age (Scheuer and Black 2000). The occurrence of the metopic suture well into adulthood is not pathological but is one of the many variations of the human skeleton in different individuals and in different populations.

Mandible The mandible articulates with the cranium at the **temporomandibular joint** by its **mandibular condyles**. The **mental eminence** (chin) shows some sexual dimorphism (discussed further in Chapter 15), in that in males it is usually more squared, with slight projections on either side of the midline, and in females, the mental eminence usually has only a single point at the midline. Of course, as with many other aspects of the human skeleton, there is significant variation in this feature. The **mental foramen** allows passage of the mental nerve and blood vessels on either side of the midline, while the **mandibular foramen** is on the lingual (tongue) side of the mandible about midway in the ascending ramus (the rising part of the mandible above the mandibular angle). The **ascending ramus** bifurcates into the mandibular condyles and the **coronoid process** (which is the area of insertion of the **masseter muscle**, one of the muscles used in chewing).

Teeth Each tooth has three areas, the **crown, neck**, and **root** (see Figure 3.35). The crown is covered with very hard, white enamel and is that part of the tooth above the gum line (see Figure 3.36). The neck is a constricted area just below the crown. The root is below the neck and is contained within the tooth socket of the mandible or maxilla.

There are 20 deciduous (baby) teeth in children, and 32 permanent teeth in adults (see Figure 3.37). A **dental formula** is a count of the number and types of teeth, written in shorthand form. Only the teeth in one upper quadrant and often a lower quadrant are counted (see Figure 3.38).

In each adult quadrant (upper left, upper right, lower left, lower right) there are two **incisors** (one central, one lateral), one **canine,** two **premolars**, and two or three **molars** (first, second, and third or wisdom tooth) (see Figure 3.38). Hence the dental formula of the maxilla and mandible for a modern human adult is:

$$\frac{2\!:\!1\!:\!2\!:\!3}{2\!:\!1\!:\!2\!:\!3}$$

if upper and lower quadrants are counted, or abbreviated 2:1:2:3 if upper and lower quadrants are the same.

Primitive mammals have four premolars. In the line of evolution leading to humans, the first two premolars were lost, leaving the third and fourth.

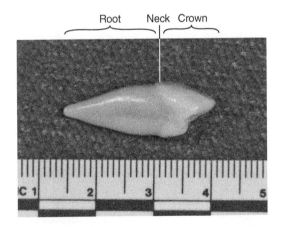

Root   Neck   Crown

FIGURE 3.35 Features of a tooth.

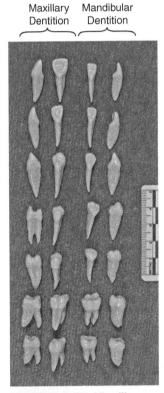

Maxillary Dentition   Mandibular Dentition

FIGURE 3.37 Maxillary dentition left two rows; mandibular dentition right two rows.

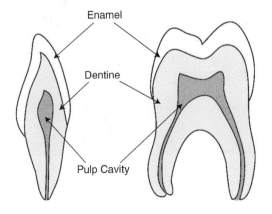

Enamel

Dentine

Pulp Cavity

FIGURE 3.36 Cross section of teeth.

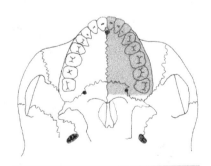

FIGURE 3.38 Tooth row. Shaded area is one quadrant.

In each quadrant of a child's mouth (ages about two to six years), there are two incisors (one central, one lateral), one canine, and two molars (first, second). There are no deciduous premolars in humans. The dental formula is therefore:

$$\frac{2{:}1{:}0{:}2}{2{:}1{:}0{:}2}$$

After about six years of age, there is a mixture of deciduous and permanent dentition.

POSTCRANIAL BONES

Postcranial bones in humans are under the cranium, but in animals that walk on four legs, the postcranial bones are behind the cranium.

Hyoid

The hyoid bone (see Figure 3.39) is a very small bone that does not articulate directly with any other bone but is suspended below the mandible by many muscles acting on the tongue, pharynx, and neck.

Vertebrae

The vertebral column is divided into five sections: **cervical** (usually 7 in number), **thoracic** (usually 12), **lumbar** (usually 5), **sacral** (4 to 6 but fused in the adult to form the sacrum), and **coccygeal** (3 to 5). The bodies of the cervical, thoracic, and lumbar vertebrae increase in size from the head toward the feet. See Figure 3.40 for features common to all vertebrae.

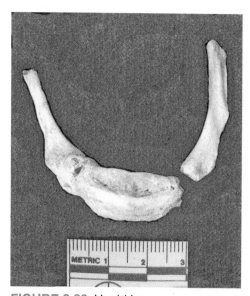

FIGURE 3.39 Hyoid bone.

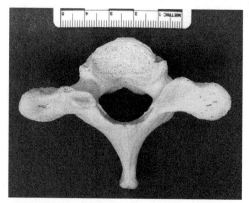

FIGURE 3.40 Typical vertebra, superior view. The anterior is at the top of the photograph, the posterior at the bottom.

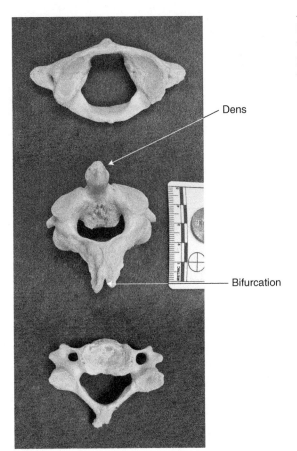

FIGURE 3.41 Cervical vertebrae, superior view. The atlas is at the top, axis in the middle, and a typical cervical vertebra at the bottom.

Dens

Bifurcation

Cervical Vertebrae Cervical vertebrae (see Figure 3.41) are the smallest weight-supporting vertebrae. The coccygeal and terminal sacral vertebrae are smaller, but they support no weight. The cervical vertebrae are also recognizable in that:

- There is a foramen (plural: *foramina*) in the **transverse process**. These foramina transmit the vertebral arteries that help supply blood, and therefore oxygen to the brain.

- The spinous processes are often bifurcated (forked).

- The body is oval in shape with the long axis in the transverse direction (except the first and second cervical vertebrae).

- The articular processes (between vertebrae) are nearly more horizontally oriented. The cranial articular processes face dorsally and cranially, and the caudal face ventrally and caudally.

The first cervical vertebra, the **atlas** (it holds the "world," that is, cranium, on its shoulders), has no body. The second cervical vertebra, the **axis,** has a prominence on its body, called the **dens** or **odontoid process** ("tooth," as it looks like a tooth). The atlas (and hence the cranium) rotates around the dens.

Cranium: "Nods" on the atlas and shakes "no" on the axis.

Spinous processes: Sites of attachment on the vertebrae for various muscles and ligaments of the neck and back.

Note: Occasionally, loose lower coccygeal vertebrae are confused with the body of the unfused hyoid bone.

Thoracic Vertebrae Thoracic vertebrae (see Figure 3.42) are easy to recognize because:

- They have facets for the articulation of the ribs. These articulations are also called **costal pits**.
- The articular processes (between vertebrae) are roughly parallel to each other, vertical, and flat (except for the 12th, which has a lumbar vertebra–type process on the inferior surface).
- Most of the **spinous processes** are long, pointed caudally, and tend to overlap the spinous process on the next vertebra below.
- There is no transverse foramen.

Lumbar Vertebrae Lumbar vertebrae (see Figure 3.43) are the largest of the movable vertebrae because they carry the most weight. In addition:

- The processes for articulation with the other vertebrae are angled, vertical, and curved to interlock with each other, giving a much stronger intervertebral articulation.
- The spinous processes are short and blunt.
- Lumbar vertebrae have no rib facets.
- Lumbar vertebrae have no transverse foramina.

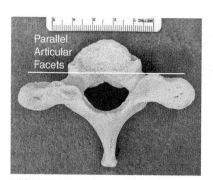

FIGURE 3.42 Thoracic vertebra, superior view (left), lateral view (right).

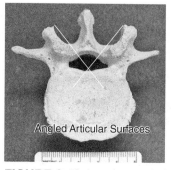

FIGURE 3.43 Lumbar vertebra, superior view (left), lateral view (right).

Sacral Vertebrae Sacral vertebrae, usually five but sometimes four or six in number, are fused in the adult to form a single bone, the sacrum (see Figures 3.44 through 3.46). The weight of the upper body in humans is passed to the ossa coxarum (innominate bones) and femora (plural for femur—the thigh bone) through the upper part of the sacrum, so this bone must be strong and stable.

The sides of the upper sacral vertebrae are flared into wings, or **alae** (singular: *ala*), to form a large surface that articulates with the ilium.

Coccygeal Vertebrae Coccygeal vertebrae (see Figure 3.47) give no support to the vertebral column but are the site of origin of a few muscles and ligaments.

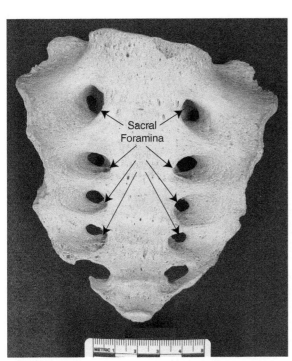

FIGURE 3.44 Sacrum, anterior view.

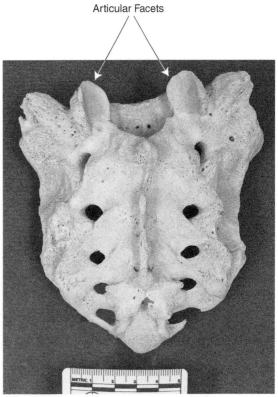

FIGURE 3.45 Sacrum, anterior view.

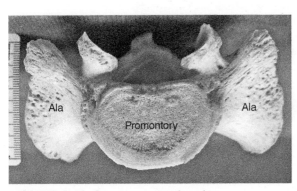

FIGURE 3.46 Sacrum, superior view.

FIGURE 3.47 First coccygeal vertebra, anterior view.

A note about general side identification in paired postcranial bones: It is easiest to identify the side the bone is from if you visualize how the bone is positioned in your own body. The hints given will include how prominent features of the bone are related to the function of the bone in the body or to other anatomical features easily recognized in your own body.

Clavicle

The **clavicle** maintains a constant distance between the scapula and the sternum and thereby adds strength to the shoulder girdle. In generalized quadrupeds that use their forelimbs primarily for support or striding locomotion, that strength is supplied by the musculature without a clavicle, while animals that use their forelimbs for manipulation or more complicated forms of locomotion sometimes have a clavicle. The medial end is rounded for articulation with the sternum; the lateral end is flattened (and roughened inferiorly) for articulation with the scapula (see Figure 3.48). The conoid tubercle is inferior and on the lateral third and is part of the area of attachment for the conoid ligament that secures it to the coracoid process of the scapula (see Figure 3.49).

To determine side, position the rounded sternal end medially and the flat end laterally, and let the bone round out anteriorly as it progresses laterally. If you hold the sternal end medially and the bone rounds out posteriorly, you have it on the wrong side. Also, because the conoid tubercle is the point of attachment for the conoid ligament, make sure that the roughest flat side of the lateral aspect is positioned inferiorly (because muscle and ligament attachment points are rougher).

FIGURE 3.48 Left clavicle, superior view.

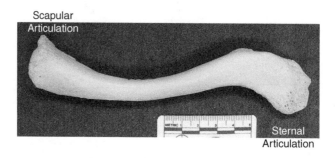

Scapular
Articulation

Sternal
Articulation

FIGURE 3.49 Left clavicle, inferior view.

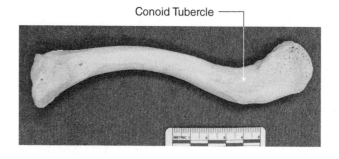

Conoid Tubercle

Sternum

The **sternum** is composed of three segments and is similar to a broadsword (see Figure 3.50):

- The **manubrium** ("handle") articulates with the clavicle and the first two ribs.
- The **body** ("blade, gladiolus") articulates with ribs (3 to 7 directly, 8 to 10 indirectly).
- The **xiphoid process** ("tip"), often a cartilaginous tab, becomes bony in later years (the exact time of ossification varies).

The three segments of this bone can be separate or fused in the adult.

Scapula

The scapula is a triangular, relatively flat bone that rests on the upper back (see Figures 3.51 through 3.53). It has two major projections on the proximal lateral angle: the **coracoid process** (anterior projection) and the **acromion process** (posterior projection), which are both points of origin of muscles of the upper back and arm. The acromion process articulates with the clavicle and is one of the points used by a tailor to calculate sleeve length.

The **scapular spine** is posterior and supports several muscles of the back, including the trapezius. The **glenoid fossa** is lateral and is the point of articulation of the head of the humerus.

To side a scapula, position the glenoid fossa laterally, the inferior angle caudally and the scapular spine posteriorly. It is easy to mistakenly

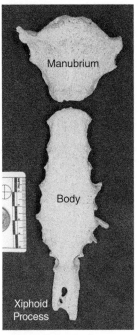

FIGURE 3.50 Sternum, anterior view.

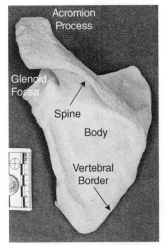

FIGURE 3.51 Left scapula, dorsal surface.

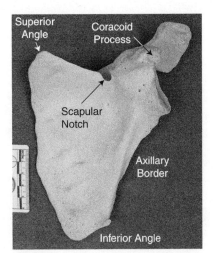

FIGURE 3.52 Left scapula, ventral surface.

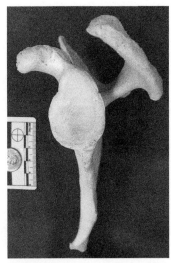

FIGURE 3.53 Left scapula, lateral view.

put the scapular spine anteriorly, but remember that there are no *prominent* muscle insertion areas between the scapula and the ribs!

Ribs

The ribs are in general easy to recognize (see Figures 3.54 and 3.55). In all but the first rib, the superior surface is rounded, the inferior surface is rather sharp, and the rib is flat dorsoventrally. The head articulates with the lateral vertebral body, and the tubercle articulates with the transverse process of the thoracic vertebra.

The first rib is flat craniocaudally and is shorter than the other ribs. The superior surface shows grooves for the subclavian artery and vein (which, as its name implies, runs under the clavicle). To determine side for first rib, be sure that the groove (which is sometimes more easily felt than seen) is positioned superiorly, the sternal end medially, and the vertebral articular surface posteriorly.

The first seven ribs are *true* ribs in that they articulate with the sternum at the readily observable costal (rib) notches.

The 8th, 9th, and 10th ribs are *false* ribs in that they do not articulate directly with the sternum but through a common cartilage, which itself articulates with the distal sternum.

FIGURE 3.54 Left ribs, superior view; first rib (bottom), standard rib (top).

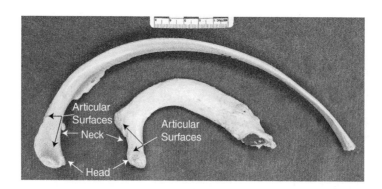

FIGURE 3.55 Left ribs, superior view.

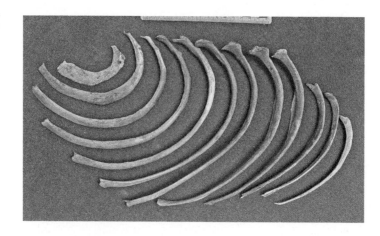

The 11th and 12th ribs are *floating* ribs, so named because they have no connection to the sternum.

To determine on which side ribs 2 through 12 reside in the body, place the rib so that the sternal end is medial, the vertebral end is lateral, and the more rounded surface is superior.

All ribs except the first rib are rounded on the superior surface and exhibit a costal ("rib") groove on the inferior surface.

Humerus

The **humerus** (see Figures 3.56 through 3.58) is the largest bone of the upper limb. The rounded head at the proximal end articulates with the glenoid fossa of the scapula, and the distal end articulates

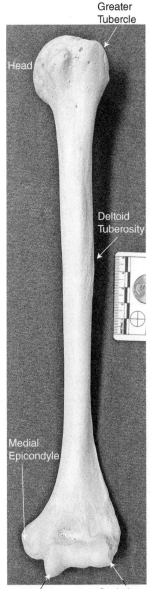

FIGURE 3.56 Left humerus, anterior view.

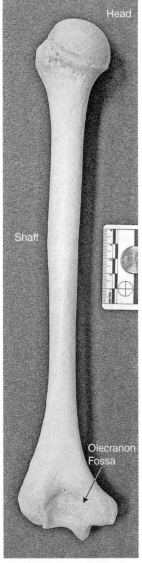

FIGURE 3.57 Left humerus, posterior view.

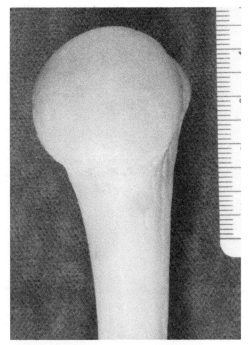

FIGURE 3.58 Humerus head.

with the radius and ulna. The deltoid muscle, a large muscle of the upper arm and shoulder, inserts at the deltoid tuberosity and **abducts** the arm and hand when contracted (think of the *abduct*ion of someone). Think of the action of the muscle, and it makes sense that the deltoid tuberosity is on the lateral aspect of the humerus. The medial epicondyle, a point of origin of major muscles of the forearm and hand, is, as its name implies, medial. The ulnar nerve (the nerve insulted when you hit your "funny bone") passes under the medial epicondyle just medial to the trochlea. The trochlea articulates with the medial bone of the forearm, the ulna, and the rounded capitulum articulates with the rounded head of the radius, which is the lateral bone of the forearm.

To determine side, hold the bone as it is in the body (head is proximal), and the medial epicondyle is medial. If you have only the distal section of the humerus, make sure that the medial epicondyle is medial, and the olecranon fossa is posterior. Then align it with your body. If you only have the proximal section, make sure that the articular surface is medial and the bicipital groove is anterior.

Radius

The **radius** (see Figures 3.59 through 3.62) is the lateral bone of the forearm and "follows" the thumb in the movements of the forearm in **pronation** and **supination**. The radius crosses over the ulna in pronation. The proximal surface is rounded for articulation with the capitulum of the humerus, so think of the "radius of a circle" when remembering the radius (see Figure 3.61). A roughened projection just below the proximal articular surface on the antero-medial surface is the radial tuberosity and is the point of insertion for the biceps muscle (when you think of the action of the biceps, it makes sense that the point of insertion is anterior). Distally, the radius articulates with navicular and lunate of the wrist via a concave articular surface (see Figure 3.62). Just above this articular surface is the ulnar notch, a concave articular surface that accommodates the rounded head of the ulna.

To determine side, make sure that the rounded head is proximal and that the radial tuberosity is anterior. Distally, the radius is roughened on the posterior surface and has a smoother, slightly concave surface anteriorly (you can feel this in your own radius). Make sure that the smoother anterior surface is placed anteriorly, and align it with your body.

Pronation: The rotation of the hand and forearm so that the palm faces posteriorly or toward the body; the hand is in the anatomical position at **supination** with palm up or forward. Think of holding a cup of soup ("supination") on your palm.

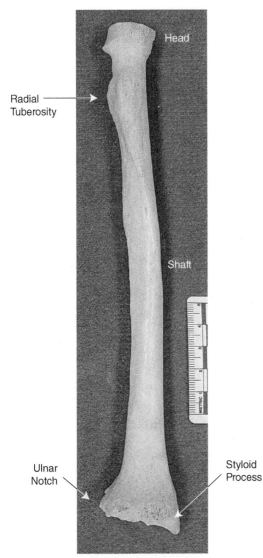

Head

Radial Tuberosity

Shaft

Ulnar Notch

Styloid Process

FIGURE 3.59 Left anterior radius.

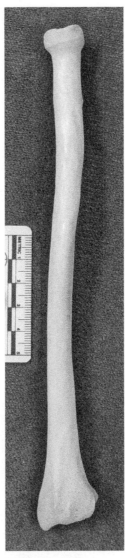

FIGURE 3.60 Posterior radius.

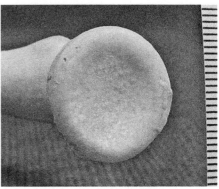

FIGURE 3.61 Radial head (proximal radius).

Ulnar notch

FIGURE 3.62 Distal radius.

Ulna

The **ulna** (see Figures 3.63 through 3.65) is the medial bone of the forearm when the body is in anatomical position, and it articulates proximally with the humerus and laterally with the radius. The **semilunar notch** ("half moon notch") at the proximal end forms a "U" (which should help you remember "ulna") and articulates snugly with the trochlea. The olecranon process slides into the olecranon fossa of the humerus when the forearm is extended.

The proximal area of articulation with the radius is at the radial notch, just below the semilunar notch. Distally, the ulna ends with a small, rounded articular surface (the head) and the styloid process

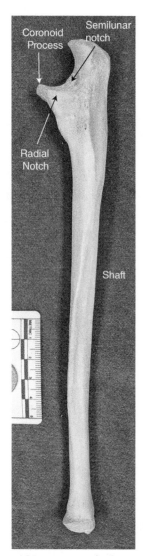

FIGURE 3.63 Left ulna, lateral view.

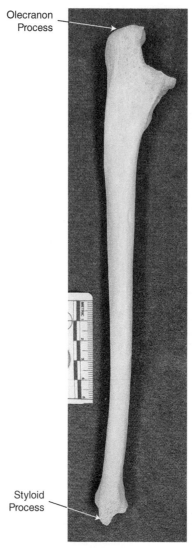

FIGURE 3.64 Left ulna, medial view.

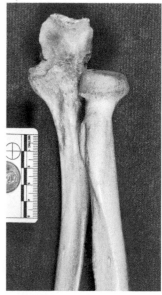

FIGURE 3.65 Proximal ulna and radius articulated.

that is on the posteromedial surface. The rounded head of the ulna articulates with the distal radius.

To determine side, place the semilunar notch in the proximal position with the open part of the "U" facing anteriorly. Then make sure that the radial notch is lateral (remember that the radius is the lateral bone in the body when it is in anatomical position), and align it with your body.

Wrist and Hand

The wrist and hand consist of many different kinds of bones (see Figures 3.66 through 3.68). The **carpals** are the eight wrist bones. From medial to lateral when the wrist is in the anatomical position, the proximal row consists of **pisiform, triquetrum, lunate**, and **navicular** (or **scaphoid**), and the distal row of **hamate, capitate, lesser multangular** (or **trapezoid**), and **greater multangular** (or **trapezium**).

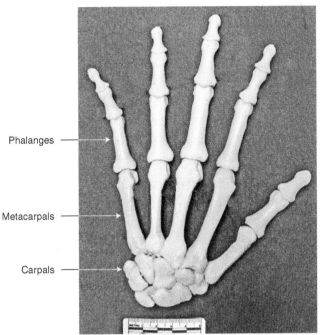

Phalanges

Metacarpals

Carpals

FIGURE 3.66 Right hand, posterior view.

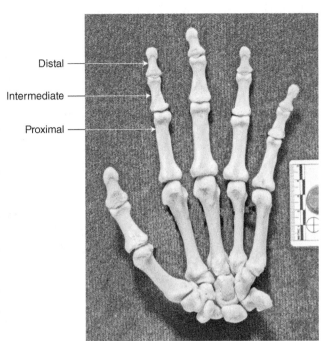

Distal

Intermediate

Proximal

FIGURE 3.67 Left hand, palmar view.

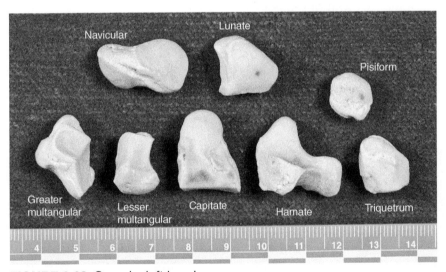

Navicular

Lunate

Pisiform

Greater multangular

Lesser multangular

Capitate

Hamate

Triquetrum

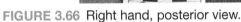

FIGURE 3.68 Carpals, left hand.

The **metacarpals** make up the main part of the living hand, including the palm, between the wrist and the projection of the fingers. They are simply numbered 1 through 5, beginning at the thumb (lateral or radial) side.

The **phalanges** are the bones of the fingers. The thumb has two (proximal and distal); all other fingers have three each (proximal, middle or intermediate, and distal).

Os coxae: Bone of the hip.

Ossa coxae: Bones of the hip.

Ossa coxarum: Bones of the hips.

Ossa Coxae (Innominate)

The **ossa coxarum (innominata)** (singular: *ossa coxae,* or innominate) are the two large bones of the pelvis, which join with the sacrum to form the pelvic girdle (see Figures 3.69 through 3.71).

Although the ossa coxae is one unit in the adult, it actually consists of three separate bones, all coming together in the **acetabulum**, the large cup-shaped cavity that articulates with the head of the femur (see Figure 3.69). These are:

- **Ilium:** Upper portion. The **iliac crest** is the most superior edge of the ilium and can be felt through the skin. Posteriorly, the **greater sciatic notch** is a deep incurve. The auricular surface (so called because it looks like an ear) is the point of articulation with the sacrum, forming the sacroiliac joint.
- **Ischium:** The inferior bone of the ossa coxae. The **ischial tuberosity** supports the body in the sitting position. The area is roughened because of the attachment of many muscles and ligaments, including the origin of the powerful hamstring muscles that extend the thigh.
- **Pubis:** The most anterior portion. It articulates with the pubic bone from the opposite side at the **pubic symphysis** to form the anterior wall of the pelvis.

To determine side of a complete ossa coxae, make sure that the acetabulum is lateral (as it articulates with the head of the femur) and that the ischial tuberosity is posterior and caudal. It is tricky at first to determine which part of the ossa coxae is the ischial

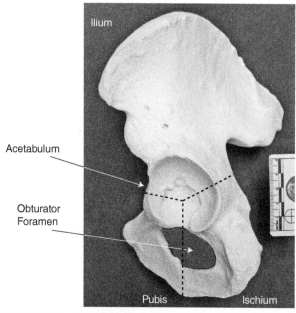

FIGURE 3.69 Left ossa coxae, lateral view.

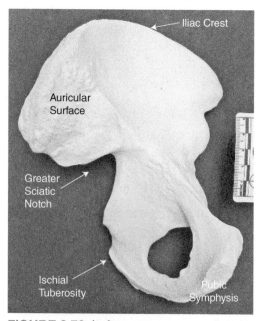

FIGURE 3.70 Left ossa coxae, medial view.

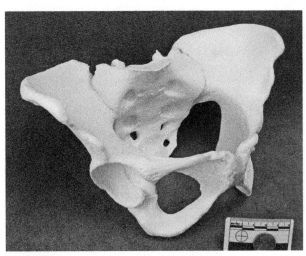

FIGURE 3.71 Articulated pelvic girdle.

tuberosity and which is the pubic symphysis. Remember that the ischial tuberosity is a muscle insertion area, so it is larger and more rounded, and has a more roughened surface than seen on the pubic symphysis. Often the pubic symphysis has a flatter surface, except in very young individuals.

Femur

The femur is the largest and longest bone in the human body (not so for all other animals, as we will see later). The head of the femur articulates proximally with the acetabulum, and the condyles articulate with the condyles of the tibia distally (see Figures 3.72 to 3.75).

The head of the femur is a more complete ball than is the head of the humerus. The head exhibits a pit, the **fovea capitis** (Figure 3.75), in the center, at which the very strong **ligamentum teres** connects the femur to the acetabulum and carries blood to the femur. The femur is much more difficult to dislocate than is the head of the humerus in a living person because of the depth of the acetabulum and the strength of the ligamentum teres. The greater trochanter is a large projection on the lateral proximal surface, roughened because of the insertion of muscles that, among other actions, abduct the thigh. The lesser trochanter is a posteromedial conical projection distal to the greater trochanter.

The **linea aspera** is a long raised and roughened line running parallel to the femur on the posterior aspect. It is the area of insertion of many muscles, including the powerful hamstring muscles that extend the thigh. The condyles of the distal femur are more extensive posteriorly, to allow the tibia to flex.

To determine side, make sure that the head faces medially (as it articulates with the acetabulum) and that it is proximal. The lesser trochanter is posterior, as are the more rounded aspects of

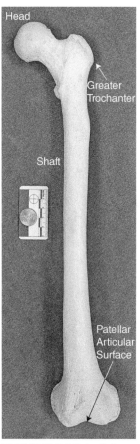

FIGURE 3.72 Left femur, anterior view.

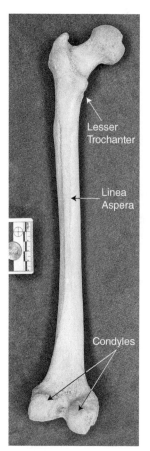

FIGURE 3.73 Left femur, posterior view.

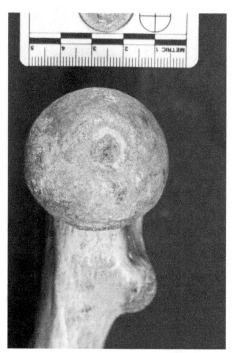

FIGURE 3.74 Right femoral head.

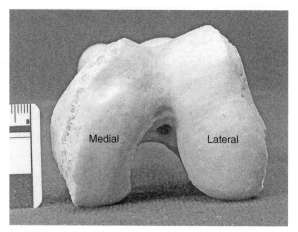

FIGURE 3.75 Distal femur.

the condyles. If you have only the proximal aspect, use the lesser trochanter to show you the posterior aspect. If you have only the distal aspect, make sure that the condyles are more rounded posteriorly and that they are distal. Also, notice that the medial condyle is larger

FIGURE 3.76 Patella, anterior view.

FIGURE 3.77 Patella, posterior view.

and has more of a curve anteroposteriorly. The lateral condyle is shorter (anteroposteriorly) and straighter.

Patella

The **patella** is the kneecap, which rests just anterior to the distal femur (see Figures 3.76 and 3.77). The patella points distally and is rounded proximally, and it is the largest of the **sesamoid bones**. A sesamoid bone is one that develops within a tendon (in this case, the patellar tendon) and acts as a pulley to enhance the mechanical force or action of the tendon that passes over it. Other smaller sesamoids sometimes occur in the hands and feet.

To side a patella is easy. Simply place the bone on a table with the apex pointing away from you. The bone will fall to the side it is from. The lateral articular surface is larger than the medial articular surface.

Tibia

The **tibia** (see Figures 3.78 to 3.81), the second largest bone of the lower limb, has a **tibial tuberosity** and a sharp shin, both of which can be palpated anteriorly in a living subject. The tibial tuberosity is the point of common insertion (through the patellar tendon) of many of the muscles that flex the thigh at the hip and extend the leg. The articular facet for the fibula can be seen on the posterolateral tibia just below the condyles. The **medial malleolus** of the distal tibia forms the medial projection of the ankle felt in a living person.

To determine side, make sure that the condyles are proximal, the medial malleolus is on the medial side, and the tibial tuberosity is anterior. Then align the bone with your body.

Intercondyloid
Eminence

FIGURE 3.80 Proximal left tibia.

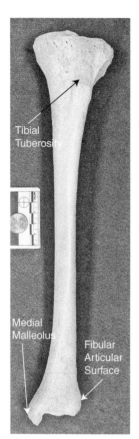

Tibial
Tuberosity

Medial
Malleolus

Fibular
Articular
Surface

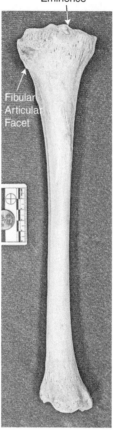

Fibular
Articular
Facet

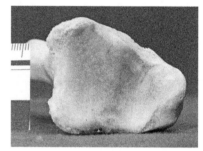

FIGURE 3.81 Distal left tibia.

FIGURE 3.78 Left
tibia, anterior view.

FIGURE 3.79 Left
tibia, posterior view.

Fibula

With the tibia, the **fibula** (see Figures 3.82 to 3.84) is the analog of
the radius and ulna, although the leg has lost most of the pronation–
supination function. The **lateral malleolus** of the distal fibula forms
the lateral projection of the ankle felt in a living subject. Distally,
the fibula is grooved on the posterior surface (the malleolar fossa;
see Figure 3.84), where a tendon crosses from the posterior leg to
the plantar surface of the foot.

To determine side, make sure that the styloid process is proximal and that the articular surface is medial (to articulate with the
tibia). Also, make sure that the malleolar fossa is posterior, and
place it in anatomical position.

Ankle and Foot

The **tarsals** are the seven bones that make up the ankle: the **calcaneus, talus, navicular, first cuneiform, second cuneiform, third
cuneiform**, and **cuboid** (see Figure 3.87).

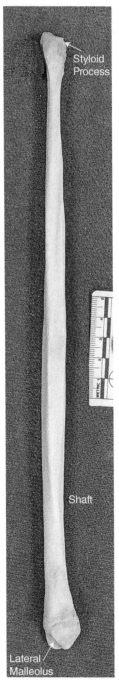

FIGURE 3.82 Fibula, lateral view.

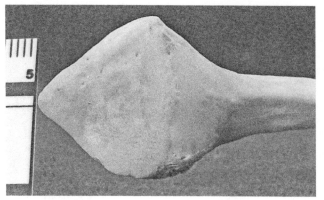

FIGURE 3.83 Proximal left fibula.

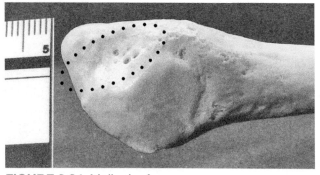

FIGURE 3.84 Malleolar fossa.

The **metatarsals** are analogous to the metacarpals of the hand and make up the body of the foot. Again, they are simply numbered 1 (medial) through 5 (lateral).

The **phalanges** of the foot are again analogous to the phalanges of the hand (see Figures 3.85 and 3.86).

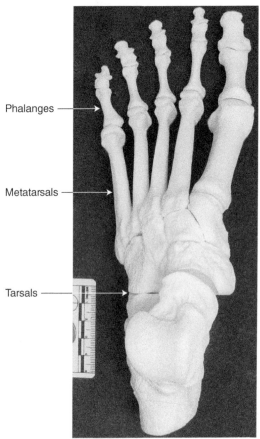

Phalanges

Metatarsals

Tarsals

FIGURE 3.85 Left foot, dorsal view.

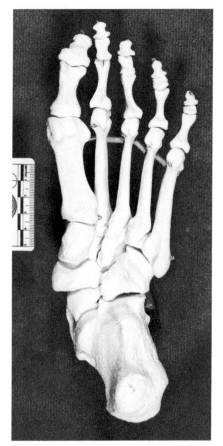

FIGURE 3.86 Left foot, plantar view.

FIGURE 3.87 Tarsals, left foot.

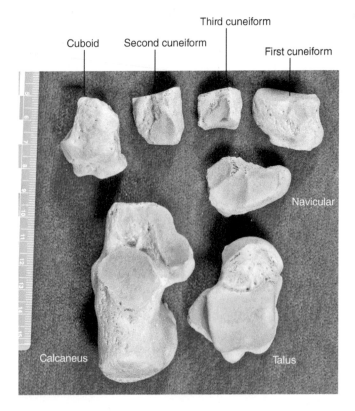

Third cuneiform

Cuboid   Second cuneiform

First cuneiform

Navicular

Calcaneus   Talus

EXERCISE 3.2   NAME _____   SECTION _____   DATE _____

The Human Skeleton

1. Why do we usually see trabecular bone near articular surfaces of bone? To answer this question, think about the biomechanics of the areas around joint surfaces (in other words, what kinds of stresses/forces are applied to bone in these areas?).

2. Why do we see dense cortical bone in the midshaft of the femur (again, think about the biomechanics of this area of the femur)?

3. What bones were you looking at in the chicken bone exercise?

4. Short Answer

   Raised, rounded areas just above the eye orbits are the:

   The suture that joins the two parietal bones is the:

   The skull articulates with the vertebral column by means of:

   The place where the scapula that articulates with the humerus is:

   The rotation of the hand and forearm so that the palm faces downward is:

   The medial bone of the forearm (in the anatomical position) is:

5. What is the definition of a dental formula?

6. How many deciduous premolars are there in humans?

7. What is the dental formula of

   a. an adult human?

   b. a human child of five years?

FIGURE 3.88 Unknown.

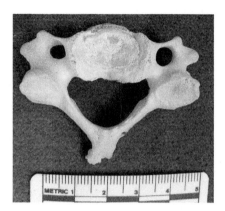

8. What vertebra is in Figure 3.88 (cervical, thoracic, lumbar, sacral, or coccygeal)? What leads you to this conclusion?

FIGURE 3.89 Unknown.

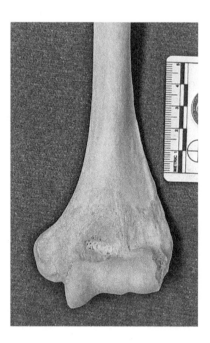

9. What bone is shown in Figure 3.89? What leads you to this conclusion? From what side is it?

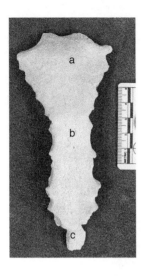

FIGURE 3.90 Unknown.

10. What are the three segments of this sternum (Figure 3.90)?

a.

b.

c.

FIGURE 3.91 Unknown.

11. Is the bone in Figure 3.91 the head of a femur or of a humerus? How can you tell?

12. How is the first rib different from the other ribs?

13. How are the 11th and 12th ribs different from the other ribs?

FIGURE 3.92 Unknown.

14. What bones are shown in Figure 3.92? This is from what side of the body? How can you tell?

BONE FRAGMENT IDENTIFICATION

The identification of bone fragments is likely the single best way to really learn the skeleton. To identify fragments, you have to pay attention to the gross morphology of the entire bone, the different parts of each bone, and the texture of the different areas in bone (refer to Figure 3.16).

Identifying the Bones of the Cranium

The cranium is a complicated set of bones. There are smooth, gently curved sections (such as the parietals and frontal), very small bones with relatively sharp edges such as the lacrimals and ethmoids, morphologically complicated such as the sphenoid, rough muscle insertion areas such as the mastoids, and so on.

Here are a few hints (these are not at all exhaustive—there are so many different shapes and textures within the cranium that it would take an entire book to list all of the traits of each section):

- If you see sutures, you are looking at a section of cranium. Some sutures are extremely complex and isolate little sections of bone (called extra-sutural or Wormian bones). Those sutures can occur in many areas of the cranium, but if the sutures are large and complex, they are more likely on or near the lambdoidal suture (see Figure 3.93).
- Very thin bones are often in the cranium (although the scapula has a thin section, so be careful if you have a small fragment).
- The parietal bones are relatively smooth on the outside surface but have grooves for the middle meningeal arteries on the inside surface. Those grooves run from the lower anterior to the upper posterior cranium, so they can be used not only for bone identification but also for side identification (see Figure 3.94).
- The bones of the superior orbits are very thin and gently curved against the eye and wavy on the inside of the cranium (see Figure 3.95).
- The occipital bone is thick and has a set of raised surfaces internally that form the shape of a cross. This is the cruciform eminence and is the point of separation of the occipital lobes of the cerebral hemispheres and the lobes of the cerebellum (see Figure 3.96).

Identifying Long Bones

Following are some hints for identifying long bones:

- Be alert for areas of articulation, particularly those areas with freely movable joints. Note the shape of that articular surface. Is it round like a ball (suggesting the head of the humerus or femur)? Is it a hinge joint (suggesting, for example, the distal humerus)?

FIGURE 3.93 Close-up of posterior cranial sutures.

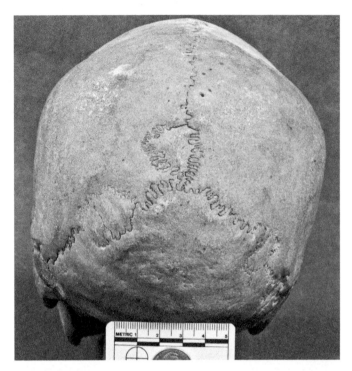

FIGURE 3.94 Intracranial view of parietal bone.

FIGURE 3.95 Intracranial view of orbits.

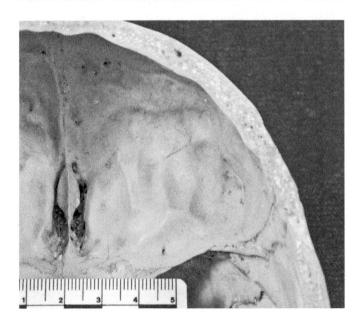

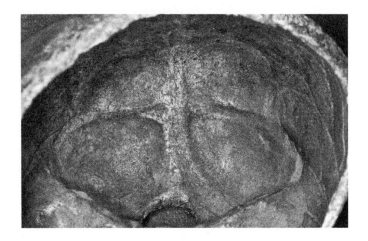

FIGURE 3.96 Intracranial view of occipital bone.

- Do you have a section of trabecular bone (see Figure 3.97)? Where do you normally see trabecular bone? (This was discussed earlier in this chapter.)

- Look for compact bones typical of a long bone shaft. Is it robust and large in cross section (suggesting perhaps a femur)? If so, look for evidence of the linea aspera.

- Notice the texture of the bone. Is it full of foramina (perhaps like the femoral neck)? Is it rough, suggesting an area of muscle or ligament insertion?

- Do you have a bone that is relatively small in cross section but has cortical bone at midshaft? It might be a bone of the hand or foot (the metacarpals, metatarsals, or proximal and middle phalanges).

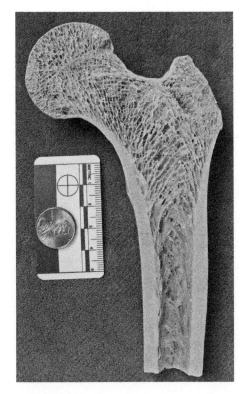

FIGURE 3.97 Cross section of femur.

The hints for irregular bones (such as the scapula, sternum, ossa coxae, vertebrae, and so on) are just modifications of the hints for the other areas of the body. Keep an eye out for areas of articulation, areas of muscle attachment (insertion or origin), thick cortical bone, trabecular bone, and general morphology. If the bone wasn't broken, what shape would it likely be just beyond the break?

The following exercises will help you practice fragment identification, intact bone identification, and the biomechanics of the skeleton (human and nonhuman). If you have bone fragments in your laboratory, practice on them. Also try putting bones in other students' hands behind their back or in a box covered with cloth so that the bone cannot be seen. Figure out what bone you are holding just by the sense of touch (it's fun!).

Fragment Identification

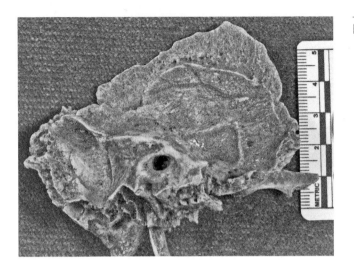

FIGURE 3.98 Unknown.

Figures 3.98 and 3.99 are opposite sides of the same bone.

1. Are all human cranial sutures the same? Figure 3.98 shows a section of cranium. Where on the cranium could this be located?

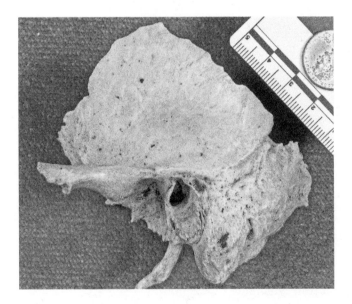

FIGURE 3.99 Unknown.

2. What bones are represented in Figure 3.99? From what side of the body?

FIGURE 3.100 Unknown.

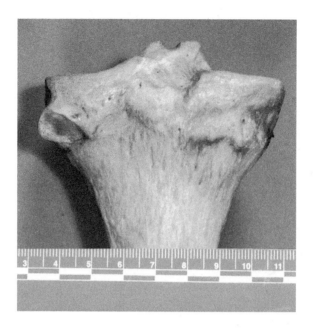

3. What bone is represented in Figure 3.100? From what side of the body?

FIGURE 3.101 Unknown.

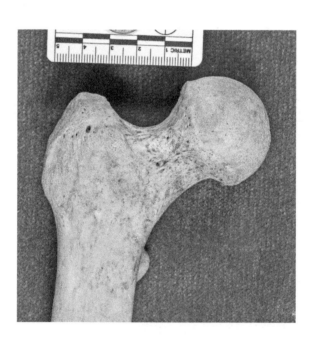

4. What bone is represented in Figure 3.101? From what side of the body?

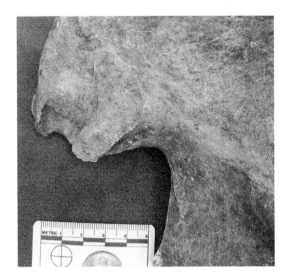

FIGURE 3.102 Unknown.

5. What bone is represented in Figure 3.102? From what side of the body?

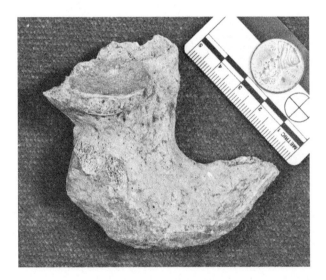

FIGURE 3.103 Unknown.

6. What bone(s) is/are represented in Figure 3.103? From what side of the body?

FIGURE 3.104 Unknown.

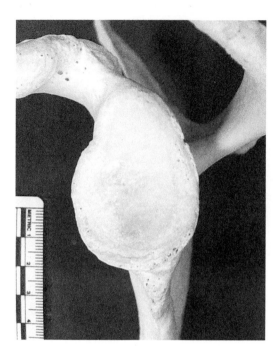

7. What bone is represented in Figure 3.104? From what side of the body?

REEXAMINING THE ISSUES

In this chapter, we learned the following:

- The names of the bones and the relationship of those bones to adjacent bones in the body.
- Bone is a living, dynamic tissue that responds to its environment.
- If you want to learn about an animal's skeleton and what it does for a "living" (that is, its locomotor modes, and so on), the first step is to learn about the bones themselves.

CHAPTER 4

Growth and Development

OBJECTIVES

1. If someone claims that he can legally drink alcohol because he is 21 years of age, but he has no identification, how can we determine whether or not that person is likely telling the truth?

2. How can we determine a person's age at death by looking at the skeleton?

3. How confident can we be in using modern standards to diagnose the age at death of a fossil hominid?

We will build on our understanding of the skeleton by investigating how humans and other mammals grow and develop. By studying the rate at which humans and great apes grow and develop and by comparing those ages to modern humans, we may better understand the aging process in fossil hominins. By learning that the rates vary at which certain bones develop in different individuals, we can avoid the common mistake of stating an exact age at death of fossil hominins or even modern humans. We should instead state the age as a range. And as we learn about the effects of the nutritional and disease status of an individual during this growth process, we may use those clues to more effectively estimate some of the history of an unknown individual.

We will delve into the morphological (primarily degenerative) changes in the adult skeleton and dentition in Chapters 14 and 15.

INTRODUCTION

When we talk about growth and development, we often assume that they mean the same thing. However, *growth* is defined as the increase in size (of a cell, bone, and so on), whereas *development* can mean a morphological change that does not necessarily occur with absolute growth. Also, we must observe that not only is an individual becoming taller and more developed through time (until the late teens or early 20s in a healthy, well-nourished individual), the *rate* at which these factors proceed increases and decreases during certain periods. The growth and development of the body proceed very quickly in the uterus where the fertilized egg produces cells at a rapid rate and differentiation of those cells into different kinds of tissues can be marked in days (or less). The rate of growth slows somewhat during the last three months before birth but becomes rapid again after birth. Although growth and development continue, the rate spikes again during the adolescent growth spurt around the time of puberty. At this time, males and females undergo rapid growth in height and development of the skeleton and soft tissues, and rapid differentiation in sexual features. In other words, at birth there is very little sexual dimorphism (differences between males and females) in the skeleton, while at puberty the skeleton becomes very different between males and females. This is a very important fact in human-identification cases because it is very difficult to diagnose the sex of an individual much before puberty. Also, females at about this time grow and mature more quickly than males (by about two years), which is an important feature to remember.

Bone is composed of both an organic and inorganic component—that is, living bone is not entirely mineral; there is a soft-tissue component as well. The mineral component is a compound of calcium and phosphates called hydroxyapatite that is formed in and around an organic matrix containing collagen. Collagen is similar in consistency to very thick, relatively hard gelatin (like a hard Jell-O® made with much less water than normal). This is important to understand not only because it helps to explain the way in which bone develops, but it also helps to explain the way bone decomposes and the way it reacts to various stresses (fractures, cuts, diseases, and so on).

The growth and development of the skeletal elements are also interesting. Most bones will grow and develop from primary centers (which occur first within a particular bone and are approximately midshaft in long bones) and often from one or more secondary centers (which usually occur on the ends of long bones or on projections such as the greater trochanter of the femur). Different bones will develop at different rates and ages throughout the body, which is particularly useful in determining age because the age can be bracketed by the age of appearance and union of the different elements.

At the very earliest stages, the centers of bone growth start as a single bone cell and, for a time, are indistinguishable from other centers of bone growth of the same size in the body. Of course, their location in the body can be determined if the body is intact, and this can give valuable information about the age of the individual. But if the amorphous centers are discovered archaeologically when the position within the body is not known, they are, naturally, considerably less useful in age determination (if they are found at all).

SKELETAL DEVELOPMENT FROM THE FETUS TO THE ADULT

Dental and skeletal tissues arise from **mesenchymal cells** (see, for example, Carlson 2004), which are unspecialized cells in the embryo that give rise to all connective tissue (including cartilage, bone, and elements of the teeth, but also including blood vessels, blood, the heart, and other tissues). Interestingly, the mesenchymal cells within the embryo migrate to different locations and receive signals from other tissues and growth factors, which dictate the type of cell into which they will develop; that is, mesenchymal cells have different points of origin and develop from different cells and into different cells in the embryo. For example, in the cranium, some of the bones originate from mesenchymal cells derived from one part of the embryo, while the facial bones and cranial vault bones are from mesenchymal cells from a different part of the embryo (from Carlson 2004).

Some areas of the cranium are ossified (turned into bone) from membranes transformed from mesenchymal tissues and are called **intramembranous bones**. These bones include the cranial vault, facial bones, mandible, and part of the clavicle. Remodeling bone also involves intramembranous ossification. Other bones in the body are developed from mesenchymal tissues that develop into cartilage models first and are then overtaken by osteogenic (bone-forming) cells that develop that cartilage into bone. These are called **endochondral bones** (this is a simplified explanation of the complex nature of intramembranous and endochondral bone formation, and some bones, such as the clavicle, are a mixture of the two processes). Figure 4.1 shows a six-month-old fetus stained to show the developing skeleton.

Throughout these processes of bone development in the embryo through adulthood, some mesenchymal cells differentiate into osteogenic cells called **osteoblasts**. In intramembranous ossification, the osteoblasts begin to lay down a network of very small, fine spicules of bone in the membrane. Initial bone formation occurs very quickly and produces loosely woven bone, which is more of a collection or weaving of those spicules of bone. A significant amount of cartilage remains within these areas of rapid bone growth, and if dry bone (in which much of the organic component is removed) is observed at this stage, it will appear to be very porous (see Figure 4.2). This is true in intramembranous or endochondral bone. This bone growth is so rapid that it traps osteoblasts, which then become osteocytes (bone cells).

Mesenchymal cells: Unspecialized cells in the embryo that give rise to all connective tissue, including cartilage, bone, and teeth (as well as some other types of cells).

Endochondral means "inside cartilage." Chondral tissue is cartilage tissue.

Intramembranous means "inside membrane."

Membranous bone = specialized mesenchymal cells → membrane → bone.

Endochondral bone = specialized mesenchymal cells → cartilage → matrix bone.

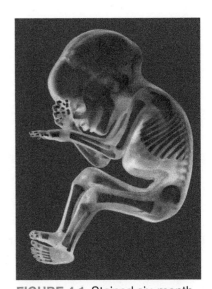

FIGURE 4.1 Stained six-month human fetus. *Photo D. L. France of specimen courtesy of National Museum of Health and Medicine*

Osteoblasts: Bone-forming cells.

Osteoclasts: Bone-removing cells.

Chondroblasts: Cartilage-forming cells.

Chondroclasts: Cartilage-removing cells.

Odontoblasts: Dentin-forming cells.

Periosteum: A thin layer of soft tissue that surrounds bone.

FIGURE 4.2 Porous nature of infant bone.

THE CHICKEN DRUMSTICK EXERCISE

In Chapter 3, Human Osteology, you were introduced to the chicken drumstick exercise (you can read about or perform the initial parts of the exercise on page 83). The growth and development part of the exercise involves the cartilage at the proximal and distal ends of the drumstick and in the nature of the bone itself.

The cartilage at the proximal end was removed to study the proximal aspect of the bone and to view the very porous nature of the tibia. Compare the chicken bone in Figure 4.3 to the porosity of the human infant femur shown in Figure 4.2. It is useful to compare the proximal aspect of the tibia from an older chicken than the one we have been studying.

After studying the bone itself, clean the bits of proximal tibia off of the inside (or distal side) of the cartilage so that you are looking at a relatively clean surface (see Figure 4.4). Look through the cartilage at a relatively strong light. Do you see the small dark spot? You will be asked about this dark spot in the exercises.

FIGURE 4.3 Proximal chicken tibia.

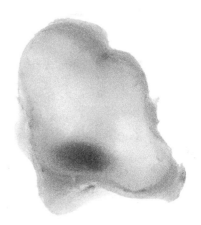

FIGURE 4.4 Chicken proximal tibia epiphyseal cartilage.

CONSIDER THIS

The porous nature of infant bones somewhat mimics some path-ological conditions (such as an inflammation of the periosteum, or periostitis) in which the bone reacts to stress by rapidly laying down bone. It is important to recognize that infant bones are very porous in a healthy, well-nourished individual, as well.

A bone may have several secondary centers of growth (see Figure 4.5). In endochondral bone, each secondary center of bone growth (termed **epiphysis**; plural: *epiphyses*) will grow and de-velop and eventually fuse to the growing and developing primary center (termed **diaphysis**; plural: *diaphyses*). Bone growth in a shaft begins where bone-forming cells enter the matrix of cartilage and begin to secrete a substance that is quickly mineralized (the hydroxyapatite crystals). The primary blood vessel that initially carries these osteoblasts into the diaphysis becomes surrounded by bone and becomes the nutrient foramen (see Figure 4.6). This pro-cess proceeds away from the initial site of bone growth toward both ends of the bone.

Epiphysis (plural: epiphyses): Secondary centers of bone growth at the ends of long bones. These centers eventually unite with the diaphysis.

Diaphysis (plural: *diaphyses*): The primary centers of bone growth; the shafts of long bones.

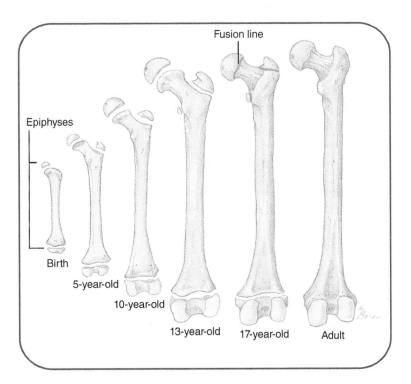

FIGURE 4.5 Developmental stages of the human femur. *Source: From Kathryn Born and Joseph Henry Press. Copyright 2006 by the National Academy of Sciences. Courtesy of the National Academies Press, Washington, D.C.*

FIGURE 4.6 Nutrient foramen in infant femur.

Nutrient foramen

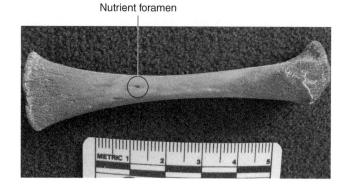

FIGURE 4.7 Normal adult femur (left), shortened femur from an achondroplastic dwarf.

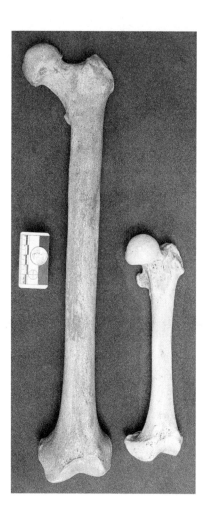

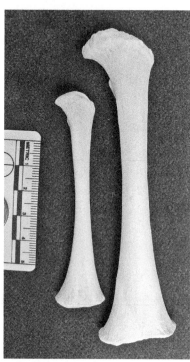

FIGURE 4.8 Femur at two stages of development. Note that the shape of the two femora changes with age, necessitating removal of bone in some places with deposition of bone in others.

At about this time, different mesenchymal cells are differentiating into a thin layer of soft tissue called the **periosteum**, which coats the bone and is filled with blood vessels. This layer will be active in bone formation throughout the life of the individual and will itself react to various stresses (for example, bacteria, trauma, and so on).

The area of rapid growth between the diaphysis and the epiphysis is the growth plate or **metaphysis**. As the cartilage matrix

Metaphysis (plural: metaphyses) Location of bone growth between the diaphysis and epiphysis.

is turned into bone at the diaphysis and the epiphysis, the cartilage between the two continues to grow and add new cells. In this way the bone growth between the diaphysis and epiphysis can continue. When the bone formation at the diaphysis meets the formation of bone at the epiphysis, the two unite, and longitudinal bone growth ceases (see Figures 4.9 to 4.11 and Table 4.1 for information about what epiphyseal union looks like and the approximate ages at which it occurs in various bones). If this happens too quickly, the bones may be shorter than normal (refer to Figure 4.7). If it happens too late, bones may be longer than normal.

A bone must also have a way to increase its diameter as it grows in length. It does this by appositional growth (or putting layers over the older layers) and taking away some bone from the areas to be reshaped. There is a constant process of remodeling of bone practically from the very beginning of bone formation, and it proceeds throughout life. This process is undertaken by **osteoclasts** taking bone away from where it is not useful and additional **osteoblasts** putting bone down where it is needed (refer to Figure 4.8).

After birth, girls mature at an earlier age than do boys (this is very important!). The adolescent growth spurt occurs later in boys than in girls, which means that the skeletons in boys have somewhat more time to increase in size before the spurt in maturity (Tanner 1978).

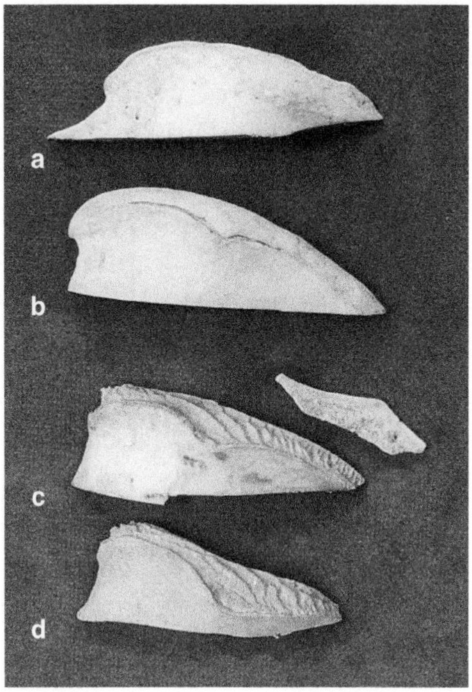

FIGURE 4.9 Stages of epiphyseal union at the iliac crest: (a) unfused with no epiphysis present, (b) unfused with separate epiphysis, (c) partially united, (d) obliterated line with complete union. These are part of an epiphyseal age determination system developed by P. O. Webb and J. M. Suchey (1985).

Adults

As was discussed in Chapter 3, the areas of cranial sutures are actually joint surfaces, though not the same kind of highly movable joint as in, for example, the knee or shoulder. In adults, those sutures may eventually disappear, and the bones separated by them will fuse in a way similar to the fusion of epiphyses to diaphyses. Cranial bones will often fuse at different rates inside the cranium (*endocranially*)

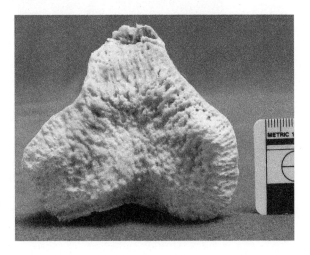

FIGURE 4.10 Epiphyseal surface on proximal tibia.

FIGURE 4.11 Epiphyseal union in various bones. *Photo, D. L. France. Drawings, © Cengage*

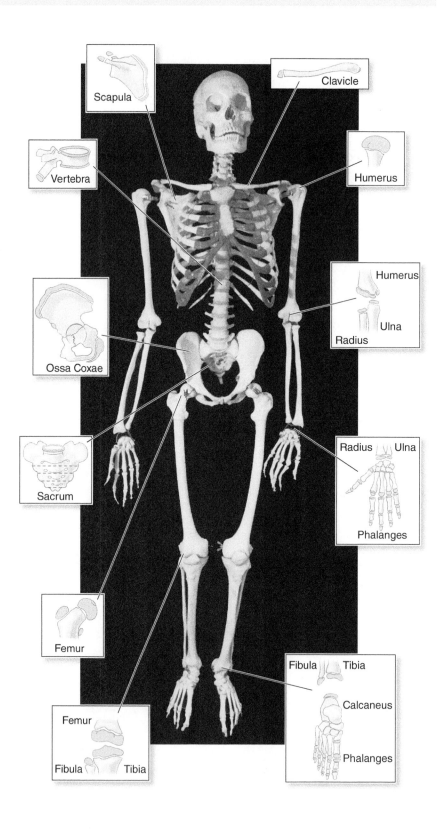

and outside of the cranium (*ectocranially*). Although the age at which this occurs varies from suture to suture, it also varies considerably between individuals, making it somewhat problematic for use in age determination in the adult.

TABLE 4.1   Appearance of Ossification Centers and Epiphyseal Union in Various Postcranial Bones (IU = In Utero)

Bone	Element	Appearance	Union	Notes
Clavicle	Diaphysis	Week 5 IU		
	Sternal epiphysis		17–30 for males, 16–33 females (Webb and Suchey 1985)	
Sternum	Acromial epiphysis		19–20	
	Manubrium	Month 5 IU		
	Body sections	1: week 5 IU	All sections to manubrium 15–20 yrs.	
		2 & 3: by week 8 IU	Body section 2 fuses to 3 & 4 at 11–16 yrs.	
		4: after 1 yr.	Body section 3 fuses to 4 at 4–10 yrs.	
Cervical vertebrae	Atlas	Week 7–10 IU	Three major sections 5–6 yrs.	
	Axis	Week approx. 8 IU	Major elements 9–10 yrs.	
	Axis dens tip	Approx. 2 yrs.	To dens approx. 12 yrs.	
	C7–C3 (progressing cranially)	By month 4 IU	Neural arches 2–3 yrs.; arches to centrum 3–4 yrs.	
Thoracic vertebrae	Centrum and both neural arches	By week 10 IU	Fuse from caudally to cranially neural arches 1–3 yrs.; arches to centrum 5–6 yrs.	
Lumbar vertebrae	Centrum and both neural arches (progressing caudally)	By month 4 IU	Progressing caudally, arches 1–5 yrs.; arches to centrum 2–4 yrs.	
Ilium	Primary center	Months 2–3 IU		
	Iliac crest	12–13 yrs. in females; 14–15 yrs. in males	Completed 18–24 yrs. in females, 17–24 in males (Webb and Suchey 1985)	
Ischium	Primary center	Months 3–5 IU	Fuses with pubis 4–8 yrs.	
	Ischial tuberosity	13–16 yrs.	Completed by 21–23 yrs.	
Pubis	Primary center	Months 4–6 IU	Fuses with ischium 4–8 yrs.	
Ossa coxae	All major elements		11–15 yrs. in females, 15–17 yrs. in males	
Sacrum**	Centra (center) for S1–S3	Month 3 IU	S1–3 centra to arches and alae 2–5 yrs.	
	Neural arches for S1–S3	Months 4–6 IU		

continues

TABLE 4.1 (Continued)

Bone	Element	Appearance	Union	Notes
	Alae for S1–S3	Months 6–8 IU		
	Centra for S4, S5	Months 4–5 IU	S4, S5 centra to arches 2–6 yrs.	
	Neural arches for S4, S5	Months 6–8 IU		
	Sacral elements		At spinous processes 7–15, alae and centra approx. 12–20 yrs., 12–18 years from S5 to S1; S1–S2 in the 20s.	
	Auricular surface and lateral epiphyses	15–16 yrs.		
Scapula	Body	Week 7–8 IU		
	Coracoid process	Birth–1 yr.	To body 16–17 yrs.	
	Acromion process	13–16 yrs.	18–20 yrs.	
	Inferior angle	15–17 yrs.	20–23 yrs.	
	Vertebral margin	15–17 yrs.	20–23 yrs.	
Humerus	Diaphysis	Week 7 IU		
	Head epiphysis	Birth–6 mos.	To diaphysis: 15–19 in females; 18–22 in males	
	Distal epiphyses	6 mos. to 2 yrs.	To diaphysis: 11–15 in females; 12–17 in males	
	Medial epicondyle	After 4 yrs.	To diaphysis: 13–15 in females; 14–16 in males	
Radius	Diaphysis	Week 7 IU		
	Proximal epiphysis	Approx. 5 yrs.	To diaphysis: 11–15 in females; 14–17 in males	
	Distal epiphysis	1–3 yrs.	To diaphysis: 14–17 in females; 16–20 in males	
Ulna	Diaphysis	Week 7 IU		
	Proximal epiphysis	8–10 yrs.	To diaphysis: 12–15 in females; 13–17 in males	
	Distal epiphysis	5–7 yrs.	To diaphysis: 15–17 in females; 17–20 in males	
Hand	Carpals	After birth		
	Metacarpal diaphyses	Week 8–10 IU		
	Metacarpal distal epiphyses 2–5 Phalanges vary	10 mos.–2.5 yrs.	To diaphysis: 14–15 in females, 16–17 in males*	

Bone	Element	Appearance	Union	Notes
Femur	Diaphysis	Week 7–8 IU		
	Head	Birth–1 yr.	To diaphysis: 12–16 in females; 14–19 in males	
	Greater trochanter	1–5 yrs.	To diaphysis: 14–16 in females; 16–18 in males	
	Lesser trochanter	7–12 yrs.	To diaphysis: 16–17 yrs.	
	Distal epiphysis	Week 36–40 IU (usually before birth)	To diaphysis: 14–18 in females; 16–20 in males	
Tibia	Diaphysis	Week 8 IU		
	Proximal epiphysis	Near birth	To diaphysis: 13–17 in females; 15–19 in males	
	Distal epiphysis	Approx. 2 yrs.	To diaphysis: 14–16 in females; 15–18 in males	
Fibula	Diaphysis	Week 8 IU		
	Proximal epiphysis	Approx. 4–5 yrs.	To diaphysis: 12–18 in females; 15–20 in males	
	Distal epiphysis	1–2 yrs.	To diaphysis: 12–16 in females; 15–18 in males	
Foot	Calcaneus	Varies: week 3–28 IU		
	Calcaneus posterior epiphysis	4–12 yrs.	Beg. 10–12 in females; 11–14 in males; and completed by 16 in females and 22 in males	
	Metatarsal diaphysis	Week 8–10 IU		

*Scheuer and Black 2000.

**Sacral elements fuse at spinous processes first, then lateral borders, and then centra.

These ages are approximations and are compiled from Baker et al. (2005); Bass (1996); McKern and Stewart (1957); Scheuer and Black (2000) (who often report narrower age ranges than other sources); and Webb and Suchey (1985). Also, see hand-wrist radiographs from Greulich and Pyle (1959). Females usually mature more quickly than males by about 1 to 2 years.

© Cengage

EXERCISE 4.1   NAME _____   SECTION _____   DATE _____

Skeletal Development

FIGURE 4.12 Two stages of femur development superimposed.

1. In Figure 4.12, would you expect greater action from osteoblasts or from osteoclasts in the shaded area?

FIGURE 4.13 Unknown for Question 2.

2. In Figure 4.13, what is the feature designated by the arrow, and what is the significance of that feature in growth and development?

3. Why is it important to know the sex of the individual before estimating the skeletal age?

4. How do you change your reported estimated age if you do not know the sex of the individual?

FIGURE 4.14 Distal radius.

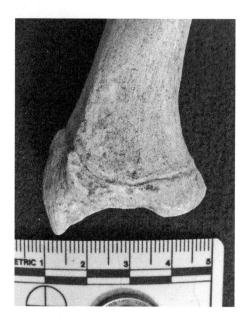

5. What is the age range of the individual represented in Figure 4.14? On what are you basing that estimate?

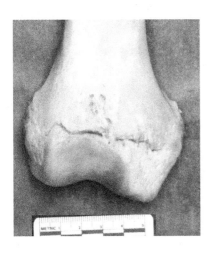

FIGURE 4.15 Unknown for Question 6.

6. What is the age range of the individual represented in Figure 4.15? On what are you basing that estimate?

FIGURE 4.16 Unknown for Question 7.

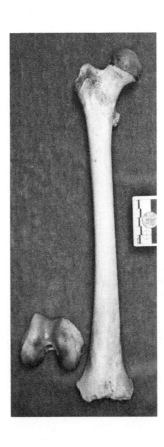

FIGURE 4.17 Unknown for Question 7.

7. Is the individual represented in Figure 4.16 younger or older than the individual represented in Figure 4.17? How can you tell? What cautionary notes would you put into your report concerning this determination?

DENTAL DEVELOPMENT FROM THE FETUS TO THE ADULT

Dental tissue also arises from mesenchymal cells, but these cells differentiate into **ameloblasts**, which are cells that secrete enamel.

Odontoblasts secrete the dentin of the tooth (Carlson 2004). Hydroxyapatite (also the mineral component of bone) is the dominant inorganic component of enamel (Carlson 2004).

As was discussed in Chapter 3, there are two sets of teeth in humans: the deciduous (or baby) teeth followed by the permanent dentition. All teeth develop from the crown to the tip (apex) of the root (see Figure 4.18) and begin to develop deep inside the maxilla or mandible before reaching a point in their development at which they erupt beyond the gum line (or the alveolus in bone) and become noticeable in the mouth. Note that in a young mandible, there are large voids (called crypts) in which the crown of the tooth develops, and those voids close around the root of the tooth as it erupts beyond the alveolus. If you find that large void, you know that a tooth was developing in it (see Figure 4.19), but be careful you do not mistake it for a void caused by a disease process such as an abscess or mistake it for a fracture before or after death.

Beneath (in the mandible) or above (in the maxilla) the deciduous tooth, the permanent tooth is forming, and while it is expanding in size, the root of the deciduous tooth begins to resorb (see Figure 4.20). When enough of the deciduous root is gone, the deciduous tooth falls out.

Ameloblasts: enamel-forming cells.

Odontoblasts: dentin-forming cells.

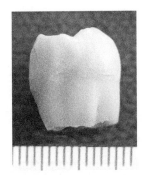

FIGURE 4.18 Partially developed molar.

FIGURE 4.19 Developing dentition in crypts.

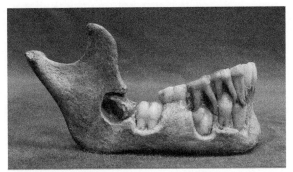

FIGURE 4.20 Cutaway mandible showing dental development.

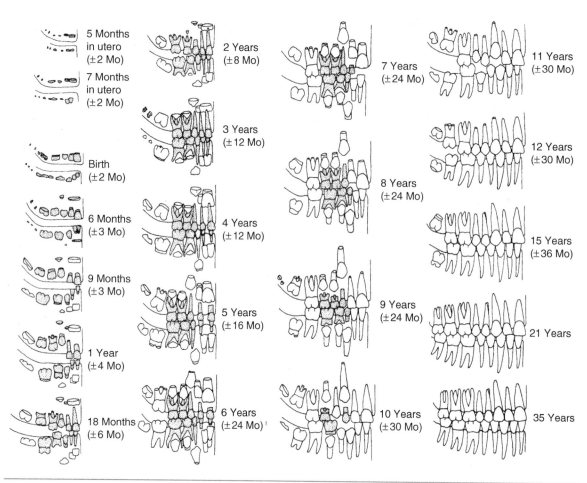

FIGURE 4.21 Dental eruption chart. *Source: Courtesy, D. Ubelaker*

Dental Eruption

The determination of the ages at which the deciduous and permanent dentition erupts is useful in identifying age to approximately 15 years. The third molar (wisdom tooth) erupts after this time, but the age at its eruption (if it erupts, as many never do) is so variable that it is not a very reliable indicator of age. The chart shown for dental eruption times (see Figure 4.21) is based on a Native American population, so be aware that other populations will vary from these time frames.

EXERCISE 4.2   NAME _____   SECTION _____   DATE _____

Dental Development

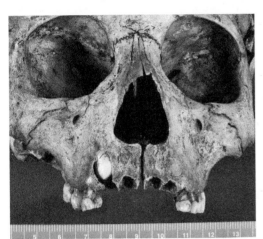

FIGURE 4.22a Unknown.

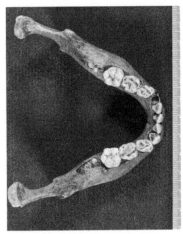

FIGURE 4.22b Unknown.

1. Concerning Figures 4.22a and 4.22b:

   a. Do the cranium and mandible represent an adult or subadult?

   b. How can you tell?

   c. What is the approximate age of this individual?

FIGURE 4.23a Unknown.

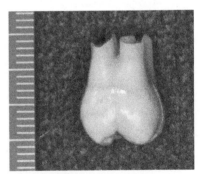

FIGURE 4.23b Unknown.

2. There are two individuals represented in Figures 4.23a and 4.23b.

   a. Which tooth is the most developed? How can you tell?

   b. Which individual is the oldest? How can you tell?

FIGURE 4.24a Unknown.

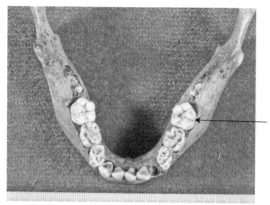

1st permanent molar

FIGURE 4.24b Unknown.

1st permanent molar

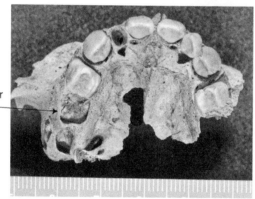

3. There are two individuals represented in Figures 4.24a and 4.24b. Which individual is the oldest? How can you tell?

THE EFFECTS OF VARIOUS INSULTS
ON BONE AND TEETH

The rate and degree of growth and development in a young individual is largely determined by genetics, but we know that the actual rate at which an individual grows and develops is influenced heavily by other factors of the environment, including nutrition, disease, ingestion of hormones in food, and so on.

It is commonly known that there are secular changes throughout recent decades in adult size (we are taller than our parents and grandparents), but the age at which adult size is reached has decreased in many societies (Floud et al. 1990; Hoppa and Garlie 1998; Tanner 1962). The age at menarche and the age of the adolescent growth spurt tend to occur earlier as well (Hoppa and Garlie 1998; Roede and Van Wieringen 1985; Tanner 1978).

A low socioeconomic status of an individual may result in compromised nutrition and greater exposure to disease. Decades ago, Garn et al. (1973a, b) found that lower socioeconomic status resulted in smaller babies, smaller children, and delayed maturation. Problems during pregnancy (including nutritional deficiencies, disease agents, drug or alcohol use), or after pregnancy can result in the bone or tooth growing or developing abnormally. Some insults will result in slowed growth and development of bones and teeth, but it has been known for some time that dental development is more resistant to these stresses than is bone development, so the diagnosis of age from dental development is more accurate (see Hillson 2003, and Saunders and Katzenberg 1992 for good discussions of dental formation and eruption).

A commonly described result that has been linked to disease or nutritional problems in the growing bone is called "growth arrest lines" or "Harris lines" after the person who described them. These are lines of bone where the bone cells are denser than in other areas of bone, and they occur at the point at which the cartilage matrix is being overtaken by bone. The osteoblasts are still laying down bone, but the cartilage matrix is adversely affected to a greater degree and does not allow the formation of bone to advance forward as quickly, so the bone is denser. These insults can be linked to nutritional problems or even a child's high fever. After the body has recovered to the point at which normal bone growth can occur, growth proceeds beyond the growth arrest line, but that line may exist for years and can be seen both in radiographs and by the naked eye in cross sections of the bone. It will potentially disappear with continuous remodeling that occurs in a normal, healthy body (see Figure 4.25).

FIGURE 4.25 Radiograph of radius showing growth arrest line.

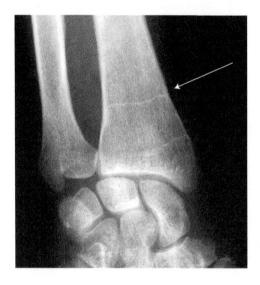

FIGURE 4.26 Enamel hypoplasia.

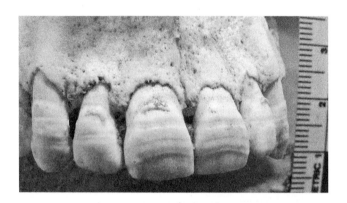

A similar effect takes place in dentition with enamel hypoplasias. If an insult similar to those described previously occurs when a tooth is developing, the enamel of that tooth takes on a wrinkled or ribbed appearance (see Figure 4.26). If that occurs while a permanent tooth is developing, that effect will stay with that tooth forever because unlike bones, teeth do not remodel throughout the life of the individual.

THE USE OF SERIATION TECHNIQUES

Seriation in age estimation involves placing an individual within a group of individuals based on age. Placing an individual in a series is, of course, easy when you know the absolute ages of a group of people, but when used on undocumented skeletal remains in a mass grave, a mass fatality incident, or an undocumented cemetery, it can be difficult, particularly if the remains are fragmentary.

A FINAL COMMENT

At least in part because of the variables in the life of an individual before death (insults, nutrition and health status, and so on), there is a range of variation in the dental or skeletal maturity, stature, and other aspects of individuals studied (here we are talking primarily about skeletal samples, but this applies as well to living subjects). When anthropologists develop standards (age, stature, and so on) for a population from a sample of individuals, there is a temptation to throw out the measurements from those individuals who are on the outer edges of the normal range. If this is done, the standards developed from that sample have narrower ranges of variation than normal. This practice might make the standards look more *precise* (and might make it more attractive for use in court, for example), but it artificially narrows the age range and therefore makes the standards less *accurate*. Researchers must resist this temptation and accept the variation that makes us human. We can explain the natural variation within the human species far more convincingly than we can explain away the fact that the individual we just studied remains unidentified because we wanted narrow age ranges and our victim falls outside that range.

EXERCISE 4.3   NAME _____   SECTION _____   DATE _____

Growth and Development

1. Why should skeletal age be reported as a range instead as of a single age?

2. What problems can you identify in developing stature reconstruction formulae from collections of skeletons established in the 1940s for use in modern populations?

3. When developing age-determination standards for use in modern populations, what variables in the population would you like to control?

4. When using modern age-determination standards on early fossil hominids, what cautionary notes would you want to include in your analysis?

5. In many countries, different punishments for crime are applied to adults and to those under 18 years of age. If you were asked by the court to identify whether or not someone was over 18 years of age:

   a. What tests would you perform (that is, what features of the body would you use)?

   b. What would you want to know about the individual?

   c. What would you say to the court if you discovered Harris lines in a radiograph of the individual?

6. What would cause a difference between the biological age (the age of the body) and chronological age (the time since birth) of an individual?

7. If you are trying to identify the individual skeletal (including dental) elements of two individuals aged 10 and 16 years of age, what specific clues would you be trying to find?

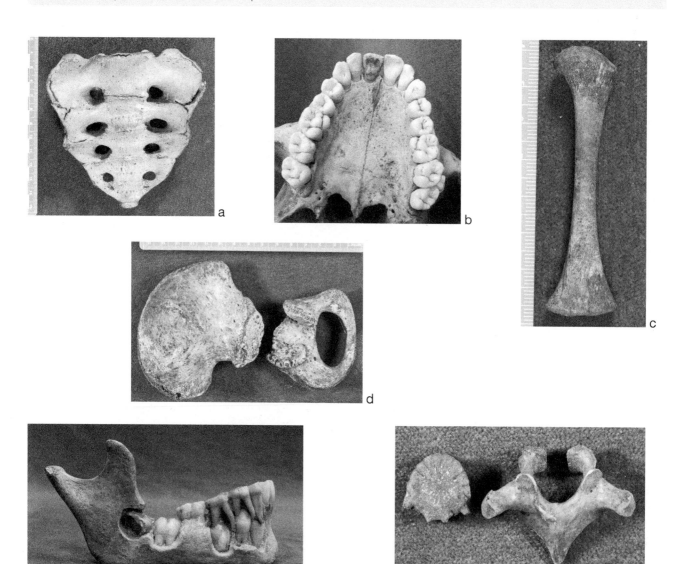

FIGURE 4.27a-f Unknown.

8. In Figures 4.27a through 4.27f, seriate the individuals from youngest to oldest, and include why you made those decisions.

REEXAMINING THE ISSUES

- Bones and teeth are ultimately derived from mesenchymal tissues.
- The rate and age at which individual bones and teeth develop differ within a body and between individuals but are predictable enough that they are useful for determining the biological and chronological age of an individual.
- There are secular changes in the maturation rate and age over time.
- The growth and development of an individual will react to different stresses.

CHAPTER 5

Biological Classification

OBJECTIVES

1. Why do we talk about all living creatures in terms of genus and species?

2. What does the classification system we use tell us about the relationships between all living creatures?

3. How have recent comparisons of genomes changed the way we classify primates (including the genetic distance between humans and nonhuman primates)?

Phylogenetic: A classification system based on evolutionary relationships, usually including a time line.

Cladistics: A classification system based on homologous derived characteristics. This system does not always include a time line.

Classification systems are developed because they improve communication. Many classification systems are based on common names of items, people, events, and so on, but at some point, scientists need an unambiguous language to speak to each other about their studies. Think about the scientific method and how much more difficult it would be for scientists to test hypotheses and theories without being certain that they are studying the same animal! If scientists did not have a way to organize individuals or fossils into species, it would be more difficult to know how that fossil compares with other previously described fossils or with contemporary or extant species. That we can talk about "species" and "genera" in modern and fossil organisms is made possible by early classification systems.

How do those classification systems make sense of the biological world? Which classification system is the most logical given the variation in that biological world? Are these systems completely arbitrary?

INTRODUCTION

Biological classification is based on the system established by the Swedish naturalist Carolus Linnaeus (Carl von Linné, 1707–1778). Linnaeus used the Latin language in his biological classification system and assigned each organism a Latin **binomial** ("two names"): a genus and species. Our biological name, for example, is *Homo sapiens* (Latin for "wise man").

Linnaeus established a formal hierarchy for establishing taxa (singular: *taxon,* a general term for any Linnaean category) above the level of species. Although Linneaeus devised this hierarchy more than a century before Charles Darwin and Alfred Wallace proposed the theory of evolution, most taxonomists today classify organisms according to their evolutionary relationship (phylogeny). Table 5.1 shows many of the higher levels of classification and the classification of our species. As you can see, in some groups of animals and plants, these levels are further subdivided into other categories such as suborders, subfamilies, subgenera, and subspecies. Species within the same genus are more closely related to each other than they are to species in other genera. Genera are grouped into related families, families into related superfamilies, superfamilies into related orders, orders into related classes, and so on. For example, the genus for chimpanzees contains two closely related species, *Pan troglodytes* (common chimpanzee) and *Pan paniscus* (bonobo chimpanzee), while the genus *Homo* contains only one surviving species, according to most (but not all) taxonomists.

Rules for using Linnaean Classification:

1. The first letter of the genus (plural: *genera*) is capitalized.
2. The species begins with a lowercase letter.
3. The genus and species are underlined or italicized in print.
4. The genus name may be abbreviated by using only the first letter (for example, *H. sapiens*).

TABLE 5.1 A Biological Classification of Humans

Kingdom:	Animal
Phylum:	Chordata
Class:	Mammalia
Order:	Primates
Suborder:	Haplorhini
Infraorder:	Anthropoidea
Superfamily:	Hominoidea
Family:	Hominidae
Subfamily:	Homininae
Tribe:	Hominini
Genus:	*Homo*
Species:	*sapiens*

© Cengage

Although most of the rules and conventions of biological classification are well established, there remain many differences of opinion among the classifiers. Even the species concept, which is the basis of the Linnaean classification system, is still debated.

Most biologists today agree to the following definition of species: "species are groups of interbreeding natural populations that are reproductively isolated from other such groups" (Mayr 1970). However, one primary criterion of this definition, the potential to interbreed, is often impossible to determine in natural populations, particularly when those populations are separated geographically. Furthermore, there are many degrees of interbreeding potential among natural populations in that some animals may be able to interbreed but their offspring are infertile (for example, if a horse crosses with a donkey, the resultant offspring, the mule, is *almost* always infertile), or the fertility of offspring may be less than the offspring of "true species."

In practice, most species determinations in fossils are made on the basis of the similarity or dissimilarity of morphological traits, or **characters**. To be useful in biological classification, the similarity of these characters must have resulted from common descent, or **homologies**. We can see that, whether we are looking at the humerus of a horse (see Figure 5.1) or the humerus of a squirrel (see Figure 5.2), there are characteristics of those bones that make them recognizable as a humerus and not a femur or a radius. They are homologous because they are shared by millions of living and extinct species and have ultimately resulted from a common ancestor; therefore, they are useful to us in producing a classification scheme.

Homologies: Characters shared through common descent.

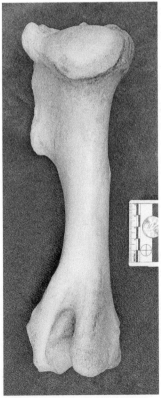

FIGURE 5.1 Horse humerus, posterior view.

FIGURE 5.2 Squirrel humerus, posterior view.

FIGURE 5.3 Bat wings.
Photo, D. L. France; access to specimen courtesy Jay Villemarette, Skulls Unlimited

FIGURE 5.4 Bird (parrot).
Photo D. L. France; access to specimen courtesy Jay Villemarette, Skulls Unlimited

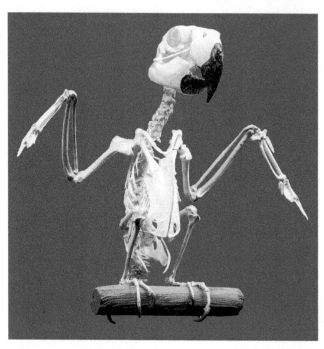

Analogies: Characters similar in appearance and with common function but through separate descent.

Interestingly, the humerus of a bird and the humerus of a bat are homologous (see Figures 5.3 and 5.4, but the entire wing structure of a bird is **analogous** to the wing structure of a bat because they have common functions (flight), but the wings are derived from different evolutionary descent, even though the bat and bird once shared a distant common ancestor in the phylum Chordata. Therefore, those wings would not be useful in a classification scheme.

Classifiers have often disagreed on what morphological criteria should be used in their classifications. For example, should the shape of the skull, the morphology of the teeth, the color of the coats, or biomolecular data be weighted more in making species designations? As genomic mapping becomes more commonplace, should we rely on genetic distance as the final determinant? But even genetic information is subject to interpretation, depending upon how much and what sections of the genome are being studied (Gatesy and Springer 2014; Springer and Gatesy 2016).

Designations of fossil species, called paleospecies, are even less "exact." Obviously, nothing can be determined about the interbreeding potential of paleospecies, and often, because of the condition of the remains, DNA is not usually available for study. Furthermore, the morphological variation of fossils reflects not only geographic variation but also variation over time. Although scientists who study fossils do their best to designate paleospecies in a manner that approximates the designation of living species, there is obviously an arbitrary factor in the designation of species and paleospecies.

Disagreements arise in making classifications above the species level as well. Most, but by no means all, biologists believe that the higher taxonomic categories of organisms should be determined on the basis of the organism's evolutionary history: Organisms that are more closely related should be placed in the same taxa, whereas those more distantly related should be placed in different taxa. This phylogenetic approach to classification is divided into two schools: cladistics and evolutionary classification (Mayr 1981). Cladistic classification (cladism) is based exclusively on genealogy (and branching order), regardless of the time scale—that is, a genus should include a group of species all descended from the same common ancestor (see Figure 5.5). Cladistic classification is also usually focused on more recently shared characters, or "derived" characters.

Derived characters evolve from more primitive characters of more ancient ancestors. For example, the presence of five digits on human hands and feet is actually a primitive condition, as many other animals share that condition regardless of their evolutionary distance from humans. Cows and many other hooved animals share the derived condition of two digits (two hooves), while horses exhibit an even more derived characteristic of only one digit (one hoof). In primates, one example of a shared derived character in anthropoids is that they have nails on all of their digits. Prosimians, on the other hand, do not have nails on all of their digits, as they retain at least one grooming claw (see Figure 5.6), which is a "primitive character." The fact that monkeys, apes, and humans have nails on all their digits is

Cladistic classifications are based on shared derived characters to establish a lineage. It does not include a time scale.

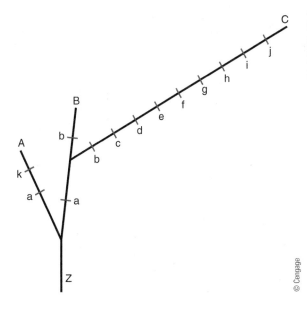

FIGURE 5.5 Cladogram of hypothetical taxa A, B, and C. *Source: Adapted from E. Mayr, "Biological Classification: Toward a Synthesis of Opposing Methodologies." Science, 214: 510–516.*

© Cengage

FIGURE 5.6 Lemur foot. Notice grooming claw on second toe. *Photo D. L. France; access to specimen courtesy Jay Villemarette, Skulls Unlimited*

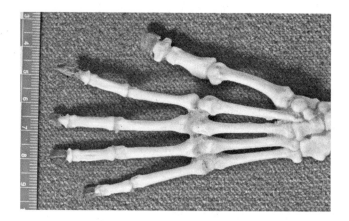

Clade: A group of organisms related through a common ancestor.

Primitive characters are found with phylogenetically older organisms and are usually shared with many organisms in an evolutionary group.

Derived characters evolved from more primitive characters and are usually acquired by few members of an evolutionary group.

an example of one shared derived character used by taxonomists to classify them together in the suborder Anthropoidea (see Chapter 7 for more discussion). These shared derived (or shared specialized) characters are usually assumed to be derived from a common ancestor. Organisms that share these derived characters are grouped into a **clade**, or a group of related organisms. Scientists must be careful, however, because organisms frequently have evolved morphological similarities independently through parallel or convergent evolution. On the other hand, even though evolutionary taxonomy or evolutionary classification is the same as cladism in that it is based on evolutionary history, it also takes into account the time factor and the different rates of evolution in different lineages. Many classification schemes will start out as cladistic schemes, and a time scale will be added later. In Figure 5.5, cladists might combine A and C into one taxon because they shared a common ancestor: Z. Evolutionary taxonomists, on the other hand, would put A and C into separate taxa because C has many derived characters (b through j) not shared with A.

Recent DNA studies and genome maps are refining the taxonomic relationships established by taxonomists. We are most interested in the way these relationships are now understood in primates, but first we must explore the way primates are classified in the class Mammalia and the way in which primates differ from other mammals.

GENERAL MAMMALIAN CLASSIFICATION

Before we delve into primate classification schemes, let us briefly discuss the characteristics that define a mammal (class Mammalia). These are the elements that separate mammals from reptiles, amphibians, birds, and so on, and are also characteristics of the order Primates.

Mammals:

- Have hair at some point in their lives (some marine mammals lose most of their hair)
- Have mammary glands (these are specialized sweat glands)

FIGURE 5.7 Malleus, incus, stapes.

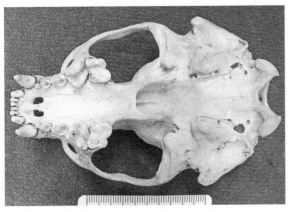

FIGURE 5.8 Heterodonty, the most common form in mammals.

FIGURE 5.9 Homodonty is the exception to the rule in mammals.

- Give birth to live young (this is true in most mammals, although monotremes such as the platypus lay eggs)
- Possess three middle ear bones (the malleus, incus, and stapes). Figure 5.7 shows these bones in humans.
- Are characterized by **heterodonty**, which means that the teeth are in more than one form (for example, incisors, canines, premolars, and molars, although the combinations of these forms vary considerably in different mammals). Many marine mammals are homodontic (which means that the tooth shape is the same throughout the mouth). See Figures 5.8 and 5.9 for examples of heterodonty and homodonty in mammals.

PRIMATE CLASSIFICATION

Traits common to primates include:

- Retention of pentadactyly (five digits on the hands and feet).
- Sensitive tactile pads.
- Nails instead of claws on at least one digit.
- Trend toward opposable thumb, and, except for humans, a trend toward opposable big toe.
- Trend toward precision grip.

Diurnal: Active during daylight hours.

Nocturnal: Active during the night.

- Trend toward a reduction in olfaction and, with that, a reduction in the size of the nose. This is accompanied by the eyes becoming closer together in the front of the face and an accompanying overlap in visual fields (which creates binocular vision and a good depth perception).

- Color vision in **diurnal** primates (those who are active during daylight hours). **Nocturnal** primates do not have color vision.

- Retention of a more omnivorous diet (one with a wide assortment of foods), and retention of a generalized dentition for processing those foods.

- Increased complexity of the brain.

The most recent and widely accepted primate classification scheme (see Figure 5.10) puts primates into two suborders: Strepsirhini (with wet noses) and Haplorhini (with dry noses). The tarsiers

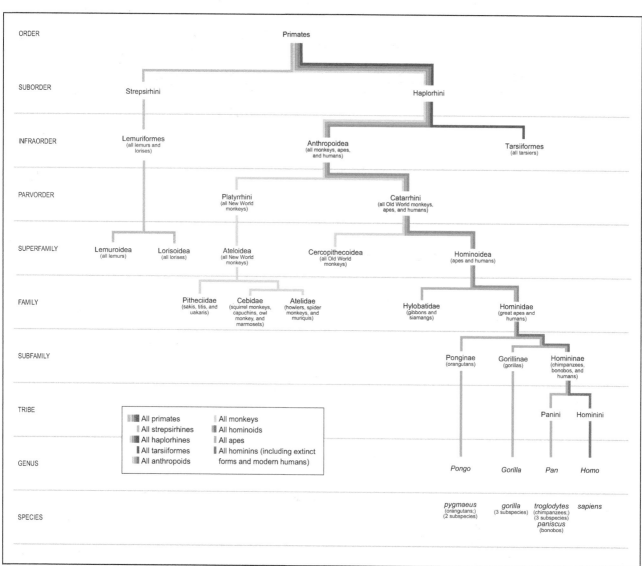

FIGURE 5.10 Updated primate classification.

are grouped into the Haplorhines, with the understanding that they are less closely related to lemurs and lorises than to any other primate. This is supported by genomic research (Hartig et al. 2013) as well as morphological characteristics.

Tarsiers today live only in island areas of Southeast Asia. They share a number of characteristics with other prosimians (lemurs and lorises), including a primitive dental pattern and social behavior, small bodies, and large ears. However, tarsiers also show many similarities to the higher primates. Unlike other prosimians, their eye orbits are mostly enclosed by bone (see Figures 5.11a to 5.11d and Chapter 7; they possess a bony ear canal more like that of anthropoids; and they lack a rhinarium, which is a wet, naked portion that surrounds the nostrils, and which is possessed by all other nonanthropoid land-living mammals).

Comparison of the morphology of living and fossil higher primates, as well as more recent research on the genetic sequence data, suggests that African apes shared a common ancestor with humans after both taxa had shared a common ancestor with the Asian great ape, the orangutan, and that chimpanzees and humans shared a common ancestor after gorillas branched off. Therefore, the more recent primate classification system lumps humans and chimpanzees in the same subfamily (Homininae) and into different genera (*Pan* and *Homo*). Some researchers (Wildman et al. 2003, and others) propose one *Homo* genus with three species: *Homo sapiens* (humans), *Homo troglodytes* (common chimpanzees), and *Homo paniscus* (bonobo chimpanzees).

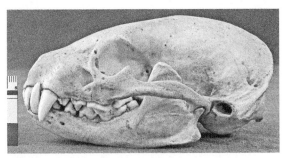

FIGURE 5.11a Skull of a mammal (badger).

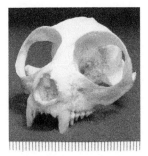

FIGURE 5.11b Cranium of a prosimian.

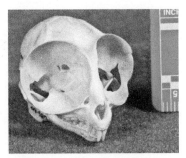

FIGURE 5.11c Skull of a tarsier.

FIGURE 5.11d Skull of a monkey.

Biological Classification

1. Evolutionary, or phylogenetic, relationships of organisms are represented graphically by branching diagrams. These diagrams are usually known as phylogenies or cladograms if cladistic analysis is used. Figures 5.5 and 5.10 are examples of phylogenies and cladograms.

   Construct a cladogram (using cladistic analysis) for the following hypothetical organisms with the following hypothetical characters. Lowercase letters signify primitive characters, or characters of more ancient members of a lineage (an evolutionary line linked by common ancestry). Uppercase letters signify derived states of those same characters.

Organism	Character
1	Abcdefgh
2	ABCDEfgh
3	abCDefGh
4	abcdeFgh
5	abCDefgH
6	abCDefgh

   Example: Suppose we have five organisms with the following primitive and derived characters:

Organism	Character
1	Abcd
2	Abcd
3	aBcd
4	aBCd
5	aBcD

   A cladogram for these organisms would look like this:

   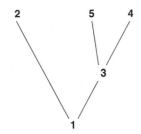

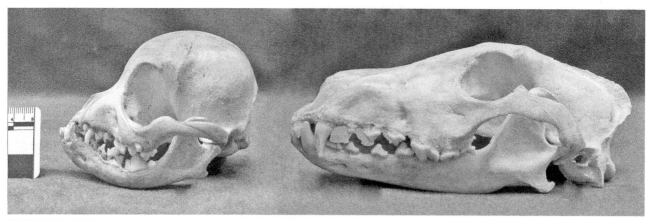

FIGURE 5.12 Unknown specimens for Question 2.

FIGURE 5.13 Unknown specimens, inferior view, for Question 2.

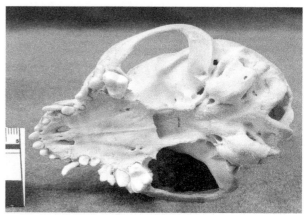

a

b

2. If you were a paleontologist and had to try to classify the specimens in Figures 5.12 and 5.13a and 5.13b, would you put them into the same or different species, based only on the features you can see in the photograph?

Give several reasons why you would classify them in this way.

3. Name some derived characters of humans not shared with the apes.

4. Do you favor classifying humans in a separate or in the same biological family as the African apes? Based on scientific evidence, discuss the pros and cons of each system.

5. Do you favor classifying humans in the same genus as chimpanzees? Based on scientific evidence, why or why not?

6. Consult the textbook you use in this course (or the lecture if the lecture and lab are combined). Does it use evolutionary classification or cladistic classification?

7. Could scientists confuse **intraspecies variation** (for example, age, sex, individual differences) with **interspecies** differences while identifying fossils? What might cause them to be confused?

FIGURE 5.14 Unknown specimens for Question 9.

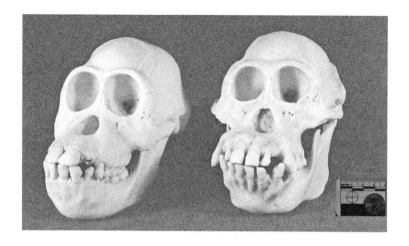

8. If you were a paleontologist and had to classify the specimens in Figure 5.14, would you put them into the same or different species, based only on the features you see in the photograph? Why would you classify them this way?

FIGURE 5.15 Unknown specimens for Question 10.

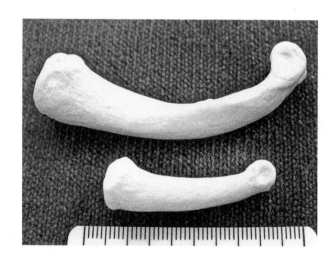

9. Would you put the hand bone specimens shown in Figure 5.15 into the same or different species (they are the corresponding bone in two individuals)? Why?

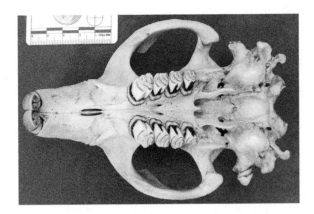

FIGURE 5.16 Unknown specimen for Question 11.

10. Would you classify the animal in Figure 5.16 as a mammal?

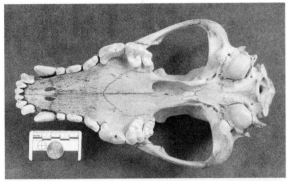

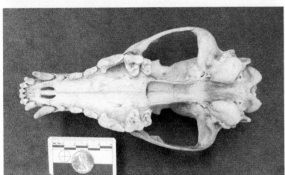

FIGURE 5.17 Unknown specimens for Question 12.

11. Would you place the animals shown in Figures 5.17 in the same species? Why or why not?

REEXAMINING THE ISSUES

In this chapter, we learned the following:

- Classification systems improve communication.
- Biological classification systems are based on the work of Carolus Linnaeus.
- Phylogenetic classification systems are based on evolutionary relationships and include a time component.
- Cladistic classification systems are based on homologous derived characteristics and do not always include a time line.

CHAPTER 6

Comparison of the Skeletons of Quadrupeds, Bipeds, and Brachiators

OBJECTIVES

1. How are patterns of locomotion reflected in the skeleton?

2. Some animals (such as dogs) rely on their sense of smell, while other animals (notably most primates) have a reduced sense of smell and increased reliance on vision. How is this illustrated in the skeleton?

3. Can we determine dietary patterns from the skeleton?

Before we get into the specifics of skeletal morphology in humans and our ancestors, it is important to understand the basic differences between living quadrupeds (such as horses and dogs), bipeds (humans), and brachiators (gibbons and siamangs). Only mammal skeletons are discussed in this book. In addition to interpreting skeletal fragments of primates and primate ancestors, we may also use the information from this chapter to determine the forensic significance of skeletal remains. If you found a skeleton of a cow in a cornfield, for instance, you know that the bony structures are inappropriate for a human skeleton. But if you found only a fragment of that cow skeleton, would you still be able to recognize the clues? Much of this chapter concentrates on the locomotor patterns, but a part of it also includes dietary patterns and other differences not related to locomotion. All of these characteristics vary greatly in each group, so they are given here only for general comparative purposes. The information in this chapter is a compilation of data from Campbell (1976, 1985), Clark (1959), and Schultz (1937, 1973) and from observations by the author.

THE VERTEBRAL COLUMN

It usually makes sense to start discussions of anatomy with the cranium and move caudally. As discussed in this chapter, however, the skeletal differences between the animals with different loco-motor patterns are due in large part to a shift in the center of gravity in the animal. In the typical **quadruped**, the center of gravity is roughly over the forelimbs, whereas the center of gravity in the **biped** is closer to the hindlimbs. The center of gravity in **brachiators** is low (sort of like a clock pendulum) in their body. Changes in the rest of the skeleton can be followed relatively easily from a discussion of the changes in the thoracic region of each animal and working toward each end.

In typical large quadrupeds (horses, cattle, and so on) the vertebral column is a single curve from the cervical to the sacral vertebrae, somewhat like a cantilever bridge. The thorax is relatively narrow from side to side but deep anteroposteriorly, and ligaments hold the intestinal contents in suspension from the lumbar region. The

Quadruped: an animal that habitually walks on four limbs.

Biped: an animal that habitually walks on two limbs.

Brachiator: an animal that habitually swings under branches in arm-over-arm locomotion.

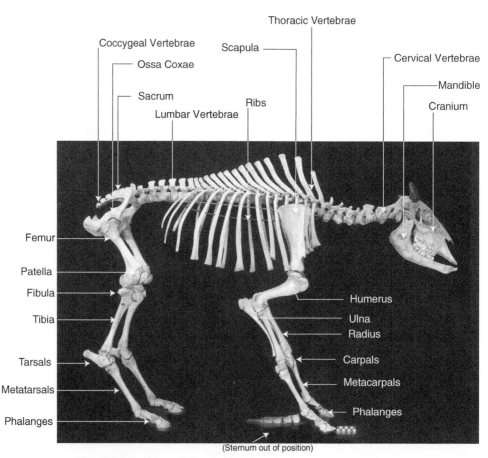

FIGURE 6.1 Bison skeleton.

vertebral bodies are cylindrical in shape and similar in size from the neck to the pelvis. The head is also affected by gravity, as it is suspended from the cervical and thoracic vertebrae. To counter the effects of gravity, large muscles originate on the occipital region of the cranium and insert on the spinous processes of cervical and thoracic vertebrae. These large muscles must attach to a relatively large area at the origin and insertion, so the nuchal area of the cranium and the affected spinous processes are very large and proportional to the weight carried (see Figures 6.1 and 6.5). Although large quadrupeds

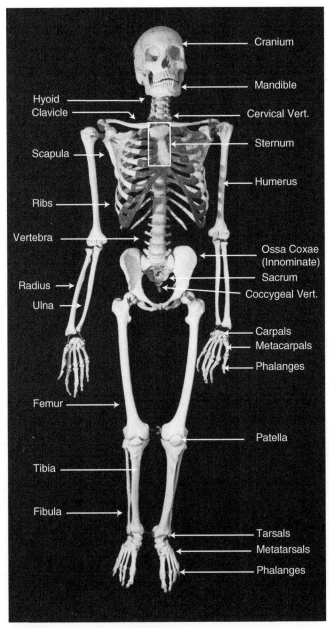

FIGURE 6.2 Human skeleton.

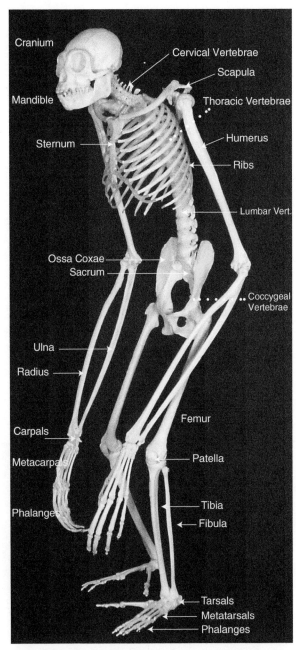

FIGURE 6.3 Gibbon skeleton. *Courtesy Jay Villemarette, Skulls Unlimited*

FIGURE 6.4a Bison thoracic vertebra. Note very long spinous process.

FIGURE 6.4b Wolf thoracic vertebra.

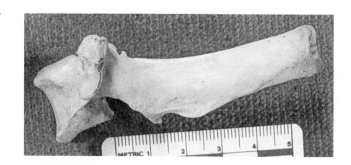

FIGURE 6.4c Chimpanzee thoracic vertebra.

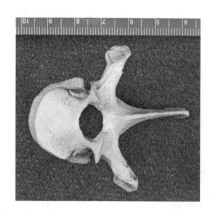

FIGURE 6.4d Human thoracic vertebra.

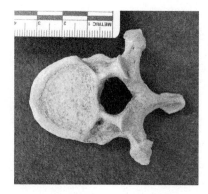

TABLE 6.1 Comparative Anatomy: The Vertebral Column and Thorax

	Typical Quadruped (e.g., dog or bison)	Typical Biped (human)	Typical Brachiator (gibbon)
Shape of the vertebral column	Single curve from neck to pelvis; similar to cantilever bridge	S-shaped curve	Single gentle curve from neck to pelvis
Shape of vertebral bodies	Cylindrical, relatively regular in shape from neck to pelvis (see Figure 6.4)	More wedge-shaped, differences in shape between neck and pelvis greater than in quadrupeds (see Figure 6.4)	Intermediate
Size of spinous processes	Large, particularly those at the origin of nuchal muscles	Small, as the large area for the origin of nuchal muscles is not needed; cranium is more balanced over the vertebral column	Fairly small
Size of vertebral bodies	Similar in size from neck to pelvis	Great differences in size between neck and pelvis	Intermediate
Center of gravity of animal body	Over the forelimbs: the forelimbs catch the body in locomotion and aid in propulsion	Closer to the hindlimbs: propulsion through the hindlimbs	Relatively low
Shape of thorax	Narrow, deep thorax, narrow sternum	Shallow, broad thorax, wide sternum	Shallow, broad thorax, wide sternum
Tail	In some quadrupeds, not in apes	Caudal vertebrae curved ventrally, aid in support of viscera	No tail

FIGURE 6.5 Origin of nuchal muscles in modern humans and gorilla. The arrows represent the center of gravity through the skull.

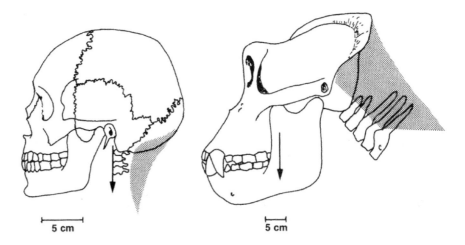

5 cm   5 cm

have very large spinous processes because of the suspended large heads, most small quadrupeds (small monkeys, for example) have smaller heads and smaller spinous processes because the muscles supporting them against gravity are smaller.

In bipeds, the center of gravity runs from approximately the vertex of the head through the center of the sacrum, and the vertebral column is S-shaped. This double curvature of the spinal column is perfect for balancing the body around the center of gravity and allowing a smooth bipedal locomotion, but it creates associated differences throughout the skeleton. For example, the vertebral bodies are larger as one moves caudally because they support more weight, and they are wedge-shaped (see Figure 6.4). Although this is a more flexible arrangement, it can result in back problems in humans. The nucleus pulposus, the fluid of toothpaste consistency inside the intervertebral disks (the cushions between the vertebrae), can be more easily extruded beyond its normal limits with downward force, often exerting pressure on a spinal nerve root and causing pain. In addition, although the abdominal contents in the quadruped are suspended relatively evenly from the lumbar vertebrae, the abdominal contents suspended from the same ligaments in bipeds are working against gravity, pulling the contents caudally (instead of ventrally). This makes them more difficult to support and increase the likelihood of herniation of the abdominal wall (in which the abdominal contents erupt through the abdominal muscles).

In brachiators, the center of gravity is relatively low like a pendulum (see Figure 6.6). The vertebral column has a gentle curve from the neck to the pelvic girdle. Although there is some difference in the size of the vertebral bodies as one moves caudally, the difference is not as great as in bipeds. See Table 6.1 for a comparison of these differences between quadrupeds, bipeds and brachiators.

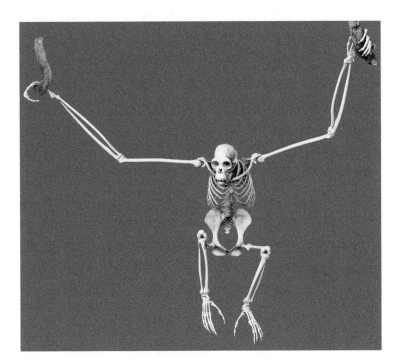

FIGURE 6.6 Gibbon skeleton in brachiation. *Photo, D. L. France; access to specimen courtesy Jay Villemarette, Skulls Unlimited*

THE CRANIUM

As stated previously, the area of the occipital region of large quadrupeds is modified for the attachment of large nuchal muscles devoted to counteracting the effects of gravity on a large skull. The foramen magnum of a typical quadruped (see Figure 6.7a) is located more posteriorly (which makes sense because the skull is in front of the spinal column). The foramen magnum in a biped (see Figure 6.7b) is more centrally located under the cranium, which helps in balancing the cranium on the vertebral column. Figure 6.7c is a photograph of the position of the foramen magnum in a gibbon. Because of the center of gravity and the placement of the foramen magnum, the nuchal region of a biped is not as extensive as in a quadruped. See the differences between quadrupeds and bipeds in muscle insertions shown in Table 6.2.

The form of the dentition of an animal and the associated morphology of the bone supporting the dentition is different with different diets. As the dentition (and maxilla and mandible) of an animal becomes larger, larger muscles are needed to operate that dentition. In young male gorillas, the temporal muscle (one of the major muscles for chewing) originates on the sides of the cranium in a way

FIGURE 6.7a Elk cranium inferior view. Note position of the foramen magnum.

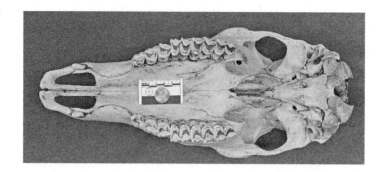

FIGURE 6.7b Human cranium inferior view. Note position of foramen magnum.

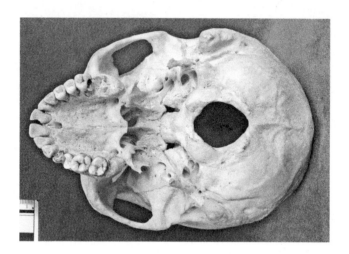

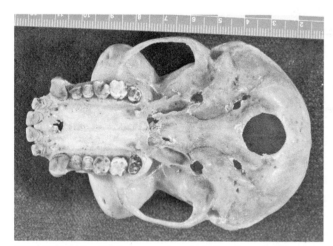

FIGURE 6.7c Gibbon cranium inferior view. Note position of foramen magnum.

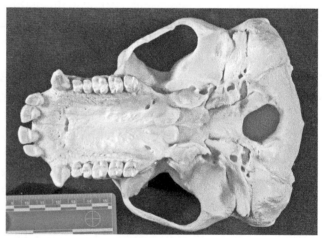

FIGURE 6.7d Chimpanzee cranium inferior view. Note position of foramen magnum.

TABLE 6.2   Comparative Anatomy in the Cranium

	Typical Quadruped (dog or bison)	Typical Biped (human)	Typical Brachiator (gibbon)
Prognathism (projection of lower face)	Extensive progna-thism, very long tooth row, very long snout	Reduced progna-thism, short tooth row, nasal area and tooth row more directly under forehead	More similar to biped than to quadruped
Foramen magnum (see Figures 6.7a–6.7c)	Near rear of cranium	More centrally located under cranium; cranium almost balanced on spinal column	Intermediate
Nuchal crest (area for origin of nuchal muscles on occiput)	Very large, rough area indicating origin of substantial nuchal muscles	No nuchal crest, only a slightly roughened area on the occiput, often difficult to see	Similar to biped
Mastoid process (insertion of sternocleidomastoid muscle) (see Figures 6.8 a–6.8c)	Very small, as there is little need to bring the cranium from a dorsal to a ventral position with muscles when gravity will function as well	Fairly large, as now the cranium is more balanced on the spinal column, and if skull is tilted dorsally, these muscles may bring it to upright position	Not pronounced
Supraorbital torus (see Figure 6.9)	Sometimes present, particularly in great apes	Sometimes present, particularly in early humans and to some degree in modern males	Not pronounced
Sagittal crest (origin of temporal muscle, which is major mastication muscle)	Very large, notably in gorilla	Absent: temporal muscle originates alongside cranium on parietal bones	Not pronounced

© Cengage

FIGURE 6.8a Mastoid area in human.

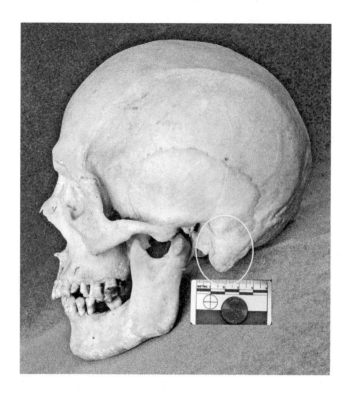

FIGURE 6.8b Mastoid area in siamang.

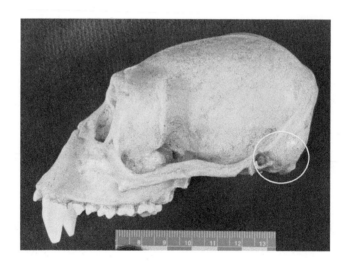

FIGURE 6.8c Almost nonexistent mastoid area in wolf.

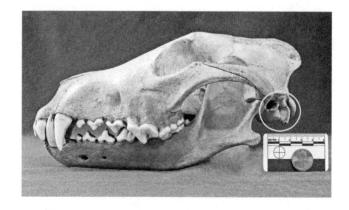

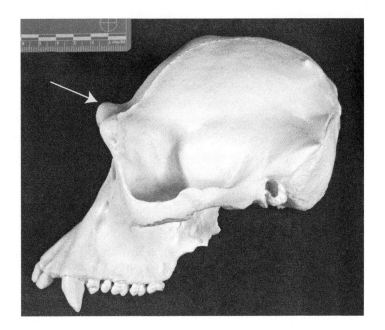

FIGURE 6.9 Supraorbital torus in chimpanzee.

similar to that in humans (see Figure 6.10a), but as the dentition and associated bony structure become larger as the animal becomes larger, the muscle literally runs out of bone on which to anchor itself. The bone is then stimulated to produce more bone to provide this area for attachment, thus producing the crests seen in the occipital and sagittal regions of the gorilla cranium (see Figures 6.10a and 6.10b). Although most of the features of the skeleton listed in the tables in this chapter relate to locomotion, the size of the supraorbital torus and the sagittal crest are *not* directly related to the differences in locomotor patterns!

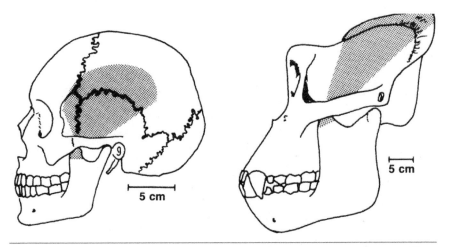

FIGURE 6.10a Origin of temporal muscle in modern humans and gorilla.

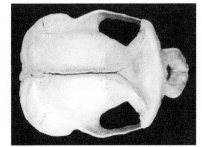

FIGURE 6.10b Young gorilla male with temporal muscle insertion areas in development (before reaching center of cranium).

THE PELVIS

The pelvic girdle (ossa coxae and sacrum) in quadrupeds is long and narrow and reflects the function of the leg muscles that attach to the pelvis. The lower limbs in the large quadrupeds move antero-posteriorly with very little lateral motion, so the strength of the muscles of the leg that make this movement possible are benefited by a long lever arm (see Table 6.3 and Figures 6.12 and 6.13). The pelvic girdle in humans has become shorter and wider, reflecting the different locomotion patterns (balancing the weight over each leg independently as forward movement occurs) as well as the difference in support of the abdominal contents and the need for a large pelvic outlet for childbirth in females. The auricular surface of the sacrum and ilium in humans has moved until it is closer to the acetabulum, which brings the weight from the spinal column closer to the femur head.

THE LIMBS

The concept of lengthening certain bones (and therefore muscle attachment areas) to increase the power of the muscle is easy to understand if we use an analogy of using a jack to lift a car. Would you use more energy if you used a jack with a short handle or a long one? Naturally a long handle would use less of your energy, and it would move through a greater distance to get the car the same distance off the ground. The biomechanics of a long lever arm in animal locomotion works the same way. The animal uses less energy to move what is on the end of the long lever arm (that is, parts of the leg). In addition (and this is particularly

TABLE 6.3	Comparative Anatomy in the Pelvis		
	Typical Quadruped (dog or bison)	**Typical Biped (human)**	**Typical Brachiator (gibbon)**
Ilium (see Figure 6.11)	Long and narrow, greater sciatic notch is very wide, forming an obtuse angle.	Short and splayed, greater sciatic notch is more acute.	Intermediate
Gluteus muscles	Gluteus maximus, medius, and minimus are all abductors (draw leg away from midline of body).	Gluteus maximus is an extensor (see Figure 6.12).	

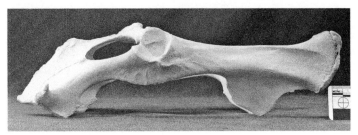

FIGURE 6.11a Pelvic girdle of a quadruped (deer).

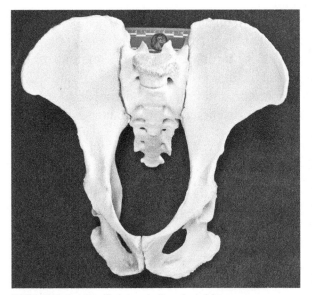

FIGURE 6.11b Pelvic girdle of a chimpanzee.

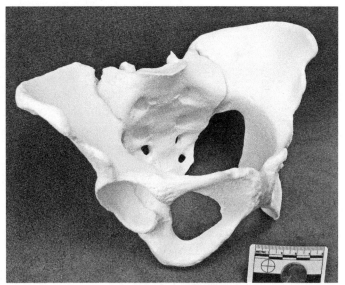

FIGURE 6.11c Pelvic girdle of human.

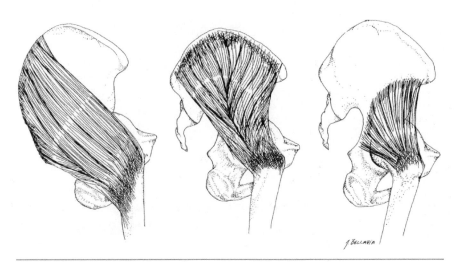

FIGURE 6.12 Biped gluteal muscles: gluteus maximus (left), gluteus medius (middle), gluteus minimus (right). *Drawing, Courtesy of Jayne Bellavia*

important in animals that run at high speed), that lever (or leg) moves through a greater range of motion than a leg that is shorter or that has a shorter lever arm. See Figures 6.13a and 6.13b and Table 6.4 for examples of differences in the limbs in the various locomotor patterns.

In general the articular surfaces of the limbs of quadrupeds such as dogs, cats, and horses are more sculpted than those of primates (and higher primates and humans in particular). Observe the articular surfaces of the distal femur of two quadrupeds (the moose and dog), and compare those to the human distal femur (see Figures 6.16a–6.16c).

There are three distinct functions of the forelimbs in most mammals: They support the body in a quadruped, suspend the body in brachiators, and manipulate objects in bipeds.

Figure 6.1 and Figures 6.17 through 6.26 show skeletons of various quadrupeds (nonprimate and primate). Figures 6.3 and 6.23 show the skeleton of a brachiator, and Figure 6.2 demonstrates a human skeleton. The principles discussed in this chapter can be seen in these photographs.

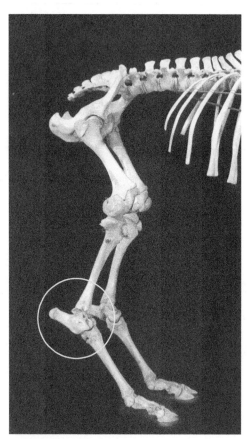

FIGURE 6.13a Achilles area in quadruped (bison).

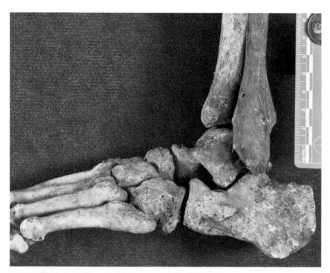

FIGURE 6.13b Achilles area in human.

TABLE 6.4   Comparative Anatomy of the Hind Limbs

	Typical Quadruped (dog or bison)	Typical Biped (human)	Typical Brachiator (gibbon)
Intermembral Index (to be measured; formula given later)	In typical primitive mammals, the forelimbs and hindlimbs are of equal length; there are notable variations in primates.	Hindlimbs are longer than forelimbs.	Forelimbs are longer than hindlimbs.
Tibia and fibula	Many primitive mammals and most primates use both bones for rotary movement of the foot: The tibia transmits weight while the fibula allows rotation. In large quadrupeds, the fibula is greatly reduced or absent, and there is virtually no rotary movement of the foot.	Humans have lost most lateral rotation of the foot afforded by the fibula.	Rotary movement of the foot is retained.
Foot	Highly variable; differences between monkeys and apes are noted later.	Transmits weight through the triad: heel, outside of foot, and then roll off of great toe.	Grasping ability is retained.

© Cengage

DISTINGUISHING HUMAN FROM NONHUMAN BONE AND DENTITION: ADDITIONAL FEATURES

In addition to the features of the skeletal elements previously mentioned, specific areas of bones and within bones are also important.

Articular Surfaces

As was stated earlier, nonprimate quadrupeds (particularly large quadrupeds) tend to have more "sculpted" articular surfaces than do humans, allowing for more stability but decreased range of motion in the joint (see Figures 6.27a to 6.27e). The metacarpals and metatarsals of many nonprimate animals demonstrate this fact, as well (but are frequently mistaken for humans when they are out of

TABLE 6.5 Comparative Anatomy of the Forelimbs

	Typical Quadruped (dog or bison)	Typical Biped (human)	Typical Brachiator (gibbon)
Scapula	Located on the side of the body, the glenoid fossa is more nearly in line with the lateral line of the scapula; points downward.	Located on the dorsum of body, the glenoid fossa is more open, allowing wider movement of the arm.	Located on the dorsum, the glenoid fossa is fairly open; points more cranially than in humans.
Clavicle	Absent in many quadrupedal mammals in which there is very little lateral movement of forelimbs. The clavicle is present in primates.	Present, allows stable lateral motion of the humerus.	Relatively longer than in humans.
Forearm	In large quadrupeds, the distal shaft of the ulna is reduced, and often the proximal ulna is fused to the radius. In smaller quadrupeds, the radius and ulna are distinct bones and often allow for some pronation and supination.	The radius and ulna allow pronation and supination, increasing the ability to manipulate materials.	The radius and ulna allow pronation and supination.
Hands (Figures 6.14 and 6.15)	The form of the hands varies from one digit present, as in the horse, to five digits in monkeys and humans. The specific characteristics of brachiators, quadrupedal monkeys, apes, and humans will be discussed in a later chapter.	Hands have five digits, opposable thumbs, and precision grip.	Hands are hook-like with very long curved fingers and a reduced thumb.

© Cengage

context). In Figures 6.27a through e, notice that the distal articular surface of the human metacarpal is smooth and rounded, and notice that there is a ridge that runs through the center of the articular surface in the wolf and bear (also animals with the primitive five-digit arrangement or derived conditions of two- or one-toed animals). The deer (Figure 6.27d) and moose (Figure 6.14b) have a derived condition in the forelimbs and hindlimbs of two digits instead of five. Further, the two metacarpals have fused into one bone, but notice

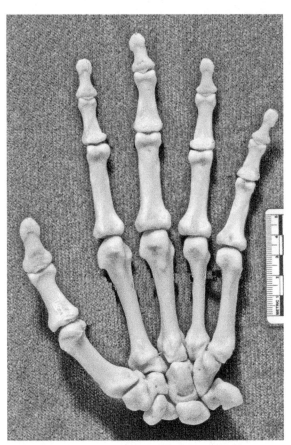

FIGURE 6.14a Primitive condition in digit number (5).

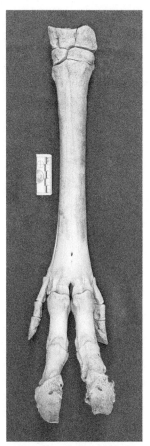

FIGURE 6.14b Derived condition in digit number (2). Notice vestigial digits on the moose, often absent in other large quadrupeds.

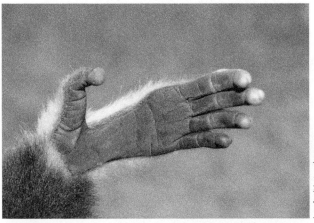

FIGURE 6.15 Closeup of the hand of a white-handed gibbon.

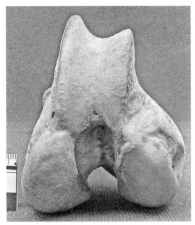

FIGURE 6.16a Distal femur of moose.

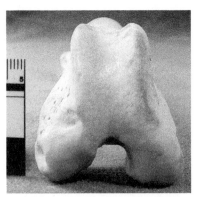

FIGURE 6.16b Distal femur of dog.

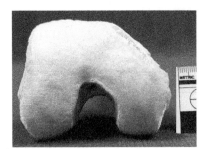

FIGURE 6.16c Distal femur of human.

FIGURE 6.17 Domestic dog.

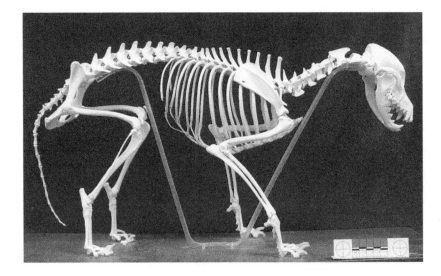

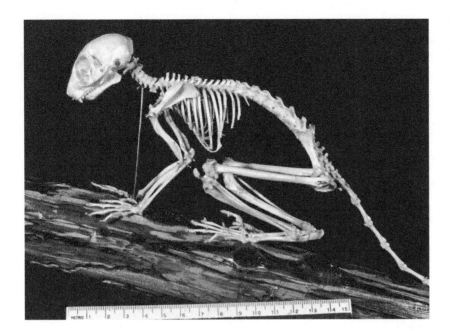

FIGURE 6.18 Bush baby (Galago sp.).

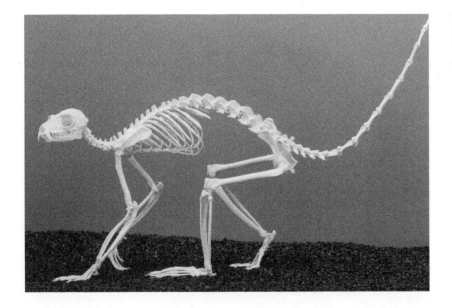

FIGURE 6.19 Lemur skeleton. *Photo, D. L. France; access to specimen courtesy Jay Villemarette, Skulls Unlimited*

FIGURE 6.20 New World monkey (squirrel monkey).

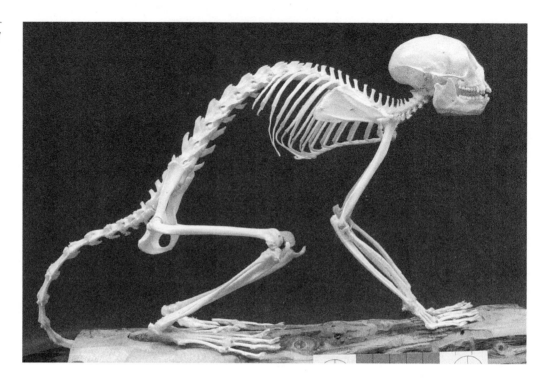

FIGURE 6.21 Old World monkey (macaque).

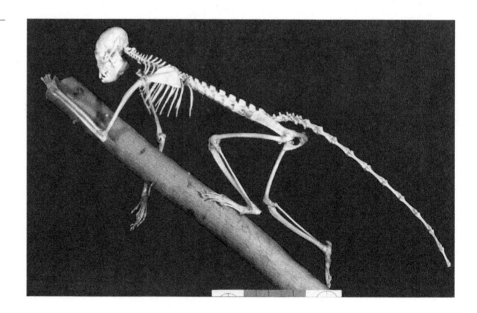

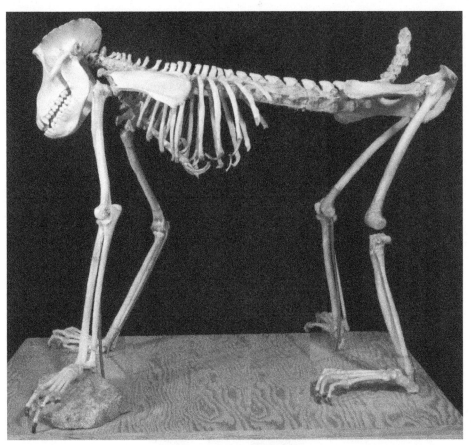

FIGURE 6.22 Old World monkey (common baboon).

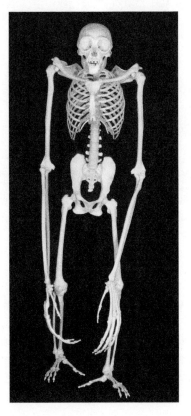

FIGURE 6.23 Gibbon (Hylobates). See additional view in Figure 6.3. *Courtesy Jay Villemarette, Skulls Unlimited*

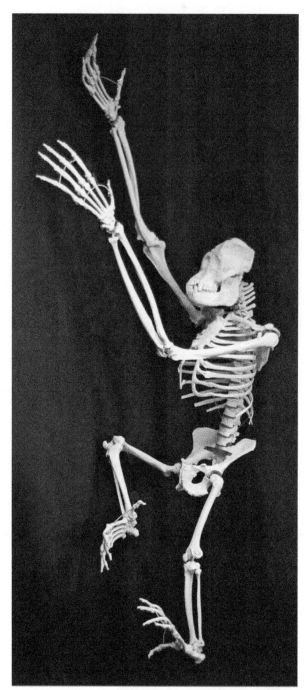

FIGURE 6.24 Orangutan (*Pongo pygmaeus*).
Photo, D. L. France of cast by France Casting

that the distal articular surface still shows the individual distal meta-carpals with the central ridge on each (Figure 6.27d)! The horse has a further derived condition of only one digit, also reflected in the single metacarpal. Notice that the distal articular surface in the metacarpal of the horse also shows the central ridge (Figure 6.27e).

Interestingly, the diaphyseal and epiphyseal surfaces on many large nonprimate mammals are more sculpted as well (see Figure 6.28).

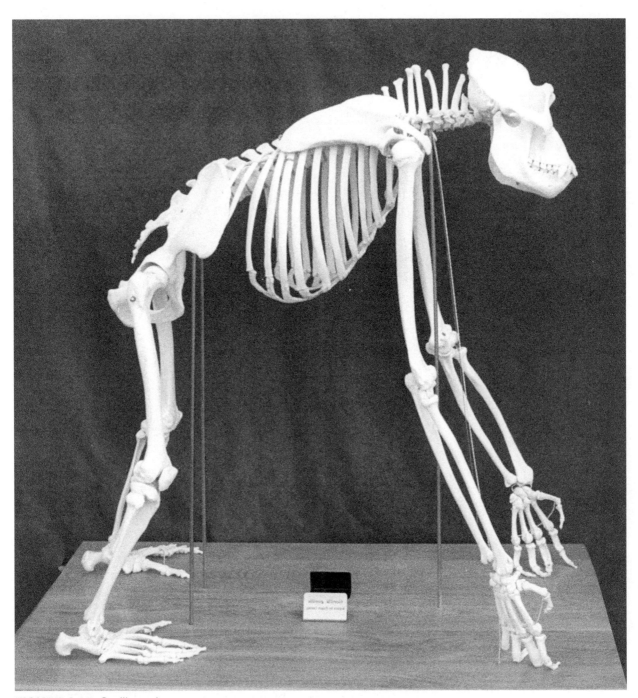

FIGURE 6.25 Gorilla male.

The biomechanical differences go far beyond that fact, however. It is interesting to try to determine the lifestyle of an animal by looking at the morphology of the skeletal elements. Three radii from three different animals are represented in Figures 6.29a to 6.29c. Note the differences in morphology that represent differences in the patterns of use of those skeletal elements, the interrelationship between skeletal elements in that area of the animal's body, and in muscle use (remember that more powerful muscles require

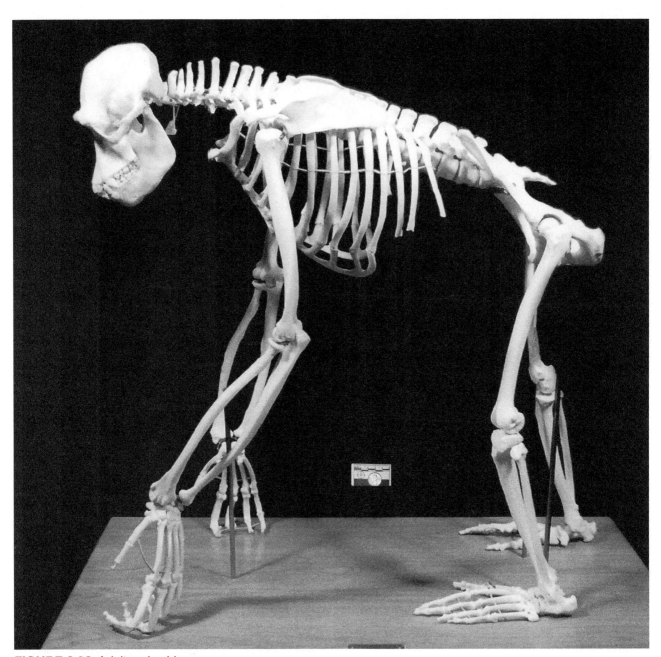

FIGURE 6.26 Adult male chimpanzee.

more robust areas onto which to attach to bone). Figure 6.29c is a radius from a horse. Notice that the proximal radius and ulna are fused and that the distal ulna no longer exists. Look at the large olecranon process, and remember that the muscles that insert on the olecranon process are responsible for the extension of the radius and ulna. Notice also that the shaft of the radius is robust, reflecting a heavy animal that requires massive support with a limited range of motion. The radius in Figure 6.29a is from a coyote. The shaft is long and slender, and the ulna (not shown) is a separate bone. The radius from a harbor seal (see Figure 6.29b) increases distally toward the wide flipper.

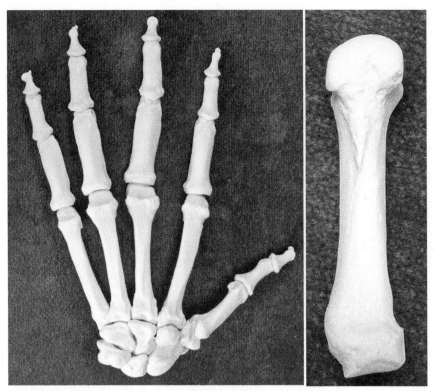

FIGURE 6.27a Human hand (left) and metacarpal (right). Notice smooth surface on distal aspect of metacarpal.

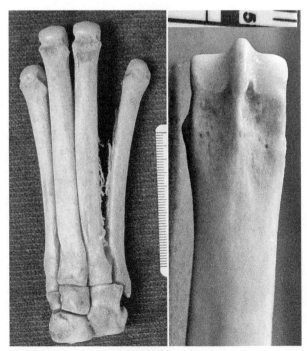

FIGURE 6.27b Wolf metacarpals. Note ridge on the distal articular surface (right).

FIGURE 6.27c Bear metacarpals. Note ridge on the distal articular surface (right).

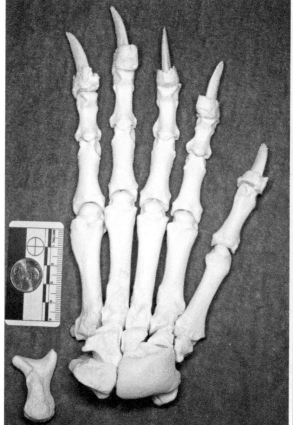

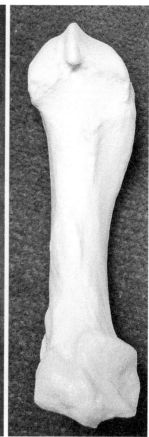

FIGURE 6.27e Horse metacarpal. Note the single metacarpal with a single ridge on the distal aspect.

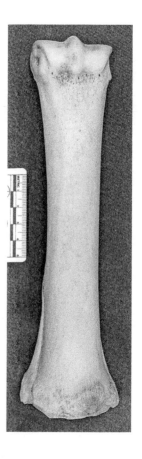

FIGURE 6.27d Deer metacarpal. Note fused metacarpals (2) and central ridge on each original distal metacarpal.

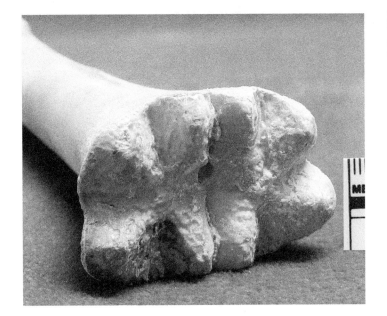

FIGURE 6.28 Nonhuman epiphyseal surface showing "crown" effect.

FIGURE 6.29a Radius of coyote.

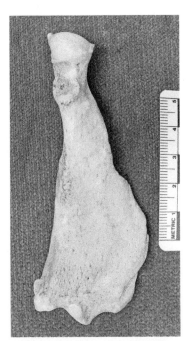

FIGURE 6.29b Radius of a seal. Notice that the radius widens distally.

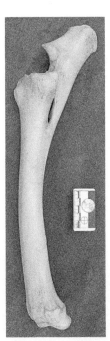

FIGURE 6.29c Radius of a horse. Notice that the radius and ulna are fused and that the ulna has been reduced to the point where it disappears distally.

EXERCISE 6.1   NAME _____   SECTION _____   DATE _____

Quadrupeds, Bipeds, and Brachiators

1. If you found a fossil with a very large sagittal crest, what would that feature indicate about the animal's masticatory apparatus relative to its cranial size?

2. a. If you found a fossil that had a very large nuchal crest, what would you expect of the size of the spinous processes of the thoracic vertebrae? Why?

    b. What might this large nuchal crest tell you about that animal's pelvic girdle?

      Its legs?

      Its vertebrae?

      The position of the foramen magnum?

      The scapula?

      The shape of the thorax?

3. a. If a fossil had very long hook-like fingers with a short thumb, what would this probably indicate about its locomotor ancestry?

    b. What might this tell you about the rest of the animal's skeletal morphology?

FIGURE 6.30 Ossa coxae.

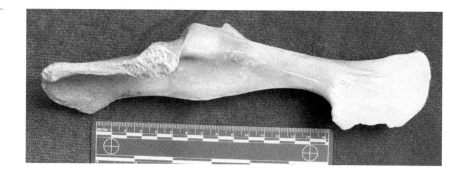

4. What does the morphology of the ossa coxae shown in Figure 6.30 tell you about the locomotor pattern of the individual?

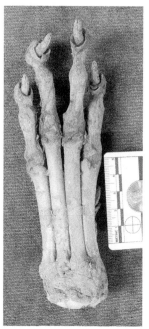

FIGURE 6.31a Unknown.

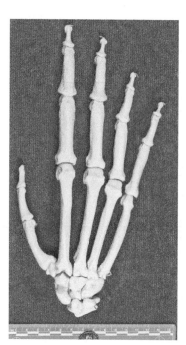

FIGURE 6.31b Unknown.

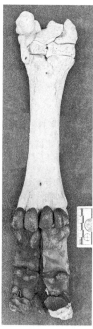

FIGURE 6.31c Unknown.

5. Look at the hands represented in Figures 6.31a to 6.31c. What does each "hand" tell you about the lifestyle and/or ancestry of the animal (arboreal, terrestrial, other)?

FIGURE 6.32 Unknown.

6. The local sheriff has brought you these bones (see Figure 6.32) and has asked you whether or not they are human. Are they? How can you tell?

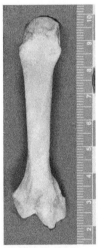

FIGURE 6.33 Unknown.

7. The local sheriff has brought you this bone (see Figure 6.33). Is it human? How can you tell?

MEASUREMENTS AND INDICES

Although Chapter 13 contains a more complete discussion of measurements and indices, it is important to introduce some of those measurements at this point. We use indices to help us compare the ratio of one measurement to another, and, in this chapter, to numerically compare the skeletons of quadrupeds, brachiators, and bipeds. We then use these comparisons to analyze fossil remains to determine their likely modes of locomotion.

Postcranial Measurements

Maximum length of long bone: With all except the tibia, this is the maximum measured length taken on the osteometric board (see Figure 6.34). On the tibia, length is taken from the most prominent part of the lateral half of the lateral condyle to the distal end of the medial malleolus. This length does not include the intercondylar eminence.

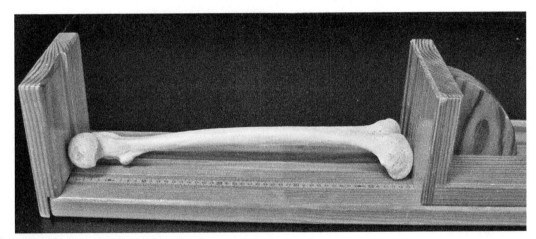

FIGURE 6.34 Osteometric board.

Cranial landmarks (descriptions from Bass 1987). The following points are illustrated in Figure 6.35.

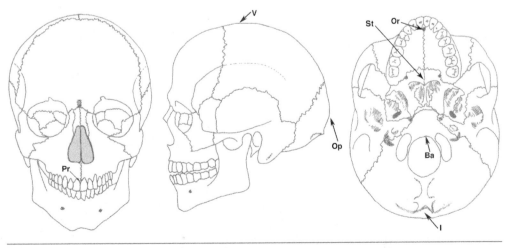

FIGURE 6.35 Landmarks on the cranium.

Basion (Ba)	The midpoint of the anterior margin of the foramen magnum.
Inion (I)	An intersection in the midline with a line drawn tangent to the uppermost convexity of the right and left superior nuchal lines.
Opisthocranion (Op)	The most posterior point on the cranium not on the external occipital protuberance.
Orale (Or)	A point on the hard palate where a line drawn tangent to the curves in the alveolar margin in back of the two medial incisors crosses the midline.
Prosthion (Pr)	The most anterior point on the upper alveolar process in the midline.
Staphylion (St)	The midpoint of a line drawn connecting the most forward points on the curves in the posterior margin of the palate.
Vertex (V)	The uppermost point on the midline of the cranium when it is in the Frankfort plane.*

Condylar index: measures the position of the foramen magnum (see Figure 6.35).

$$\frac{\text{Basion to opisthocranion}}{\text{Basion to prosthion}} \times 100$$

Palatal index: measures the shape of the palate (and hence of the mouth and lower face). Palatal length is taken from orale to staphylion (see Figure 6.35), while palatal width is the greatest transverse breadth between the inner borders of the alveolar arch at the second molars.

$$\frac{\text{Palatal width}}{\text{Palatal length}} \times 100$$

Supraorbital index: measures the height of the skull.

$$\frac{\text{Vertex to superior border of eye}}{\text{Vertex to inferior border of eye}} \times 100$$

---

*A standard plane of reference on the cranium in which the upper border of the external auditory meatus is on the same level as the lower border of the eye. This is also called the Frankfort horizontal.

Nuchal index: measures the area given for origin of nuchal muscles.

$$\frac{\text{From a line level with inferior border of eye to a line with inion}}{\text{From vertex to a line with inferior border of eye}} \times 100$$

Postcranial Indices

Brachial index: measures the relative lengths (using the osteometric board) of the upper and lower arm.

$$\frac{\text{Length of radius}}{\text{Length of humerus}} \times 100$$

Crural index: measures the relative lengths (using the osteometric board) of the thigh and leg bones. The bicondylar length of the tibia is measured with both condyles resting flat against the upright part of the osteometric board.

$$\frac{\text{Length of tibia}}{\text{Bicondylar length of femur}} \times 100$$

Intermembral index: measures the relative lengths of the upper and lower limbs.

$$\frac{\text{Length of humerus} + \text{Radius}}{\text{Bicondylar length of femur} + \text{Tibial length}} \times 100$$

EXERCISE 6.2   NAME _____   SECTION _____   DATE _____

Metric Comparison of Skeletons

The measurement descriptions used in the following exercises can be found in the indices just described.

Note: In several of these exercises, measurements may be taken from the photographs if the skeletal material is unavailable. This is not a rigorous method and not recommended for research purposes but is intended to give general observations of the relationships between different animals.

1. Fill in the following chart using Figures 6.1 through 6.3 and Figures 6.17 through 6.26.

	Quadruped		Brachiator	Biped
	Bison	Monkey	Gibbon	Human
Brachial Index				
Crural Index				
Intermembral Index				

2. Describe what the differences in the brachial, crural, and intermembral indices between these groups mean.

3. a. Take appropriate measurements of the skeletal elements in Figure 6.36a through 6.36d, and determine the probable pattern of locomotion in this animal.

   b. Can you determine anything else about this animal when comparing it with the other skeletons shown in this chapter?

FIGURE 6.36a Unknown humerus.

FIGURE 6.36b Unknown radius.

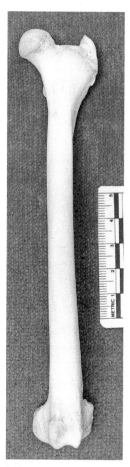

FIGURE 6.36c Unknown femur.

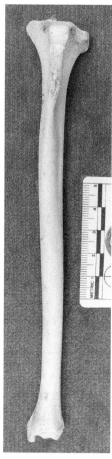

FIGURE 6.36d Unknown tibia.

4. Is there a significant difference between an arboreal and a terrestrial quadruped in the crural and intermembral indices? What are they?

REEXAMINING THE ISSUES

In this chapter, we learned the following:

- If form follows function, then skeletal morphology provides important information about how an animal lives.

- We can gain insights about the general locomotor patterns from the vertebral column, the head, the pelvic girdle, and the hands and feet. In fact, changes in one area of the body often significantly affect other areas of the body, so that it is possible to deduce (within reason) what one element of a fossil looked like even if that element is never discovered.

CHAPTER 7

Comparing the Living Primates

OBJECTIVES

1. Why are primates classified into the specific groups in the classification schemes?

2. What are some of the clues for classifying fossil primates into different taxonomic groups?

3. What are the major differences between primates?

We have made very general comparisons of the anatomies of quadrupedal, brachiator, and bipedal animals (Chapter 6). Now we will take a closer look at the anatomical similarities of and differences between the major primate groups, and examine their evolutionary trends. We will then compare the postcranial area of primates to correlate certain characteristics with their primary locomotor modes. With this information, we will not only know more about living primates, but we will also be better prepared to interpret the fossil record.

INTRODUCTION

As introduced in Chapter 5, all living primates retain some primitive characters of our ancient ancestors. For example, all living primates retain five digits on the hands and feet, the same number of digits found on the first primates in the fossil record. Derived characters evolve beyond more primitive characters, and they are usually classified in the same clade by cladists because they are usually acquired by a few members of an evolutionary group. In this chapter, we will look more closely at some of the primitive and derived characters in our primate classification models.

As was discussed earlier, recent cladistic classifications divide the primates into two suborders, the Strepsirhini and the Haplorhini (see Figure 7.1). Strepsirhini primates include lemurs and lorises, which are the most primitive primates. Lemurs are only found naturally on the island of Madagascar (and adjacent islands) off of the southeast coast of Africa. There are around 60 species of lemurs, and they fill many different niches. There are nocturnal and diurnal species and species that eat insects while others eat a greater variety of vegetation. Lorises are much more widely distributed and, like the lemurs, occupy many different niches.

The Haplorhini suborder is divided into two infraorders (see Figure 7.1): Tarsiiformes and Anthropoidea. Members of the

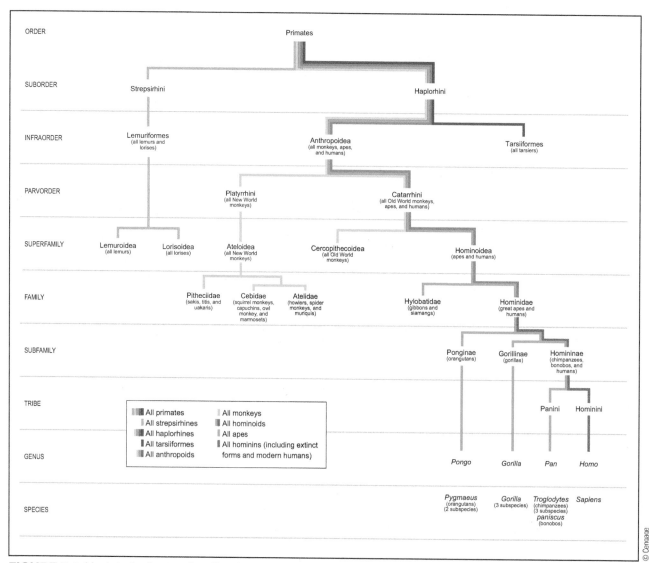

FIGURE 7.1 Updated primate classification.

genus *Tarsius* are grouped with the Haplorhini because, although they are in many respects very primitive primates, they share a few derived characters with monkeys and apes. We will explore a few of those traits in this chapter and compare them to other Haplorhini primates as well as the more primitive Strepsirhini primates. To begin this discussion, Table 7.1 lists a few of the evolutionary trends in all primates, while Table 7.2 is a list of some of the more primitive traits of the Strepsirhini compared to the more derived traits of the Haplorhini.

The Anthropoids include all New World and Old World monkeys, apes, and humans. The New World monkey species (around 70) are all in the parvorder Platyrrhini (or "flat nose" as shown in

TABLE 7.1   Primate Evolutionary Trends (Shared Derived Characters or Synapomorphy among Primates)

1. Retention of five digits on hands and feet (pentadactyly).
2. Nails on all digits (exceptions occur in some Strepsirhini) (see Figures 7.2, 7.5, and 7.8).
3. Primate hands and feet are usually prehensile (the first digit on the hand or foot can touch the other four digits). This is an adaptation for grasping (see Figure 7.2).
4. Tactile pads on the digits are expanded and more sensitive (see Figure 7.2).
5. Reduction in the importance of the sense of smell. Primates usually have shorter snouts and a smaller area of the brain (the olfactory bulbs) devoted to the sense of smell. Some primates have long snouts, but in the upper primates this is often related to the size and configuration of the dentition.
6. An increase in the importance of vision. Primate eyes are usually close together in the front of the face, allowing overlapping vision (binocular vision), which enhances depth perception. Most higher primates also possess color vision (see Figure 7.3).
7. Primates usually have large brains relative to their body size.

In part because of these trends, the following behavioral trends are also involved:

8. Primates usually have only one infant at a time. Twins are rare, except in one of the New World monkey families, the Callithricidae (tamarins and marmosets), in which twins are the rule.
9. An increase in the time of infant dependency. Primate infants are born in a more helpless and dependent condition and remain so for a longer period of time relative to most other mammals. There is, therefore, an increased learning and socialization period. Other life phases are similarly extended.
10. Primates usually live in social groups consisting of both sexes and all age grades (infants, juveniles, and adults). Some other mammalian groups show this tendency (for example, elephants, wolves, dolphins), but it is the rule in primates.

TABLE 7.2   Anatomical Characteristics in Strepsirhini and Haplorhini

Strepsirhini	Haplorhini
1. Rhinarium (fleshy, wet nose) on a relatively long snout. This indicates an increased importance in the sense of smell (see Figures 7.4 and 7.5).	1. Shortened snout, no rhinarium (see Figure 7.3).
2. Unfused mandibular symphysis (unfused in the middle).	2. Fused mandibular symphysis.
3. Eyes placed more on side of face (see Figure 7.5).	3. Eyes facing more forward on face (Figure 7.3).
4. Smaller brain relative to body size.	4. Larger brain relative to body size.
5. Postorbital bar (partial orbital closure) (see Figures 7.6 and 7.7).	5. Postorbital closure (see Figures 7.6 and 7.7).
6. Retention of grooming claws on the second toe (see Figure 7.8).	6. Nails on all digits (see Figure 7.2).
7. Specialized dentition with high-cusped molars.	7. More generalized dentition for more varied diet.
8. Dental comb formed by small, forward-projecting lower incisors (see Figure 7.12).	8. No dental comb.
9. Shortened gestational and maturation periods.	9. Increased gestation and maturation periods.

© Cengage

FIGURE 7.2 Saki hand. Notice nails on all digits and opposable thumb.

Figure 7.3) and are found in southern Mexico, Central America, and South America. They differ in several ways from those primates in the parvorder Catarrhini (or "narrow nose").

There are some exceptions to the general primate classification trends in the more primitive platyrrhines. The marmosets and tamarins are the smallest of the New World monkeys, and they differ from the primate norm in that they have claws instead of nails, and they usually give birth to twins. New World monkeys in general have a dental pattern that is different from the catarrhines in that New World

FIGURE 7.3 Saki monkey (a New World monkey).

FIGURE 7.4 Notice the wet rhinarium in a dog.

FIGURE 7.5 Lemur. Notice the shape of the face, the rhinarium, and the hands.

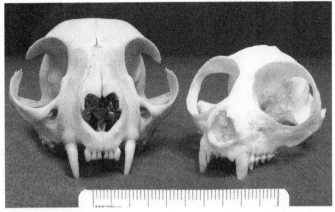

FIGURE 7.6 Lack of postorbital closure in cat (left), postorbital bar in prosimian (right).

monkeys have an extra premolar in each quadrant (see page 215). The sizes of the monkeys as well as their diets, locomotion patterns, and behavioral patterns differ. All New World monkeys have tails, and a couple of species have prehensile tails (or tails that can be used to grip, for example, tree branches for extra support).

Old World monkeys are grouped in the superfamily Cercopithecoidea and are found in much of the Old World, including

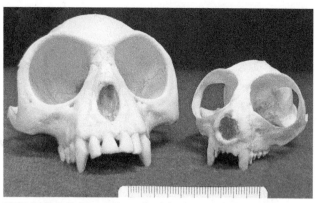

FIGURE 7.7 Unenclosed orbits in prosimian (right), postorbital closure in monkey (left).

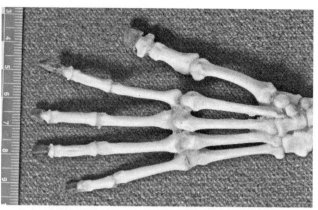

FIGURE 7.8 Lemur foot. Notice grooming claw on second toe. *Photo, D. L. France; access to specimen courtesy Jay Villemarette, Skulls Unlimited*

southern Africa (sub-Saharan), southern Asia, and Japan. They occupy even more varied niches than do the New World monkeys in that New World monkeys inhabit arboreal areas while Old World monkeys inhabit arboreal areas as well as savannah, the temperate climates of Japan, and even urban areas! Their social groups are extremely varied as well, from the smaller groups of the arboreal colobine monkeys to the larger groups of the terrestrial baboons. We will discuss some of the dental and locomotion differences shortly.

The primates in the superfamily Hominoidea include the "lesser apes" in the family Hylobatidae (the gibbons and siamangs) and the great apes and humans in the family Hominidae. The gibbons and siamangs are the smallest of the hominoids. The great apes and humans are classified in an interesting way: The orangutans (subfamily Ponginae) are the most distantly related of the hominids; that is, there is good evidence (morphological as well as biochemical and genetic) that they split off of the line leading to gorillas, chimpanzees, and humans before any of those other groups split from the line. They have an interesting pattern of locomotion, as we shall soon see, and they exhibit great sexual dimorphism (different morphology in males and females). Orangutans are confined to the forested areas of Borneo and Sumatra (both islands in Indonesia). Gorillas are the largest of all living primates, and they are confined to forested areas of western and eastern equatorial Africa. Both orangutans and gorillas are the victims of poaching and shrinking habitats.

The current classification scheme puts the two species of chimpanzee (*Pan troglodytes* and *Pan paniscus*, or bonobos) in the same subfamily (Homininae) with humans. Some researchers (with some pretty strong genetic evidence) argue that chimpanzees are even more closely related than this classification scheme shows. Currently humans are in a different tribe (Hominini) than chimpanzees (Panini).

EXERCISE 7.1   NAME _____   SECTION _____   DATE _____

Living Primate Clades

FIGURE 7.9 Living tarsier.

FIGURE 7.10 Tarsier skeleton. Notice elongated tarsals (arrows show limits) and large orbits. *Photo, D. L. France; access to specimen courtesy Jay Villemarette, Skulls Unlimited*

1. Tarsiers (see Figures 7.9 and 7.10) are newly classified with higher primates in the suborder Haplorhini, although they do not share enough characteristics with the monkeys, apes, or humans to be classified with them in the infraorder Anthropoidea.

   a. Using the following traits for tarsiers, do you think they should be placed in the suborder Strepsirhini or Haplorhini (or do you think they are so different from either that they should be in their own suborder)?

Characteristics of Tarsiers	Strepsirhini?	Haplorhini?
Very large brain to body size.	_____	_____
Very large eyes for nocturnal habitat. Eyes do not move within sockets, but head can rotate 180 degrees.	_____	_____
No dental comb on mandible.	_____	_____
Presence of grooming claws on feet.	_____	_____
Lack of rhinarium.	_____	_____
Enclosed eye sockets.	_____	_____
Social unit is mated pair and offspring.	_____	_____

b. What other information would you want to see that would help you decide whether to put the tarsiers in the suborder Strepsirhini or Haplorhini?

FIGURE 7.11 Unknown skeleton.

2. Using the photograph in Figure 7.11, would you put this primate into the Strepsirhini or Haplorhini? Why?

3. What information, if any, might convince you that humans and chimpanzees should share the same genus? Why? If you could not be convinced, then what *scientific* evidence leads you to that conclusion?

DENTAL TRENDS THROUGH PRIMATE EVOLUTION

We discussed dentition in humans in Chapter 3, including the definition of a dental formula. Deciduous dentition in humans has a dental formula of 2:1:0:2 (two incisors, one canine, zero premolars, and two molars), while adult humans have the formula of 2:1:2:3 (two incisors, one canine, two premolars, and three molars). Why is the dental formula important for us to know? The different dental formulae of the New World monkeys (2:1:3:3) and Old World monkeys (2:1:2:3) gives us some important information about the sequence of divergence of those primate groups from each other. In a somewhat related way, the dental formula can give us some information about where to place a fossil primate in the taxonomic scheme.

Incisors

Most generalized mammals have four incisors in each quadrant, while most primates have two. Most living primates have at least somewhat procumbent (forward-projecting) incisors, but incisors generally became more vertically oriented through hominid evolution.

An interesting characteristic of the incisors of lemurs and lorises (Strepsirhini) is the "tooth comb" (see Figure 7.12) on the mandible. This tooth comb is used for grooming their own fur or the fur of another member of the social group. It is also used to take tree gum off of trees for eating.

Canines

We have seen that a reduction in the importance of the sense of smell and accompanying reduction in the size of the snout are features in the evolutionary trends of primates. Small canines are one of the distinguishing characteristics in humans and our closely related ancestors, as through hominid evolution the canines have become more incisor-like and extend only very little beyond the occlusal line of the other teeth.

In some primates, however, the size of the dentition, and in some primates such as the baboon, gorilla, and chimpanzee, the size of the canines dictates the size and shape of the dental arcade and of the snout. In these primates, the canines are used for gripping and defense. Note the diastema (the gap that receives the canine of the opposite jaw), which accommodates the very large canine (see Figures 7.13 and 7.14).

Premolars

Early mammals had four premolars in each quadrant. The first premolar in the tooth row was lost first to give the New World monkey

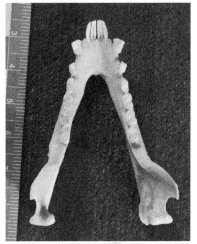
FIGURE 7.12 Bush baby tooth comb.

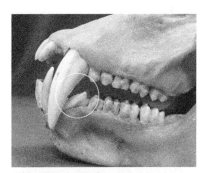
FIGURE 7.13 Sectorial lower first premolar in baboon.

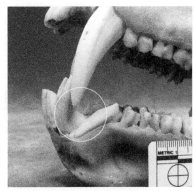
FIGURE 7.14 Diastema.

formula (2:1:3:3). The second premolar in the tooth row was lost next to give the dental formula of Old World monkeys, apes, and humans (2:1:2:3). The practice by paleontologists is, therefore, to state that our dental formula includes premolars 3 and 4.

Modern pongids and some monkeys have a **sectorial lower first premolar** (P3), a single-cusped premolar that forms a cutting, slicing complex with the cutting edge of the upper canine (see Figures 7.13 and 7.14). Note that the upper canine of these forms is honed by the sectorial premolar. Later in human evolution, this premolar is a true "bicuspid" ("two cusps," the term dentists frequently use for these teeth). A trend through much of hominin evolution includes "molarization" of the premolars; that is, the premolars in many hominins became wider, with a more effective grinding surface.

Molars

Many of the major differences of molar morphology among primates reflect differences in their diets. Primates who primarily eat insects have high, pointed cusps, which enables them to better puncture and digest the insect's body. Similarly, folivore primates have high shearing crests or blades on their molars that enable them to break up leaves and other plant material more easily. In contrast, the frugivore primates have low, rounded cusps for crushing fruit, and primates who eat a lot of tough, hard foods such as seeds and nuts have low, rounded cusps on their molars for grinding the materials. Primates who eat these foods also have thicker enamel on their molars, which is an important feature in human evolution).

A clear distinction can be made between the morphology of the molars of Old World monkeys and apes. The cercopithecoids have **bilophodont molars** (see Figures 7.15 and 7.16), which usually have four cusps situated in two parallel rows (sometimes a fifth cusp is present). Hominoids, on the other hand, often have

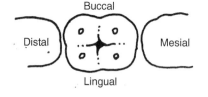
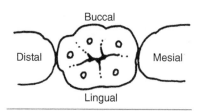

FIGURE 7.15 Bilophodont (X-4) molar (left); Y-5 molar (right).

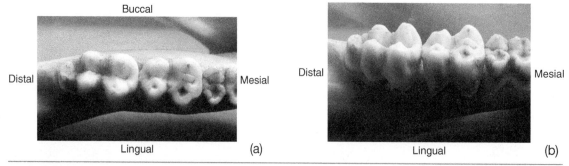

FIGURE 7.16 X-4 Bilophodont molars in baboon (two views).

two or more 5-Y (or Y-5) molars in their mandibles. The 5-Y molars have five cusps in a pattern that resembles a "Y" (see Figures 7.15 and 7.17).

Tooth Row Shape (Dental Arcade)

Very early primates have tooth rows that are divergent toward the back. Throughout evolution, the shape of the tooth row has changed from those like the modern gorilla (rectangular, long tooth row), to a parabolic shape as in modern humans (see Figures 7.18a–7.18d). As a coincident change with this difference in tooth row form, the entire face has become less prognathic (in which the lower part of the face protrudes forward). The snout has become generally smaller, and the cranial vault has expanded out over the face. Throughout human evolution the parabola of the tooth row has become wider.

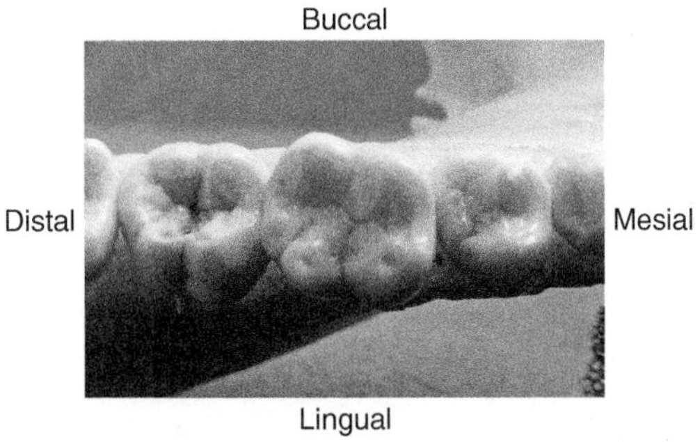

Buccal

Distal   Mesial

Lingual

FIGURE 7.17 Y-5 molar in chimpanzee.

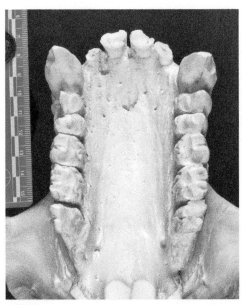

FIGURE 7.18a Gorilla dental arcade.

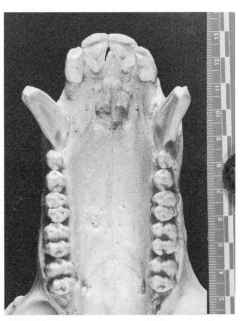

FIGURE 7.18b Baboon dental arcade.

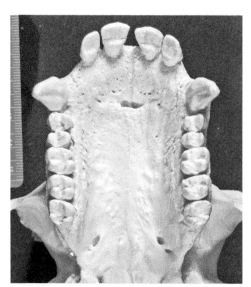

FIGURE 7.18c Chimpanzee dental arcade.

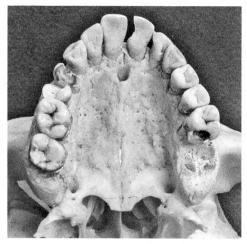

FIGURE 7.18d Human dental arcade.

EXERCISE 7.2   NAME _____   SECTION _____   DATE _____

Dental Trends

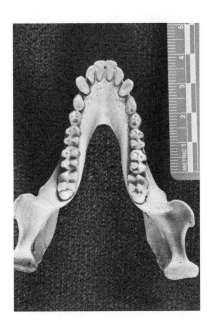

FIGURE 7.19 Unknown.

1. Are the molars shown in Figure 7.19 bilophodont, Y-5, or some other form?

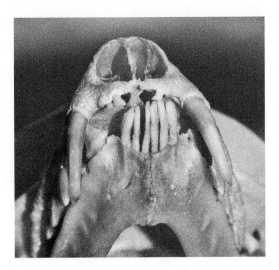

FIGURE 7.20 Unknown.

2. What do the incisors shown in Figure 7.20 tell you about the taxonomic classification of this animal? Why?

FIGURE 7.21 Unknown.

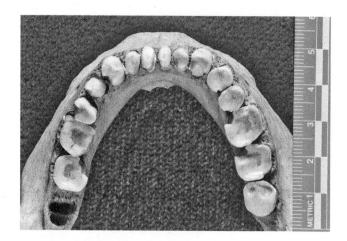

3. What characteristics of the mandible shown in Figure 7.21 tell you about the taxonomic classification of this animal?

4. If you found a section of a mandible with only a sectorial first premolar, what would that tell you about the other dentition in the mouth?

FIGURE 7.22 Unknown.

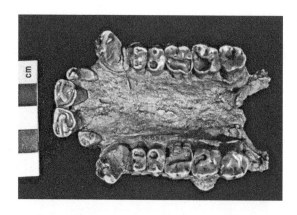

5. The individual in Figure 7.22 is a fossil from the Miocene (a time period roughly 23 to 10 million years ago). How would you classify this fossil? Is it a primate? Be as specific as possible, and give reasons for your decision.

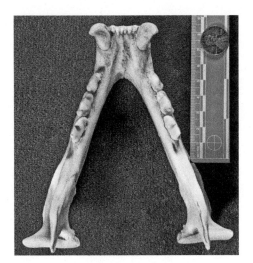

FIGURE 7.23 Unknown.

6. How would you classify the mandible shown in Figure 7.23? Is it a primate? Give reasons for your decision, and be as specific as possible.

POSTCRANIAL COMPARISONS AND LOCOMOTION

Seven modes of primate locomotion are:

- *Slow quadrupedal climbing (SQC):* pottos of Africa and lorises of South Asia
- *Vertical clinging and leaping (VCL):* galago sp. of Africa and some other strepsirhines
- *Quadrupedal walking, running, leaping:* many monkeys and some strepsirhines
- *Brachiation:* gibbons and siamangs
- *Knuckle-walking:* a subcategory of quadrupedalism found in African apes (chimpanzees and gorillas)
- *Slow quadrumanual climbing:* orangutan
- *Bipedalism:* humans

Primates exhibit great variety and versatility in their locomotor behavior, particularly in the trees, where most of them spend all or part of their existence. Simply stating that a primate is a quadruped or a brachiator, for example, hardly describes all of the movements a primate must make to earn a living in natural habitats. Siamangs, for example, although generally classified as brachiators (using the forearms to swing beneath branches), tend to move primarily by climbing when feeding (Fleagle 1976) and may sometimes move bipedally on top of branches. Some sifakas also move bipedally when on the ground.

Slow Quadrupedal Climbing

This specialized mode of locomotion is seen only in the pottos of Africa and lorises of South Asia. Unlike all others, these primates never run or leap in their arboreal habitat but always move very slowly and deliberately. These strepsirhines are nocturnal, and their slow, quiet mode of locomotion allows them to stalk prey (insects, birds, and lizards) and to avoid predators in the trees. Slow quadrupedal climbers are characterized by robust musculature and limb bones; mobile ankle, wrist, and hip joints; and short or absent tails.

Vertical Clinging and Leaping

The bush baby (galago sp.) (see Figure 7.24) of Africa and other prosimians of similar anatomical structure exhibit a locomotor mode that has been called vertical clinging and leaping (VCL) (Napier and Walker 1967). Prosimians that typically move in this way push off with their powerful hindlimbs from a vertical or near-vertical support to which they were clinging, turn around

FIGURE 7.24 Bush baby
(*Galago* sp.).

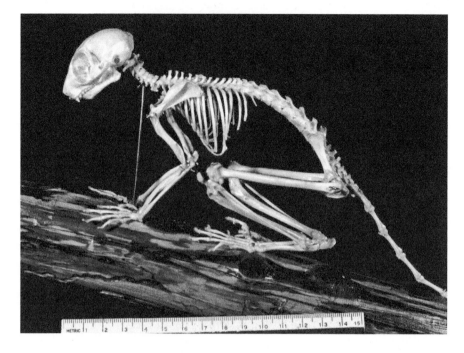

FIGURE 7.25 Vertical clinging
and leaping. *Adapted from from
J. R. Napier and A. C. Walker,
"Vertical Clinging and Leaping: A
Newly Recongnized Category of
Locomotor Behavior of Primates,"
Folia Primat., 1967, 6:204–219*

FIGURE 7.26 Ring-tailed
lemurs.

while in midair, and then land feet first on another branch or tree trunk (see Figure 7.25).

Recent analysis of the anatomy of VCL prosimians indicates that vertical clinging and leaping cannot be considered as one coherent locomotion category. For example, Anemone (1990) argues that there may have been two or three separate evolutionary pathways among prosimian groups to arrive at a VCL locomotor mode. Nevertheless, for the purposes of this introductory course, VCL is considered as one locomotor mode.

Quadrupedal Walking, Running, and Leaping

Most monkeys and many strepsirhines are quadrupeds (Figure 7.26 shows a quadruped lemur), and those that are primarily arboreal (a majority of them) can be called quadrupedal runners and leapers; that is, they move on top of the branches quadrupedally and leap from tree to tree when there is a break in the forest canopy by using their strong hindlimbs to propel themselves and using their tails as stabilizers. There are subtle differences between the skeletons of terrestrial Old World monkeys (for example, baboons) and those that are completely arboreal. In general, Old World monkeys are adept at moving their limbs in a relatively limited plane, and they rarely suspend themselves beneath a branch by hanging from their forelimbs. Parallel evolution is thought to explain the similarities between the arboreal ways of life in New World and Old World monkeys, which are adaptations to a similar way of life in similar habitats. There are a few differences, however, between the two groups. Some of the New World monkeys (but no Old World monkeys) have prehensile tails, used as a "fifth hand" in manipulating

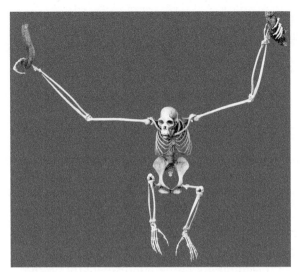

FIGURE 7.27 Gibbon skeleton in brachiating mode. *Photo, D. L. France; access to specimen courtesy Jay Villemarette, Skulls Unlimited*

FIGURE 7.28 Closeup of the hand of a white-handed gibbon.

objects or hanging from branches. Ground-living behavior is rare among New World monkeys but is more common in the Old World monkeys. There are no monkeys adapted to the savanna in the New World, whereas there are a few such species in the Old World (for example, baboons).

Brachiation

The small lesser apes (gibbons and siamangs of Southeast Asia) habitually swing, or brachiate, beneath the branches (see Figure 7.27), and sometimes feed while hanging by their forelimbs. This activity is aided by the position of their scapulae, by the upward orientation of their glenoid cavities, and by their hook-like hands with small thumbs and long fingers (see Figure 7.28). When climbing in the trees, they use their forelimbs and strong upper bodies much more than their legs. In short, the locomotion and posture habits of the small apes can be said to be forelimb and upper-body dominated (Fleagle 1976).

Knuckle-Walking

Although the great apes share most of the morphological characteristics of the small apes and occasionally brachiate for short distances, they are too large to brachiate habitually through the forest canopy.

African apes (chimpanzees and gorillas) carry out most long-distance movements on the ground by "knuckle-walking." The knuckle-walkers (see Figures 7.29 and 7.30) are characterized by tough, hairless skin on the dorsum of the middle fingers, and their wrists are strengthened by differences in the carpals. When these apes climb trees, however, they, like the lesser apes, use their forearms and strong upper bodies more than their hindlimbs and often use a variety of hanging or suspensory postures.

Slow Quadrumanous Climbing

The orangutans of Sumatra and Borneo move through the forest canopy by a locomotor mode that has been called slow quadrumanous climbing. Figure 7.31 shows an orangutan climbing the platform in a quadrumanous manner. Note the morphology of the hand and foot of the orangutan in Figure 7.32. These large great apes use their hands and feet to grasp branches and other supports as they slowly move through the trees. The female orangutans are almost exclusively arboreal. The huge males, which are about twice as large as females (about 120 kg), carry out much of their long-distance movements on the ground. Orangutans move quadrupedally on the ground with their hands held in a fist, not in the knuckle-walking posture of the African apes (see Figure 7.32).

Bipedalism

The anatomical modifications for habitual bipedal locomotion found in humans are unique among extant primates. These anatomical modifications are observed mostly in the pelvis and feet of humans.

However, anatomists have long recognized the similarities between humans and apes in the upper body: a short, inflexible trunk (relative to most monkeys), the position of the scapula on the dorsum of the thorax, the triangular shape of the scapula, and the relative anteroposterior shallowness of the thorax. These upper-body similarities are not due to similarities in locomotor behavior but to the long period of evolutionary relatedness.

FIGURE 7.29 Gorilla knuckle-walking (and holding on for dear life).

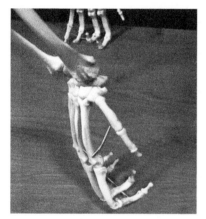

FIGURE 7.30 Skeleton of a knuckle-walker.

FIGURE 7.31 Orangutan quadrumanous climbing.

FIGURE 7.32 Orangutan walking. Note that he is walking on his wrist.

EXERCISE 7.3   NAME _____   SECTION _____   DATE _____

Comparing Extant Primates

1. Which of the three bones that make up the ossa coxae has changed most in humans, compared with monkeys and apes? In what way has it changed?

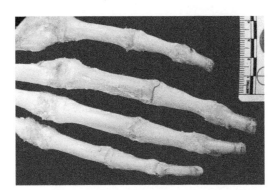

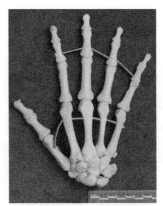

FIGURE 7.33 Unknown.

2. Is the skeletonized hand in Figure 7.33 from a primate? What characteristic(s) lead(s) you to that conclusion?

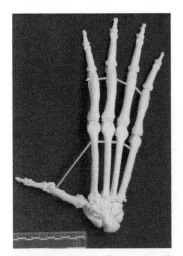

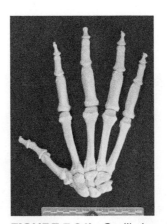

FIGURE 7.34a Orangutan hand.   FIGURE 7.34b Gorilla hand.   FIGURE 7.34c Human hand.

3. Compare the phalanges of the hands of the orangutan, gorilla, and human in Figure 7.34. What are the differences, and what does that tell you about the ways these animals use their hands differently?

4. What are four differences between the skeletons of an Old World monkey and an ape?

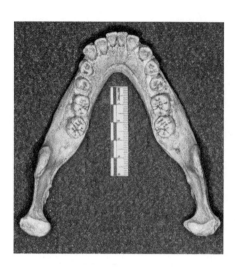

5. How would you classify the individual in Figure 7.35? Is it a primate? Is it a New World monkey? Old World monkey? Ape? Human? Why would you classify it the way you did? Be specific in your answer.

FIGURE 7.36a Squirrel monkey skeleton.

FIGURE 7.36b Old World monkey (macaque) skeleton.

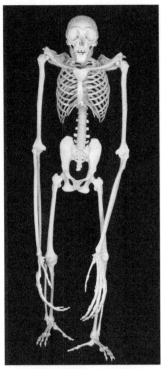

FIGURE 7.36c Gibbon skeleton. *Courtesy Jay Villemarette, Skulls Unlimited*

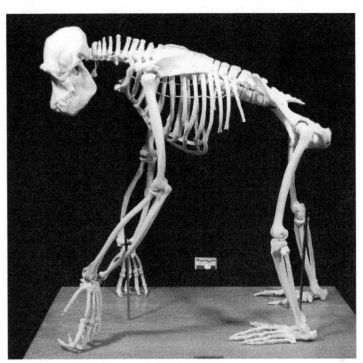

FIGURE 7.36d Chimpanzee skeleton. *Photo, D. L. France; cast from France Casting*

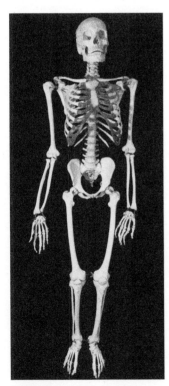

FIGURE 7.36e Human skeleton.

FIGURE 7.37a Galago maxilla. *Photo, D. L. France; access to specimen courtesy Jay Villemarette, Skulls Unlimited*

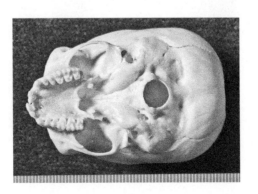

FIGURE 7.37b Squirrel monkey maxilla. *Photo, D. L. France; access to specimen courtesy Jay Villemarette, Skulls Unlimited*

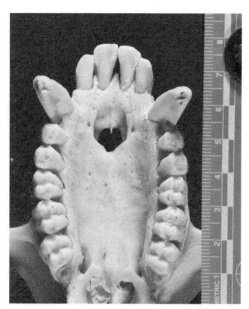

FIGURE 7.37c Macaque maxilla.

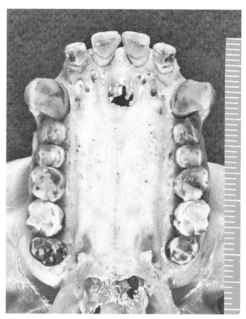

FIGURE 7.37d Gibbon maxilla.

FIGURE 7.38a Galago skull. *Photo, D. L. France; access to specimen courtesy Jay Villemarette, Skulls Unlimited*

FIGURE 7.38b Squirrel monkey skull. *Photo, D. L. France; access to specimen courtesy Jay Villemarette, Skulls Unlimited*

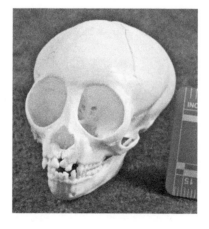

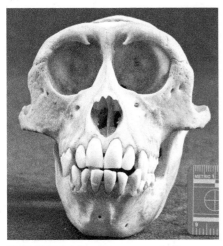

FIGURE 7.38c Macaque skull.

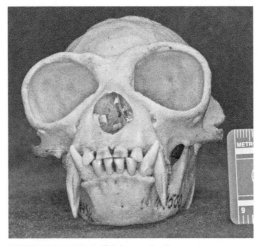

FIGURE 7.38d Gibbon skull.

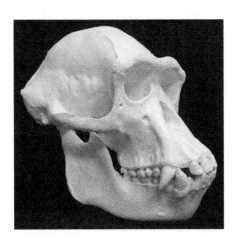

FIGURE 7.38e Chimpanzee skull. *Photo, D. L. France; access to specimen courtesy Jay Villemarette, Skulls Unlimited*

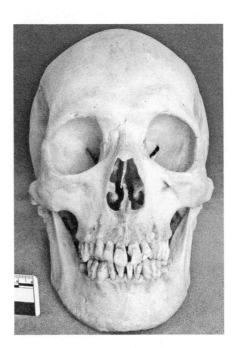

FIGURE 7.38f Human skull.

6. Fill out the following chart for the prosimians, a New World monkey, an Old World monkey, an ape, and a human. If you do not have these skeletons in your laboratory, use Figures 7.18 and 7.24, and Figures 7.36 through 7.38.

Comparisons of Extant Primates

	Prosimian	New World Monkey	Old World Monkey	Ape	Human
Intermembral index					
Condylar index					
Brachial index					
Dental formula					
Enclosed eye orbits?					
Location of scapula on thorax					
Number of thoracic vertebrae					
Nails on all digits?					
Tail?					

REEXAMINING THE ISSUES

In this chapter, we learned the following:

- Extant primate dentition gives us clues about the diet of the primate.
- Extant primate locomotion is reflected in their skeletons and in turn gives us information about the environment in which the primate lives.
- The morphological differences in the skeletons of primates offer clues about their evolutionary relationships.

With this information, we are now prepared to begin to interpret the fossil record. In future chapters, you will be asked to do just that.

CHAPTER 8

Observation of Living Primate Behavior and Morphology

OBJECTIVES

1. Do different species of animals exhibit different behaviors?

2. Do different species of primates exhibit different interpersonal behaviors?

3. What role does the environment in which they live influence interpersonal behavior?

Primates are fascinating individuals whose behavior and interactions with other primates help us understand our own behavior and our roles in society. Also, we cannot deduce all we need to know about the behavior of our ancestors by studying their skeletal morphology, but we can obtain some of the information we need by studying the social behavior of primates.

After learning about general behavioral categories and ways to observe and record primate behavior in a zoo or in the wild, we will practice our techniques at a dog park in case a zoo is not available.

INTRODUCTION

This chapter involves exercises in observing behavior and morphology of zoo primates. Before visiting the zoo, we will review the typical locomotor behavior and other physical characteristics and classification of major groups of primates discussed in previous chapters. In addition, there are links on the Internet to short video clips of primates in various situations.

Primate morphology in zoos may be different from their morphology in the wild, but probably not as different as their behavior. Studies of baboons in a very crowded enclosure in the London Zoo in the 1930s gave the impression that primate societies were centered on sex and violence. Studies of primates in their natural habitats that began in earnest in the 1950s and 1960s have shown that although sex and violence are certainly parts of the behavioral repertoire of primates, they are exhibited rarely relative to other aspects of their behavior, such as foraging for food, grooming behavior, and mother–infant interactions.

The locomotor behavior of primates in zoos obviously depends to a large extent on what they have available in their cages and enclosures. An arboreal primate will not be able to exhibit its full repertoire of arboreal agility, for example, if its cage consists only of bars and a concrete floor. Also note that many of the behaviors listed next will be season-specific and will be determined to some extent by the number, ages, and sexes of individuals present within each enclosure. The zoo personnel can often provide some of the information needed to complete the checklist, such as the species and common names and their distributions.

BEHAVIOR CATEGORIES

There are basically two methods for observing primates:

- Specific behavioral categories
- All behavior of a specific (focal) animal or group of animals

If, for example, a female primate in the zoo has recently given birth, the researcher may wish to concentrate on mother–infant interactions. If, on the other hand, a group of primates includes many juveniles, research may focus on play behavior.

To fully understand the behavior sequences observed, one must usually be familiar with the individual and group histories. For example, an adult female may interact with another adult female to which she is closely related quite differently than to one to which she is not related. Again, zoo personnel may be able to give some information on the relationships between different individuals. Following is a short list of behavioral categories to choose from:

1. Mother–infant interactions
2. Play behavior
3. Sexual behavior/mounting behavior
4. Adult male–adult female interactions (including nonsexual)
5. Adult male–juvenile interactions
6. Adult male–adult male interactions
7. Adult female–adult female interactions
8. Adult female–juvenile interactions
9. Agonistic behavior (combative or contestant)
10. Dominance behavior

SAMPLING TECHNIQUES

Attempting to record all behavior for each animal over a long period of time is impractical and overwhelming, so sampling techniques are used. The following is a brief summary of three of the more common techniques:

1. **Scan sampling:** The researcher records the behavior of a group of primates or an individual at regular time intervals, usually 30 seconds, 1 minute, or 5 minutes. If you want to use this method with a group of primates, the group should not be too large, and all members should be visible at all times.

2. **Focal sampling:** The researcher records the behavior of a specific animal.

3. **Ad-lib sampling:** The researcher records any behavior of a group of primates that is observable and that seems interesting. Recordings are made on a blank sheet of paper or in a field notebook. Even though regular time intervals are not used in ad-lib sampling, the time should be recorded often. Also, the researcher usually develops a form of abbreviations because this method involves significant amounts of writing.

Your instructor may divide the class into groups, which may use different sampling techniques to compare the results.

If your class does not have access to zoo primates, but your campus has a tree squirrel population, observe the behavior of the squirrels. This has one advantage in that you will be exposed to the difficulties of observing animals in a "wild" habitat. Tree foliage at times makes observing the animals impossible. Keep in mind that the trees in a tropical rain forest, where most primates live, are two to five times taller than most trees found in temperate zones. A disadvantage to observing squirrels is that they are often observed alone, whereas one rarely observes a solitary primate in the wild.

EXERCISE 8.1   NAME _____   SECTION _____   DATE _____

Observation Skills at a Dog Park

As an introduction to observing primate behavior, visit a dog park where dogs are allowed to be off of a leash (you do not want to take your own dog at this point so you can observe other dogs without being distracted). Take a notebook, and observe the following behaviors:

- Play behavior
- Aggressive behavior
- Dominance displays around other dogs (stiff posture, tail erect, ears up, and so on)
- Submissive displays around other dogs (slumped posture with tail down or tucked between the legs or lying on back)

1. When do these displays occur? How far was the dominant dog from its owner?

2. If there is a dominant dog, how many times did he display dominance to another dog within 10 minutes?

3. Did the submissive dog display submission to more than one other dog?

4. Did a certain breed show dominance more often than other breeds?

5. Did very young dogs display dominance? How often? Were they more likely to show dominant or submissive behavior?

6. What other behaviors did you witness?

7. When did those other behaviors occur?

NAME _____ SECTION _____ DATE _____

Classification, Morphology, and Locomotion of Primates

Provide the following information for one to four primates at the zoo, from videotapes, or from library or Internet research.

Common name _____

Scientific name _____

Infraorder _____

Superfamily _____

Family _____

Subfamily _____

Genus _____

Species _____

Distribution _____

Number of animals in cage _____

Tail? _____

Prehensile tail? _____

Nails on all digits? _____

Relative length of forelimbs to hindlimbs ____

Hand grip used _____

Habitual mode of locomotion _____

Sexual dimorphism in body size? _____

Common name _____

Scientific name _____

Infraorder _____

Superfamily _____

Family _____

Subfamily _____

Genus _____

Species _____

Distribution _____

Number of animals in cage _____

Tail? _____

Prehensile tail? _____

Nails on all digits? _____

Relative length of forelimbs to hindlimbs ____

Hand grip used _____

Habitual mode of locomotion _____

Sexual dimorphism in body size? _____

Additional Comments

EXERCISE 8.3   NAME _____   SECTION _____   DATE _____

Primate Observation

Scan Sampling (Record the behavior of a group of primates or an individual at regular time intervals, usually 30 seconds, 1 minute, or 5 minutes.)

Beginning Time: _____

Ending Time: _____

Species: _____ Common name: _____

Composition of group: Number of adult males _____ Adult females _____

Immature individuals _____ Group size _____

Brief description of weather:

Focal Sampling (Record the behavior of a specific animal.)

Description of the focal animal:

Age grade (adult, juvenile, infant):

Sex:

Additional Observations

EXERCISE 8.4   NAME _____   SECTION _____   DATE _____

Checklist of Primate Behaviors

Choose a focal animal. Using a watch, observe what this animal is doing during the relevant time intervals, and make a check in the appropriate category. Feel free to use behavioral categories you have created in addition to those presented.

Interval used: ___ 30 seconds ___ 1 minute ___ 2 minutes ___ 5 minutes

	Number of Occurrences during Time Interval																			
	1	2	3	4	5	6	7	8	9	10	11	12	13	14	15	16	17	18	19	20
Walking																				
Sitting																				
Prone																				
Standing																				
Eating																				
Scratching																				
Vocalizing																				
Sleeping																				
Autogrooming																				
Grooming/Groomed																				
Displaying																				
Threat/Threatened																				
Chase/Chased																				
Attack/Attacked																				
Inspecting																				
Playing																				
Courtship/Courted																				
Mount/Mounted																				
Present																				
Displace/Displaced																				
Other																				
Other																				

REEXAMINING THE ISSUES

In this chapter, we learned the following:

- In previous chapters, we have seen that we can determine how an animal moves by looking at the skeletal morphology. There are serious limits, however, to what we can surmise about behavior from the skeleton, so we must look to living models for behavior.

- The behavior of living animals (from squirrels to dogs to primates) depends in part upon the environment in which they are observed and in part upon the behavior of the surrounding animals.

CHAPTER 9

The First Primates

OBJECTIVES

1. How and why did primates evolve?

2. When we examine a fossil primate, how do we know it is a primate?

3. When did the earliest primates show up in the fossil record?

Geological Time	Dates
Paleozoic Era	570–225 MYA
Mesozoic Era	225–65 MYA
Cenozoic Era	65 MYA to present
Paleocene Epoch	65–56 MYA
Eocene Epoch	56–33 MYA
Oligocene Epoch	33–23 MYA
Miocene Epoch	23–5 MYA
Pliocene Epoch	5–2.58 MYA
Pleistocene Epoch	2.58 MYA–11,700 YA
Holocene (Recent)	11,700 YA–present

MYA = millions of years ago
YA = years ago

INTRODUCTION

In this book (and in any introductory text in physical anthropology), the differences between species of extant primates and between extant and extinct primates focus on major characteristics, but many researchers are also studying minute but significant morphological differences between species to try to place them into the appropriate taxonomic classification. As only one example, many researchers (Bloch and Silcox 2001; Bloch and Silcox 2006; Kay et al. 1992; Silcox 2003) are studying the anatomy of the middle ear in extant primates and the earliest primate-like ancestors in the Paleocene to try to find a tiny canal through which the internal carotid artery and nerves are transmitted. If that canal is present, it is an indication that the fossil is more similar to primates than to the sister orders. On an even smaller scale, DNA sequencing is being used to determine the relatedness of species not only by the genes that are active, but also by "fossilized" genes that tell us about that animal's genetic past (see Chapter 2). This is a demonstration that evolutionary changes do not have to be huge to be significant for species differentiation!

With the extinction of the dinosaurs at about 65 MYA, niches once occupied by the dinosaurs opened up to mammals, including the common ancestor of present-day primates. Naturally, the first primates would have many of the primitive traits of other mammals, but enough derived traits to be recognizable as primates.

Why did primates evolve? A couple of theories are worth considering. The first is known as the **arboreal theory**, which dates from the early part of this century. Briefly, this theory states that the characteristics found on most primates are adaptations that allow primates to pursue an arboreal lifestyle and to compete with other arboreal animals. These characteristics include an increased reliance on vision with binocular vision, a reduction in the importance of the sense of smell, and prehensile hands and feet with nails instead of claws (claws can get in the way of the precision grip: see Figure 9.1).

This theory had become dogma in anthropological thought by the 1950s, but in the early 1970s, Matt Cartmill of Duke University proposed the **visual predation theory** (Cartmill, 1972, 1974, 1992). He pointed out that many mammals (for example, tree squirrels) make their living partially or fully in the trees and do not possess these primate characteristics. He suggests that prehensile extremities with precision grip, reduced claws, and binocular vision evolved in the very first primates to enable them to prey on insects on the terminal branches of the lower layers of tropical rain forests. Indeed, most of the true primates of the early Eocene are quite small, a clear benefit for moving on the outermost limbs of trees. Today, primates that specialize in eating insects weigh less than 500 g, or about 17.5 oz (Kay 1984). Furthermore, the molar morphology of these early primates is functionally similar to extant insectivorous primates. Sussman (1991), however, added that some primate traits (including color vision) developed because of the occurrence of flowering plants (angiosperms), and that the

FIGURE 9.1 Prairie dogs.

TABLE 9.1   Anatomical Characteristics in Strepsirhini and Haplorhini

Strepsirhini	Haplorhini
1. Rhinarium (fleshy, wet nose) on a relatively long snout. This indicates an increased importance in the sense of smell. (See Figures 7.4 and 7.5 in Chapter 7).	1. Shortened snout, no rhinarium (see Figure 7.3).
2. Unfused mandibular symphysis (unfused in the middle).	2. Fused mandibular symphysis.
3. Eyes placed more on side of face (see Figure 7.5).	3. Eyes facing more forward on face (see Figure 7.3).
4. Smaller brain relative to body size.	4. Larger brain relative to body size.
5. Postorbital bar (partial orbital closure) (see Figures 7.6 and 7.7).	5. Postorbital closure (see Figures 7.6 and 7.7).
6. Retention of grooming claws on the second toe (see Figure 7.8).	6. Nails on all digits (see Figure 7.2).
7. Specialized dentition with high-cusped molars.	7. More generalized dentition for more varied diet.
8. Dental comb formed by small, forward-projecting lower incisors (see Figure 7.12).	8. No dental comb.
9. Shortened gestational and maturation periods.	9. Increased gestation and maturation periods.

different beneficial aspects of those plants (fruits, seeds, and so on) contributed to the new niches exploited by various animals. This seems to be supported by theories proposed by Dominy et al. (2003) that the eyes of catarrhines, platyrrhines, and strepsirhines were modified through evolution to be attracted to figs and palms. However, Kirk and Simons (2001) state that probably all late Eocene Fayum (on the eastern edge of the Sahara desert) anthropoids were probably fruit eaters, but that late Eocene prosimians were diverse eaters (some were insectivores, some leaf eaters, and some fruit and insect eaters). They state that this dispels the notion that diet was one of the major driving factors in the evolution of anthropoids. Further, they say that anthropoids probably developed in Africa, and that the resemblance to Asian primates is probably not a result of a direct ancestral line to anthropoids in Asia, but rather a "dietary convergence." In fact, at least parts of all of these hypotheses may be true at the same time or in different times along the evolutionary paths in primates.

Fossil Primates Discussed in this Chapter		
PALEOCENE PRIMATES: About 12 Families of Plesiadapiformes		
Order	*Plesiadapiformes* (late Cretaceous, Paleocene)	
Family	Purgatoriidae	
Genus	*Purgatorius* (Early Paleocene, North America)	
Superfamily	Plesiadapoidea	
Family	Plesiadapidae	
Genus	*Plesiadapis* (late Paleocene-early Eocene, North America, Europe)	
Family	Carpolestidae	
Genus	*Carpolestes* (late Paleocene-early Eocene, Wyoming: 55.8–60.2 MYA)	
Family	Paromomyidae	
Genus	*Ignacius* (middle Paleocene to late Eocene, North America, Europe, Asia)	
EOCENE PRIMATES		
Suborder	Strepsirhini	
Infraorder	Adapiformes	
Superfamily	Adapoidea	
Family	Notharctidae	
Genus	*Cantius* (North America and Europe 50 MYA)	
Family	Adapidae	
Genus	*Adapis* (Europe: 33.9–40.4 MYA)	
Genus	*Afradapis* (Egypt: 37 MYA)	
Genus	*Darwinius* (Germany: 47 MYA)	
Suborder	Haplorhini	
Infraorder	Omomyiformes	
Superfamily	Omomyoidea	
Family	Omomyidae (North America, Pakistan, China: Eocene)	
Subfamily	Anaptomorphinae	
Genus	*Teilhardina* (Asia, Europe, North America: early Eocene)	
Subfamily	Microchoerinae	
Genus	*Necrolemur* (Europe: middle to late Eocene)	
Subfamily	Omomyinae	
Genus	*Shoshonius* (North America: 46.2–55.4 MYA)	
Family	Archicebidae	
Genus	*Archicebus*	
Species	*achilles*	
Infraorder	Anthropoidea (Middle to late Eocene)	
Superfamily	Parapithecoidea	
Family	Unsure placement	
Genus	*Algeripithecus* (Algeria: 45 MYA)	

Fossil Primates Discussed in this Chapter (Continued)	
EOCENE PRIMATES	
Family	Parapithecidae
Genus	*Biretia* (Fayum, Egypt: 37 MYA)
Parvorder	Catarrhini
Superfamily	Propliopithecoidea
Family	Oligopithecidae
Genus	*Catopithecus* (Fayum, Egypt: 37–35 MYA)
OLIGOCENE PRIMATES	
Suborder	Haplorhini
Infraorder	Omomyiformes
Superfamily	Omomyoidea
Family	Afrotarsiidae (not everyone agrees with this classification)
Genus	*Afrotarsius* (Fayum, Egypt: Oligocene)
Infraorder	Anthropoidea
Superfamily	Parapithecoidea
Family	Parapithecidae (also in Eocene)
Genus	*Apidium* (Fayum, Egypt: 30 MYA)
Parapithecus	
Parvorder	Platyrrhini
Superfamily	Ateloidea
Family	Unsure placement
Genus	*Branisella* (South America–Bolivia: 27 MYA)
Parvorder	Catarrhini
Superfamily	Propliopithecoidea
Family	Oligopithecidae
Genus	*Catopithecus* (Fayum, Egypt: 37–35 MYA)
Family	Propliopithecidae
Genus	*Aegyptopithecus* (Fayum, Egypt: 28.4–33.9 MYA)

WHEN DID THE EARLIEST PRIMATES APPEAR?

"Euarchonta" is a superorder term used to describe the very earliest mammals that show primate characteristics. This superorder includes the tree shrew (order Scandentia) (see Figure 9.2), "flying lemurs" (order Dermoptera), and living and extinct primates (order Primates), all of which are thought to be relatively closely related. "Flying lemurs" could be misleading because they are not really lemurs (they were so named in part because their head looks lemur-like) and they don't fly; they glide on membranes

FIGURE 9.2 Tree shrew (order Scandentia).

between their limbs. In a recent study of the genomes of many primates and Dermoptera and Scandentia, Dermoptera were found to be more closely related to primates than Scandentia (Perelman et al. 2011).

CONSIDER THIS

A FURTHER LOOK AT EVOLUTIONARY THEORY

When Charles Darwin first proposed and refined the theory of evolution through natural selection in the latter part of the nineteenth century, he envisioned a constant, gradual process in which organisms would be evolving characteristics that would enhance their survival. In the 1930s and 1940s, when Darwinism was combined with genetics (called the modern synthesis, or neo-Darwinism), this constant, gradual evolutionary process was still believed to be the norm (with a few exceptions, such as genetic drift). In the 1970s, two paleontologists claimed that data from the fossil record does not support gradual continuous morphological evolution (Eldredge and Gould 1972; Gould and Eldredge 1977). They stated that many fossil records indicate that the morphology of a species is often in **stasis** (no morphological change in an organism for long periods of time). They argued that the fossil record indicates that this stasis is "punctuated" by the appearance of one or more new species. Further, they theorized that new species would evolve in a small peripheral population that was genetically separated from the parent population. After the new species appears, it may replace the parent species if the new morphological characters possessed by the new species give its members survival advantages over the parent species. These paleontologists called their new ideas **"punctuated equilibria."** Much debate has occurred over the past few years about this new model of the rate of evolutionary change.

PALEOCENE (65 TO 55.8 MYA)

The search for the first primates has traditionally started in the late Paleocene with a very diverse group of mammals classified as plesiadapiformes (semiorder plesiadapiformes) (Bloch and Silcox 2006). They occur in deposits in North America, Europe, and Asia (the world landmasses were continuing to move to their current position, but a connection still existed between North America and Europe). They were considered to be close to primates because of certain morphological characters of their molars (which had somewhat more rounded cusps than did mammalian insectivores in general), the morphology of the internal ear, and a handful of other derived characters they were thought to have shared with primates. However, other parts of their bodies were distinctly unlike modern primates: Their eyes are not completely enclosed by a bony ring (a postorbital bar), and they have enlarged incisors (somewhat rodent-like, though not ever-growing nor self-sharpening) (Szalay 2000), unlike later primates. Many authors today put the plesiadapiformes into their own **semiorder** within the order Primates, but separate from later true primates. There are 12 families in this group, but we will only mention four. Although some of the families are found in Eocene deposits, none are now thought to be direct ancestors of later primates. In late Paleocene deposits in Africa, *Altiatlasius* may be the oldest true primate, but little is known of it at this time (Fleagle 2013), and its taxonomic status is uncertain.

Semiorder: Taxonomic classification between suborder and order.

Purgatoriidae is the most primitive family of the plesiadapiformes. The genus *Purgatorius* was described in 1979 by Szalay and Delson as a mouse-sized probable insectivore that was discovered in what is now Montana. It was described at that time as possibly the earliest primate because it was discovered in deposits that dated to 65 MYA, although the origin of the genus may be earlier—some time in the late Mesozoic (the animal represented by a fossil didn't suddenly appear at that moment; the close relatives would have developed earlier). Recently discovered tarsals in the same deposits as the dentition suggest closer affinities to primates as well as tree shrews (order Scandentia) and "flying lemurs" (order Dermoptera) (Chester et al. 2014).

Also in the New World, a fossil discovered in Wyoming (*Carpolestes simpsoni*) (Bloch and Boyer 2002; Bloch and Gingerich 1998,) is described as a nearly complete skeleton with characteristics consistent with early primates. They still have the enlarged incisors and greatly modified premolars possibly adapted to process a high-fiber vegetable diet. Interestingly, their thumbs and big toes are opposable and the big toe has a nail instead of a claw. In general, the morphology of the hands and feet make them better adapted to life in the trees (Kirk et al. 2008), and their big toe has a nail instead of a claw. Sargis et al. (2007) do not believe that this animal was a vertical clinger and leaper like later primates in the Eocene.

The paromomyids (genus *Ignacius*) was among the most widespread and long-lived plesiadapiformes, having been found in North America, Europe, and Asia in deposits from the middle Paleocene to the late Eocene.

Plesiadapis (see Figure 9.3) is one of the best known of the plesiadapiformes and is thought to be among the most successful.

FIGURE 9.3 *Plesiadapis tricuspidens.*

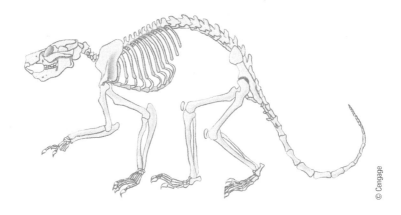

© Cengage

EOCENE (55.8 TO 33 MYA)

The climate of the world inferred from paleobotany indicates that the Eocene was the warmest and wettest epoch of the Cenozoic era, and rain forest habitats extended into the northern continents even more than they did during the Paleocene era. A gradual cooling and drying trend began in mid-Eocene times, a trend that continues with many fluctuations. This climate was ideal for the spread of primates of modern aspect around the world. Until the middle of the Eocene, North America was connected to Europe, and in the middle to late Eocene, North America was at times connected to Asia, so many of the Eocene primates are represented in these continents as well as in Africa.

The Eocene has been considered the time in which the lemurs and lorises (strepsirhines) split from the early haplorhines (tarsiers and anthropoids) (see Table 9.1). The Eocene fossils are divided into two groups, which represent the most lemur-like (**Adapoidea**) and the most tarsier-like (**Omomyoidea**). These superfamilies are divided into many families and subfamilies, and there are more than 40 proposed genera weighing between 70 to 10,000 g (2.25 oz to 20 lbs), the latter figure larger than some modern monkeys. Both superfamilies possess the postorbital bar (although the eyes are not completely enclosed in bone), eyes that are more toward the front of the face, digits with nails that are opposable for grasping, and in general, dentition that shows movement toward a more generalized diet.

Adapoidea

The superfamily Adapoidea includes more than 35 genera, and, by dental evidence, these are the most primitive of the Eocene primates. They have a dental formula of 2:1:4:3 (remember that the dental formula for a general mammal is 3:1:4:3; most strepsirhines are 2:1:3:3; a New World monkey is 2:1:3:3; and the Old World monkey, ape, and human are 2:1:2:3), and, in general, they do not yet show the derived trait of a toothcomb. Cranially they resemble lemurs, with a relatively long snout and a complete bony ring around the orbits, although their brain is smaller than in lemurs. They also have a sagittal

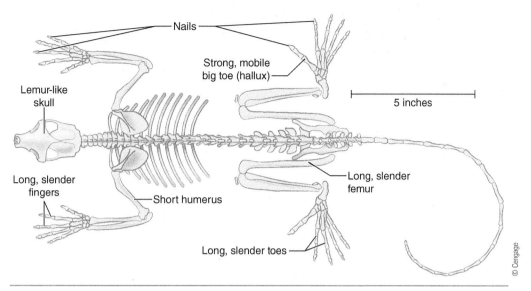

FIGURE 9.4 *Notharctus.*

crest. Postcranially they also resemble lemurs and lorises with tarsals that are not as long as in tarsiers (Omomyoidea). They have a divergent big toe with nails instead of claws on at least some digits.

The adapoids are divided into families primarily based on their geographic distribution (although there are differences in morphology between them): In North America and Europe, they are represented by the **notharctids**; in Europe and Africa they are the **adapids**; and in Asia they are the **amphipithecids**. The interesting question is how these relate to each other, and which, if any, gave rise to later primates.

Cantius (primarily from North America with a couple of species in Europe) is the earliest notharctid (see Figure 9.4 for a drawing of *Notharctus,* which was larger than *Cantius*). Dental morphology and a dental formula of 2:1:4:3 have led some researchers to think that *Cantius* was likely a fruit eater. They were probably arboreal quadrupedal runners and leapers, as they had long hindlimbs. They had a cranium similar to lemurs, although more robust. Like lemurs, they had an opposable big toe and nails on all digits except the second toe (Maiolino et al. 2012).

The adapids are represented in Europe in the late Eocene by *Adapis* (see Figure 9.5). They have a dental formula of 2:1:4:3 but

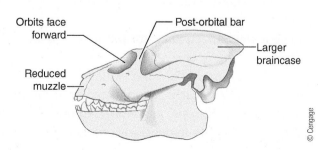

FIGURE 9.5 *Adapis.*

may have had an incipient toothcomb. Cranial elements indicate a reduction in the importance of smell and an increase in the importance of vision (small orbits that face forward) (Gingerich and Martin 1981). Skeletal elements suggest that it was a slow arboreal quadruped, although Bacon and Godinot suggest that there is a diversity of locomotor patterns (Bacon and Godinot 1998; Gebo et al. 2008). Its phylogeny is uncertain.

In May 2009, a sensationalized fossil named *Darwinius masillae* was described as "not simply a fossil lemur, but part of a larger group of primates, Adapoidea, representative of the early haplorhine diversification" (Franzen et al. 2009). The preservation of this complete fossil is extraordinary, to be sure, as even the contents of the digestive tract were preserved (although there have been other well-preserved fossil adapoids). The skeleton has a toothcomb and nails on all of the digits (no grooming claw). Many researchers believe the claim that this fossil is a close relative of anthropoids, and a distant relative of tarsiers is incompatible with the current thinking (supported by most genetics and morphology) that tarsiers are more closely related to anthropoids than to lemurs and lorises. Fleagle (2013) places *Darwinius* with the adapoids.

Seiffert et al. (2009) have discovered a poorly preserved fossil that they have named *Afradapis* near the Fayum Depression in northern Egypt. This large-bodied fossil dates to about 37 million years ago and represents another family of the adapids. The dentition of *Afradapis* suggests that it was a leaf eater (Seiffert et al. 2010).

Poux et al. (2005) used DNA data to suggest that lemurs had arrived in Madagascar, the limits of their current natural habitat, between 60 MYA (when they likely split from lorises) and approximately 50 MYA. If this date proves to be accurate, it pushes the prosimian line back further than previously thought and may change the current thinking about strepsirhine and haplorhine origins.

Omomyoidea

Omomyoids are the earliest haplorhine group (leading to modern tarsiers). They have a dental formula of 2:1:4:3, very large eye orbits, and small snouts. There is a wide range of morphology in the omomyoids, from very generalized forms (thought by Ross [2000] to be a generalized ancestor for all haplorhines) to more specialized forms with more derived traits.

The genus *Teilhardina* is the most primitive of the omomyoids, and is similar to early adapoids in dentition. It is found on three continents (Asia, Europe, and North America), and the different species vary considerably in dentition and general morphology.

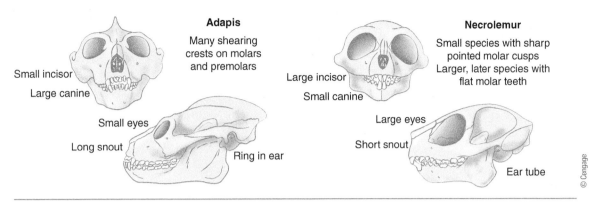

Adapis

Many shearing crests on molars and premolars

Small incisor

Large canine

Small eyes

Long snout

Ring in ear

Necrolemur

Small species with sharp pointed molar cusps
Larger, later species with flat molar teeth

Large incisor

Small canine

Large eyes

Short snout

Ear tube

© Cengage

FIGURE 9.6 *Adapis* compared to *Necrolemur.*

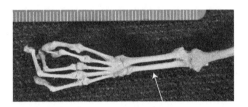

FIGURE 9.7 Hind foot of tarsier. Notice the elongated tarsals (arrow) that are advantageous for leaping.   *Photo, D. L. France; access to specimen courtesy Jay Villemarette, Skulls Unlimited*

Although from different subfamilies, *Shoshonius* (in North America) and *Necrolemur* (in Europe) have large orbits and characteristics of the ear that are similar to tarsiers (see Figure 9.6 for comparison of *Adapis* and *Necrolemur* skulls). In other ways, each was different from extant tarsiers, particularly in locomotor adaptations. Each was probably a great leaper, but not the vertical clinging and leaping as in modern tarsiers (see Figure 9.7) (Rasmussen et al. 1998).

Anemone and Covert (2000) and Gunnell (1997) have described the tarsier-like primates (*Omomyidae*) from Wyoming, which probably moved in an "active quadrupedal and leaping" manner. Tarsier-like primates have also been discovered in Eocene deposits in Pakistan (Thewissen et al. 1997). Rossie et al. (2006) state that a facial fragment found in China in middle Eocene deposits is very similar to modern tarsiers. It is likely that tarsiers had evolved to nearly their modern morphology in the Eocene.

Several fossil tarsiids have been discovered in Asia that pushes that family back at least 50 million years (Fleagle 2013).

ANTHROPOIDS

Recently, Xijun Ni et al. (2004) described a fossil called *Archicebus achilles* discovered in China from about 55 million years ago (right on the cusp of the Eocene). They interpret this fossil as the oldest known haplorhine primate with some features that are closer to anthropoids and some that are closer to tarsiiforms. This would push back the split between tarsiiforms and anthropoids to an earlier time and would, in turn, push back the split of the strepsirhines

FIGURE 9.8 *Catopithecus.*

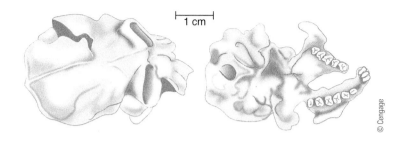

1 cm

© Cengage

from the haplorhines. This also further supports the theory that tarsiers are more closely related to anthropoids than they are to lemurs
and lorises.

A fossil that was an undisputed anthropoid (*Algeripithecus,*
dated to more than 45 million years ago) from Algeria appears about
three million years before the middle Eocene anthropoids in Asia
(Godinot 1994; Godinot and Mahboubi 1992). However, Tabuce
et al. (2009) now describe evidence from additional fossils that
points to *Algeripithecus minutus* (a tiny animal) as having a toothcomb, which, if true, would mean that it is not an anthropoid.

Biretia is a species of anthropoid dated to 37 MYA from the
Fayum Depression in Egypt. It is represented by a nearly complete
fossil (Seiffert et al. 2005). Simons has placed this into the extinct
superfamily Parapithecoidea, and believes that it is the rootstock for
all New World anthropoids.

Again from the Fayum in the very late Eocene, *Catopithecus*
(Seiffert et al. 2005; Simons 1990), from the family Oligopithecidae,
possessed complete postorbital closure, a fused frontal bone (no
patent metopic suture) and a 2:1:2:3 dental formula (see Figure 9.8).
With *Biretia,* this shows that by 37 to 35 MYA, different species
of anthropoids are living in the Fayum Depression in Egypt.
Oligopithecidae continued into the Oligocene.

Elsewhere, a couple of jaw fragments of late Eocene age have
been found in Burma, each containing two molars. The dental
morphology suggests that these may have been anthropoids, but the
material available is insufficient to confirm this possibility.

The climate at the beginning of the Oligocene was becoming
cooler and drier, and many primate species had appeared and disap-
peared by this time. The anthropoids become much more prevalent
in the Oligocene, so we will turn to that epoch now.

OLIGOCENE (33 TO 23 MYA)

We will discuss the fossil evidence, but, as DNA testing becomes
more widely used in all contexts, it is also becoming more widely
used to investigate the relationships and genetic distances between
extant primates. This leads to theories about the dates of divergence
of the ancestors of various primates.

The Biomolecular Data

The basic premise in biomolecular analysis of the phylogenetic relationship of organisms is that the closer organisms are biochemically and genetically, the more closely they are related. Many different techniques of biomolecular analysis have been used over the years to classify extant hominoids, but the most recent and the most accurate is genome sequencing. Data from such studies on hominoids have shown a fairly consistent branching sequence among the hominoids and all anthropoids. These data show that the Cercopithecoidea (Old World monkeys) branched off of the ancestral tree before the living apes diverged. Among the hominoids, gibbons and siamangs branched off before the orangutan, the orangutan before the gorilla, and chimpanzees and humans were the last to share a common ancestor (see Figure 9.9). Steiper et al. (2004) have used DNA data to estimate the hominoid-cercopithecoid divergence at between 29.2 and 34.5 MYA, although Janecka et al. (2007) estimated the split at about 27 MYA. Not everyone agrees with these dates of divergence, however. Using current genomic data of many extant primates, Perelman et al. (2011) calculated the emergence of catarrhine emergence at about 20 to 38 MYA, the platyrrhine emergence at 20 to 27 MYA, hominoid emergence at 13 to 18 MYA, and the chimp/human split

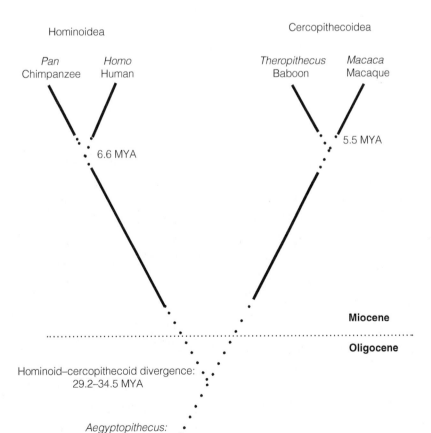

FIGURE 9.9 Dates of divergence of cercopithecoids and hominoids. *Adapted from Steiper et al., 2004 and Steiper and Young, 2006.*

at about 6 to 7 MYA. Moorjani et al. (2016) now state that some of the dates are off because of the "human slowdown," which suggests that the mutation rate slowed in the human line. If true, the dates of divergence closer to humans should be pushed back.

The Fossil Data

Most of our knowledge of the Oligocene (and some Eocene) primates still comes from one site, the Fayum Depression (or badlands) of Egypt (see Figure 9.10), but we will discuss a few fossils found elsewhere, which add to our information about this epoch. In general, the late Eocene and early Oligocene period were characterized by the divergence of New World (platyrrhine) and Old World (catarrhine) monkeys. The primates are classified into several families, two of which (Oligopithecidae and Parapithecidae) we have already discussed from the Eocene.

The Fossil Primates of the Fayum

The Fayum is on the eastern edge of the Sahara (see Figure 9.10) and contains not only Oligocene primates but also late Eocene primates. Although the area is now on the edge of a desert, during Oligocene times, the Fayum was much wetter, with mixed habitats of freshwater swamps bordered by grasslands and woodlands (Olson and Rasmussen 1986).

There were tarsier-like primates at the Fayum. Significantly, the genus *Afrotarsius* was initially represented by a mandible with five teeth and classified with the generalized anthropoids because of similar dentition (Kay et al. 1997; Simons and Brown 1985). Simons (1995, 1998) thought that the teeth were not similar enough to anthropoids to declassify them as tarsier ancestors. *Afrotarsius* has the modified tibiofibula and tarsals that tarsiers have, and on that basis, researchers classify *Afrotarsius* with extant tarsiers instead of with the generalized anthropoids. Roos et al. (2004) used genetic markers in living strepsirhines to conclude that this suborder originated in Africa, and that Madagascar and Asia were colonized by migration. Madagascar, they state, was inhabited between the late Cretaceous and middle Eocene (by "rafting" across the Mozambique channel), and Asia was colonized between the early Eocene and middle Oligocene by land.

Obviously, anthropoids would be expected to appear more like extant primates with the passage of time. The eyes face more forward (the ranges of vision overlap to allow stereoscopic vision) and are completely enclosed in bone. The mandible is fused in the front, and there appear to be nails on all digits (instead of a grooming claw as in lemurs). The Fayum anthropoids are mostly known by teeth and jaws, but there are some skulls and postcranial fossils. Their postcranial material suggests that they were arboreal and ranged in size from that of a New World marmoset (300 g or 9.6 oz) to that of a gibbon (6,000 g or 12 lb).

FIGURE 9.10 Fayum, Egypt.

Strepsirhines = lemurs, lorises, galagos.

Haplorhines = tarsiers and anthropoids (New World and Old World).

Catarrhines = Old World anthropoids.

Platyrrhines = New World anthropoids.

The Parapithecidae resemble Eocene prosimians (they are first seen in the Eocene), and they are the most primitive of all known higher primates (Fleagle 2013). Yet, they possess the diagnostic characteristics of anthropoids, including a fused mandibular symphysis, no patent metopic suture, and four small upper incisors. The genus *Apidium* is the most common and well-known primate from the early Oligocene (Fleagle and Simons 1995; Fleagle 2013) and possesses a primitive dental arrangement (retention of a 2:1:3:3 dental formula like New World monkeys) that some paleontologists have suggested puts it in the likely ancestry of both New World (platyrrhines) and Old World (catarrhines) anthropoids (Simons 1995). The dental form of *Apidium* suggests that they ate primarily fruit and some seeds. From their postcranial skeleton, they seem to be arboreal quadrupeds. *Apidium* (see Figure 9.11) is the most common primate from the early Oligocene, according to Fleagle and Simons (1995), and may be similar enough to platyrrhines to be an ancestor. Simons (2001) described a parapithecid (genus *Parapithecus*) from the early Oligocene from Egypt that he says is larger than *Apidium* and the most complete higher primate skull yet found for this time and place. The cranial and dental characteristics also place it in the anthropoid line.

If the parapithecids were the common ancestor to Old World and New World monkeys, the New World monkey ancestor likely originated in the Old World and migrated to the New World. South America was much closer to Africa during the Oligocene, and oceanic ridges were probably exposed during Oligocene times. These exposed ridges as well as other islands are believed by some to have provided primates a series of "stepping stones" across the Atlantic (Tarling 1980), although this idea is not universally accepted. At any rate, fossil primates represented by the genus *Branisella,* first appeared in South America (Bolivia) during the late Oligocene (about 27 MYA), and they resembled the parapithecids.

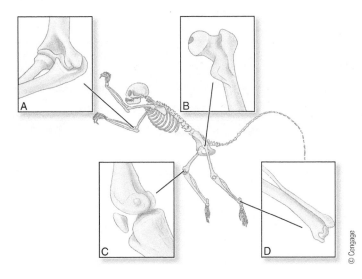

FIGURE 9.11 *Apidium* postcranial elements showing primate characteristic and adaptation for quadrupedal running and leaping.

© Cengage

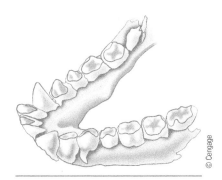

FIGURE 9.12 *Propliopithecus* mandible.

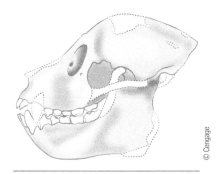

FIGURE 9.13 *Aegyptopithecus* mandible.

FIGURE 9.14 Unenclosed eye orbits in cat (left), enclosed in monkey.

For ancestors to later catarrhines, we have to look to members of the Propliopithecidae (see Figure 9.12). The propliopithecids have a dental formula of 2:1:2:3, and they do not have bilophodont molars (remember, the New World monkeys do have bilophodont molars). For this reason and because their dentition morphologically resembles those of later apes, they are usually classified in the superfamily Hominoidea. Otherwise, they possess none of the specializations of Old World monkeys or apes. Postcranially, they resemble primitive platyrrhine morphology more than they resemble catarrhine morphology (Fleagle 2013). Studies of the postcranial remains of *Aegyptopithecus* (see Figure 9.13) suggest that it was a robust arboreal quadruped (Ankel-Simons et al. 1998). Also compare the orbits of *Aegyptopithecus* to the orbits of a monkey, and cat, which doesn't have a postorbital bar or enclosed orbits (see Figure 9.14), noting that they are very similar to the monkey. Studies of propliopithecid dentition suggest that they primarily ate fruit.

The family Saadaniidae was discovered in Saudi Arabia (genus *Saadanius*) from deposits dating to 29 to 28 MYA (Zalmout et al. 2010). It is represented by a partial cranium and has no derived features of either cercopithecoids (Old World monkeys) or hominoids, so they believe this fossil predates the split between the two. It has auditory modifications of monkeys, apes and humans, and may be intermediate between *Aegyptopithecus* and Miocene apes.

These first anthropoids are too primitive to draw direct ancestral-descendent relationships from them to any extant primate. Also, their fossil record, although considered "good," is not refined enough to specify which genus or species is ancestral to a specific genus or species of the primitive hominoids of the early Miocene.

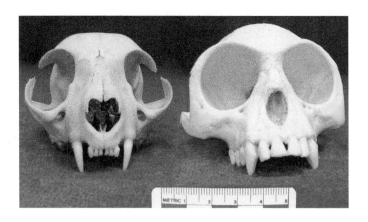

The First Primates

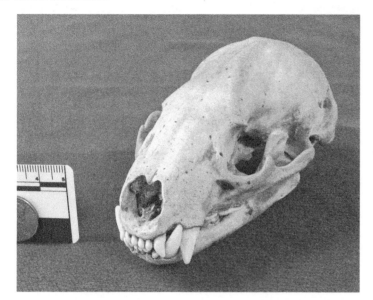

FIGURE 9.15 Unknown animal.

1. Is the animal in Figure 9.15 likely a primate? How do you know?

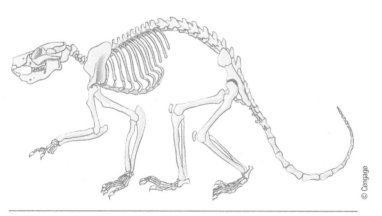

© Cengage

FIGURE 9.16 *Plesiadapis tricuspidens.*

2. Observe the Paleocene-age plesiadapiform pictured in Figure 9.16.

   a. Make a short list of characteristics in which it does not resemble lemurs.

   b. Are there ways in which it does resemble lemurs?

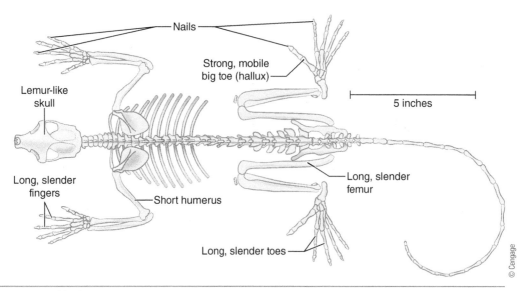

FIGURE 9.17 *Notharctus.*

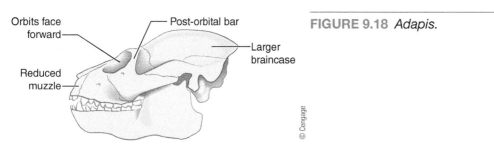

FIGURE 9.18 *Adapis.*

3. Observe the two Eocene primates of Figures 9.17 and 9.18. Make a short list of characteristics in which these fossils are like Figure 9.16. How are they different?

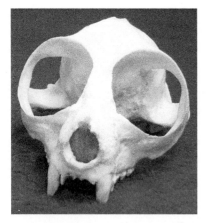

FIGURE 9.19 Bush baby skull.

4. Do you think that the animal in Figure 9.19 is nocturnal or diurnal? Why?

5. Why is it significant that there were tarsier-like primates among the primate fauna of the Fayum?

6. Given all of the information about the fossils in the Eocene and the potential dates of divergence of the primate groups (based on genetic information), draw a phylogeny of the Eocene primates. Realize that some of the information is contradictory, depending upon the evidence and points of view of the researchers.

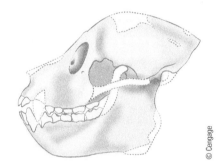

FIGURE 9.20 *Aegyptopithecus.*

© Cengage

7. What do the cranial characteristics of Aegyptopithecus (see Figure 9.20) suggest about the relative importance of the senses of smell and sight?

8. What are the similarities of Aegyptopithecus (see Figure 9.20) orbits (in size, relative enclosure, and position) with those of living prosimians, monkeys, apes, and humans?

9. Aegyptopithecus has been found in two sizes, both in skull and canine size, and in canine shape. What might this suggest about their social structure?

10. In describing *Darwinius masillae* (page 000), Franzen et al. (2009) concluded that the fossil was representative of Adapoidea and also an early haplorhine diversification. Why would that be incompatible with the belief that tarsiers are more closely related to anthropoids than to lemurs?

11. If you found cranial remains from the Paleocene, what features would you look for to classify it as a primate?

REEXAMINING THE ISSUES

- Eocene primates are found in North America, Europe, and Asia.
- Adapoidea fossils are lemur-like.
- Omomyoidea fossils are tarsier-like.
- *Aegyptopithecus* could be the ancestor of Old World monkeys, apes, and hominins, and they are found in Oligocene deposits in the Fayum Depression in Egypt.

CHAPTER 10

Miocene Hominoid Evolution

OBJECTIVES

1. What did the last common ancestor of apes and humans look like?

2. When did we last share a common ancestor with apes?

3. When, during the Miocene, did hominoids first appear outside of Africa?

4. Where did hominins first appear?

The Miocene (23 to 5 MYA [millions of years ago]) is the epoch during which the ape and human lineages diverged, according to most evidence. It is an epoch, therefore, of primary interest and importance to paleoanthropologists and to anyone curious about human evolution. In previous editions of this book, the Miocene was described only in terms of **hominoid** evolution, with the idea that as yet undescribed **hominins** probably branched off of the hominoid line just before the end of the Miocene. The Miocene fossil record has improved considerably over the past decades, and it is now apparent that the Miocene may be more richly populated with hominins than even recently believed.

From the last chapter, remember that the biomolecular data and current genome sequencing data have given us a good idea of the relatedness of extant primates. Researchers have taken that biomolecular evidence and calculated dates of divergence of our primate relatives based on relatively standard mutation rates (see Figure 10.1). That evidence, plus the dates established for the fossil evidence, results in increasing understanding of when our extinct relatives lived (see Jameson et al. 2011; Perelman et al. 2011; see also Steiper and Young 2008 for an interesting discussion on when and why the estimated dates between biomolecular and paleontological evidence don't always agree). Of course, the fossil evidence also gives us information about how they lived.

Hominoid: Lesser apes, great apes, and humans.

Hominin: *Homo sapiens* and all of our ancestors after the split with species of the genus *Pan*.

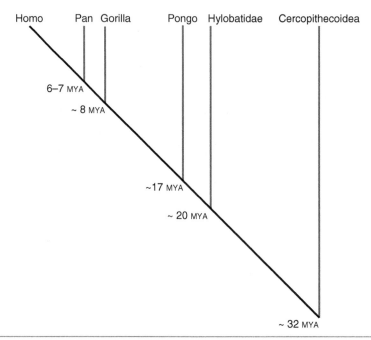

FIGURE 10.1 Molecular clock phylogeny based on Perelman et al. (2011). Horizontal distance does not reflect genetic distance.

THE FOSSIL DATA

MIOCENE TAXONOMY	
Superfamily	Pliopithecoidea
Family	Unsure placement
Genus	*Lomorupithecus* (Uganda, 19–20 MYA)
Family	Pliopithecidae
Genus	*Pliopithecus* (Europe, 12.5–13 MYA)
Superfamily	Cercopithecoidea
Family	Victoriapithecidae
Genus	*Victoriapithecus* (northern and eastern Africa, 19 MYA)
Family	Cercopithecidae
Genus	*Theropithecus* (Kenya, 3.3 MYA)
Superfamily	Hominoidea
Family	Proconsulidae
Genus	*Proconsul* (Africa, 20–17 MYA)
Genus	*Micropithecus* (Uganda, 20 MYA)
Genus	*Afropithecus* (Kenya and Saudi Arabia, 16–18 MYA)

Family	Pliobatidae
Genus	*Pliobates* (Spain, 11.6 MYA)
Family	Hylobatidae
Genus	*Yuanmoupithecus* (China, 9 MYA)
Family	Hominidae
Subfamily	Kenyapithecinae
Genus	*Kenyapithecus* (Kenya, 14 MYA)
Subfamily	Ponginae
Genus	*Sivapithecus* (Europe and Asia, 12 MYA)
Genus	*Gigantopithecus* (Asia, 8–1 MYA)
Genus	*Lufengpithecus* (southern China, 9–5 MYA)
Genus	*Griphopithecus* (Europe, 17 MYA)
Subfamily	Homininae
Genus	*Dryopithecus* (East Africa and Eurasia, 16–17 MYA)
Genus	*Ouranopithecus* (Greece, 9.6–8.7 MYA)
Genus	*Nakalipithecus* (Kenya, 9.9–9.8 MYA)
Genus	*Chororapithecus* (Kenya, 10.5–10 MYA)
Genus	*Sahelanthropus*
Species	*tchadensis* (Chad, 6–7 MYA)
Genus	*Orrorin*
Species	*tugenensis* (Tugen Hills, central Kenya 6 MYA)
Genus	*Ardipithecus* (Ethiopia, 5.77–5.54 MYA)
Species	*kadabba*

OLD WORLD CATARRHINES

Old World catarrhines (Old World monkeys and apes) appeared in the early Miocene (Conroy et al. 1996; Rae 2004; Rossie and Maclatchy 2006), primarily from Asia and Europe, though the origin of the line was thought to have been in Africa. The oldest catarrhine may be a genus (*Lomorupithecus*) in Uganda, which dates to between 19 and 20 MYA (Rossie and Maclatchy 2006). A somewhat more recent family, the Pliopithecidae, was still more primitive than other catarrhines and they likely branched off before the cercopithecoid–hominoid split (Begun 2002). Their teeth were primitive with broad upper incisors, small lateral incisors, and sexual dimorphism in the canines and lower first premolars (Fleagle 2013). At this time, the Old World catarrhines were rare relative to the primitive hominoids, but their numbers increased through the Miocene. In Europe, *Pliopithecus* (also of the family Pliopithecidae) dates from the middle Miocene (12.5 to 13 MYA), and interestingly, the postcranial remains suggest some adaptations for suspension from the arms. It did not have the

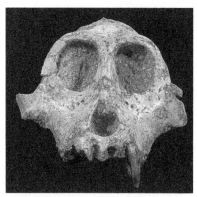

FIGURE 10.2 *Victoriapithecus* cranium showing catarrhine characteristics.

prehensile tail of some New World monkeys. All of the pliopithecoids became extinct in the Pliocene, apparently with no descendants.

By the late Miocene, the cercopithecoids were relatively much more common than the hominoids, the situation that exists today. Two families represent the line of Old World cercopithecoids in the Miocene that actually led to significant descendants: the victoriapithecids (which are extinct) and the cercopithecids. *Victoriapithecus* (see Figure 10.2) appears in northern and eastern Africa at about 24 MYA, and predates the probable split between the two Old World monkey subfamilies: the colobines and the cercopithecines, which occurred around 15 MYA (Gutierrez 2011). It was a small monkey that exhibited bilophodont molars (like all current Old World monkeys) and some postcranial features that are similar to living terrestrial monkeys (Benefit and McCrossin 1997). It likely ate fruits and seeds. Alba et al. (2015) state that by 12 MYA, *Victoriapithecus* was likely replaced by monkeys whose descendants live today.

A baboon-like cercopithecid was discovered from late Miocene deposits in Kenya. *Theropithecus* was the dominant cercopithecid of the Plio-Pleistocene (which we will discuss in the next chapter). Most of them died out, but one species led to *Theropithecus gelada*, which is the gelada baboon of today (Fleagle 2013).

By 9 MYA, the first true colobine fossil is seen in Africa, and fossils of colobines from Europe and Asia appear soon afterward.

HOMINOIDS

Almost 30 genera and many more species of Miocene hominoids have been described, which makes them more abundant than extant species. Although most Miocene fossil hominoids are known from teeth and jaws only, with more postcranial and cranial material being discovered, it is apparent that these hominoids exhibit even more diversity than the dentition alone had indicated (Brunet et al. 2002; Kelly and Pilbeam 1986; Kordos and Begun 1997).

The apes of the early Miocene had a 2:1:2:3 dental formula, thick enamel, low cusps, and Y-5 molars similar to extant apes. Other than that, they did not greatly resemble later apes, as postcranially they looked more like monkeys. These primitive apes gave way to a radiation of apes of a more modern form in the middle Miocene.

© Cengage

FIGURE 10.3 *Proconsul africanus.*

Virtually all the primitive apes of the early Miocene have been found in East Africa and Namibia. Most of the species of proconsuloids were likely to have been forest living and arboreal, and were derived from the propliopithecids from the Oligocene. Some were quite large; for example, *Proconsul major*, which was female gorilla–sized, was likely primarily an arboreal quadruped (from the skeletal morphology—see Nakatsukasa 2004), although it may have been at least partially terrestrial. Observe the casts of any *Proconsul* species you have in your lab or look at Figures 10.3 through 10.6.

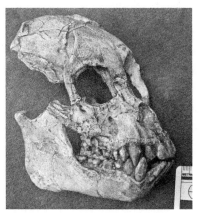

FIGURE 10.4 *Proconsul africanus.* *Photo, D. L. France; cast from National Museums of Kenya*

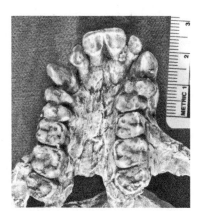

FIGURE 10.5 *Proconsul africanus,* maxilla. *Photo, D. L. France; cast from National Museums of Kenya*

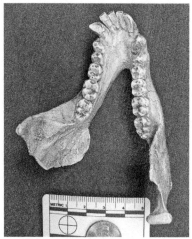

FIGURE 10.6 *Proconsul africanus,* mandible. *Photo, D. L. France; cast from National Museums of Kenya*

Proconsul africanus was about the size of a large female baboon and was a robust quadruped that probably ate fruit in a rain forest or woodland habitat. The specimen pictured (RU7290) (see Figures 10.4 to 10.6) is nearly complete, though the cranium and mandible were slightly deformed in the process of fossilization. The dentition is apelike, but the remainder of the specimen exhibits none of the specializations characteristic of living apes, except for the lack of a tail. For this reason, hominoids of the early Miocene are often referred to as "dental apes." Like the propliopithecids of the Oligocene, *Proconsul* and other primitive "dental apes" of the early Miocene are quite variable in size, general morphology, and dietary patterns. Some researchers have said that because *Proconsul* is just a dental ape with postcranial remains that are not particularly apelike, they should be in their own superfamily, Proconsuloidea, but many researchers still place this fossil in the Hominoidea superfamily. Some (Harrison 2010; Zalmout et al. 2010) think that they are the general precursors to later hominoids, although most think that they are not ancestors to any specific later hominoids. *Micropithecus,* which is the smallest ape (at 6 to 8 pounds) ever uncovered (extinct or extant), is also in this family (Fleagle and Simons 2005).

From 16 to 18 MYA, *Afropithecus* lived in Kenya and Saudi Arabia. This could have been the first apelike ancestor to leave Africa (Begun 2012). It had a relatively small brain (Fleagle 2013), thick enamel on its teeth, a long snout, and procumbent incisors (they protrude horizontally away from the face) (Andrews and Martin 1987; Leakey et al. 1988).

The first apes arrive in the fossil record at about 17 MYA in Europe, too, possibly from a *Pronsul* ancestor from Africa (Begun et al. 2012). The earliest is *Griphopithecus,* which had thick enamel, more generalized dentition, and more monkeylike postcranial features. There is no evidence of a tail and no evidence of arboreal

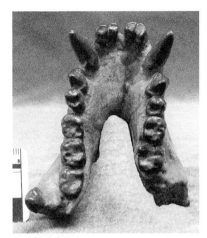

FIGURE 10.7 *Dryopithecus fontani,* mandible. *Photo, D. L. France; cast from University of Pennsylvania*

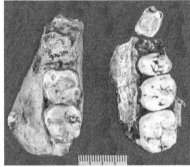

FIGURE 10.8 *Kenyapithecus wickeri,* mandible (left) and maxilla (right) fragments. *Photo, D. L. France; casts from Wenner-Gren Foundation*

adaptations. Begun et al. (2012; Begun 2010) think that *Griphopithecus* could be a common ancestor to both European and Asian apes.

Dryopithecus (see Figure 10.7) was the first fossil ape to be described in the scientific literature (Lartet 1856). This specimen was found in southern France, and *Dryopithecus* species of middle Miocene age have been found throughout southern Europe. Its dental enamel is thin, and Galbany et al. (2005) suggest that microwear on its teeth indicate that it ate abrasive, tough foods. The thin dental enamel is different from most of the hominoids from this time period, and its descendants are not clearly known.

Sivapithecus, Kenyapithecus (Figure 10.8), *Ouranopithecus,* and *Gigantopithecus* share the following characteristics, even though they are from different parts of the world:

• Teeth have thick enamel. In fact, the enamel of *Ouranopithecus* has been termed "hyperthick" by Kay and Ungar (1997).

• Molars are wide, have low cusps, and are large relative to anterior teeth.

• Mandibles are deep, with a heavy buttress.

Living primates that eat tough foods such as seeds and nuts have thick-enameled molars and low cusps similar to those of *Sivapithecus.* Studies of the postcranial remains of *Sivapithecus* reveal that they show anatomical patterns characteristic of living hominoids. They seem to have possessed generalized ape bodies underlying generalized locomotor and postural capabilities (Rose 1983). These hominoids have usually been found at fossil sites that indicate that they were not tropical rain forest animals. Rather, paleobotanical and paleontological evidence from these sites indicate that they lived in mixed habitats of seasonal woodlands interspersed with open grasslands.

A partial face of *Sivapithecus indicus* that resembles the face of an orangutan (see Figures 10.9 and 10.10) was recovered in Pakistan.

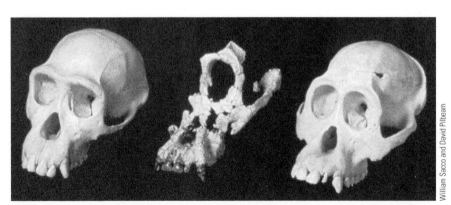

FIGURE 10.9 Chimpanzee (left), *Sivapithecus indicus* (center), orangutan (right).

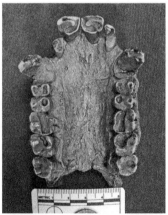

William Sacco and David Pilbeam

FIGURE 10.10 *Sivapithecus indicus* maxilla. *Photo, D. L. France; cast from National Museums of Kenya*

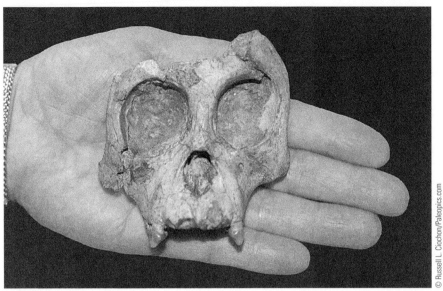

FIGURE 10.11 Skull of a *Lufengpithecus* juvenile from the late Miocene of Yunnan Province, China.

In fact, the resemblances are so striking that most experts believed that *Sivapithecus* was ancestral to *Pongo* (Andrews 1983; Pilbeam 1984). Thus, paleoanthropologists had identified one Miocene genus that was probably in or close to the lineage that led to a living ape, although analysis of postcranial material indicates little similarity to the modern orangutan (Kelly 1995).

However, *Lufengpithecus* (see Figure 10.11) discovered in southern China and dated at about 9 to 5 MYA does show postcranial aspects similar to the orangutan. The genus is represented by many teeth, crania, mandibles, and more recently some postcranial material, including a femur and some finger bones (Xu and Lu 2007). It has a very narrow interorbital distance, oval orbits, and curved phalanges like extant orangutans (Harrison et al. 2008; Harrison 2010). In many ways, it is also very similar to *Sivapithecus,* and because *Sivapithecus* fossils date to around 12 MYA, *Sivapithecus* may be ancestral to *Lufengpithecus* and to *Pongo* (modern orangutans) (Chaimanee et al. 2003).

Gigantopithecus is the largest primate ever to have lived. The eight-million-year-old *Gigantopithecus gigantus* (*G. bilaspurensis*) was gorilla-sized. However, a younger species, *G. blacki* from China of about middle Pleistocene age (about 1 MYA) was two to three times the size of a gorilla (this is based on dentition only) (see Figures 10.12 through 10.14)! Jaws and teeth are all we know of this, but they were so large that the animals must have been entirely terrestrial.

There is no record of hominoids in Africa between about 13 MYA and 10 MYA, although there is fossil evidence of hominoids in Europe and Asia. A partial face with the upper dentition of *Ouranopithecus* was found in Greece and dated between

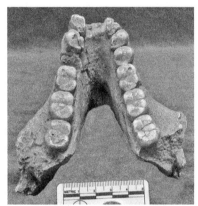

FIGURE 10.12 *Gigantopithecus gigantus. Photo, D. L. France; cast from University of Pennsylvania*

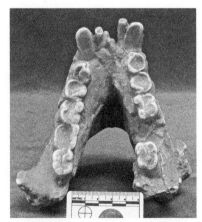

FIGURE 10.13 *Gigantopithecus blacki. Photo, D. L. France; cast from University of Pennsylvania*

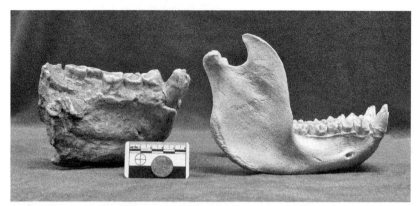

FIGURE 10.14 *Gigantopithecus blacki* (left) and gorilla (right). *Photo, D. L. France; cast from University of Pennsylvania*

9.6 and 8.7 MYA. It exhibits some similarity in dentition and facial form (including a big browridge with a frontal sinus) to the African apes and to hominins (De Bonis et al. 1990; De Bonis and Koufos 1994; Kay and Ungar 1997; Kordos and Begun 1997; Smith et al. 2004). Begun et al. (2012) describe it as a possible sister clade to extant apes and humans.

Chororapithecus teeth have been discovered in Kenya, and date to about 10.5 to 10 MYA (Bernor 2007). Although *Ouranopithecus* (9.6 to 8.7 MYA in Greece) was thought to perhaps be an ancestor to modern apes and possibly the common ancestor between apes and humans, some believe that *Chororapithecus* is so similar to gorillas in their dental morphology that it was likely the gorilla ancestor. If that is true, then it pushes the ape/human split further back in time.

Also in Kenya, *Nakalipithecus,* dated between 9.9 and 9.8 MYA, displays some similarities to *Ouranopithecus,* although it has fewer derived characters. It might be an ancestor to *Ouranopithecus* and could be a common ancestor to apes and humans (Kunimatsu et al. 2007).

GIBBONS AND SIAMANGS

Remember, Perelman et al. (2011) puts the gibbon great divergence at about 20 MYA. *Pliobates*, dated at about 11.6 MYA, was discovered in Spain (Alba et al. 2015), and was a small-bodied ape said to have a combination of early catarrhine-like and living hominoid-like features. Although it was not a full brachiator as in modern gibbons, it was likely able to suspend itself on branches. Alba et al. suggest that although it is more similar in some ways to hylobatids (gibbons and siamangs), given all of the evidence it could predate the divergence between hylobatids and hominids.

Yuanmoupithecus (Chatterjee 2006; Harrison et al. 2008) was discovered in China and dates to about 9 MYA. The fossil shows some of the postcranial traits needed for brachiating locomotion. Also, remember that gibbons and siamangs today live in Borneo and Java, and this fossil shows some of the postcranial traits needed for the brachiating locomotion.

We will now leave the evolution of our primate relatives to concentrate on the evolution of the hominins.

MIOCENE HOMININS

As might be expected, becoming human does not happen overnight. In previous chapters, we talked about mosaic evolution, in which the characteristics we attribute to primates that live today did not appear fully developed and all at the same time. Instead, some fossils have some attributes (but perhaps not all) of the extant hominoids and hominins. How can we say that a fossil is a hominin? Probably the most important clues are changes that signal bipedalism, and in particular obligate bipedalism, which means that the individual is bipedal because other modes of locomotion are either impossible or are not biomechanically sensible (for example, a healthy adult human *can* walk on his hands and feet, but it would take much more energy and would be much more difficult than walking bipedally). In addition to saving energy walking as an obligate biped, it has been suggested that it is easier to see over tall grasses on the savannah, and walking frees the hands for carrying loads (that is, carrying tools or food) (Preuschoft 2004; Wang and Crompton 2004).

We also look for differences in dental morphology, particularly a reduction in size of all teeth and evidence that the lower premolars are not sectorial. The reduction in the size of the dentition is accompanied by a reduction in the size of the face. The brain increases in size and complexity relative to the size of the body, and the foramen magnum moves more to the center of the basicranium, concomitant with an upright posture and expansion of the brain.

PRE-*AUSTRALOPITHECUS* HOMININS

Exciting discoveries of hominin fossils within the past decade have dramatically changed our view of early hominin evolution. In 2002, a collection of fossils was described from Chad (central Africa) (Brunet et al. 2002; Brunet et al. 2005; Vignaud et al. 2002). These fossils have been dated by associated fauna at between 6 and 7 MYA, by radioactive isotope (beryllium nuclide) to between 6.8 and 7.2 MYA, and have been named *Sahelanthropus tchadensis* (commonly called "Chad Man") (see Figure 10.15). These hominins display a combination of derived and primitive characters, including a small brain, smaller canines than the great apes (it also shows wear on the occlusal surface or tip, which means it is unlikely to have had a sectorial lower first premolar like an ape), a large and continuous

FIGURE 10.15 A nearly complete cranium of *Sahelanthropus* from Chad, dating to 7 to 6 MYA.

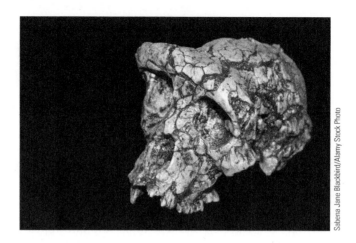

Sabena Jane Blackbird/Alamy Stock Photo

supraorbital torus (an apelike characteristic), large central incisors (apelike), and intermediate enamel thickness. Its foramen magnum is more toward the back of the cranium than in a typical hominin, but farther forward than in apes. The postcranial characteristics suggest bipedality (Cobb 2008; Crompton et al. 2008; Guy et al. 2005). These finds are important for several reasons. First, if the suggested dates are accurate, and if this is a hominin (and it appears that it is), then this discovery pushes the dates for a hominin back by about a million years. Also, it extends the geographical distribution of early hominins beyond what has been described to date. In addition, this discovery would push the likely dates of divergence from the common hominoid ancestor to an earlier date.

A different fossil has also been unearthed recently and is also dated to about 6 MYA (by radiometric dating). This fossil has been dubbed *Orrorin tugenensis* and was discovered in the Tugen Hills of central Kenya. It is represented by many skeletal and dental elements, exhibiting many characteristics similar to *Sahelanthropus*. Femur and other lower limb elements show clear bipedalism (Galik et al. 2004; Richmond and Jungers 2008). The foramen magnum is relatively forward on the cranium, but cranial and dental elements are thought by several researchers (White et al. 2009) to be more primitive than the later hominin, *Ardipithecus ramidus*.

Ardipithecus kadabba (Haile-Selassie et al. 2004) has been discovered in East Africa and dates to between 5.77 and 5.54 MYA. Represented by cranial and postcranial teeth and bone, it shows features of bipedalism, and may be an ancestor of *Ardipithecus ramidus,* which we will discuss in Chapter 11.

Miocene Hominoid Evolution

1. Is it reasonable to expect that mutation rates are relatively constant over long periods of time?

   What events would significantly alter the mutation rates of a species?

2. Aside from the primitive hominoids of the early Miocene, what other group of primates that we have discussed is close to the divergence of the Old World monkeys and apes and might be ancestral to both?

3. How would a paleoprimatologist identify a cercopithecoid fossil?

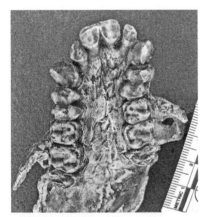

FIGURE 10.16 *Proconsul africanus,* maxilla. *Photo, D. L. France; cast from National Museums of Kenya*

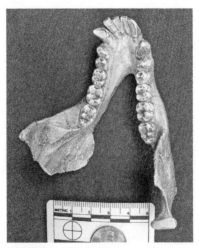

FIGURE 10.17 *Proconsul africanus,* mandible. *Photo, D.L. France; cast from National Museums of Kenya*

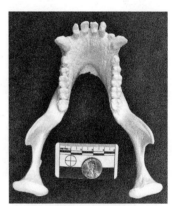

FIGURE 10.18 Mandible of chimpanzee.

4. Compare the upper and lower jaws of *Proconsul africanus* (see Figures 10.16 and 10.17) to an extant chimpanzee mandible (Figure 10.18). Make a list of the dental similarities of the two forms.

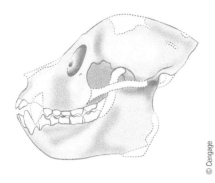

FIGURE 10.19 *Aegyptopithecus.*

© Cengage

5. How is the skull of *P. africanus* (Figures 10.16 and 10.17) more derived than the skull of *Aegyptopithecus* (Figure 10.19) of the Oligocene?

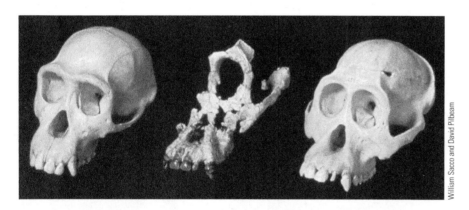

William Sacco and David Pilbeam

FIGURE 10.20 Chimpanzee (left), *Sivapithecus indicus* (center), orangutan (right).

6. Compare the face of *Sivapithecus sivalensis* (= *indicus*) (GSP15000) (see Figure 10.20) with an orangutan cranium. What are some of the similarities between this eight-million-year-old fossil face and the face of the extant orangutan?

7. What part or parts of the postcranial skeleton would be especially useful in identifying a hominin?

8. The early hominins appear to be bipedal but have small brains. Which would you consider to be more important in the identification of a fossil as "hominin"—a large brain or evidence of bipedalism? Why?

9. How would you organize or classify the Miocene hominoids into a cladogram (tree)? Do they relate to extant primates? Of course, a definitive solution is not possible at this time, but by using the disparate pieces of the puzzle we have given, you can make educated guesses about the appearance of the missing pieces.

10. Given the extremely large mandibles discovered for *Gigantopithecus,* what characteristics would the rest of the body have exhibited?

REEXAMINING THE ISSUES

- The Miocene is the epoch in which ancestors are seen for later lesser apes (gibbons and siamangs) and great apes.
- We will likely find increasing evidence for the last common ancestor for great apes and hominins in the Miocene.
- The oldest catarrhine appeared in Africa in the Miocene, and by the late Miocene the cercopiths were abundant.

CHAPTER 11

The Early Hominins of the Pliocene

OBJECTIVES

1. How can we recognize a fossil as a hominin?

2. Where did humans first appear?

3. When did we last share a common ancestor with the chimpanzee?

INTRODUCTION

In the past few years, an explosion of discoveries from this general time period has created interesting concerns in the categorization (and naming) of fossils. Should we continue to add more genera with fewer species within each, or should we "lump" more species (with more morphological variation) into fewer genera? All researchers would not agree on the classification schemes presented in this chapter, but they are probably the most parsimonious. Of course, as more discoveries are made, the taxonomic classifications will likely change. In fact, as we will see, there is disagreement about what morphological characteristics are important and what they say about a particular genus and species, but it is fascinating to try to figure out the clues!

Pliocene hominins from East Africa	
Suborder	Haplorhini
Family	Hominidae
Subfamily	Homininae
Genus	*Ardipithecus*
Species	*ramidus* (Afar region, Ethiopia: 4.4 MYA [millions of years ago])
Genus	*Australopithecus*
Species	*anamensis* (N. Kenya, Ethiopia, Tanzania: 4.17–4.07 MYA)
Species	*afarensis* (Ethiopia, Laetoli, Tanzania: 4–3 MYA)
Species	*deyiremeda* (Ethiopia: 3.5–3.3 MYA)
Species	*garhi* (Ethiopia: 2.5 MYA)
Genus	*Kenyanthropus*
Species	*platyops* (Lake Turkana, Kenya: 3.5 MYA)
Genus	*Paranthropus*
Species	*aethiopicus* (Ethiopia, Lake Turkana, Kenya: 2.5 MYA)
Species	*boisei* (Ethiopia, Kenya, Tanzania: 2.3–1.2 MYA)

Pliocene hominins from South Africa	
Genus	*Australopithecus*
Species	*africanus* (South Africa: 3.0–2.3 MYA; Sterkfontein, South Africa: 4 MYA)
Species	*sediba* (Malapa Cave, South Africa: 1.98–1.97 MYA)
Genus	*Paranthropus*
Species	*robustus* (South Africa: 2–1 MYA)

PLIOCENE PRE-*AUSTRALOPITHECUS* HOMININS

We begin our discussion of Pliocene hominins with a set of remains from a hominin-rich area of the world. We continue to learn more about the amazing diversity of individuals from the Afar Rift region in northeastern Ethiopia.

Ardipithecus ramidus

In 2009, an issue of the journal of the American Association for the Advance of Science (*Science* magazine) was devoted to a 4.4 MYA assembly of fossils from the Afar Rift region (*Science* 326(64)). More than 100 specimens of *Ardipithecus ramidus* have been discovered that show very early hominin characteristics, and are likely descendants of *Ardipithecus kadabba,* whom we learned about in the last chapter. *A. ramidus* had a relatively small brain (between 300 and 350 cm^3), which is smaller than the australopiths and a little smaller than *Sahelanthropus* (Miocene hominin), which is estimated at a little less than 400 cm³. Its canines are small relative to chimpanzees, and the cheek teeth are not as enlarged as in later australopithecines (Suwa et al. 2009a and b). Lovejoy (2009) infers from the small canines that there was little need for the aggressiveness between males implied by large canines and significant sexual dimorphism.

Because the canines and the cheek teeth are relatively small, the face in *Ardipithecus* is smaller than in *Australopithecus,* and it does not project as far forward. The dental enamel is relatively thin (thinner than the Miocene anthropoids, with the possible exception of *Dryopithecus*), which is a trait unlike later hominins.

The foramen magnum is placed more forward than in apes (Suwa et al. 2009a and b), which suggests bipedalism. The pelvis and foot are also consistent with bipedalism, but there was a divergent big toe that was able to grasp objects (or tree limbs) (Haile-Selassie 2001; Lovejoy et al., 2009a through d; Semaw et al. 2005; Suwa et al. 2009a; White et al. 2009). Lovejoy also thought that the morphology of the foot suggested that *Ardipithecus* may have been able to walk, but may have had difficulty running. Kimbel et al. (2014) disagrees with the idea that *A. ramidus* was an obligate biped, and suggests that the foot and pelvis indicate arboreal locomotion and perhaps parallel evolution with later forms.

With the hominin characteristics of *Sahelanthropus, Orrorin,* and *Ardipithecus,* as well as the dates assigned to these fossils, it is interesting to think about what this means in terms of the last common ancestor between chimps and humans, or, indeed, if there was a side branch leading to more modern hominins. Sarmiento (2010) stated that because of some of the primitive characteristics, *Ardipithecus* may not have been a hominin, but instead may predate the human/African ape split.

Most researchers still believe that at least one australopithecine is in the line leading to *Homo,* so we will now look at the evidence in *Australopithecus*.

AUSTRALOPITHS

The australopiths are represented by two closely related genera, *Australopithecus* and *Paranthropus,* which lived between about 4.2 MYA and 1 MYA. Fossils of these genera have been discovered in East and Central Africa. Although *Paranthropus* looks more primitive (with a big browridge, large face, and a sagittal crest), it is actually the more derived genus. *Australopithecus* is the more primitive in morphology and therefore thought to be more in line with humans. It is obvious that there is considerable diversity throughout the australopiths and they were around for a considerable period of time. All australopiths were bipedal, although they still had some primitive features postcranially that likely modified that bipedal locomotion. They all had smaller brains than *Homo* and larger teeth with thick enamel.

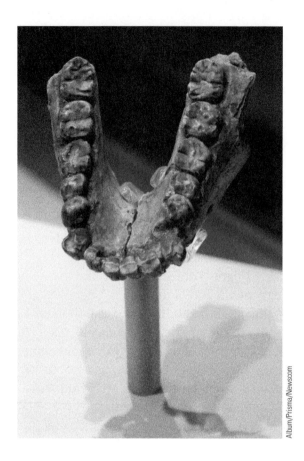

Australopithecus anamensis

Australopithecus anamensis

The name *Australopithecus anamensis* (see Figure 11.1) has been given to a group of fossils discovered in northern Kenya, Ethiopia, and Tanzania. All but one of these fossils date between 4.17 and 4.07 MYA (White et al. 2006), which makes them the oldest East African australopith known to date. As with many other fossils, these show a mosaic of primitive and derived characters. The postcranial remains strongly suggest bipedality, but the face still projects forward significantly. The dentition is more apelike in many ways, with large canines and teeth that are in a parallel dental arcade. However, the enamel is relatively thicker than in ape dentition (Macho et al. 2005), and the molars are wider relative to length than in *A. ramidus,* so they may have been adapted to eating hard foods. They are more primitive than the slightly more recent *Australopithecus afarensis,* so Ward et al. (2001) believe that *A. anamensis* could be an ancestor to *A. afarensis.* However, Senut (2002) believes that because of the postcranial morphology, *A. anamensis* should be considered ancestral to the Hominine lineage and separate from *Australopithecus afarensis* or *Ardipithecus ramidus.*

Australopithecus afarensis

Beginning in the 1970s, specimens of *A. afarensis* were discovered at Hadar, Ethiopia, and Laetoli, Tanzania. Radiometric dates of these sites are roughly between 3 and 4 MYA. The famous specimen

"Lucy" was discovered by Don Johanson in 1974 as it was eroding out of a hillside (see Figure 11.2).

A. afarensis (see Figures 11.2 through 11.5) exhibits a number of primitive as well as derived characters. The most striking derived characters are the adaptations of the pelvis and foot for habitual bipedal locomotion, but they also retained longer, more curved metatarsals and phalanges (see Figure 11.5). Latimer and Lovejoy (1990a and b) think that the long, curved phalanges are retentions from a common ancestor with the apes and that they are not indications that *A. afarensis* lived a life in the trees. Although there are arguments that these individuals could have lived in the trees in addition to the savannah (Green and Alemseged 2012), important footprints at Laetoli, Tanzania, clearly indicate a bipedal gait (Day and Wickens 1980).

Cranial capacity is estimated to be approximately 400 cc (Holloway 1983), which is within chimpanzee range. The cheek teeth of *A. afarensis* and all australopithecines were large relative to body size. The canines were smaller than in male apes, but they are still large, pointed teeth. In many of the specimens, there appears to be a diastema, and the lower first premolar is semisectorial (creating a cutting surface against the upper canine). In fact, Rak, Ginzburg, and Geffen (2007) think that the morphology of the mandible suggests that some derived traits similar to the morphology of a gorilla should cast doubt on it being an ancestor to humans. Body weight estimates of *A. afarensis* range from 30 kg to 80 kg (66 to 176 lb) (Conroy 1990), and with that variation in body size, there is a variation in morphology as well (Alemseged et al. 2005; White et al. 2009). That morphological and size variation suggests to some researchers that fossil specimens from Laetoli and Hadar actually represent two species (Falk 1986; Falk and Conroy 1983; Olson 1981). The paleoanthropologists who originally described *A. afarensis* maintain that it was a highly sexually dimorphic species (Johanson and White 1979), although Lee (2005) suggested that sexual dimorphism in this species is probably patterned

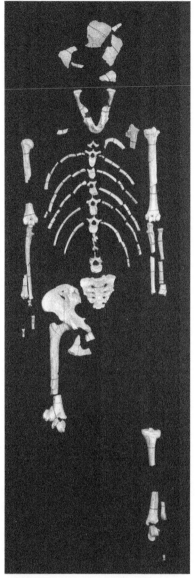

FIGURE 11.2 *Australopithecus afarensis. Photo, D. L. France; cast from Institute of Human Origins*

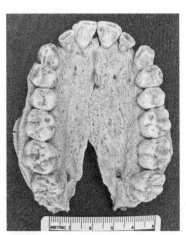

FIGURE 11.3 *A. afarensis* maxilla. *Photo, D. L. France; cast from Institute of Human Origins*

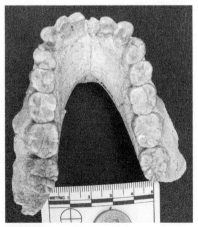

FIGURE 11.4 *A. afarensis* mandible. *Photo, D. L. France; cast from Institute of Human Origins*

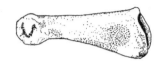

FIGURE 11.5 Pedal phalanges of modern human (top), *A. afarensis* (center), chimpanzee (bottom). *Drawing, from R. L. Susman et al., "Arboreality and Bipedality in the Hadar Hominids," Folia Primat., 1984, 43:113–156.*

differently than in living humans or apes or in the pre-*Australopithecus* hominins. One specimen at Hadar attributed to *A. afarensis* was dated to 3 MYA, which is one of the most recent and largest individuals from that species (Drapeau et al. 2005).

Another, almost complete skeleton found near Hadar was dated at about 3.3 MYA (Alemseged et al. 2006). It is a very well preserved child, estimated to be about three years of age when it died. It is said to be female by the size of the teeth, but it is almost impossible to accurately assess sex even in a modern three-year-old child, and the sexual dimorphism in this population is still not well understood. The cranium is nearly complete, and there are even foot bones that attest to a likely bipedal stance.

Villmoare et al. (2015) describe a hominin mandible dated from 2.8 to 2.75 MYA from the Afar region in Ethiopia that may be transitional between *A. afarensis* and *Homo,* based on the size and characteristics of the mandible and teeth. It is now placed in the *Homo* genus, and could push the *Homo* line considerably earlier than previously thought.

Australopithecus deyiremeda

Fossils represented primarily by dentition and elements of maxillae and mandibles were described by Haile-Selassie et al. (2015) as a new species from the Afar region in Ethiopia. It is dated to between 3.3 and 3.5 MYA and has thicker enamel, a more complex second premolar and a more robust mandible than *Ardipithecus ramidus,* and the front of the mandible is more vertical than in *Australopithecus anamensis*. They suggest that because of the dating, there were likely at least two species of hominin living in the region at the same time: *A. afarensis* (close geographically and temporally) and *A. deyiremeda*. In addition to the dental and associated bone evidence, a partial foot was also discovered in that location, although it was not directly associated with the other remains, so Haile-Selassie et al. (2012) have not assigned a genus and species to it. It also dates to 3.4 MYA and suggests a distinct form of bipedalism.

Kenyanthropus platyops

Discovered west of Lake Turkana, Kenya, by Maeve Leakey's team in 1999, *Kenyanthropus* is dated to approximately 3.5 MYA, which makes it contemporary with *A. afarensis*. *Kenyanthropus* is represented by a temporal bone, two partial maxillae, isolated teeth, and a largely complete cranium (Leakey et al. 2001). It has a narrower second molar than does *A. ramidus* and thick enamel. Also, it differs from the australopithecines in facial morphology, with the derived feature of a flatter face. The size of the cranium is between that of *A. afarensis* and *A. africanus* (Leakey et al. 2001). Further information about this specimen must wait until further publications.

Australopithecus garhi

Australopithecus garhi, which was named in 1999 (Asfaw et al. 1999), was discovered in Ethiopia and was dated to approximately 2.5 MYA. The cranium exhibits a large, projecting face, relatively large front teeth, and very large back teeth. The dental arcade is slightly parabolic, and there is marked postorbital constriction. The limb proportions are unusual, in that the forelimbs and hindlimbs are both long.

Using craniodental characteristics, Strait and Grine (2004) have suggested that *Australopithecus anamensis* and *A. garhi* should be allocated to new genera and that they are likely not in the line leading directly to *Homo.*

Paranthropus aethiopicus

Paranthropus aethiopicus has been described from Omo, Ethiopia, and Lake Turkana, Kenya. The specimen at Omo was discovered first, in 1967, but the more famous specimen, WT 17000, or the "Black Skull" (named because the deposits turned the fossil black), was discovered in 1986 west of Lake Turkana (Walker et al. 1986). The "Black Skull" (see Figure 11.6) is dated at approximately 2.5 MYA and has a small cranial capacity (~410 cc). It also had a marked postorbital constriction (similar to the other robust *Paranthropus* species) and a large sagittal crest for large muscles of mastication. The dental enamel was thick, however, and it had a parabolic dental arcade. The anterior dentition was small relative to the larger premolars and molars. It had a mosaic of features between *A. afarensis* and later species of *Paranthropus.*

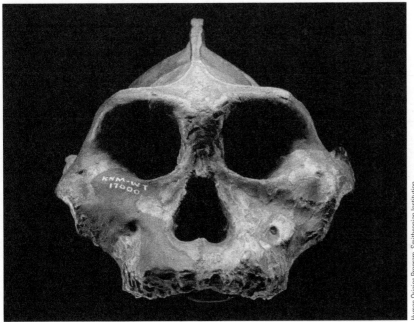

FIGURE 11.6 WT-17000. The "Black Skull."

Human Origins Program, Smithsonian Institution

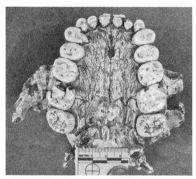

FIGURE 11.7 *Paranthropus/ Australopithecus boisei,* maxilla. *Photo, D. L. France; cast from Wenner-Gren Foundation*

Paranthropus boisei

Paranthropus boisei was originally named *Zinjanthropus boisei* after Mary Leakey discovered it in the late 1950s, but has since been re-named to the established robust genus of *Paranthropus*. Fossils in this species, dated from 2.3 to 1.2 MYA, have been discovered at Omo in Ethiopia, Koobi Fora in Kenya, and Olduvai Gorge in Tanzania, and have several features in common (and also several features in common with the robust South African forms). The anterior dentition is reduced (incisors and canines), the molars and premolars are large, the enamel is thick (see Figure 11.7), and the mandible is very large (Wood and Constantino 2007). In addition, there is a large sagittal crest and significant postorbital constriction in these forms. The brain size is similar to that of apes, although postcranially and cranially, the skeleton does show adaptations for bipedalism.

THE SOUTH AFRICAN AUSTRALOPITHECINES

Hominins are not exclusively found in East and Central Africa. Hominins from South Africa demonstrate interesting similarities and differences from those we have discussed so far.

Australopithecus africanus

The first australopithecine discovered in South Africa was the Taung child (Dart 1925) (see Figures 11.8 and 11.9). Although the specimen was that of a young child (judging from dental eruptions), many features were evident. The dentition was more hominin-like than apelike with wider molars and smaller canines, and the foramen magnum was farther forward than in apes. The estimated adult cranial capacity was more similar to that of an ape, but the pattern of brain development was more like later hominins (Falk et al. 2012). This specimen was named *Australopithecus africanus* ("southern ape of Africa").

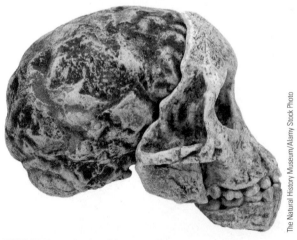

FIGURE 11.8 *A. africanus:* Taung.

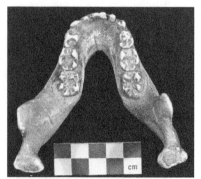

FIGURE 11.9 *A. africanus:* Taung mandible. *Photo, D. L. France; cast from University of Pennsylvania*

Other fossils that have been named *Australopithecus africanus* have been found at Makapansgat and at Sterkfontein, both in South Africa, and date to about 2.3 to 3.0 MYA. They all have a projecting face and some postorbital constriction, which are primitive characteristics, but the canines do not project much beyond the tooth row and they have no diastema. The teeth exhibit thick enamel, although they have relatively parallel tooth rows. Postcranially, they have relatively long arms, but they also have the modifications in the spinal column and lower limb bones that suggest bipedalism.

A largely complete set of remains was discovered in the late 1990s at Sterkfontein, South Africa. The specimen is largely complete and is dated to 3.5 MYA, although a more recent publication (Partridge et al. 2003) puts the date at about 4 MYA, which is about the same time period as *A. anamensis*. The skull and parts of the arm and leg bones have been uncovered. This fossil is a complete adult, so continued analysis has the potential to yield significant information about *Australopithecus africanus* in South Africa.

Australopitheus sediba

In 2008, the fossilized remains of a female and a juvenile male from just under 2 MYA were discovered at the bottom of Malapa cave near Johannesburg, South Africa. Berger et al. (2010) argue that it is a new species transitional between *Australopithecus africanus* and *Homo* (and probably descended from *A. africanus*) because of a range of characteristics including *Australopithecus*-like smaller cranial capacity (about 440 cubic centimeters), a small apelike calcaneus, larger medial malleolus, and a hand that indicates arboreal capabilities. The more advanced characteristics include a longer thumb and shorter fingers that imply precision grip (see Figures 11.10 and 11.11) and a pelvic girdle and foot features that imply a form of bipedalism (Berger et al. 2010; Kibii et al. 2011; Kivell et al. 2011).

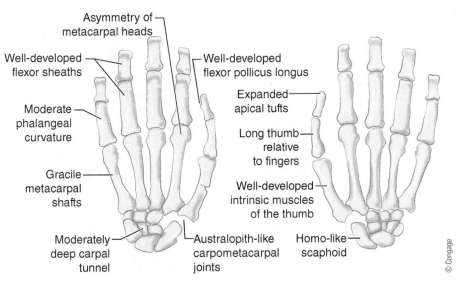

FIGURE 11.10 *A. sediba* hand.

Asymmetry of metacarpal heads

Well-developed flexor sheaths

Moderate phalangeal curvature

Gracile metacarpal shafts

Moderately deep carpal tunnel

Well-developed flexor pollicus longus

Expanded apical tufts

Long thumb relative to fingers

Well-developed intrinsic muscles of the thumb

Australopith-like carpometacarpal joints

Homo-like scaphoid

© Cengage

FIGURE 11.11 Gorilla, chimpanzee and human hand.

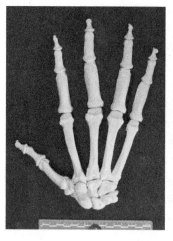
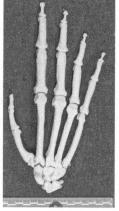
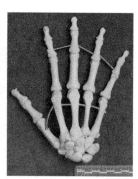

Others have argued that this specimen is within the range of variation of *A. africanus* and does not warrant a new species.

Paranthropus robustus

The more robust species found in South Africa has been found in deposits dating from 2.0 to 1.0 MYA (see Figures 11.12a and b and Figures 11.13a and b). Most of the differences between *Paranthropus robustus* and *Australopithecus africanus* are in the cranium and mandible. The most striking difference is in the presence of a large sagittal crest for the attachment of large chewing muscles, and as you would expect, the mandible is very large. In addition, the molars

FIGURE 11.12a and b
A. africanus. *Photo D. L. France; cast from Wenner-Gren Foundation*

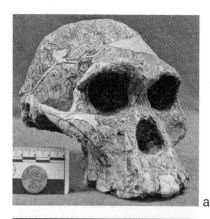

FIGURE 11.13a and b
P. robustus. *Photo D. L. France; cast from University of Pennsylvania*

and premolars are large relative to the incisor size and to the size of the body, and the teeth have thick enamel. There is a marked postorbital constriction, and the brain size is comparable to that of apes, though there are modifications in the skeleton for bipedalism (see Figure 11.14 for a modern femoral neck compared to that of *Paranthropus robustus*).

Sites in South Africa that have yielded the robust form of paranthropine include Swartkrans, Kromdraai, and a relatively recent find at Drimolen (Keyser 2000). All of these sites have fossils that are similar to each other but are somewhat dissimilar to the robust forms discovered in East Africa.

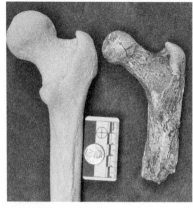

FIGURE 11.14 Proximal right femora: Modern human (left), *P. robustus* (right). *Photo D. L. France; original bone (left), cast from University of Pennsylvania (right)*

COMPARISON OF EAST AND SOUTH AFRICAN PLIOCENE FOSSILS

There have been no unquestioned specimens of *A. africanus* found in East Africa, and no fossils of the genus *Australopithecus* more recent than 3 MYA in East Africa. However, there is no doubt that a hyperrobust species, *Paranthropus boisei*, lived in East Africa from 2.5 MYA to just about 1 MYA at several sites. It is very similar to *P. robustus* of South Africa in that the dentition of the robust forms represents the continuation of dental trends first observed in the Miocene: a reduction of the anterior dentition, enlargement of the cheek teeth with thick enamel, and thickening of the jaws. The premolars of *boisei/robustus* are referred to as molariform premolars because of the molar-like form and function of these teeth (see Figure 11.19 in the exercises at the end of the chapter). These large, thick-enameled cheek teeth probably provided the surface area for grinding small, tough foods that need little preparation. Compare the relative sizes of the teeth of a robust australopithecine (Figure 11.19) to *Australopithecus africanus* (Figure 11.15).

Estimates of the cranial capacities of the australopithecine specimens run from just under 400 cc to more than 500 cc, and when body size is considered, these cranial capacities are not much more than those of the extant apes. Brain expansion, so characteristic of our lineage, began with the first appearance of our genus.

The interpretations of the relationships between the Pliocene hominins vary. *Ardipithecus ramidus, Australopithecus anamensis,* and *Australopithecus afarensis* occur in the fossil record before 4 MYA, and one or more may be in the line leading to the later australopithecine forms or even to a later *Homo* line. The hominin forms that are found in deposits from the Miocene (*Sahelanthropus tchadensis, Orrorin tugenensis,* and *Ardipithecus sp.*) may take that line millions of years before the Pliocene. Were there other australopithecines in the hominin lineage that led to modern humans? Did *A. afarensis* lead more directly into *Homo?* Were the Miocene hominins the ones in the ancestral line to *Homo?*

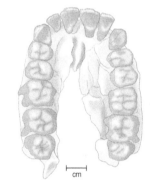

© Cengage

FIGURE 11.15 *A. africanus.*

The Early Hominins

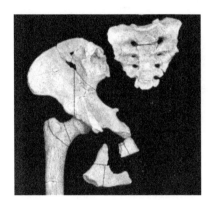

FIGURE 11.16 *Australopithecus afarensis,* pelvis. *Photo D. L. France; cast from Institute of Human Origins*

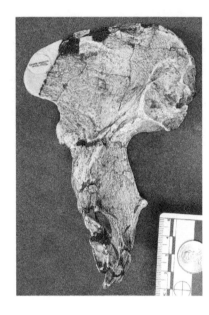

FIGURE 11.17 *Australopithecus africanus,* ossa coxae. *Photo D. L. France; cast from Wenner-Gren Foundation*

1. Observe the remains of an *A. afarensis* pelvis in your laboratory or as shown in Figure 11.16. Pelvic remains of a later species, *A. africanus* (Figure 11.17), are very similar to those of *A. afarensis.*

    a. Name similarities of the *A. afarensis* pelvis to that of modern humans.

    b. How are they different?

    c. What does this mean in terms of biomechanical differences?

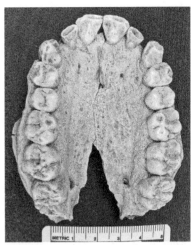

FIGURE 11.18 *A. afarensis,* maxilla. *Photo, D. L. France; cast from Institute of Human Origins*

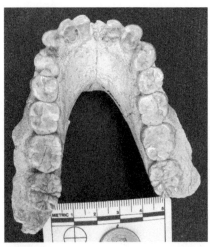

FIGURE 11.19 *A. afarensis,* mandible. *Photo, D. L. France; cast from Institute of Human Origins*

2. Using the criteria of ape and human dentition from previous chapters, analyze the dentition of *A. afarensis* (Figures 11.18 and 11.19). In what ways is the dentition apelike? In what ways is it humanlike?

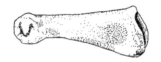

FIGURE 11.20 Pedal phalanges of modern human (top), *A. afarensis* (center), chimpanzee (bottom). *Drawing, from R. L. Susman et al., "Arboreality and Bipedality in the Hadar Hominids," Folia Primat., 1984, 43:113–156*

3. Compare the phalanges of *A. afarensis* (Figure 11.20) to those of apes and humans. How are they apelike? How are they humanlike?

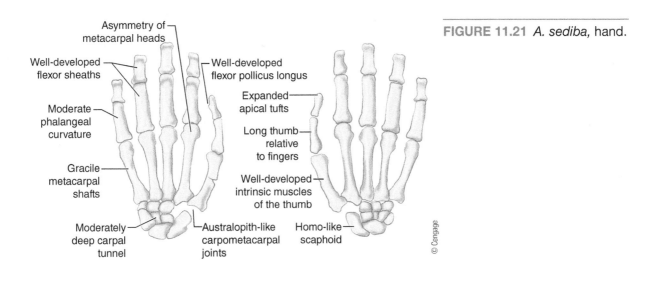

Asymmetry of metacarpal heads

Well-developed flexor sheaths

Moderate phalangeal curvature

Gracile metacarpal shafts

Moderately deep carpal tunnel

Well-developed flexor pollicus longus

Expanded apical tufts

Long thumb relative to fingers

Well-developed intrinsic muscles of the thumb

Australopith-like carpometacarpal joints

Homo-like scaphoid

© Cengage

FIGURE 11.21 *A. sediba,* hand.

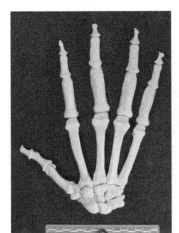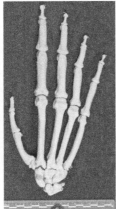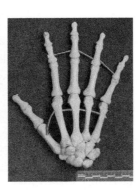

FIGURE 11.22 Gorilla, chimpanzee, and human hand.

4. Compare the hands of *Australopithecus sediba* (Figure 11.21) to those of gorilla, chimp, and human (Figure 11.22). How do they compare?

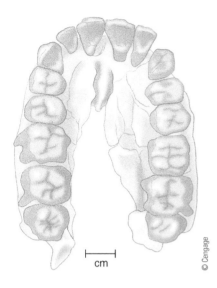

FIGURE 11.23 *A. africanus.*

cm

© Cengage

5. Compare the dentition of *A. africanus* (Figure 11.23) with that of the more ancient *A. afarensis* (Figures 11.18 and 11.19). In what ways can the dentition of *A. afarensis* be said to be more primitive than that of *A. africanus?* Based on this evidence, do you believe *A. afarensis* is a good ancestral candidate for *A. africanus?*

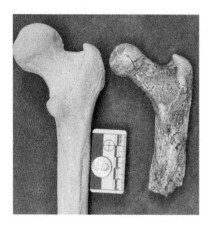

FIGURE 11.24 Proximal right femora: Modern human (left), *P. robustus* (right). *Photo D. L. France; original bone (left), cast from University of Pennsylvania (right)*

6. Observe the proximal femur of *Paranthropus robustus* (Figure 11.24). How is it different from the proximal femur of humans?

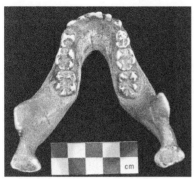

FIGURE 11.25 *A. africanus:* Taung mandible. *Photo, D. L. France; cast from University of Pennsylvania*

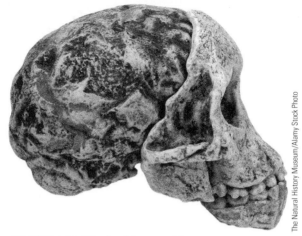

FIGURE 11.26 *A. africanus:* Taung.

7. Observe the dentition of the Taung child (Figures 11.25 and 11.26). All but the molars (one in each quadrant) are deciduous. The first permanent molar erupts at about age six years in modern humans and at about age three in chimpanzees (Schultz 1937). How old do you think the Taung child was at death? Why?

8. Develop a likely ancestor-descendant chart with the fossils from this chapter.

9. Which of the fossils are most likely in the line of evolution leading to modern humans?

10. What does it mean to the Pliocene ancestral/descendant relationships that *Kenyanthropus* has thicker enamel and a narrower second molar than does *Ardipithecus*?

REEXAMINING THE ISSUES

- The current evidence indicates that hominins first appeared in the Miocene and developed much more modern morphological characteristics in the Pliocene.
- The very early hominin species have been discovered in central and eastern Africa.
- Bipedalism seems to have developed first in the hominin line, and increased brain size followed.

CHAPTER 12

The Genus *Homo*

OBJECTIVES

1. When did humans begin to develop a significantly larger brain?

2. Did Neanderthals live at the same time as some anatomically modern (AM) modern humans?

3. Did Neanderthals and more modern humans mate?

4. Did modern humans develop in Africa and migrate from there, or did modern humans evolve independently from *Homo erectus* in all areas of the Old World?

If one word could sum up this chapter, it would be *variation*. It is tempting to try to oversimplify the situation by drawing a simple taphonomic tree of the interrelationships between the various *Homo* species, but that would completely misrepresent the evidence. The evolutionary theories of the genus *Homo* are some of the most fascinating in paleoanthropology and some of the most varied, and once again, the Human Genome Project and related studies have a great deal of information to contribute to the discussion. New genetic evidence combined with fossil discoveries shed light on many of the ancestral relationships among species of *Homo*, while dispelling some of our old beliefs.

INTRODUCTION

By the time we reach the genus *Homo*, pretty much everyone agrees that the hominins were bipedal, although at the *Homo* stage, there is a refinement of the striding gait. The more interesting aspect of evolution at this stage is in the increasing size and complexity of the brain. After seeing relatively little increase in brain size in the pre-*Australopithecus* and *Australopithecus* species, we see exciting changes through the more recent species. Along with that, there is evidence of culture and more sophisticated tool use (chimpanzees make and use tools, so the earlier hominins must have used tools). We see migration out of Africa to Europe, Asia, and Indonesia, and evidence suggests that different species of our genus lived at the same places at the same time, even for hundreds of thousands of years! What's more, although there was a debate at one time about whether Neanderthals even existed with more modern *Homo* lines, current genetic evidence shows that many people living today carry Neanderthal genes!

A section of mandible was recently discovered in the Afar region of Ethiopia that has been dated to 2.8 to 2.75 MYA (millions of years ago), which, if true, actually predates *Australopithecus sediba* in South Africa, and both the robust *Paranthropus aethiopicus* and the more gracile *A. garhi* in Ethiopia (DiMaggio et al. 2015; Villmoare et al. 2015). It is only represented at this point by the left side of a mandible with teeth and has not yet been assigned a species, but it combines the primitive traits of *Australopithecus* with the more derived features of later *Homo* species.

Homo species	
Genus	*Homo*
Species	*(LD350-1) unassigned species* (Afar region, Ethiopia: 2.8–2.75 MYA)
Species	*habilis* (East Africa: 2.1–1.44 MYA; South Africa ~2MYA)
Species	*erectus* (East Africa: 1.7–<1 MYA; Europe: 1.2–0.3 MYA; Israel:1.5 MYA; Republic of Georgia: 1.75–1.7 MYA; Java, China: 1.8–0.3 MYA)
Species	*heidelbergensis* (Africa: 300–125 KYA; Europe: 850–200 KYA; China: 200 KYA)
Species	*floresiensis* (Flores, Indonesia:700–60 KYA)
Species	*sapiens neanderthalensis* (Europe to Central Asia: 430–40 KYA)
Species	*Denisova* (Siberia: 50 KYA)
Species	*sapiens sapiens* (AM) (Africa: 120–80 KYA [perhaps to 200 KYA]; Israel: 130–92 KYA; Europe: 35 KYA; China: 40–20 KYA; Borneo: 45–35 KYA; Australia: ~50 KYA)

HOMO HABILIS

H. habilis is generally believed to be a transitional species between the australopithecines and *H. erectus*. Wood (2014), however, believes that *H. habilis* remains are too different from *Homo erectus* to be its direct ancestor, although *H. habilis* specimens show considerable morphological variation, perhaps as much as in modern *H. sapiens* (Miller 2000).

This species received its designation in the early 1960s when most of a mandible (OH 7; see Figure 12.1), skull fragments, and some postcranial materials were discovered at Olduvai Gorge in East Africa, and classified as *H. habilis* ("handy man"—because the hand bones exhibit features characteristic of a precision grip) (Leakey et al. 1964). These were considered to be in the genus *Homo* primarily because of more humanlike dentition and a brain larger than that of australopithecines. Spoor et al. (2015) recently reanalyzed the original fossils recovered and determined that the dental arcade is more similar to *Australopithecus afarensis* than to *Homo sapiens* or *Homo erectus*. But he says that one specimen of *A. afarensis* is actually more derived than OH7, and because it existed 500,000 years before this specimen of *H. habilis,* and if *H. habilis* is descended from *A. afarensis*, it would place *H. habilis* before 2.3 MYA. Other than OH7, other fossils of *H. habilis* in East Africa date to approximately 2.4 MYA, which makes it roughly contemporaneous with australopithicines, while the most recent fossils date to approximately 1.44 MYA, which makes it also contemporaneous with *Homo erectus* (Spoor et al. 2007)! In fact, in East Africa, South Africa, and other areas of the world, we see overlaps like this that lead us to wonder what these hominins were doing with, and to, each other?

Probably the most important *Homo habilis* specimen is KNM-ER 1470 (see Figures 12.2 and 12.3). Some researchers placed this individual with the australopithecines, or in a separate species, *Homo rudolfensis* (Alexeev 1986), but most now place it with *Homo habilis* (for example, Blumenschine et al. 2003). This specimen is characterized by a larger brain (775 cm^3) than seen in *Australopithecus* species and by evidence of smaller premolars and molars (although they are larger than in later species). KNM-ER 1470 is from deposits dated to approximately 1.9 MYA.

A few fossil fragments found in South Africa (at Sterkfontein and Swartkrans) (Curnoe and Tobias 2006) probably represent an early *Homo* species contemporaneous with *Paranthropus robustus* more than 2 MYA.

The discovery of a *H. habilis* specimen (OH 62), has shown a more *Homo*-like cranial morphology, with a more *Australopithecus*-like postcranium (Johanson et al. 1987; Stringer 1995). Haeusler and McHenry (2004), however, thought that the relative leg length of OH62 was more humanlike. In 2009, Christopher Ruff studied the cross sections of the femur and humerus of OH62 and compared them to the corresponding area in humans, *Homo erectus*, and chimpanzees, and stated that the distribution of strength as indicated by the thickness of the cross sections was an indication of the locomotor behavior of the different species. He concluded that, although *Homo habilis* walked bipedally, there was evidence that the species was still

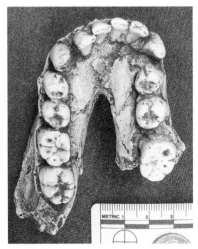

FIGURE 12.1 OH 7 mandible. *Photo, D. L. France; cast from Wenner-Gren Foundation*

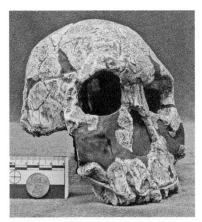

FIGURE 12.2 KNM-ER 1470. *Photo, D. L. France; cast from National Museums of Kenya*

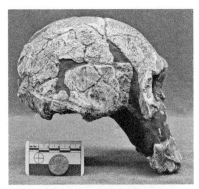

FIGURE 12.3 KNM-ER 1470. *Photo, D. L. France; cast from National Museums of Kenya*

FIGURE 12.4 Oldowan tool.

FIGURE 12.5 KNM-ER 3733.
Photo, D. L. France; cast from National Museums of Kenya

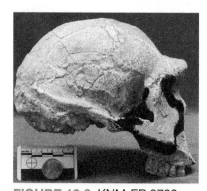

FIGURE 12.6 KNM-ER 3733.
Photo, D. L. France; cast from National Museums of Kenya

partly arboreal, which could indicate that *Homo habilis* and *Homo erectus* lived in potentially different environmental niches at about the same time. Most of a foot attributed to *H. habilis* (OH 8). indicates that they had feet much like our own bipedally adapted feet.

Although there is still some debate about the sophistication of the morphology of some *Homo habilis* skeletons, it appears that they were making stone tools at about this time (although it is difficult to always identify the manufacturer of a very primitive tool). These first 2 MYA stone tools were very crude (see Plummer 2004, for discussion of early *Homo* tool use; Figure 12.4). Gradually, stone tools and other artifacts left by populations of *Homo* became more complex. The culture of these ancient hominins must be increasingly considered in the study of their evolution as we approach the present day.

HOMO ERECTUS

The variability in skeletal morphology continued in *H. erectus* and some researchers interpret that variability as two species: *Homo ergaster* from Africa and *Homo erectus* from Asia, who existed at about the same time. Other researchers indicate that even though there is variability, it is still consistent with grouping these two species into *Homo erectus*. In general, *Homo ergaster* is said to have a smaller browridge, a smaller area for muscle insertion on the occipital, and the crania are not as thick as in *Homo erectus*. Is this enough variation for a new species designation, or is there enough variation inherent in *Homo erectus* to account for this variation in the non-Asian fossils? This book will acknowledge that there is disagreement in these designations but will group *H. ergaster* and *H. erectus* together.

The features that characterize *H. erectus* include a reduction in premolars and molar size, an increase in brain size from *H. habilis*, and often some keeling of the midline of the cranium (similar to the keel of a ship), although the keeling does not resemble the sagittal crest in the robust *Paranthropus*. Likewise, the supraorbital torus is pronounced, and the forehead is receding, but again, not as much as in *Paranthropus*. The cranium is usually wider at the base than at the top, whereas in modern humans, the widest part of the cranium is superior to that area. A study of the internal cranial features of a child from Java (attributed to *Homo erectus*) suggests that the brain developed differently in *Homo erectus* than in *Homo sapiens* (Balzeau et al. 2005).

One of the early *Homo erectus* specimens (KNM-ER 3733) in East Africa (see Figures 12.5 and 12.6) is dated to about 1.7 MYA (Lepre and Kent 2010). When compared to KNM-WT 15000 (on the next page) and to KNM-ER 3733 from the same site, it is smaller with somewhat more delicate features, and is therefore thought to be a female.

The nearly complete skeleton of *H. erectus* (KNM-WT 15000) was found in Kenya in 1984 (see Figure 12.7; Brown et al. 1985) and is thought to represent a young boy because of the incomplete

union of epiphyses in the postcranial skeleton and erupted second
(but not third) molars. The brain size of this 1.6 MYA individual has
been estimated to be about 880 cm^3, and the arms and legs are
within modern human limits, although the bones are quite robust.

A well-preserved calvarium was also discovered east of Lake
Turkana and dates to 1.55 MYA (Spoor et al. 2007). This cranium
displays many of the typical *Homo erectus* characteristics, particularly of the Asian forms (described in the next paragraph), although
it is closer in size to *Homo habilis*. At the same site, remember, a
maxilla dated to 1.44 MYA is also attributed to *Homo habilis*. Other
African *H. erectus* remains have been discovered in Olduvai Gorge
(1.2 MYA to less than 1 MYA), Kenya, Algeria, Morocco, Ethiopia,
and South Africa. A female pelvis from Chad has been assigned a
date of 1.3 MYA (DeSilva 2011; Simpson et al. 2008). This is exciting because it seems to show the sexual dimorphism in the pelvis
that would allow a large-brained infant to develop significantly before leaving the womb.

Currently, *H. erectus* is thought to have migrated out of Africa
between 2 and 1.5 MYA. Sites in Java and China are now dated to as
early as 1.8 MYA (Kaifu et al. 2005). The *H. erectus* (Figures 12.8
and 12.9 show the old fossil casts of *Homo erectus* from China)
stage of human evolution lasted more than a million years (1.8 to 0.3
MYA). Notice that these dates are roughly contemporaneous with
the African forms. A study of a South China (Hexian) *Homo erectus*
suggests that the brain height, frontal breadth, cerebral height, frontal height, and parietal chord increased from *Homo erectus* times to
modern, but there was little change in the length, breadth, frontal
chord, and occipital breadth (Wu et al. 2006).

Fossils in the Republic of Georgia (Dmanisi) in the former
Soviet Union are tentatively dated at about 1.75 to 1.7 MYA
(Gabunia and Vekua 1995; Spoor et al. 2007; Vekua et al. 2002).
Cranial material from that region vary, but at least one has a smaller
face than KNM-ER 3733 or KNM-ER 1470, although there is no
indication of a chin (the chin is important for defining AM humans).
Rightmire et al. (2006) suggested that specimens from the Republic
of Georgia might be close to the origins of *Homo erectus*, although
this idea is not accepted by everyone, and in fact, Lordkipanidze
et al. (2013) have suggested that the great range of variation in
Homo erectus at Dmanisi demonstrates that it could incorporate all
Homo habilis fossils, so *H. habilis* should be put into *Homo erectus*.

In Israel, remains have been discovered that date to 1.5 MYA
(Belmaker et al. 2002). In Europe, the fossil hominin record for this
time period is still fairly poor. A partial jaw and some teeth have
been assigned a date of about 1.2 MYA (Carbonell et al. 2008) in
Spain. Many hominin cultural remains have been found in Europe
dating to around 0.8 to 0.3 MYA, and the fossil remains that have
been found (mostly teeth and partial crania) are either *H. erectus* or
a very closely related species. Some researchers place the European

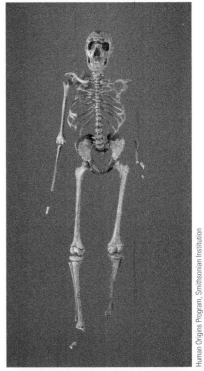

FIGURE 12.7 KNM-WT 15000.

FIGURE 12.8 *Homo erectus
pekinensis.* Photo, D. L. France;
cast from University of
Pennsylvania

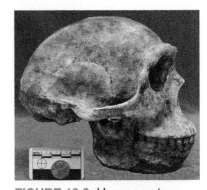

FIGURE 12.9 *Homo erectus
pekinensis.* Photo, D. L. France;
cast from University of Pennsylvania

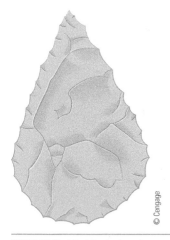

FIGURE 12.10 Acheulean hand ax.

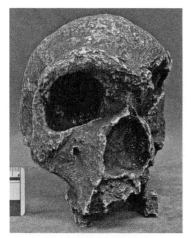

FIGURE 12.11 Steinheim.
Photo, D. L. France; cast from University of Pennsylvania

FIGURE 12.12 Steinheim.
Photo, D. L. France; cast from University of Pennsylvania

forms of *H. erectus* into the separate species *Homo heidelbergensis* (discussed in the next section).

A new tool type, the "Acheulian hand ax" (see Figure 12.10), appears with the fossil remains of early *H. erectus* in East Africa. Acheulian stone tools are found in Africa, western Europe, and western India. Less advanced stone tools are found associated with eastern European and East Asian *H. erectus* remains. Sites in both France and China that are slightly younger than this age show that this *Homo* species used fire, lived in temporary camps, built temporary living shelters, and relied on gathering and hunting for subsistence.

HOMO HEIDELBERGENSIS

H. heidelbergensis is a transitional form between *H. erectus* and early archaic *H. sapiens,* and it seems to be gaining in popularity as a valid species designation. The characteristics are generally transitional between *Homo erectus* and archaic *Homo sapiens* and include an increase in brain size, a reduction in cranial and postcranial robustness, a shift to the widest cranial breadth in the parietal region instead of near the cranial base, and a more rounded occipital region. The type specimen was discovered in 1907 at the Mauer region in Germany. The dates assigned to this species are generally thought to be between about 850 and 200 KYA. An example of one of the early European forms is Steinheim (see Figures 12.11 and 12.12), dated approximately 300 to 250 KYA, in Germany. Also in Europe, sites in Spain have been yielding literally thousands of fossil fragments from as early as 850 KYA for one site (Gran Dolina) and from between 600 and 530 KYA from a cave nearby (Bischoff et al. 2007; Rightmire 1998).

In Africa, one of the early archaic fossils has been discovered in Zambia, and is dated to be between about 300 and 125 KYA. This site at Broken Hill has yielded a cranium and some postcranial remains that retain some characteristics of *H. erectus,* while exhibiting some characteristics of early *H. sapiens* (see Figures 12.13 and 12.14). The browridges are still robust, the forehead is still receding, and the occipital torus is large, but the cranial base (particularly in the occipital region) is not as flat as in *H. erectus.* The cranial capacity is larger (~1280 cc), and the cranial bones are thinner than in *H. erectus.* Many are now putting this fossil in the *H. heidelbergensis* category.

Fossils from China have a mix of *Homo erectus*-like and *Homo sapiens*-like characteristics. Jinniushan (northeast China) has been dated to about 200 KYA (Rosenberg et al. 2006; Tiemel et al. 1994). The cranial capacity is approximately 1,260 cm^3. There are great discussions about how the fossils from China relate to the fossils from the rest of the world, but they may be regional variants of *Homo heidelbergensis* (Rightmire 2004).

FIGURE 12.13 Broken Hill; early archaic *Homo sapiens. Photo, D. L. France; cast from University of Pennsylvania*

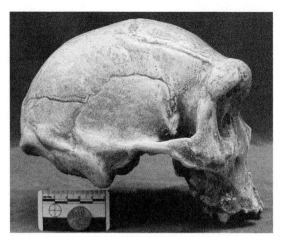

FIGURE 12.14 Broken Hill; early archaic *Homo sapiens. Photo, D. L. France; cast from University of Pennsylvania*

HOMO FLORESIENSIS

Homo floresiensis (see Figure 12.15) was a surprising find (Brown et al. 2004; Morwood et al. 2004). Nicknamed the "Hobbit" after the small characters in *The Lord of the Rings,* this hominin stood only about 1 m (3 ft) tall and had a cranial capacity of about 380 cc (this is about the size of *Australopithecus*). They lived on the island of Flores in Indonesia (east of Bali), and one explanation for their small size is that they may have been isolated for a long period of time, and perhaps experienced genetic drift (relative genetic isolation; see Chapter 2). In fact, Van den Bergh et al. (2016) believe that this species probably developed from early *H. erectus,* because their features are more derived than *H. habilis.* An earlier study (Argue et al. 2009), though, suggests that *H. floresiensis* emerged even before *Homo habilis.*

Recent descriptions date the earliest fossils at Mata Menge to around 700 KYA (Van den Bergh et al. 2016), but Sutikna et al. (2016) say that all *H. floresiensis* remains date to 100,000 to 60,000 years ago. If this species existed until around 50,000 years ago, it could potentially have been in contact with the Denisovans (discussed later) (Sutikna et al. 2016).

Some studies suggested that the type specimen (LB1) was an individual with microcephaly (pathologically small brain size, usually resulting in mental retardation) (Weber et al. 2005), but Falk et al. (2005a, b) dispute this. More recently, however, Gordon et al. (2008) compared the size of the cranium with the size of the rest of the skeleton (an individual with microcephaly would have a small cranium with a more normal postcranial skeleton) and decided that it is a normal but diminutive population with a head shape that is outside of the range of *Homo sapiens.* They also believe that this population is more closely related in morphology to early *Homo erectus* from East Africa and/or Dmanisi or perhaps to *Homo habilis.*

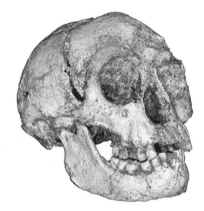

FIGURE 12.15 Cranium of adult female *Homo floresiensis* from Flores, Indonesia, dated 18,000 YA. *From Jurmain/Kilgore/Trevathan/Ciochon. Introduction to Physical Anthropology 2009-2010 Edition, 12E. © 2010 Wadsworth, a part of Cengage Learning, Inc. Reproduced by permission. www.cengage.com/permissions*

ARCHAIC *HOMO SAPIENS*

In no other case has the interpretation of the ancestry of modern humans been changed more than in archaic *Homo sapiens*. For decades after Neanderthal remains were discovered in Europe, researchers wondered if the Neanderthals were within the ancestral line leading to modern humans, or if they lived alongside *Homo sapiens*. With DNA obtained from Neanderthal remains that are not completely fossilized (DNA cannot be retrieved in completely fossilized remains) we can now say that bits of both scenarios apply, but it's actually even more complicated!

Prüfer et al. (2013; and confirmed by Sanchez-Quinto and Lalueza-Fox 2015) studied the genome sequence of Neanderthals and found evidence of mating among close relatives, which likely produced individuals with decreased fitness (see Chapter 2 for discussions about inbreeding and evolutionary fitness). There is also evidence that Neanderthals mated with Denisovans (below) and modern humans, and many humans living today (particularly Europeans) have some of the same DNA that has been retrieved from Neanderthal remains.

Homo sapiens Denisova is thought to be a second group of archaic *Homo sapiens* living at the same time as Neanderthals at around 50,000 years ago (Cooper and Stringer 2013). Their remains were discovered in Denisova Cave in Siberia, a cave that also contained Neanderthal and modern human remains. They are only represented by a phalanx and teeth, so we don't know much about their morphology, but DNA analysis shows that they are not Neanderthals nor are they modern humans. They seem to have ranged across East Asia, but breeding with our ancestors may have only occurred in Southeast Asia (Cooper and Stringer 2013). About 3 to 5 percent of the DNA of modern Melanesians (and in general Oceanians) and Australian Aborigines is from Denisovans (Sankararaman et al. 2016), and Qin and Stoneking (2015) found only a low level of Denisovan genes in eastern Eurasian and Native American populations.

The fossilized remains of Neanderthals are found throughout Africa, Asia, Europe, and the Near East in deposits typically from about 75 to 10 KYA, although remains from about 28 individuals were discovered in a cave in Spain (Sima de los Huesos meaning "pit of bones" in Spanish) date to approximately 430,000 years ago (Meyer et al. 2016). DNA evidence from two specimens shows that these individuals were closely related to Neanderthals, although mtDNA results from a different individual within the cave indicates a close relationship to the Denisova populations. Meyer et al. (2016) suggest that this indicates a shared ancestry between the Neanderthal and Denisova populations to 430 KYA.

A different Neanderthal deposit in Spain was at the El Sidrón, in which the remains of 12 individuals were discovered

(Lalueza-Fox et al. 2011). They obtained mtDNA from the remains and discovered that the males in the group were closely related, but the females were not, showing that unrelated women were living with their mates. They also showed that there was little genetic diversity within the lineage, which could make them less likely to be able to withstand changing conditions.

Neanderthal fossils represent a greatly varied group with the earlier remains retaining some *H. erectus* traits while moving toward some *H. sapiens* traits (some put the earlier fossils into a separate species: *Homo antecessor*), whereas the later fossils exhibit more of the anatomically modern (AM) *H. sapiens* traits, as might be expected.

The early Neanderthal fossils in general are different from *H. erectus* in that they show larger brains, with the greatest width of the cranium now in the parietal region instead of near or below the ear (as in *H. erectus*). In fact, the cranial capacity is very large (actually larger as a group than modern humans, likely because there are fewer folds in the brain, although this is difficult to discern from endocranial characteristics). Neanderthals have long crania and a bun-shaped occipital bone. The browridges are still pronounced, but not as pronounced as in *H. erectus*. The forehead rises more vertically from the browridges than in *H. erectus*, but again, not as much as in modern *H. sapiens*. The face projects forward. The premolars and molars continue to decrease in size, but the postcranial skeleton is still large and robust.

The classic Neanderthal fossil is La Chapelle-aux-Saints in France (see Figures 12.16 and 12.17). This individual had an extremely large cranial capacity (1,620 cm^3) and is thought to have lived about 50 KYA. Interestingly, this individual seems to have been intentionally buried with some flint tools and some fragmentary nonhuman bones.

Sites in Israel (Tabun at Mt. Carmel), Iraq (at Shanidar), and Uzbekistan (Teshik-Tash) are populated by hominins that are also morphologically like Neanderthal. An individual at Shanidar had massive antemortem (it shows signs of healing) blunt trauma to the cranium and elsewhere, and the fact that it shows signs of healing dictates that someone had taken care of the individual for a significant period of time. This is an indication of a cooperative culture. The oldest intentional burial site (dating to around 130,000 years), discovered to date is from Krapina, a site in Croatia (see Figures 12.18a and b).

In addition to definite signs of intentional burial and caring for the injured, Neanderthals showed other signs of group behavior and culture. They developed a new technique of making stone tools (the Levallois technique), which had more complex and varied tool kits than any hominin culture that had come before. More than 60 different types of scrapers, knives, points, and other stone

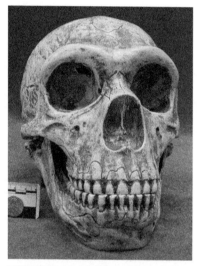

FIGURE 12.16 Law Chappelle-aux-Saints. *Photo, D. L. France; cast from University of Pennsylvania*

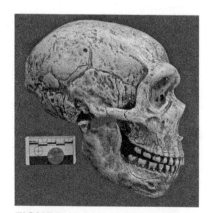

FIGURE 12.17 La Chappelle-aux-Saints. *Photo, D. L. France; cast from University of Pennsylvania*

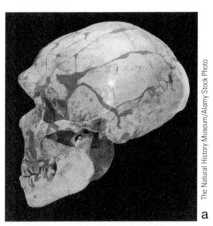

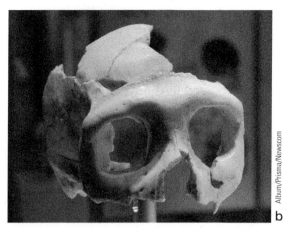

a

b

FIGURE 12.18 Krapina cranium. (a) Lateral view showing characteristic Neanderthal traits. (b) Three-quarters view.

FIGURE 12.19 Mousterian tool.

tools have been identified in these cultural assemblages (for example, see Figure 12.19). This culture is referred to as Mousterian culture and/or Middle Paleolithic culture. Some studies (Bocherens et al. 2005; Richards et al. 2000) have suggested through isotope analysis that Neanderthals were large-animal predators (including woolly rhinoceros, woolly mammoth, bovines, large deer and horses).

Still, archaic *H. sapiens* culture is quite crude relative to the rich cultures that flourished in the Upper Paleolithic (around 30 to 10 KYA) that are associated with AM *H. sapiens* (although Conard et al. [2004] suggest that Neanderthals may have contributed to the cultural artifacts of the Upper Paleolithic more than some believe). Anatomical evidence has been used to argue that classic Neanderthals were not capable of fully articulate speech, although the discovery of an anatomically modern hyoid bone from Israel, dated to around 60,000 years ago, as well as DNA evidence (Johansson 2013) shed doubt on that claim.

MODERN *HOMO SAPIENS*

There are basically two hypotheses, with variations, used to explain the transition from archaic to anatomically modern *H. sapiens*. The "out of Africa" theory indicated that modern humans originated in Africa, then moved to other areas of the Old World and replaced archaic *H. sapiens* everywhere (Stringer and Andrews 1988). With modern DNA evidence, we can dismiss the idea of complete replacement and instead suggest partial replacement and partial gene flow between *H.s. neanderthalensis, H. sapiens,* and probably Denisovans as well as other populations yet unknown. Smith et al. (2016) propose the "assimilation model" in recognition of the Neanderthal genes present in much of the world's populations.

Similarly, the second hypothesis (called the "multiregional evolution" theory) (Wolpoff et al. 1994, 2001; Smith et al. 1989) suggests that archaic *H. sapiens* populations *everywhere* gradually evolved into AM *H. sapiens,* and that interbreeding between populations throughout the evolutionary period would have mixed the traits and prevented speciation. Again, with current DNA evidence, this hypothesis is not that different from the assimilation model. This is not parallel evolution (as often thought) as much as it is a hypothesis that recognizes gene flow and its importance in modern human evolution.

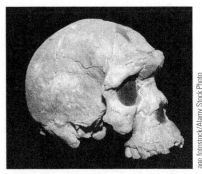

FIGURE 12.20 Herto cranium from Ethiopia, a well-preserved early modern *H. sapiens* cranium.

Although DNA evidence is vitally important in analyzing these hypotheses, we must also look at the abundant fossil remains of Neanderthals and other archaic *H. sapiens*. The specimens discovered continue the morphological changes toward modern *Homo sapiens*. The browridges are relatively small, with a vertical frontal bone. There is a feature called a "canine fossa," which is a depression in the maxilla just above the canines. Also, there is a mental eminence (chin) for the first time in human evolution. Fossils that are transitional and occurred just before AM humans were discovered in Africa and date possibly as early as 200 KYA (the site of Omo Kibish in southern Ethiopia dates to 195 KYA) (McDougall et al. 2005). A group of individuals also from Ethiopia dates to 160 to 154 KYA and exhibited a mix of characteristics, not quite modern but more modern than Neanderthals. One adult (see Figure 12.20) had a cranial capacity of 1,450 cm, which is well within the *Homo sapiens* range. White et al. (2003) placed these individuals into a new subspecies: *Homo sapiens idaltu*. The dates on these individuals predate any modern *H. s. sapiens*, and supports the origin of modern humans in Africa.

Fully AM fossils have been discovered in Africa in several localities dating from about 120 to about 80 KYA (for example, Klasies River Mouth and Border Cave in South Africa).

Some information suggests that AM humans were in Israel about 100 KYA (Stringer 1995) and therefore also predates Neanderthal populations. Skhūl Cave (see Figures 12.21 and 12.22) in Israel has been dated at about 130 to 115 KYA. Other fossils from Israel at Skhūl, Qafzeh (120 to 92 KYA), and Tabun (120 KYA) (Grun et al. 2005) suggest that anatomically modern humans were in these areas at the same time as Neanderthals, and Neanderthals, as a group, cannot be in the direct line to humans. AM *H. sapiens* have been thought to have been the only occupants of Europe by about 40 KYA (recently C14 dates of about 31 KYA have been given to modern human assemblages in the Czech Republic by Wild et al. (2005), but recent excavations in southwestern France and in southern Spain suggest that Neanderthals may have been in those areas as recently as 29 to 35 KYA. It is currently believed that AM humans were living in western Europe by about 35 KYA (Cro-Magnon dates to about 30 KYA in southern France).

FIGURE 12.21 Skhūl V. *Photo, D. L. France; cast from University of Pennsylvania*

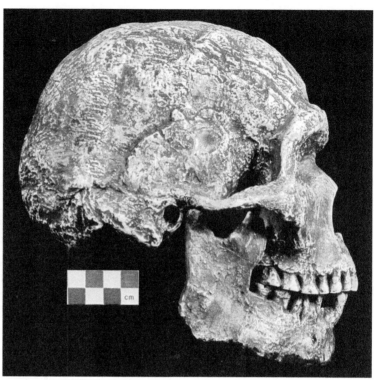

FIGURE 12.22 Skhūl V. *Photo, D. L. France; cast from University of Pennsylvania*

The data concerning archaic and AM *Homo sapiens* in China is interesting. Several sites in China have yielded AM humans. The upper cave at Zhoukoudian is dated at about 27 KYA, and Tianyuan Cave near Zhoukoudian is dated at less than 40 KYA (Remember that Jinniushan had individuals with a mix of ancient and modern characteristics at around 200 KYA!) Wolpoff (1989) states that some of the traits are inconsistent with the traditional "Out of Africa" theory because they are inconsistent with African traits.

Anatomically modern humans are exhibited in the fossil record on the north coast of Borneo by about 35 to 45 KYA (Barker et al. 2007), which may be contemporaneous with the settlement of Australia at about 50 KYA, and Hudjashov et al. (2007) believe that the current residents of Australia are descendants from a single migration. Interestingly, individuals discovered from deposits dating to 14 to 9 KYA at Kow Swamp show much more archaic traits than do current native populations.

The culture of AM *H. sapiens* in the Upper Paleolithic was remarkable relative to the cultures of previous hominins. For the first time, musical instruments, sculpture, jewelry, paintings, needles, harpoons, and spear-throwers (atlatls) appear on the fossil record. AM *H. sapiens* regularly buried their dead. Blade stone tools, which were much more varied and efficient than previous stone tools, appear in the Upper Paleolithic. The societies of the Upper Paleolithic truly represent a "cultural explosion."

The Genus *Homo*

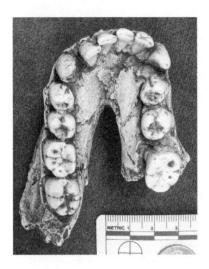

FIGURE 12.23 Lower dentition of *H. habilis*. *Photo D. L. France; cast from Wenner-Gren Foundation*

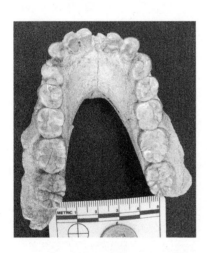

FIGURE 12.24 Lower dentition of *Australopithecus*. *Photo, D. L. France; cast from Institute of Human Origins*

1. Compare the lower dentition of *H. habilis* (Figure 12.23) with that of *Australopithecus* (Figure 12.24). How are they different?

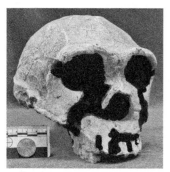

FIGURE 12.25 *H. habilis* cranium. *Photo, D. L. France; cast from National Museums of Kenya*

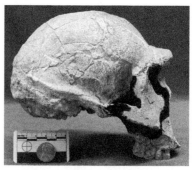

FIGURE 12.26 *H. habilis* cranium. *Photo, D. L. France; cast from National Museums of Kenya*

FIGURE 12.27a *A. africanus.* *Photo, D. L. France; cast from Wenner-Gren Foundation*

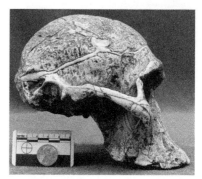

FIGURE 12.27b *A. africanus.* *Photo, D. L. France; cast from Wenner-Gren Foundation*

FIGURE 12.28a *P. robustus.* *Photo, D. L. France; cast from University of Pennsylvania*

FIGURE 12.28b *P. robustus.* *Photo, D. L. France; cast from University of Pennsylvania*

2. Compare the *H. habilis* cranium (Figures 12.25 and 12.26) with that of *A. africanus* and a robust species (Figures 12.27 and 12.28). How are they different?

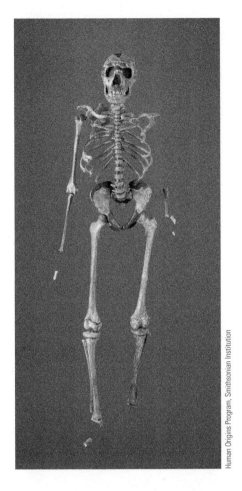

Human Origins Program, Smithsonian Institution

FIGURE 12.29 *Homo erectus,* KNM-WT 15000.

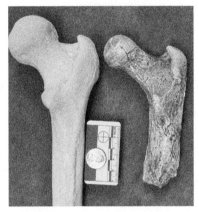

FIGURE 12.30 Proximal femur of modern human (left) and *P. robustus* (right). *Photo D. L. France; original bone (left), cast from University of Pennsylvania (right)*

3. Compare the proximal femur of the 1.6 MYA *H. erectus* specimen (Figure 12.29) with those of *Paranthropus* and modern *H. sapiens* (Figure 12.30).

4. Do you notice any other differences in the *H. erectus* specimen in Figure 12.29 from those of modern humans?

FIGURE 12.31 Later *H. erectus* specimen. *Photo, D. L. France; cast from University of Pennsylvania*

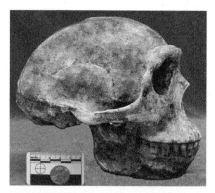

FIGURE 12.32 Later *H. erectus* specimen. *Photo, D. L. France; cast from University of Pennsylvania*

5. Compare the crania of early *H. erectus* specimens from Africa (Figures 12.25 and 12.26) with that of later *H. erectus* specimens (Figures 12.31 and 12.32). Would you support gradual morphological change, stasis, or something in between? What data might help in this assessment?

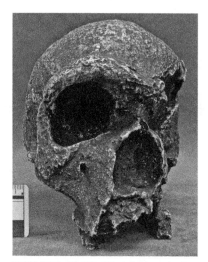

FIGURE 12.33 Steinheim skull. *Photo, D. L. France; cast from University of Pennsylvania*

FIGURE 12.34 Steinheim skull. *Photo, D. L. France; cast from University of Pennsylvania*

6. Observe the Steinheim skull (Figures 12.33 and 12.34) or any other non-Neanderthal specimen of archaic *H. sapiens*. Make a list of those characters that seem *erectus*-like and another list of those characters that seem *sapiens*-like. The cranial capacity of this specimen is about 1,000 cc.

7. Look at any Neanderthal postcranium you may have in your laboratory. Compare it with the appropriate postcranium of modern *H. sapiens*. What are the differences?

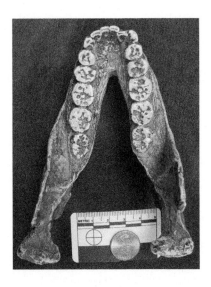

FIGURE 12.35 Unknown.
Photo, D. L. France; cast from University of Pennsylvania

8. Compare the mandible pictured in Figure 12.35 with those of other hominins discussed in this chapter. Based especially on the relative size of the cheek teeth to anterior teeth and the shape of the dental arcade, how would you classify this unknown?

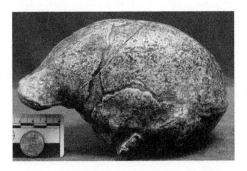

FIGURE 12.36 Unknown.
Photo, D. L. France; cast from Wenner-Gren Foundation

9. Compare the cranium pictured in Figure 12.36 with those of other hominins discussed in this chapter. How would you classify this unknown?

10. Do you think that the relatively new species designations of *H. heidelbergensis* is valid, or should it be subsumed into another species? Why or why not?

11. Develop a phylogeny that explains the Plio-Pleistocene fossils so far discovered. State why you think your phylogeny is likely correct.

12. Why do you think *Homo floresiensis* is so different from other fossils that have been discovered?

13. Do you think it likely that researchers will discover other *Homo sapiens* species? If that happens, do you think the new species will change our current thinking about evolution in the Pleistocene? How?

REEXAMINING THE ISSUES

- The early genus *Homo* is fully bipedal and exhibits increased brain size and modification of the dentition and face.
- *Homo erectus* moved out of Africa and populated many areas of the Old World.
- New genetic information casts doubt on the theory that Neanderthals are in the line leading to modern humans.
- There is still much to learn about the lineages leading to all populations of humans as we know them today.

CHAPTER 13

Anthropometry, Nonmetric Traits, and Dermatoglyphics

OBJECTIVES

1. What can we learn from taking measurements on living people and skeletal remains?

2. What are the appropriate ways to take these measurements?

3. What are nonmetric traits, and why are we interested in them?

We could take an almost infinite number of measurements of bones and of living humans (and other primates) and describe each bone or individual we study. As important as this is, however, we have to use statistics to determine what these measurements and descriptions really mean. This chapter will first introduce the instruments and methods to record living human variation and the statistics appropriate to describe that variation. We will then move to measurements and analysis of skeletal remains, and a discussion of variation in remains that we do not necessarily measure. Finally, although fingerprint analysis is usually recognized as a technique used by law enforcement in forensic identification, anthropologists have also used dermal ridge analysis in their studies, making it appropriate to discuss in this book.

Everyone knows that humans vary greatly from individual to individual. Some of that variation can be explained by the effects of environment on the genetic predispositions in size (including stature and weight and the size of the skeletal elements), and morphology (in the soft tissue and skeleton) within populations and within the sexes. In some cases, differences can be measured between the sexes and between populations. As discussed in greater detail in Chapter 15, how those differences are explained and used or misused has become inextricably intertwined with the collection of the measurements or observations and the reports generated from the statistics. Your instructor may take the opportunity to discuss these issues at the end of study of this chapter (or when you study Chapter 15).

METRIC ANALYSIS: THE LIVING

The living body is measured with the tools shown in Figures 13.1, 13.2, and 13.3, in addition to flexible tapes and other equipment. The instrument used to measure skeletal material is shown in Figure 13.4.

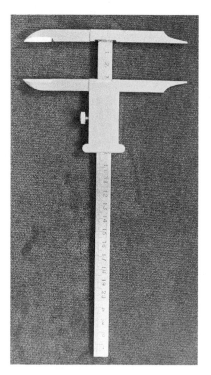

FIGURE 13.1
Sliding calipers.

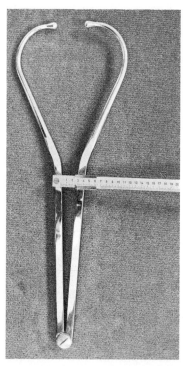

FIGURE 13.2
Spreading calipers.

FIGURE 13.3 Skinfold calipers.

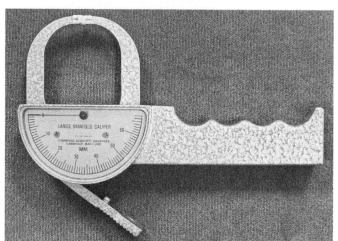

FIGURE 13.4 Osteometric board.

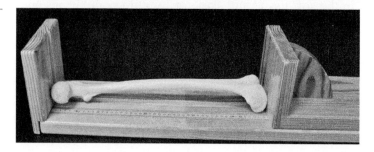

Be sure you know how to use each of these instruments, as you will use them to demonstrate the variation in living individuals, and also in skeletal material of humans and nonhumans.

The Living Body

Various measurements of the living body are useful to anthropologists, geneticists, physicians, and manufacturers of goods that fit on or around the body (clothing, car seats, and seat belts, for instance). Measurements are useful in determining the heritability of traits, the rate of growth at particular ages, the nutritional and health status of individuals, and so on. Measurements are also usually collected on infants and adolescents as they develop for comparison with national and world norms in measuring growth efficiency. You can take an almost infinite number of measurements on the human body, which are limited primarily by practicality in finding easily discovered and described landmarks.

MEASUREMENT DESCRIPTIONS

The following standard measurements are taken with spreading calipers:

1. **Head length:** Taken on the sagittal line, from between the browridges to the maximum measurement in the sagittal line of the occipital region (see Figure 13.5).

2. **Maximum head width:** The maximum width of the head, above the supramastoid and zygomatic crests (Figure 13.6).

3. **Length of nose:** From nasal root (or nasion) to tip of nose; no distorting pressure should be applied (Figure 13.7). Some spreading calipers will not accurately measure this; you may need to use sliding calipers. Use the rounded ends of the calipers.

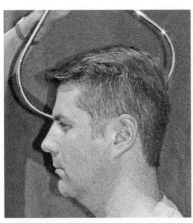

FIGURE 13.5 Head length.

FIGURE 13.6 Head width.

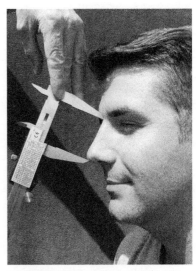

FIGURE 13.7 Nose length.

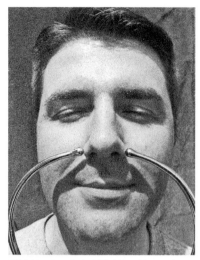

FIGURE 13.8 Width of nasal alae.

4. **Width of fleshy alae of nose:** The maximum width of alae; do not apply distorting pressure (Figure 13.8).

The following is taken with sliding or dial calipers:

5. **Length of middle finger:** Measure each hand. This should include only the combined lengths of the phalanges (do not include the metacarpal) (Figure 13.9).

The following are usually taken with an anthropometer rod or stadiometers:

6. **Standing height:** Taken in stocking feet to the vertex (highest point) of the head. The skull is in the Frankfort plane (a horizontal plane in which the lower border of the eye is on the same horizontal level as the upper border of the external auditory meatus).

7. **Sitting height:** While the subject is sitting on a table, taken from the surface of the table to the vertex of the head (Figure 13.10).

FIGURE 13.9 Middle finger length.

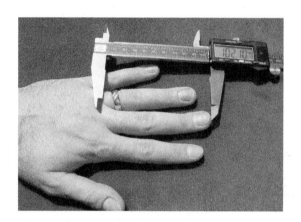

FIGURE 13.10 Sitting height.

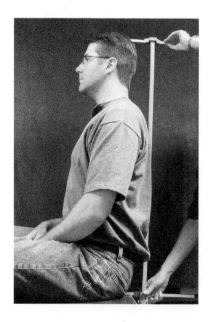

8. **Arm length:** Taken from the acromion process of the scapula to the styloid process of the ulna (each can be felt through the skin) (Figure 13.11).

The following are taken with a metal or fiberglass tape:

9. **Head circumference**: The maximum circumference of the head, not including the browridges (Figure 13.12).

10. **Upper arm circumference:** At widest point in the middle of the biceps; arm is slightly bent, and lower arm is supported so that the muscle is not flexed.

The skinfold thickness is taken on a subcutaneous fold without including muscle; the caliper is placed 1 mm below the hand gently pinching the tissue and perpendicular to the skinfold. Read the measurement within 3 seconds so that the pressure does not compress the subcutaneous tissue:

11. **Skinfold thickness of triceps area:** Taken approximately halfway down the arm while the arm is hanging relaxed at the side of the body (Figure 13.13).

12. **Subscapular skinfold thickness:** Measured laterally just below the angle of the left scapula.

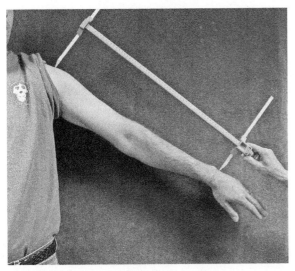

FIGURE 13.11 Arm length.

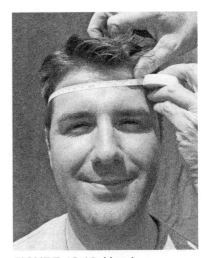

FIGURE 13.12 Head circumference.

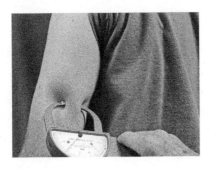

FIGURE 13.13 Skinfold thickness.

Measurement Record

Using the measurement instructions on the previous pages, complete this table for 10 individuals (5 males and 5 females), and keep track of which individual is which. Also keep track of whether the individual you have measured is left-handed or right-handed. You will use this information for exercises following a discussion of statistical techniques.

Measurement	Individual (in cm)											
	1	2	3	4	5	6	7	8	9	10	$\bar{x}$	SD
Head length	—	—	—	—	—	—	—	—	—	—	—	—
Head width	—	—	—	—	—	—	—	—	—	—	—	—
Nasal length	—	—	—	—	—	—	—	—	—	—	—	—
Nasal width	—	—	—	—	—	—	—	—	—	—	—	—
Middle finger length R	—	—	—	—	—	—	—	—	—	—	—	—
Middle finger length L	—	—	—	—	—	—	—	—	—	—	—	—
Standing height	—	—	—	—	—	—	—	—	—	—	—	—
Sitting height	—	—	—	—	—	—	—	—	—	—	—	—
Arm length	—	—	—	—	—	—	—	—	—	—	—	—
Head circumference	—	—	—	—	—	—	—	—	—	—	—	—
Upper arm circumference	—	—	—	—	—	—	—	—	—	—	—	—
Triceps skinfold	—	—	—	—	—	—	—	—	—	—	—	—
Subscapular skinfold	—	—	—	—	—	—	—	—	—	—	—	—

STATISTICAL TESTS

We need to use some basic statistics to compare the data we just gathered as well as to compare measurements we will gather from skeletal remains. Following are a few of the basic statistical tests used to describe data, but first we must discuss a pattern of normal distribution of measurements (the normal distribution).

The **normal distribution** is a probability distribution depicted graphically by a bell-shaped curve symmetrical about the mean (see Figure 13.14).

If the height of all individuals in a population were measured, those measurements would theoretically be arranged around the mean in a normal distribution. Because measurement of all individuals in a population is not usually possible, measurements are taken of a subset of that population (a sample). This sample is ideally taken at random from within the larger population, so that the sample is a true representation of the total population.

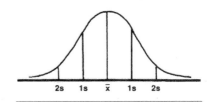

FIGURE 13.14 The normal curve.

Sample Data		Measurement A	Measurement B
Individual	1	10.0	1.2
	2	10.3	3.8
	3	11.1	1.9
	4	10.9	2.2
	5	10.5	3.2

Mean ($\bar{x}$): The average of a set of measurements, calculated by adding the measurements and dividing the sum by the number of items or individuals measured. The means of measurements of two data sets (for example, the measurements of arm length of males and females) are usually compared to determine whether or not there is a difference between two samples. To determine the mean of one sample, follow this equation:

Mean: $\bar{x}$

$$\frac{\text{sum of measurements}}{\text{no. of measurements}}$$

$$\text{Mean} = \frac{\text{sum of measurements}}{\text{number of measurments}}$$

The mean of Measurement A for the five individuals listed is

$$\frac{10.0 + 10.3 + 11.1 + 10.9 + 10.5}{5} = \frac{52.8}{5} = 10.56$$

$$\sqrt{\frac{\text{sum of } (y - \bar{y})^2}{\text{no. of measurements}}}$$

Standard deviation: S (sample), σ (population) where y = measurement, and y = sample mean.

Standard deviation (S for sample, σ for population): A gauge of variation or spread within a set of measurements. When determining the mean of a sample, the same mean could be derived from measurements that are spread a great distance from the mean or from measurements that are all very close to the mean. The standard deviation is a description of the general pattern of measurements about the mean.

One standard deviation is about 68 percent of the total area.

Two standard deviations are about 95 percent of the total area.

The area within one standard deviation about the mean in a normal distribution is approximately 68 percent of the total area; the area within two standard deviations is approximately 95 percent of the total area.

$$\text{standard deviation} = \sqrt{\frac{\text{sum of } (y - \bar{y})^2}{\text{number of measurments}}}$$

where y is a measurement, and $\bar{y}$ is the sample mean.

The standard deviation of Measurement A for the five individuals above is

Meas. A	Mean	$y - \bar{y}$	$(y - \bar{y})^2$
10.0	10.56	−0.56	0.31
10.3	10.56	−0.26	0.07
11.1	10.56	+0.54	0.29
10.9	10.56	+0.34	0.12
10.5	10.56	−0.06	0.00

$$\text{standard deviation} = \sqrt{\frac{.31 + .07 + .29 + .12 + .00}{5}} = 0.40$$

Correlation coefficient:

$$r = \frac{S_{xy}}{(S_{xx})(S_{yy})}$$

Correlation coefficient (r): A measure of linear dependence or mutual relationship between two random variables, x and y. This is a useful statistical method to show a relationship between two samples, possibly (though not necessarily) cause and effect.

A correlation coefficient of 0 indicates two variables that show no mutual relationship, whereas a coefficient of 1 or −1 shows a direct relationship or dependency between the two variables.

The formula is

$$r = \frac{S_{xy}}{(S_{xx})(S_{yy})}$$

In this example, let Measurement A = x and let Measurement B = y.

$$S_{xy} = \text{Sum of } (x)(y) - \frac{(\text{sum of } x)(\text{sum of } y)}{n}$$

$$= 129.81 - \frac{(52.8)(12.3)}{5} = -0.07$$

	Meas. A	x^2	Meas. B	y^2	xy
	10.0	100.00	1.2	1.44	12.0
	10.3	106.09	3.8	14.44	39.14
	11.1	123.21	1.9	3.61	21.09
	10.9	118.81	2.2	4.84	23.98
	10.5	110.25	3.2	10.24	33.60
Sum	52.8	558.36	12.3	34.57	129.81

$$S_{xx} = \text{Sum of } x^2 - \frac{(\text{sum of x})^2}{n}$$

$$= 558.36 - \frac{2787.84}{5} = +0.79$$

$$S_{yy} = \text{Sum of } y^2 - \frac{(\text{sum of y})^2}{n}$$

$$= 34.57 - \frac{151.29}{5} = +4.31$$

So, for this sample

$$r = \frac{S_{xy}}{(S_{xx})(S_{yy})}$$

$$r = \frac{-0.07}{(+0.79)(+4.31)} = -.02$$

is a very slight negative correlation.

Chi-square (χ^2): A measure of the statistical significance of the deviation of a frequency of occurrences from an expected frequency. For example, the frequency of male to female students in a crowd is expected to be 50 percent males to 50 percent females, but if that frequency is actually observed to be 45 percent males and 55 percent females, is that deviation within the range of normal probability, or are the differences significant enough to be linked to a specific cause or event? This test will help you determine whether or not you have a "real" difference.

Chi-square (χ^2):

$$\chi^2 = \frac{(O - E)^2}{E}$$

O = Observed frequency

E = Expected frequency

Formula:
Let O = observed frequency
     E = expected frequency

EXERCISE 13.2   NAME _____   SECTION _____   DATE _____

Statistical Analysis

1. What are the means of each sex in the measurements you took in Exercise 13.1?

2. What is the correlation between left hands and right hands in middle finger length?

3. How does middle finger length (left and right) correlate with handedness?

4. If you were to compare standing height for an individual in the morning and again in late afternoon, how do you think the measurements would compare? Why?

5. Pick one of the measurements, and have everyone in the class measure the instructor. How did your measurement results vary? This is interobserver error (the error in measurements between two or more observers).

6. Pick one measurement, and measure the same individual each day for two or three days or each week for two or three weeks.

   a. How did your measurement results vary? This is intraobserver error.

   b. Why is the recognition of intraobserver error important in either setting up a research design or calculating results?

7. If you had a large sample of individuals of the same age for maximum height, and you found that the range of measurements was large, what would you expect some of the explanations for this variability to be?

8. Would you expect maximum head length to correlate more highly with head width or upper arm circumference? Would there be a difference? Why?

METRIC ANALYSIS: OSTEOMETRY

Osteometry, as the name implies, describes the measurement of bones. Data from these measurements can be helpful in documenting various aspects of human and nonhuman remains, including, but not limited to, age, sex, population affinity, height, and nutritional status or general levels of health, particularly when compared with other individuals or other populations. This section will focus on techniques for measuring cranial and postcranial bones, and the exercises will demonstrate how these measurements can describe individuals and populations.

Postcranial Measurements

Maximum length of long bone: With all except the tibia, this is the maximum measured length taken in the osteometric board (the osteometric board was shown earlier in Figure 13.4).

Tibia: The most prominent part of the lateral half of the lateral condyle to the distal end of the medial malleolus; this does not include the intercondylar eminence.

Bicondylar length of femur: Both condyles are placed against one vertical end of the osteometric board, and the other vertical end of the osteometric board is placed against the head of the femur.

Indices

An index is the ratio of one measurement to another, expressed as a percentage. Indices have been used for decades in anthropometry, in both the living and the dead, and are still used even though multivariate statistics and other modern statistical techniques have made the index obsolete in some circumstances. An index is very useful for quick, preliminary investigations and also in describing evolutionary trends and general population variation. When using an index, however, note that a change in *any* of the parts of an index can result in a change in the value of an index.

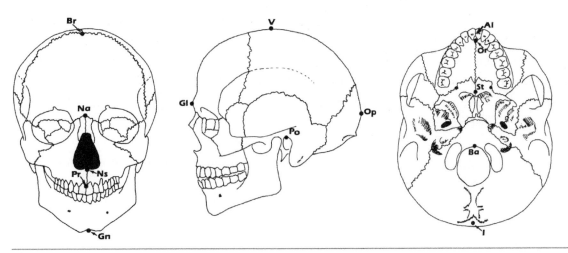

FIGURE 13.15 Landmarks on the skull.

CRANIAL LANDMARKS FROM BASS, 1987

Alveolare (Al): The apex of the septum between the upper central incisors

Basion (Ba): The midpoint of the anterior margin of the foramen magnum

Bregma (Br): The intersection of the coronal and sagittal sutures

Glabella (Gl): The most forward-projecting point of the forehead in the midline at the level of the supraorbital ridges and above the nasofrontal suture

Gnathion (Gn): Lowest midline point on the lower border of the mandible

Inion (I): An intersection in the midline with a line drawn tangent to the uppermost convexity of the right and left superior nuchal lines

Nasion (Na): The midline point of intersection of the internasal suture with the nasofrontal suture; the point where the two nasal bones and the frontal bone meet

Nasospinale (Ns): The midpoint of a line drawn connecting the two lower margins of the right and left nasal apertures

Opisthocranion (Op): The most posterior point on the cranium not on the external occipital protuberance

Orale (Or): A point on the hard palate where a line drawn tangent to the curves in the alveolar margin in back of the two medial incisor teeth crosses the midline

Porion (Po): The uppermost lateral point in the margin of the external auditory meatus

Prosthion (Pr): The most anterior point on the upper alveolar process in the midline

Staphylion (St): The midpoint of a line drawn connecting the most forward points on the curves in the posterior margin of the palate

Vertex (V): The uppermost point on the midline of the cranium when it is in the Frankfort plane

Cranial Measurements

Maximum cranial length:	From glabella to opisthocranion
Maximum cranial breadth:	The maximum measurement above the supramastoid crest
Basion-bregma height:	From basion to bregma (maximum height)
Porion-bregma height:	From porion to bregma
Bizygomatic breadth:	The maximum measurement spanning the zygomatic arches
Total facial height:	From nasion to gnathion
Upper facial height:	From nasion to alveolare
Nasal height:	From nasion to nasospinale
Nasal breadth:	Maximum breadth of the bony aperture
Palatal length:	From orale to staphylion
Palatal breadth:	Greatest transverse breadth between the outer borders of the alveolar arch at the second molars

(see Figure 13.15)

Indices on the Cranium

The following calculations demonstrate the ratios of one cranial measurement to another:

Cranial index: Measures the shape of the cranium

$$\frac{\text{Cranial Breadth}}{\text{Cranial Length}} \times 100$$

(Martin and Saller 1957; Bass 1987):

Dolichocrany	Up to 74.9 (narrow or long-headed)
Mesocrany	75.0 to 79.9 (average)
Brachycrany	80.0 to 84.9 (round-headed)
Hyperbrachycrany	85.0 and up (even more rounded)

Nasal index: Measures the shape of the nasal (bony) aperture

$$\frac{\text{Nasal Breadth}}{\text{Nasal Height}} \times 100$$

(Martin and Saller 1957; Bass 1987):

Leptorrhiny	Up to 47.9 (narrow aperture)
Mesorrhiny	48.0 to 52.9 (average or medium)
Platyrrhiny	53.0 and up (broad aperture)

Condylar index: measures the position of the foramen magnum (see landmark diagram)

$$\frac{\text{Basion to Opisthocranion}}{\text{Basion to Prosthion}} \times 100$$

Palatal index: Measures the shape of the palate (and hence of the mouth and lower face)

$$\frac{\text{Palatal Width}}{\text{Palatal Length}} \times 100$$

Supraorbital index: Measures the height of the skull

$$\frac{\text{Vertex to Superior Border of Eye}}{\text{Vertex to Inferior Border of Eye}} \times 100$$

Nuchal index: Measures the area given for the origin of nuchal muscles

$$\frac{\text{From Line Level with Inferior Border of Eye to Line with Inion}}{\text{From Vertex to Line with Inferior Border of Eye}} \times 100$$

Postcranial Indexes

The following calculations demonstrate the ratios of one postcranial measurement to another:

Brachial index: Measures the relative lengths of the upper and lower arm (use the osteometric board for these measurements)

$$\frac{\text{Length of Radius}}{\text{Length of Humerus}} \times 100$$

Crural index: Measures the relative lengths of the thigh and leg bones (use the osteometric board for these measurements)

$$\frac{\text{Length of Tibia}}{\text{Bicondylar Length of Femur}} \times 100$$

Intermembral index: Measures the relative lengths of the upper and lower limbs

$$\frac{\text{Length of Humerus} + \text{Radius}}{\text{Bicondylar Length of Femur} + \text{Tibial Length}} \times 100$$

Cranial Volume

Measurements of the cranium can be used to determine the volume of the cranium and thereby the size of the brain. This method, however, is more straightforward.

Volumetric method: To be used on complete, intact skulls

1. Plug holes and openings with cotton (except the foramen magnum).

2. Fill the cranium through the foramen magnum with suitable material (mustard seed or millet is often used).

3. Gently shake the skull to settle the seed.

4. When filled to the border of the foramen magnum, carefully empty the seed into a large volumetric cylinder. Record the volume.

Raw Data for Exercise 13.3

Following is a list of cranial measurements of maximum (glabello-occipital) length and maximum breadth for Questions 1 to 6 in Exercise 13.3.

No.	Cranium Length	Breadth	No.	Cranium Length	Breadth
1	16.4 cm	14.7 cm	11	18.5 cm	14.8 cm
2	17.1	13.8	12	18.7	13.8
3	17.6	13.8	13	18.6	13.8
4	19.1	14.3	14	17.2	13.1
5	19.7	14.0	15	19.8	13.6
6	17.6	12.6	16	18.5	13.3
7	18.9	13.7	17	16.0	12.6
8	18.7	13.3	18	17.9	14.0
9	17.4	13.4	19	17.5	12.7
10	16.1	13.8	20	17.6	12.9

Following is a list of humerus measurements from different populations to be used when answering Questions 7 to 11 in Exercise 13.3.

Population	Maximum Length No.	Mean	S.D.	Transverse Diameter of Head No.	Mean	S.D.
European American						
Male	84	32.64 cm	1.88	82	4.50 cm	0.23
Female	82	29.92	1.57	74	3.91	0.19
African American						
Male	87	33.53	1.87	81	4.50	0.24
Female	85	30.65	1.70	79	3.95	0.21
Native American (Pueblo)						
Male	89	30.69	1.19	72	4.06	0.20
Female	68	28.59	1.43	63	3.60	0.17
Native American (Arikara)						
Male	96	31.79	1.25	84	4.33	0.19
Female	86	29.54	1.17	75	3.83	0.16

EXERCISE 13.3   NAME _____   SECTION _____   DATE _____

Osteometrics

To answer the following, refer to the preceding raw data charts.

1. Use the raw data to determine the range of:

    a. The glabello-occipital length.

    b. Maximum cranial breadth.

2. Use the data to calculate:

    a. The mean glabello-occipital length.

    b. The standard deviation of the glabello-occipital length.

3. Use the data to calculate:

    a. The mean maximum cranial breadth.

    b. The standard deviation of the maximum cranial breadth.

4. Does the glabello-occipital length show a correlation with the maximum cranial breadth?

    a. Is this a positive or negative correlation? What, in words, does this mean?

    b. What is the r value for the correlation?

    c. Draw a scattergram of the relationship between cranial length and breadth. Use a separate piece of paper.

    d. What reason would you suggest for this correlation?

    e. Would you also expect glabello-occipital length to be correlated with maximum cranial height?

        With nutritional levels in the diet?

        With the sex of the individual?

5. Why should you be concerned with the standard deviation of two samples when comparing their means?

6. If you had two measurements that were greatly different from the other measurements and if you had checked to make sure they were measured correctly, would you delete them or add them to your measurements? Why?

7. What is the approximate 95 percent range for the maximum humerus length measurements for:

   a. European American males?

   b. European American females?

   c. African American males?

   d. African American females?

8. Plot the means and one standard deviation on one histogram (bar graph) for maximum length of each of the populations. Use a separate piece of paper.

9. If you had a European American humerus that measured 31 cm in maximum length, and you were asked to determine its sex, what would you say:

   a. If that humerus measured 29.92 cm?

   b. If that humerus measured 24.0 cm?

10. Plot the means and one standard deviation on one histogram for transverse diameter of the humeral head of each of the populations. Use a separate piece of paper.

11. How does the overlap of the 68 percent (one standard deviation) ranges of the transverse diameter of the humeral head compare with the overlap for the maximum length? Which of the two measurements would you be more comfortable using to determine sex? How reliable is either of the measurements in determining sex? What about determining population affinity from these measurements?

12. Repeat the previous exercises for measurements taken from your laboratory on either skeletal populations or living subjects. What are the differences between the sexes in your measurements?

13. Would you expect a relatively high correlation between different size measurements within the same body?

NONMETRIC TRAITS

Nonmetric or discontinuous traits are not measured but are rather scored as present or absent (although some nonmetric traits are scored as small, medium, or large, and sometimes as trace to complete). These traits probably have a very high genetic component, although no simple Mendelian inheritance patterns have been discovered. When we use nonmetric traits, we assume that a predisposition occurs for the inheritance of these traits and that we can infer degrees of relatedness between individuals within and between populations by the shared frequency of traits. This comparison can be "spatial," in which two individuals within or between populations from about the same time period are compared, or the comparisons can be "temporal," in which individuals from different time periods are compared. Nonmetric traits are useful in part because most of the traits described seem to be less affected by environment than are metric measurements.

You can compare the frequency of a single trait between individuals, but multivariate (involving more than one variable in one test) statistics are now commonly used to analyze the additive effects of combinations of nonmetric traits. Univariate statistical tests can be performed quickly, but multivariate tests are performed with computers because of the complicated time-consuming nature of the computations.

The nonmetric traits described here (Figures 13.16 to 13.20) are chosen because of the low level of interobserver and intraobserver error. The frequencies for some of the traits are given; for more information, see Hauser and De Stefano (1989). Many nonmetric traits that are not listed here are also commonly scored.

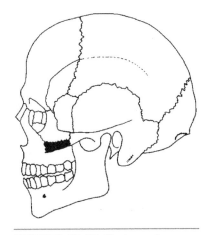

FIGURE 13.16 Os japonicum.

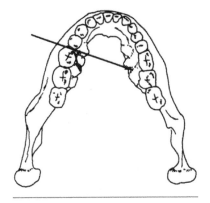

FIGURE 13.17 Mandibular torus.

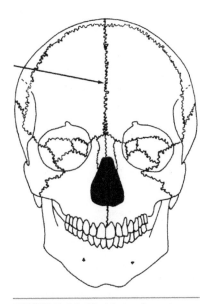

FIGURE 13.18 Metopic suture.

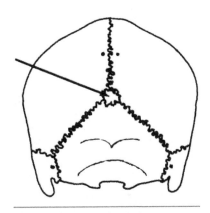

FIGURE 13.19 Ossicle at lambda.

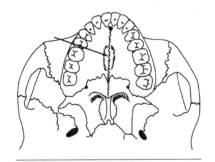

FIGURE 13.20 Palatine torus.

NONMETRIC TRAIT FREQUENCIES

Numbers refer to sides scored

	Combined Frequency	Males No.	%	Females No.	%	
Os japonicum						
North American Caucasians	1.4	154	2.6	124	0.0	(Corruccini 1974)
NW Coast	0.2	149	0.0	137	0.3	(Finnegan 1972)
Arizona	0.2	245	0.0	347	0.3	(Birkby 1973*)
African Americans	5.5	198	4.0	166	7.2	(Corruccini 1974)
Japanese	8.8	282	7.1	174	11.4	(Mouri 1976)
Indian (Uttar Pradesh)	0.4	Total N = 235**				
Ainu	24.0	116	31.0	76	13.2	(Dodo 1974)
Mandibular torus						
North American Caucasians	7.2	77	6.5	62	8.1	(Corruccini 1974)
North American Indians						
NW Coast	17.5	Total N = 618				(Finnegan 1972)
Arizona	28.6	282	34.6	387	4.0	(Birkby 1973*)
African Americans	6.6	99	6.1	83	7.2	(Corruccini 1974)
Japanese	29.2	151	26.7	90	33.3	(Mouri 1976)
Indian (Uttar Pradesh)	30.4	Total N = 158**				
Metopic suture						
North American Caucasians	7.2	77	6.5	62	8.1	(Corruccini 1974)
North American Indians						
NW Coast	2.8	149	2.0	137	3.6	(Finnegan 1972)
Arizona	0.7	159	0.6	240	0.8	(Birkby 1973*)
African Americans	2.2	99	2.0	83	2.4	(Corruccini 1974)
Japanese	9.1	151	6.6	90	13.3	(Mouri 1976)
Indian (Uttar Pradesh)	16.0	Total N = 119**				
Ossicle at lambda						
North American Caucasians	10.1	77	9.1	62	11.3	(Corruccini 1974)
North American Indians						
NW Coast	8.7	149	7.3	137	10.2	(Finnegan 1972)
Arizona	25.8	116	19.8	178	29.8	(Birkby 1973*)
African Americans	12.6	99	13.1	83	12.1	(Corruccini 1974)
Japanese	6.9	119	9.2	84	3.6	(Mouri 1976)
Indian (Uttar Pradesh)	23.5	Total N = 115**				

Palatine torus

North American Caucasians	23.7	77	4.3	62	35.5	(Corruccini 1974)
North American Indians						
NW Coast	14.8	149	9.3	137	20.4	(Finnegan 1972)
Arizona	6.5	113	7.1	163	6.1	(Birkby 1973*)
African Americans	15.4	99	11.1	83	20.5	(Corruccini 1974)
Japanese	32.8	151	35.8	90	27.8	(Mouri 1976)
Indian (Uttar Pradesh)	26.7	Total N = 116**				

*Recalculated in Hauser and De Stefano, 1989.

**Combined males and females.

RECORDING FORM

Use this recording form to score the nonmetric traits discussed in this chapter on the cranial material in your laboratory. You may also research other nonmetric traits and use those instead.

Individuals	1 L R	2 L R	3 L R	4 L R	5 L R	6 L R	7 L R	8 L R	9 L R	10 L R

EXERCISE 13.4   NAME _____   SECTION _____   DATE _____

Nonmetric Analysis

1. Can scientists extricate themselves from discussions of morality and social conscience when "doing" science?

    Is it possible for a scientist to be unaffected by the concerns of society at the time that the science is occurring (that is, can the scientist escape from the "concerns of the day")?

    At what point in matters of social conscience should a scientist refuse to conduct research (give examples)? Has that point changed in history?

2. What are the means and standard deviations of the following traits listed in the table?

	Mean		Standard Deviation (SD)	
	L	R	L	R
Os japonicum				
Mandibular torus				
Metopic suture				
Ossicle at lambda				
Palatine torus				

3. If you calculated the frequency of os japonicum in an unknown population to be 1.4 percent, would you be able to identify the population from which the population was genetically derived? Why or why not?

4. If you discovered os japonicum in an individual, would you be able to determine the group from which that individual came based on this trait alone? Why or why not?

5. The mandibular and palatine tori can be detected in the living. Calculate the frequency of occurrence of each of these traits in a large sample of your school colleagues. Are there significant differences in frequency with population affinity? Sex? If so, describe them.

6. Are there significant correlations in frequency of occurrence between any of the traits listed on the preceding chart? If so, describe them.

DERMATOGLYPHICS

The study of patterns of dermal ridges present on the fingers and palms of the hands and toes and soles of the feet of humans and other primates is called dermatoglyphics. These ridges even occur on the naked skin of the prehensile tail of some New World monkeys, and the presence of dermal ridges has a selective advantage in that they provide a surface of greater friction than if there were no ridges. The pattern of these ridges varies greatly, however, which is an indication that there are no strong selective advantages in favor of a particular pattern. Studies of fingerprint patterns in related individuals indicate that about 90 percent of the pattern is inherited (Brues 1990), most likely through a complex polygenic mode, and because several congenital disorders that cause alterations of chromosomal numbers also have specific effects on dermal ridge patterns, these alleles probably occur on different chromosomes (Brues 1990). There are some population differences between ridge patterns as well (see Table 13.1).

Aside from the common practice of comparing unknown latent fingerprints at the scene of a crime to a collection of known individuals to identify who was at that particular location, there are other uses for studying dermal ridge patterns. Because of the high heritability of configurations, one can study familial inheritance patterns as well.

In classifying fingerprints, the patterns are initially grouped into three categories: arches, loops, and whorls (see Figures 13.21 to 13.27). Along with this, the ridge count method is probably the most widely used for categorizing fingerprints.

Core At the innermost ridge of the pattern, at the approximate center of the pattern.

Delta or triradius The point at which three ridges diverge or the point nearest the center of the divergence of the type lines.

Type lines The innermost ridges that surround the pattern area.

Ridge count The number of ridges transecting a straight line drawn from the core to the delta.

Total ridge count The total number of ridges on all fingers. In prints with whorls, only one ridge count per finger is added to the total.

Hints: Arches have no ridge count.

Loops have a single delta and hence a single line for a ridge count.

Whorls have two deltas, and therefore will have two lines drawn for ridge counts.

Loops can open (or flow if the delta is thought of as analogous to the delta of a river), toward the ulna (ulnar loops), or toward the radius (radial loops).

TABLE 13.1   Percentage Ranges of Types of Fingerprints among Human Populations

Group	Arches	Loops	Whorls
Africans	3–12%	53–73%	20–40%
Europeans	0–9%	63–76%	20–42%
East Asians	1–5%	43–56%	44–54%
Australian Aborigines	0–1%	28–46%	52–73%
Native Americans	2–8%	46–61%	35–57%
San (Bushmen)	13–16%	66–68%	15–21%

Adapted from Coon (1965, p. 261)

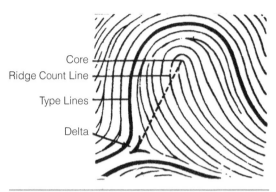

FIGURE 13.21 Print properties. *Drawing, The Science of Fingerprints, Classification and Uses, U.S. Government Printing Office, Washington, D.C.*

FIGURE 13.22 Arch. *Drawing, The Science of Fingerprints, Classification and Uses, U.S. Government Printing Office, Washington, D.C.*

FIGURE 13.23 Loop. *Drawing, The Science of Fingerprints, Classification and Uses, U.S. Government Printing Office, Washington, D.C.*

FIGURE 13.24 Whorl. *Drawing, The Science of Fingerprints, Classification and Uses, U.S. Government Printing Office, Washington, D.C.*

FIGURE 13.25 Tented arch. *Drawing, The Science of Fingerprints, Classification and Uses, U.S. Government Printing Office, Washington, D.C.*

FIGURE 13.26 Double loop. *Drawing, The Science of Fingerprints, Classification and Uses, U.S. Government Printing Office, Washington, D.C.*

FIGURE 13.27 Central pocket loop. *Drawing, The Science of Fingerprints, Classification and Uses, U.S. Government Printing Office, Washington, D.C.*

Dermatoglyphics

FIGURE 13.28 Unknown.
Drawing, The Science of
Fingerprints, Classification and
Uses, *U.S. Government Printing
Office, Washington, D.C.*

1.   What is the type of fingerprint in Figure 13.28?

What is the ridge count?

FIGURE 13.29 Unknown.
Drawing, The Science of
Fingerprints, Classification and
Uses, *U.S. Government Printing
Office, Washington, D.C.*

2.   What is the type of fingerprint in Figure 13.29?

What is the ridge count?

FIGURE 13.30 Unknown. *Drawing,* The Science of Fingerprints, Classification and Uses, *U.S. Government Printing Office, Washington, D.C.*

3. What is the type of fingerprint in Figure 13.30?

    What is the ridge count?

4. Can the population from which an individual is derived be estimated by the type of print on that individual's fingers?

    Why or why not?

5. Use the following form to record the pattern of the prints from your fingers. The friction pads extend on the sides of the fingers toward the nail, so the fingers should be rolled from side to side on the ink pad and then on paper.

Digit	Left Hand Classification	Left Hand Ridge Count	Right Hand Classification	Right Hand Ridge Count
I (thumb)	_____	_____	_____	_____
II	_____	_____	_____	_____
III	_____	_____	_____	_____
IV	_____	_____	_____	_____
V	_____	_____	_____	_____

REEXAMINING THE ISSUES

- It is important to use the correct methods and instruments to measure skeletal elements and living individuals.
- It is important to understand the statistical tests employed to describe the relationships between individuals and populations in measured characteristics and in nonmetric traits.
- Variation in humans is an important consideration when deriving standards for age, sex, ancestry, stature, and so on.

CHAPTER 14

Abnormalities in the Skeleton: Pathology, Anomalies, and Intentional Modification

OBJECTIVES

1. What are the ways in which the skeleton reacts to disease processes?

2. How can we diagnose the direction of force in blunt trauma?

3. Can the skeleton be modified intentionally?

In this chapter, we will study some of the more common pathology and anomalies in the skeleton, although we certainly will not exhaust the topic, as there are volumes of information written about these topics. The goal in this book is to merely touch on some examples you are most likely to see, with some clues about how to identify them as pathology, anomalies, intentional modification, or normal variation in the skeleton. The pathology more commonly associated with medicolegal investigations will be explored further in Chapter 15.

Why do we study these processes? Obviously, it is important to know how to determine what happened to an individual during life or at about the time of death, but frankly, some of them are just interesting! In lectures about physical anthropology, students pay particular attention to the ways in which the skeleton is altered by disease pathogens, genetic abnormalities, and intentional modification (either by violence or by gentle pressures). We are all drawn to the abnormal.

We also need to study how a body reacts to various diseases because even if we cannot immediately identify the pathogen responsible, we still need to know how to accurately describe what is happening in the bone or tooth for later diagnosis (it is always important to precisely describe what a bone or tooth looks like because diagnoses can change but the description may not). Remember that this is one of the basic tenets of the scientific method.

INTRODUCTION

Throughout most of this book, we have investigated the normal human and nonhuman skeleton, so we should know by now how to recognize them. When something abnormal happens to bone and teeth, however, the classification into genus and species could be incorrect, or the abnormality may be so extreme that a bone may not even look like bone!

We will begin by investigating various pathological processes (that is, processes that are harmful to individuals). We will then discuss a few anomalies commonly (and a few not so commonly) seen in the skeleton and teeth. These are not necessarily harmful to individuals, but they are unusual. We will complete the chapter by discussing some of the ways in which cultures or individuals intentionally modify their skeletons and teeth, both while an individual is alive and after death.

PATHOLOGY

Pathology is a term that refers to many processes that are harmful to an individual. These can include disease, fractures, sharp injury, and other insults to a person, although in this book we will discuss the reactions of bone to those processes.

Disease Agents

Disease agents can be infectious, usually bacterial if it makes changes to bone, although some bacterial infections are not contagious. They can also be noninfectious as with cancer, anemia, or many other conditions.

Infectious Processes Many of the manifestations of disease in present times are different from those seen in skeletal remains from even 100 years ago. The discovery of penicillin in 1929 and its general use during World War II, as well as the discovery of other antibiotics, have changed the course of medicine, so that in most cases, the bony changes that used to occur as a result of bacterial infections are not as severe, and most infections do not even get to the point at which they infect bone. However, antibiotic-resistant strains of bacteria have evolved in part because of the overuse and misuse of antibiotics for even minor infections (see Chapter 2 for the ways in which this could occur), so some infectious processes are progressing in the body more than they might have a few years ago. Having said that, however, the reactions to bacterial infections in bone are still usually not as severe as what were seen during, for example, the time of the American Civil War. Even so, anthropologists studying human remains still have to know what disease processes are likely to do to bone because we do not always look at modern human remains.

It is often difficult to diagnose the specific pathogen responsible for disease changes to bone, as bone can react to the entire disease spectrum in limited ways: the addition of new bone by osteoblastic activity, the destruction of existing bone by osteoclastic activity, or a combination of the two (see Chapter 4 for further discussions about osteoblastic and osteoclastic activity). In some cases, both the osteoblasts and osteoclasts are more active in different areas of the body, and in some cases the amount of bone is constant, but the shape of the bone may change relative to its normal morphology. Experienced anthropologists and pathologists will describe the changes seen in the entire skeleton, as the focal sites for bony change may be different for different pathogens or processes. As stated earlier, remember that it is more important to accurately describe the changes you see than to diagnose the specific pathogen.

Figure 14.1 shows the effects of a bacterial infection on a human humerus. This is obviously a pathogen that promotes osteoclastic activity, but interestingly, it also promotes osteoblastic activity, as the body is trying to react to the stress of the infection. The original bone shaft is essentially sequestered (like a jury in a trial is sequestered and not allowed to speak to anyone outside of the jury, and in fact this shaft of bone is called a **sequestrum**). The sequestrum is isolated from the rest of the body by a shell called an **involucrum**. Often the involucrum is penetrated by holes called **cloaca** (see Figure 14.2), which are areas from which the pus from an infection exits the bone. Figure 14.3 shows a proximal tibia and fibula and a bacterial infection resulting from the amputation of the distal tibia and fibula during the Civil War after the soldier was shot in the lower leg. Note that there is no sequestrum or involucrum in this example (according to historical records, this individual's distal tibia and fibula were exposed and "unhealthy fluids" were flowing from the infected stump).

FIGURE 14.1 Infection in humerus. *Photo, D. L. France; materials curated by the National Museum of Health and Medicine*

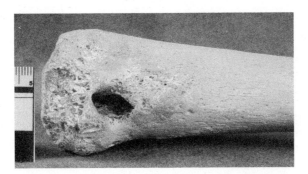

FIGURE 14.2 Cloaca in proximal tibia. *Photo, D. L. France; specimens curated by the National Museum of Natural History*

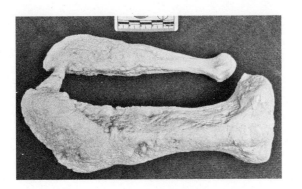

FIGURE 14.3 Proximal tibia and fibula showing infection. *Photo, D. L. France; cast of original curated by the National Museum of Health and Medicine*

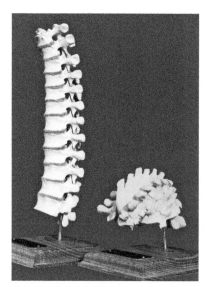

FIGURE 14.4 Effects of tuberculosis on thoracic vertebral column (right). Normal thoracic column is on the left. *Photo, D. L. France; diseased thoracic column from National Museum of Health and Medicine*

Figure 14.4 displays the effects of tuberculosis on thoracic vertebrae. Tuberculosis is an airborne disease that affects the lungs, and if it is not contained, it will spread to the surrounding soft and hard tissue (ribs, vertebrae). Because tuberculosis is primarily an osteolytic process, as it progresses in the vertebral column, it makes the bodies of the vertebrae weaker, and they may ultimately collapse. As the disease wanes, the osteoclastic activity wanes, and the body may attempt to stabilize the vertebrae by osteoblastic activity (and in fact, the vertebrae in Figure 14.4 are fused into one piece). Figure 14.5 may represent a tuberculosis lesion (this has been variously diagnosed) in the cranium.

The preceding osteoblastic and osteoclastic activity describes infections in bone, but the periosteum can also be affected by bacterial infections. When it is inflamed, it is called **periostitis**. It can be caused by something penetrating the skin and passing the pathogen to the periosteum, or it can be a more generalized infection that causes periostitis in multiple locations in the body. This can become quite severe and can spread to the underlying bone. Figure 14.6 shows an example of periostitis in a tibia.

Figure 14.7 represents a different kind of infection. Syphilis is caused by a treponemal organism (a spiral-shaped bacterium) that enters the body through skin or mucosal membranes. It can progress from soft-tissue infection in primary syphilis to tertiary syphilis, which attacks brain tissue and the skeleton, and obviously promotes osteoclastic activity.

FIGURE 14.5 Possible tuberculosis lesion in cranium. *Photo, D. L. France; material from San Diego Museum of Man*

FIGURE 14.6 Periostitis in tibia. *Photo, D. L. France; cast of original from San Diego Museum of Man*

FIGURE 14.7 Syphilis in cranial section. *Photo, D. L. France; cast from specimen at National Museum of Health and Medicine*

Infections also result from tooth decay. If the bacteria within dental caries move into the pulp cavity, it can spread easily to the alveolus and beyond. Figure 14.8 shows dental caries (cavities), while Figure 14.9 represents an abscess caused by dental decay.

Cancers are generally classified as either benign (or not rapidly spreading or life-threatening) or malignant (usually rapidly spreading and more dangerous to the individual). Cancers of bone more often start as a soft-tissue tumor that spreads to the bone (as a **metastasis**). A couple of forms of cancer of bone are shown here (Figures 14.10 and 14.11), but cancer of bone can manifest itself in many different ways. They can be either primarily osteolytic or osteogenic.

Other Conditions Blood-supply problems or interruptions caused by anemia (possibly) or by other agents can result in more porotic bone than normal. When accompanied by a thickening of the bone, it is termed *porotic hyperostosis*. (Figure 14.12 shows a dramatic example of porotic hyperostosis.) Cribra orbitalia (see Figure 14.13) is occasionally seen (particularly in younger individuals) and is probably an early example of porotic hyperostosis.

Developmental problems can arise in various ways. They can be caused by genetic abnormalities passed from the parents, but they can also arise from abnormal conditions during the development of the fetus in the uterus. The latter can be caused by, for example, too much heat (pregnant women sitting in hot tubs during pregnancy is a recognized cause of some spinal abnormalities), altered chemistry in the blood (for example, thalidomide was a drug used to decrease the effects of "morning sickness" in pregnancy, and often led to undeveloped or misshapen limbs), or other environmental problems.

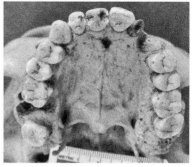

FIGURE 14.8 Dental caries. *Photo, D. L. France; material from National Museum of Natural History*

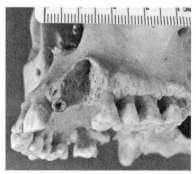

FIGURE 14.9 Abscess caused by dental decay. *Photo, D. L. France; material from National Museum of Natural History*

FIGURE 14.10 Metastasis in the femur of an individual with prostate cancer.

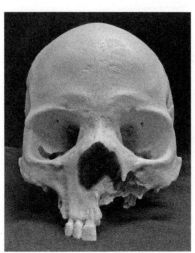

FIGURE 14.11 Cancer of the maxilla, an osteoclastic condition.

FIGURE 14.12 Porotic hyperostosis. *Photo, D. L. France; specimen from National Museum of Natural History*

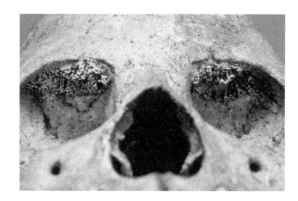

FIGURE 14.13 Cribra orbitalia.
Photo, D. L. France; material curated by the National Museum of Health and Medicine

FIGURE 14.14 Anencephaly.
Photo, D. L. France; cast of specimen curated by the National Museum of Health and Medicine

A pregnant woman can transmit the Zika virus to the developing fetus, which can cause microcephaly, or an abnormally small brain. Because the growth of the cranium responds to the growth of the brain, the crania of these infants are also abnormally small.

Problems in the developing skeleton can be as severe as anencephaly (see Figure 14.14), in which the brain (and the cranium) does not develop *in utero,* and the child dies within a few days after birth (a child cannot survive this condition). Other developmental issues, including dwarfism (see Figure 14.15), scoliosis (a lateral bending of the spine, as shown in Figure 14.16), or kyphosis (an anteroposterior bending of the spine), cleft palate (see Figure 14.17), clubfeet, or missing or altered limbs, may not be fatal, but may have a serious impact on the quality of life of an individual.

Developmental problems can also occur after the birth of an infant. Chapter 4 discusses the effects of malnutrition and disease on the development of bones (with growth arrest lines) and teeth (with enamel hypoplasias). Rickets (see Figure 14.18) is a condition in which calcium is not being applied to the growing skeleton, and the bones become curved (particularly if they support weight).

FIGURE 14.15 Normal and dwarf femur. *Photo, D. L. France; materials curated by the National Museum of Health and Medicine*

FIGURE 14.16 Severe scoliosis. *Photo, D. L. France; cast of specimen curated by the University of Colorado*

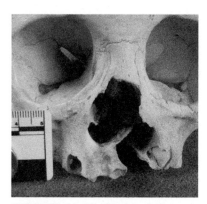

FIGURE 14.17 Cleft palate. *Photo, D. L. France; material curated by the National Museum of Natural History*

Mechanical Processes

Osteologists, anthropologists, and pathologists see many types of mechanical insults. These include blunt trauma, sharp injuries, gunshot wounds, and even combinations of these forces. For example, one can often see a combination of blunt and sharp trauma to bone if a sharp instrument (such as a saber or hatchet) both cuts and fractures the bone. Victims of plane crashes or building explosions sometimes exhibit injuries from many different types of forces.

Bone is elastic in life (because of the organic component) and can "bounce back" from many mechanical forces, particularly if the stress is slow to build and contains little power. If the force contains a great deal of power applied quickly, bone will fracture before it has a chance to exhibit its elastic qualities. Slow-loading, or slower-impact forces produce more elastic response from bone before it fractures.

Fractures and Blunt Trauma Such injuries can, of course, be accidental, as in a fall, for example, or they can be intentional. Fractures can be **incomplete**, in which the bone is not completely broken into two or more pieces. A "greenstick" fracture is this type of fracture and is particularly common in young individuals, in whom there is more organic component as the bone is growing and more bending is allowed before fracture. Fractures can also be a simple fracture or more complicated **comminuted** (fractured into many pieces) or **compound** (in which the broken ends of the bone erupt through the skin). Blunt trauma is, as its name implies, damage caused to bone or teeth by objects with relatively broad surfaces, as opposed to a sharp instrument. This is usually a relatively slow-loading force (that is, it builds relatively slowly) and can cause significant deformation of the bone before the bone fractures. Often at least a portion of this deformation remains even after the bone is cleaned, which sometimes makes it more difficult to reconstruct the fragments.

Blunt trauma in tubular bone often results in the separation of wedge-shaped fragments of bone, as bone can withstand compression forces to a greater degree than it can withstand tensile forces (forces that pull bone apart) (see Figure 14.19 for an example). Be careful when trying to determine the direction of force in a tubular bone. It has been a common mistake in textbooks to describe the results of force in a tubular bone as the same as a gunshot wound in either tubular bone or the cranium. See Figure 14.20 for an example of blunt trauma in a human cranium that resulted in plastic deformation and a complex fracture pattern.

Complex fracture patterns can sometimes contain clues as to which blow(s) occurred first, which occurred second, and so on (particularly in crania). Fracture lines in fresh bone usually radiate away from the point of initial impact, hence they are called "radiating fracture lines." Radiating fracture lines from multiple injuries usually do not cross each other but stop at other fractures or cranial sutures

FIGURE 14.18 Rickets in tibia. *Photo, D. L. France; material from National Museum of Natural History*

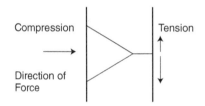

FIGURE 14.19 Reactions of tubular bone to stress.

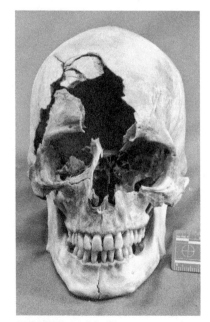

FIGURE 14.20 Blunt trauma in cranium.

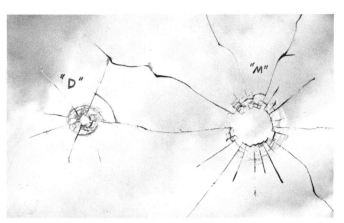

FIGURE 14.21 Fracture interrupted by another fracture in glass. *Photo, D. L. France; demonstration by Wayne Bryant.* *Key: D = 2nd shot; M = 1st shot*

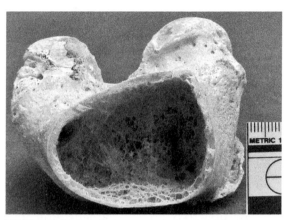

FIGURE 14.22 Osteoporosis in distal femur.

FIGURE 14.23 Stabilized fracture at neck of femur.

because the force transmitted through the radiating fracture lines is suddenly dissipated when it reaches a suture or another crack. (See Figure 14.21 for an example of this in plate glass. Although the fractures in this example are caused by gunshots, notice the interaction of the fracture lines.) Depending on the degree of force and the area of bone, concentric rings may also radiate away from the point of initial injury (this is like dropping a pebble into a pond). These are also helpful in identifying the initial point of contact even if you no longer have that part of the bone with the point of contact. This is also the way in which fresh bone injuries are distinguished from dry bone damage. Trauma to dry bone usually results in fractures with ragged edges and without the radiating fracture lines or concentric rings.

Degenerative changes in the skeleton can also lead to mechanical manifestations of force. They can be caused by disease, malnutrition, or old age, and are characterized by an imbalance in the osteoblastic/osteoclastic activities. Osteoporosis, for example, is a thinning of the cortical bone. It is caused by too much osteoclastic activity and is more prevalent in postmenopausal women. Figure 14.22 illustrates how thin the cortical bone in the distal femur of a 93-year-old woman can be (this was from a woman who donated her body to medicine). The cortical bone of this femur was so thin and brittle that even mild pressure could fracture it. One hears often of an older woman "falling and breaking her hip." But actually, often the event occurs the other way around: a person may step off of a curb and the stress on the neck of the femur may be just enough with the thinner bones of osteoporosis that the femur will fracture at the neck (see Figure 14.23). Degenerative joint disease can occur with increased age and/or with trauma. Figures 14.24a, b, and c are photographs of the knee joint of the woman from Figure 14.22, and illustrate what happens when the joint degenerates, the cartilage of the knee disintegrates, and bone moves against bone. When this occurs, the joint surfaces begin to break

FIGURE 14.24a Arthritic knee of femur from Figure 14.22.

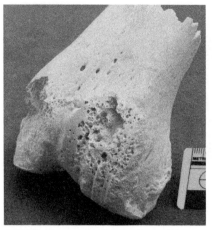

FIGURE 14.24b Arthritic femur from Figure 14.22. Notice breakdown of joint surface.

FIGURE 14.24c Posterior patella from same woman as in Figure 14.22.

down (causing the ruffled appearance), and polishing (**eburnation**) begins as the reaction of bone rubbing on bone. Figures 14.25 and 14.26 show increased bone growth along the spinal column. These areas of extra bone growth are called **osteophytes.**

Dislocations occur at any joint, depending on the relative stability of the joint and the strength of the ligaments and tendons surrounding the joint. Figures 14.27a and b show a long-term "unreduced" (that is, it was not put back into proper position) dislocation at the shoulder. Notice the modifications of the scapula where the humeral head

FIGURE 14.25 Sequence of osteophytic development in vertebrae. *Photo, D. L. France; specimens curated by the National Museum of Natural History*

FIGURE 14.26 Significant osteophyte development in cervical vertebrae.

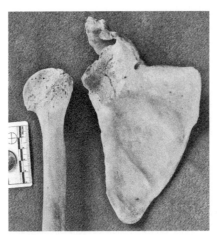

FIGURE 14.27a Dislocated shoulder. *Photo, D. L. France; specimens curated by the National Museum of Natural History*

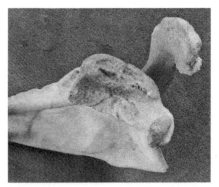

FIGURE 14.27b Glenoid fossa of dislocated shoulder. *Photo, D. L. France; specimens curated by the National Museum of Natural History*

essentially created a new joint surface. Dislocations at the shoulder are more common than at the femoral head because the acetabulum is much deeper, and the ligaments (including the ligamentum teres) are so strong that it is much more difficult to displace. When it is dislocated, it is very difficult to reduce because the strong ligaments and tendons then hold the femoral head *out* of position.

Sharp Injury Cut marks are caused when a sharp object incises bone. On close inspection (with a dissection microscope or scanning electron microscope), cut marks typically are V-shaped, or have a series of V shapes (as if made by stone tools that have a series of parallel cutting edges along the worked edges). See Figure 14.28 for an example of the series of cuts caused by a stone tool. Vascular grooves (most often the grooves along the lateral aspects of the frontal bone) are often mistaken for cut marks, but they have a rounded or U shape in cross section (see Figure 14.29 for a photograph of a vascular groove). They are caused by gentle pressure of a blood vessel against the bone (the bone responds

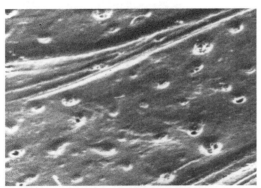

FIGURE 14.28 Scanning electron micrograph of cuts made by stone knife (10X). *Photo, Colorado State University S.E.M. Laboratory*

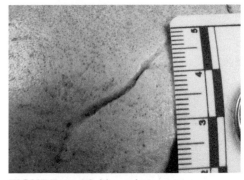

FIGURE 14.29 Vascular groove on frontal bone. *Photo, D. L. France; specimens curated by the National Museum of Natural History*

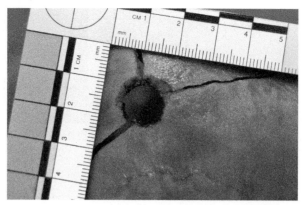

FIGURE 14.30 Rodent tooth marks on bone.

FIGURE 14.31 Gunshot entry wound in cranium.

to gentle pressure by "molding" itself to that pressure—more about this later). Rodent tooth marks are also sometimes mistaken for cut marks on bone, but they are typically paired and have a square cross section (see Figure 14.30).

Sharp force injuries usually combine cuts with force, so that one sees a V cross section with compacted bone near the center of the cut and often lifted and somewhat displaced edges. These are often insults created by an axe, saber, or other relatively heavy sharp instrument.

Gunshot Wounds More will be discussed about the different types of gunshot wounds in Chapter 15, but they vary widely by the caliber (size) of the projectile (usually, but not always, a bullet), and they are projected by a wide variety of explosive forces. They are somewhat predictable in that the missile usually creates a smaller opening at the entrance and a larger opening as it exits (that is, the missile carries a "plug" of bone with it as it travels through the bone). With a round missile, one can liken the effect to the pattern of a small BB shot through a plate glass window. If the shot is coming from outside the building, the cone of glass will be taken away from the side inside the building (see Figure 14.21). In this way, the direction of travel can often (but not always!) be determined by looking at the direction of beveling in the bone (see Figures 14.31 and 14.32).

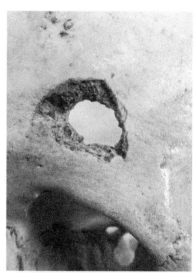

FIGURE 14.32 Gunshot exit wound in cranium.

Healing of Bone How do we determine whether or not an individual has survived a mechanical insult to bone? In all of the preceding examples, the edges left by the insult are sharp. The body reacts to fractures by immediately forming a soft-tissue callus around the point of fracture, and the bone quickly (it is noticeable with a dissection microscope within a few days) reinforces this callus with a loosely woven bone bridge. The process of remodeling this quickly formed bone begins immediately and will proceed until the morphology of the bone approaches the normal condition. The edges of the fracture at this point are becoming smoother and more rounded. The fracture is stable within a few weeks (the physician requires a person to have a cast on the bone for about six weeks to

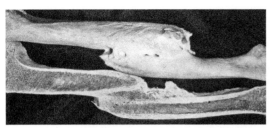

FIGURE 14.33a Stable fracture, outside (above) and inside (below). Notice the original bone shaft segments. *Photo, D. L. France; materials curated by the National Museum of Health and Medicine*

FIGURE 14.33b Healed displaced fracture of clavicle.

be sure it is stable), depending on the health, age, and nutritional status of the individual. See Figures 14.33a and b for examples of healed fractures of bone. Although these are displaced fractures, the fracture site is healed and stable.

If a fractured bone is not stabilized and allowed to heal as described previously, sometimes the fractured ends never join, and they are allowed to constantly rub against one another. This can form a **pseudoarthrosis,** or false joint (like the dislocated shoulder shown in Figures 14.27a and b). The edges usually become rounded and sometimes show eburnation at the "joint" surface.

ANOMALIES

Anomalies are odd things that happen to bones and teeth that are not necessarily injurious to the individual. For example, some developmental problems with dentition may not even be known to the individual. Figure 14.34 shows an "occult" tooth obviously growing in the wrong direction. This individual also had a "pegged" tooth (a tooth that has an incompletely formed crown) and a cleft palate (shown in a more severe form in Figure 14.17), although not all occult teeth are accompanied by pathological conditions. Figure 14.35 shows a "pegged" tooth.

Figure 14.36 shows an anomaly on the occipital bone of a man from the island of Tinian. It has been variously described as "occupational" effects from the overuse of muscles that insert in this area, to a variation due to a genetic predisposition in this population. It could be a combination of both (Gary Heathcote, personal communication).

An osteoma is a benign bone growth that can occur on the outside or the inside of the cranium. See Figure 14.37 for an example of a button osteoma on a cranium.

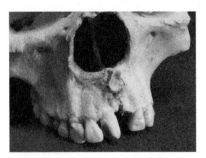

FIGURE 14.34 Occult teeth. *Photo, D. L. France; material from San Jose State University*

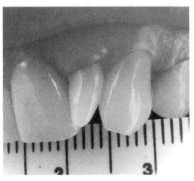

FIGURE 14.35 Pegged tooth.

INTENTIONAL MODIFICATION

The kinds of intentional modification presented here often do not result in pathological changes in the skeleton, but sometimes they do, even if that is unintentional (such as surgical intervention in the cranium). A few examples of each are presented.

FIGURE 14.36 Anomalous growths on occipital bone. *Photo, D. L. France; cast from material loaned from Gary Heathcote*

FIGURE 14.37 Osteoma. *Photo, D. L. France; specimens curated by the National Museum of Natural History*

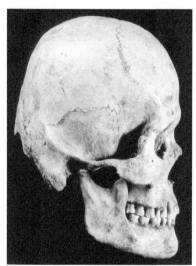

FIGURE 14.38 Cradleboard modification in prehistoric Native American.

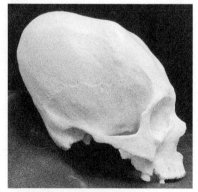

FIGURE 14.39 Modification of frontal and occipital in prehistoric Native American from the Northwest United States. *Photo, D. L. France; cast from France Casting*

Cranial Modifications Just as the frontal bone yields to gentle pressure from the blood vessels that course along its surface, and just as the displaced fracture of a tibia will gradually remodel itself toward its original (and most efficient biomechanical) morphology, so too will the cranium and postcranium respond to gentle pressure. One of the most commonly seen cranial modifications in the prehistoric southwestern United States is "cradleboard modification" or the flattening of the rear of the cranium from the gentle pressure of the board onto which a baby is swaddled (see Figure 14.38). There is no indication that this cranial modification changes the IQ of the infant in any way, and in fact, the cranium can take on many shapes, as long as it is allowed to grow in some direction to accommodate the growing brain. Figure 14.39 shows a variation of this modification in a Northwest coast (of the United States) Native American, in which there is a board on the occipital region as well as a board on the frontal region of the cranium. In this situation, the cranium is wider than usual. In Peru (and in other regions), a baby's head was wrapped in cloth, so that the posterior parietal and occipital bones were drawn toward the back of the cranium, making the cranium longer (see Figure 14.40). If the cranium is *not* allowed to grow in some direction to accommodate the developing brain, as in the pathological condition of **craniostenosis** (in which the sutures prematurely fuse), brain growth itself is stunted, and mental retardation can (and usually does) occur. See Figure 14.41 for an example of microcephaly, in which the cranial sutures are prematurely fused.

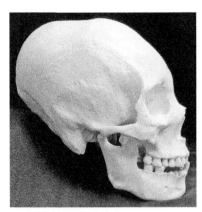

FIGURE 14.40 Wrapping modification of cranium in prehistoric Peruvian. *Photo, D. L. France; specimen from University of Wyoming*

Surgical intervention is a form of intentional modification and includes **trephination** (see Figure 14.42). Trephination is performed today as an emergency surgery designed to relieve pressure on the brain. Trephination was also performed in prehistoric societies and was once thought to have released "evil spirits" from the person. (It is interesting that if we do not understand cultural processes, we often jump to conclusions that involve religion or the supernatural with the assumption that those cultures didn't understand the biological aspects of the human body!) Most researchers now believe that trephination may have been performed in prehistoric societies to relieve symptoms of an injury.

Postcranial Modifications Probably the most well-recognized postcranial skeletal modification occurred in China, with "foot binding," in which the foot was tightly bound, making the foot seem small and petite (see the shoes in Figure 14.43 and the bones in Figure 14.44). Actually, the growing metatarsals were drawn caudally and toward the tarsals so that the foot was "folded." The women who bound their feet (or who had their feet bound) could wear tiny shoes, but they had difficulty walking.

Dental Modifications Dental modifications, such as filing, notching, staining, and adding implants of precious stones can occur in any culture, although certain of these are more prevalent in some cultures than in others. For example, the dark staining of the teeth with betel nut juice would obviously occur more often where there

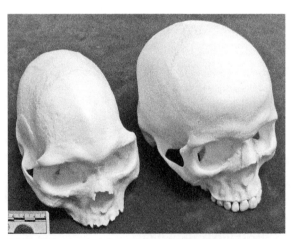

FIGURE 14.41 Microcephaly (left) compared to normal adult (right). Note the small and elongated cranium of the individual with microcephaly. *Photo, D. L. France; casts of specimens from the University of Washington and University of New Mexico*

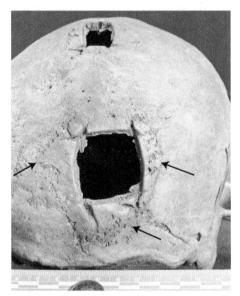

FIGURE 14.42 Prehistoric trephination. Notice the relatively sharp edges and the area of reactive bone (at arrows) around wound, indicative of probable infection. *Photo, D. L. France; specimens curated by the National Museum of Natural History*

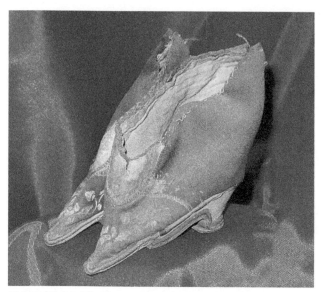

FIGURE 14.43 Shoes used in foot binding.

FIGURE 14.44 Foot binding. *Photo, D. L. France; specimen made available by Jay Villemarette, Skulls Unlimited.*

are, in fact, betel nuts (such as in New Guinea, Java, Bali, and so on). Figure 14.45 illustrates staining of the teeth by betel nut juice in an individual from Bali. Note also that the teeth were filed so that there is a horizontal groove in the teeth (Figure 14.46).

Unintentional modification of the dentition can also occur with the habitual use of tobacco pipes (particularly when pipe stems were made of ceramics), as shown in Figure 14.47. The teeth are worn down by the constant abrasion. Other notches can occur with holding yarn in the teeth while weaving, holding sewing needles in the teeth, and even by the habitual use of toothpicks. Figure 14.48 shows a tooth that has been notched on two surfaces.

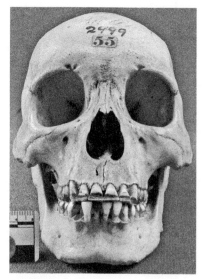

FIGURE 14.45 Teeth stained by betel nut juice. *Photo, D. L. France; specimens curated by the National Museum of Natural History*

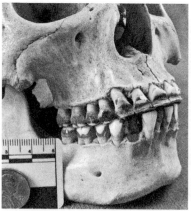

FIGURE 14.46 Horizontal filing of teeth from individual in Figure 14.42. *Photo, D. L. France; specimens curated by the National Museum of Natural History*

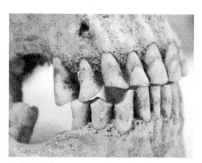

FIGURE 14.47 Pipe stem groove.

Postmortem Modifications Several cultures modify remains after death. Figure 14.49 shows a modified cranium and mandible from Tibet. Sometimes this modification/decoration was performed post-cranially as well. Figure 14.50 demonstrates a child's cranium that was incised after death.

FIGURE 14.48 Notched tooth. *Photo, D. L. France; specimens curated by the National Museum of Natural History*

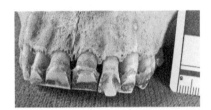

FIGURE 14.49 Cranium from Tibet. *Photo, D. L. France; specimens curated by the National Museum of Natural History*

FIGURE 14.50 Postmortem incisions on cranium from New Guinea. *Photo, D. L. France; specimens curated by the National Museum of Natural History*

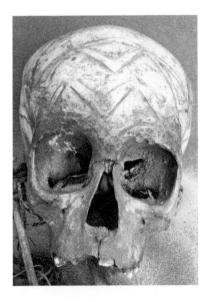

EXERCISE 14.1   NAME _____   SECTION _____   DATE _____

Abnormalities in the Skeleton

FIGURE 14.51 Unknown.
Photo, National Museum of Health and Medicine

1. What processes are occurring in the bone pictured in Figure 14.51 (osteogenic or osteolytic)?

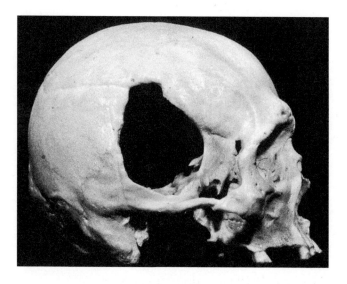

FIGURE 14.52 Unknown.
Photo, D. L. France; specimen from the University of New Mexico

2. The cranium in Figure 14.52 illustrates blunt trauma. Did the individual survive this injury? How do you know?

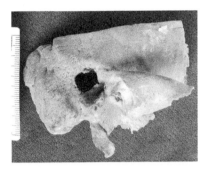

FIGURE 14.53 Unknown.
Photo, D. L. France; material from University of New Mexico

3. Figure 14.53 is a photograph of the right mastoid process. Is this primarily an osteoblastic or osteoclastic pathogen? How do you know?

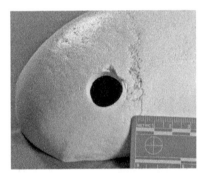

FIGURE 14.54 Unknown.
Photo, D. L. France; materials curated by the National Museum of Health and Medicine

4. Figure 14.54 is an example of trephination. Did this individual survive this surgery? How do you know?

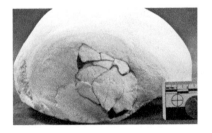

FIGURE 14.55 Unknown.

5. What has happened to the cranium in Figure 14.55? How do you know?

FIGURE 14.56 Unknown.

6. Figure 14.56 shows a tibia that has been fractured by blunt trauma. From what direction did the force hit this bone? How do you know?

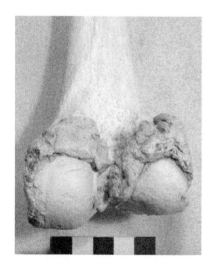

FIGURE 14.57 Unknown.

7. How would you describe the distal femur in Figure 14.57?

FIGURE 14.58a Unknown.

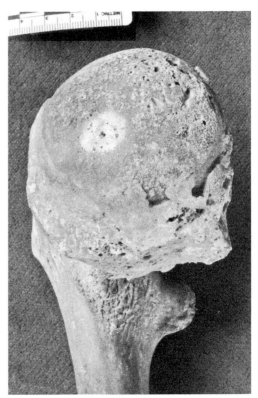

FIGURE 14.58b Unknown.

8. Figures 14.58a and b show degenerative changes in what bone? What does the polishing in Figure 14.58b tell you?

REEXAMINING THE ISSUES

- The human skeleton has a wide range of normal variation, but anthropologists will also encounter a wide range of abnormal, unusual, or pathological conditions.

- It is important to understand that there are a limited number of ways in which the human skeleton can react to stresses while alive, and we must be aware of both what constitutes abnormal variation and how to describe it (which is more important than diagnosing the specific condition or pathogen responsible for that abnormal variation).

CHAPTER 15

Human Skeletal Variation and Forensic Anthropology

OBJECTIVES

OBJECTIVES

1. How can we determine the age, sex, and ancestry of an individual from skeletal remains?

2. What information can we obtain from a partial skeleton that might help police solve a homicide?

3. What does "forensically significant" mean?

4. How can taphonomy change the appearance of remains?

INTRODUCTION

It only takes a few minutes of looking at people in a park to realize that we vary considerably! How do we look through the vast array of differences to come up with ways to determine the age, sex, ancestry, stature, and other aspects of the biological profile? How do we determine the circumstances surrounding death? This chapter will introduce areas of physical anthropology in which human skeletal remains are analyzed, including archaeological finds, remains from historic sites, and in recent forensic cases. Throughout this chapter, forensic situations will be used to demonstrate what we can determine from a skeleton, because unlike most archaeological or historic situations, forensic cases are often tested in court, thereby requiring that any statement about a skeleton be supported by very strong evidence.

Forensic anthropology is a rapidly growing subfield of anthropology, possibly in part because of the prevalence of forensic television programs that appeal to the "detectives" in all of us. In fact, when the author testifies in court, often one of the first questions is: "Is your practice the same as what we see on television?" With the growing interest in this field, there is an increasing need in colleges and universities (and even in high schools) to provide an introduction to forensics in a responsible way and to accurately represent what forensic scientists can and, as importantly, *cannot* do. It assists no one to have an anthropologist give a very narrow age range for a skeleton when a wider age range is more accurate, even though the narrow range sounds more precise.

Some aspects of forensic anthropology are not common to all standard anthropological investigations. The analysis of gunshot wounds, cuts made by saw blades, time since death, and the concern about maintaining the chain of evidence are basic to forensic anthropology but not to the analysis of archaeological remains. Strictly speaking, the term *forensic anthropology* should be reserved for the analysis of remains that have forensic significance and are important in a medicolegal context.

Forensic science is defined as the application of scientific methods to the law. Forensic physical anthropology is the application of physical anthropology to medicolegal questions and is usually used in determining the identity and circumstances of death of an individual (with or without soft tissue). This is usually abbreviated as forensic anthropology, although that term can literally mean the application of any subdiscipline of anthropology to the law.

Time is one standard measure of whether a case is forensically significant. In general terms, if a case occurred less than 50 years ago, there is a greater likelihood that the body can be identified, that evidence in the case will still be obtainable, and that a perpetrator will still be alive to be prosecuted. Even though there is no statute of limitations on homicide in this country, after 50 years the possibility of obtaining evidence declines, although it is still important to identify the victim so that the family can be notified.

THE IMPORTANCE OF TAPHONOMY

Taphonomy is defined as *anything* that happens to a body after death. It includes various natural environmental factors (sun, temperature, elevation, scavenging, burial, and so on) as well as human-influenced factors (for example, storage in a freezer versus storage in a cardboard box on a shelf). These factors influence many things such as the decomposition patterns of a body and the location of bodies or body parts (for example, scavenger versus river transport of elements). Recognition of taphonomic influences is extremely important in trying to determine time since death (or time since deposition in a certain environment), and in determining whether or not the evidence you think you have discovered on a body is important evidence or an artifact of the environment. The condition of the skeleton can help you determine whether or not the body is a forensic case or an archaeological case. The color, texture, smell, and

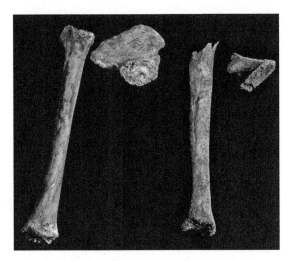

FIGURE 15.1 Copper staining on one side of the body is an example of taphonomic influence. *Photo, D. L. France; material from University of Tennessee*

weight are all important clues (see Figure 15.1 for an example of taphonomic influence on the color of bones). Are the bones dried out, bleached white, and cracking, which could mean that they have been in the elements for a longer period of time? Are the bones oily, and do they smell like decomposing tissue, which would indicate that they are much more recent? Are the bones dried out and the color of the dirt in which it was discovered, which could be one indicator that the remains of archaeological origin? Bones that have not been buried in a container for, say, one hundred years usually take on some of the color of the soil in which they are buried.

THE DETERMINATION OF FORENSIC SIGNIFICANCE AND THE IDENTIFICATION PROCESS

The steps one goes through in the analysis of a potential forensic case starts with the determination of forensic significance, and whether law enforcement and the medical examiner should start a potentially lengthy investigation. That process usually starts with determining whether or not the evidence is organic. We would want to determine if the evidence is, or contains, bone. Is it human bone? Until the evidence is determined to be not forensically significant, it is important to follow proper protocol for the handling of evidence, which means that the evidence must be protected at every step.

Are the Materials Organic?

Often materials that are not even organic can look like human remains. For example, PVC pipe that is subjected to heat will sometimes bubble slightly and fracture to look like portions of tubular bone that is burned to the calcined (or "white") stage (Figure 15.2 illustrates many pieces of PVC pipe affected by heat and fire in a building explosion and fire). How can you tell the difference? Burned bone has most if not the entire organic component destroyed, so only the inorganic component, which is extremely porous, remains (Figure 15.3 illustrates a bone that

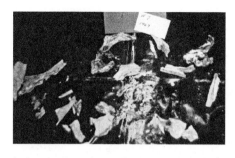

FIGURE 15.2 Many fragments of PVC pipe mistaken for bone.

FIGURE 15.3 Calcined bone.

is burned to the point at which there is no organic component remaining). If you drip water on a piece of PVC or other plastic that has been melted and burned to look like bone, the drop of water will remain as a bead of water and roll off of the material. However, completely burned bone is "thirsty." Why? It has no organic matrix to withstand moisture, and the water soaks in quite quickly. In the past, archaeologists used this test when trying to determine whether they had dried bone or stone that looks like bone (in fact, some archaeologists used to put the questioned material to their tongue, and if it stuck to their tongue, it was bone!). Burned bone also often fractures in a circular pattern. That curved pattern can indicate the direction of the fire in tubular bone. Use the "thumb" rule (Steve Symes, personal communication) in determining the direction of burn; that is, put your thumb so that it fits into the curved fracture pattern. Pull your thumb back "away from the fire" and that will tell you the direction of the burn. See Figure 15.3 for an illustration of calcined bone and Figure 15.4 for an illustration of the curved fracture pattern.

If the Materials Are Organic, Are They Bone?

Some plant materials can look like bone, even to the point of having the internal structure that looks like trabecular bone (this is particularly true in reeds, which sometimes look like ribs). Sometimes it is a little tricky to tell the difference, but if you get a piece of reed wet, it will easily bend (that's how baskets are made), but bone has more mineral component and is more resistant to bending forces even when wet.

If the Materials Are Bone, Are They Human?

There are several ways to determine whether a bone is human, and we discussed some of them in Chapters 3 and 6. As discussed, morphological features are the easiest way to determine the species.

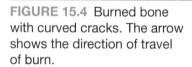

FIGURE 15.4 Burned bone with curved cracks. The arrow shows the direction of travel of burn.

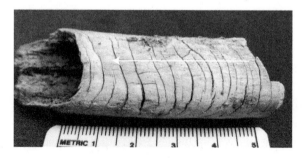

Other ways to determine species (or at least whether the bone is likely human) are by histological methods, in which you take a thin section of bone and look at the microstructure. Artiodactyls (even-hoofed animals such as deer, antelope, and so on), for example, have **plexiform** bone as the primary structure. Plexiform bone cells look like "curved bricks" stacked on top of each other (see Figure 15.5). Humans, in contrast, have a series of rounded bone cells that are interspersed within a matrix (see Figure 15.6), although other species, such as dog species, have variations of that pattern. DNA tests or antibody tests are other ways to distinguish human from nonhuman bone.

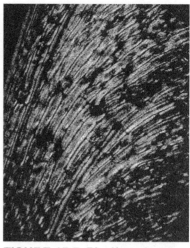

FIGURE 15.5 Plexiform bone.

THE BIOLOGICAL PROFILE

After remains are determined to be human, we can then get to the features that help us determine the biological profile of the individual. The age, sex, ancestry, stature, and so on, are all part of a person's biological profile. We discussed other individualizing characteristics (such as anomalies, healed fractures, and so on) in the previous chapter, and we are also concerned with determining the circumstances surrounding the death of that person. We will investigate all of these topics in this chapter.

IMPORTANT NOTE: The diagnoses of age, sex, population affinity, and other features in skeletons are performed through statistical probabilities; that is, we state conclusions based on what has been seen in the majority of skeletons from similar populations.

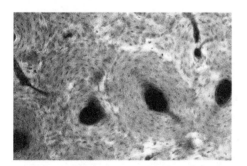

FIGURE 15.6 Human bone cells.

SOLVE THIS CASE!

Throughout this chapter, you will learn the information necessary to solve the identity of the individual in this forensic case. In addition, you will be able to provide information to the medical examiner about the circumstances surrounding the death of this person. This is not a real forensic case, though it is typical of many.

In the spring, a body was discovered in the foothills of the Rocky Mountains by hikers who were out for the first hike of the season. The body was covered by brush and had mostly decomposed (though some desiccated tissue remained). The hikers called the sheriff's office, and officers responded immediately to the scene. The medical examiner's office removed the body and called the forensic anthropologist (you).

Figures 15.7 through 15.13 are photographs of the remains (after cleaning). You will refer to these photographs and to others in the solution of this case.

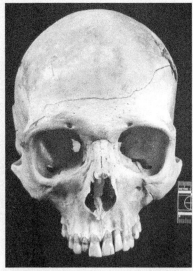

FIGURE 15.7 Unknown cranium.

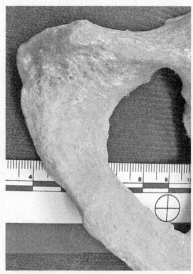

FIGURE 15.8 Unknown pubis ventral surface.

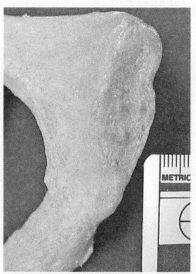

FIGURE 15.9 Unknown pubic symphysis.

FIGURE 15.10 Unknown rib end.

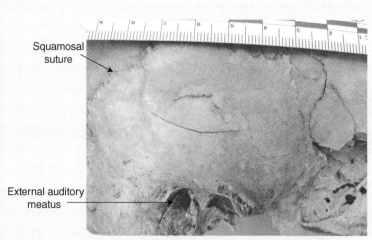

Squamosal suture

External auditory meatus

FIGURE 15.11 Right temporal region.

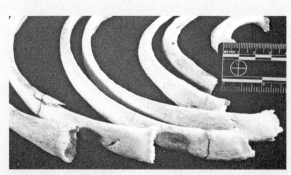

FIGURE 15.12 Ribs.

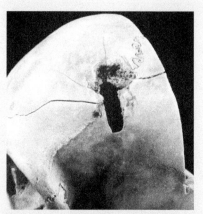

FIGURE 15.13 Left side of cranium.

DETERMINATION OF SEX

One of the first steps in the determination of the biological profile is to determine the sex of the remains. In general, males are bigger than females: The bones are larger and the areas devoted to muscle attachment are larger and more rugged. This, in part, is **sexual dimorphism**. However, to use this size difference in sex determination, a researcher must be able to identify the population from which a skeleton came, as populations differ in average skeletal size and degree of sexual dimorphism and proportions. For example, the people of India have, on average, smaller skeletons than do Australian Aborigines. An adult male Asian Indian skeleton placed alongside a male adult Australian Aborigine skeleton (or many females) would, if judged on the basis of size, be misclassified as a female. A study performed on humeri of Arikara versus Pueblo (North American native groups) misclassified almost 70 percent of the male Pueblo humeri on the basis of size alone, indicating that relatively great general size differences between these two populations could confuse sex differences (France 1983). For this reason, particular morphological differences are usually more reliable than are general size differences, particularly if one is not sure from what population an individual is derived. We now turn to these differences in shape (see Figures 15.14 to 15.17 and Table 15.1). Size differences will be studied later.

"Sex" and "gender" are often used interchangeably, but "sex" describes the biological characteristics whereas "gender" is the way in which an individual identifies himself or herself. Gender cannot be diagnosed in a skeleton.

Sexual dimorphism: Variations in morphology attributed to the two sexes. The pelvic girdle is the most reliable area for determination of sex.

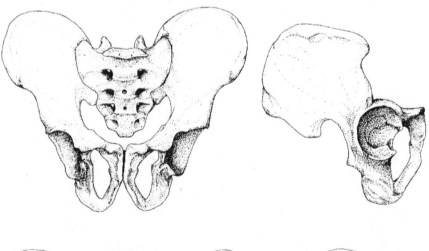

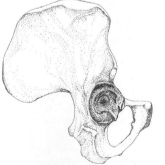

FIGURE 15.14 Male pelvic girdle. *Drawing, courtesy of Jayne Bellavia*

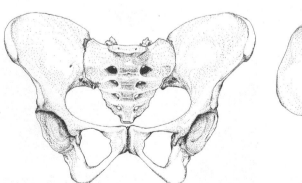

FIGURE 15.15 Female pelvic girdle. *Drawing, courtesy of Jayne Bellavia*

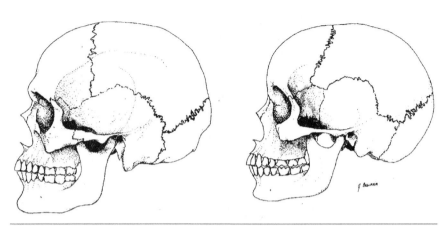

FIGURE 15.16 Cranium and mandible: male (left), female (right). *Drawing, courtesy of Jayne Bellavia*

TABLE 15.1 Sex-Determination Differences

Pelvic Girdle	Typical Male	Typical Female
A. Subpubic angle	Less than 90 degrees	More than 90 degrees
B. Pubic bone shape	Triangular	Rectangular
C. Ventral arc (see Sutherland and Suchey 1991)	Not well defined	Well defined
D. Subpubic angle shape	Convex	Concave
E. Pelvic outlet	Narrow mediolaterally	Wide mediolaterally
F. Greater sciatic notch	Less than 68 degrees	More than 68 degrees
G. Sacroiliac articulation	Relatively flat	Somewhat raised
H. Acetabulum	Large	Small
I. Obturator foramen	Oval	Triangular
J. Blade of ilium	More vertical	Flared
K. Sacrum	Small, narrower, more curved	Larger, wider, straighter
Cranium	**Typical Male**	**Typical Female**
A. Muscle attachment areas: mastoid process, etc.	More pronounced	Less pronounced
B. Superciliary arch/glabella	Raised, more pronounced	Less pronounced
C. Nuchal area	Rougher, more pronounced	Smoother, less pronounced
D. Frontal bone	Slanting	Globular
E. Superior margin of eye orbit	Rounded, blunt	Sharp
F. Palate	Deep	Shallow
G. Chin	More square	One midline point
Other Areas	**Typical Male**	**Typical Female**
A. Scapular notch on scapula	Often present	Often absent
B. Femur: angle of neck to shaft	Smaller angle	Greater angle
C. Femur: linea aspera	Raised/pronounced	Less pronounced

The most reliable area for the determination of sex is, as one might guess, the pelvic girdle. This is the one area of the body for which a sexual difference has clear natural selection ramifications, for if the birth canal is not large enough in females for the fetus to pass, the infant (and perhaps the mother as well) will die, and genes from the parents will not be passed on to the next generation. At least that was the traditional situation, although, of course, modern medical interventions through cesarean sections have circumvented much of the natural selection pressures in societies in which they are performed. In females, the pubic bone is wider mediolaterally, the subpubic angle is wider (see Figure 15.15 and compare with Figure 15.14), and if a ventral arc is present (Figure 15.17), the individual is much more likely to be female (Sutherland and Suchey 1991). Other morphological differences between males and females are listed in Table 15.1. When the entire skeleton is available for inspection, the pelvic area is the most important for sex determination, but do not ignore the other areas of the skeleton. The more information you can gather, the better.

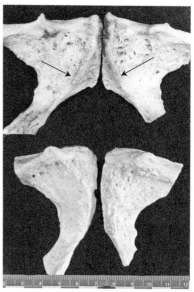

FIGURE 15.17 Ventral arc in classic female (above) and absence in classic male (below).

The preceding standards are for skeletons past adolescence; preadolescent sexing techniques are not reliable, in that they diagnose sex correctly only a little better than chance, and therefore should not be used in a forensic case.

Size Differences in Sex Determination

It has been widely taught that the second best area for sex determination is the cranium and that measurements of the postcranium should be used largely if the cranium and pelvic girdle are not usable. However, if one knows the population from which a skeleton is derived, postcranial metric measurements can be highly reliable (see Table 15.2) (some researchers report an accuracy rate of over 90 percent in some measurements [cf. Dittrick and Suchey 1986; France 1983; Krogman and Iscan 1986]). Cultural practices and differences in muscle use can reduce the reliability of both cranial morphological and postcranial metric dimorphic differences, however (France 1986, 1990). For example, in a culture in which burden baskets are carried on the female heads, the size of the mastoid process will increase so that a population would likely show less dimorphism for that trait.

Correction of Formulae Reported by Bass (1996)

In editions of *Human Osteology* by William Bass (1996), the entry concerning sex determination in the human humerus as studied by France (1983, 1985) is incorrect. When using Bass's reference, note that the result of the regression formulae for females is higher than the cutoff, and those for males are lower than the cutoff, even though males are larger than females.

Table 15.2 Size Differences in Sex Determination

This is not a complete list of sex-determination measurements. For more information, consult Bass (1996), Krogman and Iscan (1986), and Reichs (1997).

Transverse Diameter of Humeral Head (in centimeters)

Population	Sex	No.	Mean	SD	Min.	Max.	Cutoff	% Correctly Classified
African Americans*	M	81	4.50	0.24	3.76	5.04	4.22	91.88%
	F	79	3.95	0.21	3.35	4.40		
Euro-Americans*	M	82	4.50	0.23	3.88	5.45	4.22	92.31%
	F	74	3.91	0.19	3.45	4.41		
Native Americans								
Pecos Pueblo*	M	72	4.06	0.20	3.40	4.54	3.84	89.64%
	F	63	3.60	0.17	3.13	3.96		
Arikara*	M	84	4.33	0.19	3.87	4.72	4.09	94.97%
	F	75	3.83	0.16	3.42	4.26		
Central California	M	150	4.36	0.22	4.12	89.5%		
Combined Horizons**	F	155	3.87	0.18				

Articular Width of Distal Epiphysis of Humerus (in centimeters)

Population	Sex	No.	Mean	SD	Min.	Max.	Cutoff	% Correctly Classified
African Americans*	M	85	4.84	0.26	3.97	5.65	4.48	93.53%
	F	85	4.13	0.23	3.54	4.58		
Euro-Americans*	M	83	4.70	0.25	4.13	5.33	4.37	92.12%
	F	82	4.04	0.19	3.60	4.49		
Native Americans								
Pecos Pueblo*	M	83	4.13	0.19	3.72	4.66	3.91	87.33%
	F	67	3.74	0.15	3.39	4.02		
Arikara*	M	97	4.48	0.21	3.82	5.03	4.27	83.06%
	F	86	4.07	0.20	3.61	4.48		

Maximum Head Diameter of Femur (in centimeters)

Population	Sex	No.	Mean	SD			Cutoff	% Correctly Classified
African Americans ***	M	50	4.78	0.24			4.50	90%
	F	58	4.19	0.24				
Euro-Americans***	M	54	4.82	0.23			4.50	90%
	F	53	4.22	0.23				
Native Americans								
Central California	M	175	4.70	0.25			4.46	88.7%
Combined Horizons**	F	171	4.22	0.19				

*France (1983).

**Central California Combined Horizon (Early Horizon, beginning circa 2500 B.C.E. through Late Horizon beginning after A.D. 500) (Dittrick and Suchey 1986).

***Compiled from Iscan and Miller-Shaivitz (1986) and Krogman and Iscan (1986).

Note: SD = standard deviation.

© Cengage

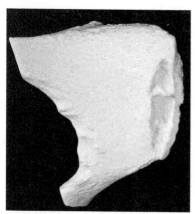

FIGURE 15.18 Dorsal pitting on left pubic bone.

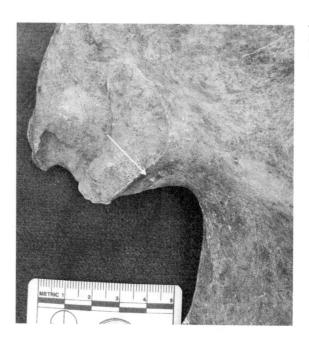

FIGURE 15.19
Preauricular sulcus.

Parturition Scars

Considerable interest has been shown in various features of the female pelvis thought to be remnants of parturition (birth). Suchey et al. (1979) studied 486 females aged 13 to 99 to determine the effect of parturition on the dorsal surface of the pubic bone and determined that the *number* of full-term pregnancies is only slightly correlated with the severity of the dorsal pitting, although it is likely that a pelvic girdle demonstrating bilateral dorsal pitting and preauricular sulci (a groove on the ilium just ventral to the auricular surface) belonged to a female who has given birth (see Figures 15.18 and 15.19). Nulliparous women (meaning those who have not given birth) under 30 more frequently have an absence of pitting than those over 30 (Suchey et al. 1979).

DETERMINATION OF AGE

The introduction to human growth and development was covered in some detail in Chapter 4, and to answer some of the questions in this chapter, you may have to review parts of Chapter 4 (particularly as the information relates to subadults). This chapter will use that information as clues to the diagnosis of age as part of the biological profile of an individual, and a few of the charts and illustrations will be repeated for your convenience.

Several methods are commonly used in the determination of the physiological age of a skeleton. Researchers hope that the physiological age will give an accurate estimate of chronological age, but as was discussed in Chapter 4, environmental, nutritional, and disease stresses will often cause changes in the skeleton that will mask the chronological age of the individual.

Subadults

Age estimation in subadults has a narrower range of variation than in adults, in part because more is happening in different parts of the body in dental formation and eruption and skeletal growth and development, which allows researchers to bracket an age more precisely. Age estimation in adults must include a wider range of variation because most of the processes are degenerative throughout the skeleton and because they have lived more years with all of the hormones and various stresses affecting the body. Of course, genetics play a large role in how a body ages.

Dental formation Dental formation (mineralization; see Figure 15.20) is more resistant to insults, such as disease and nutritional deficiencies, than are the formation and epiphyseal union of the skeleton, and so are more reliable age indicators (see Saunders and Katzenberg 1992; see also Hillson 2003 for good discussions of dental formation and eruption).

Dental eruption The determination of the ages at which the deciduous and permanent dentition erupts is useful in identifying age to approximately 15 years (see Figure 15.20). The third molar (wisdom tooth) erupts after this time but is so variable in age of eruption (if it erupts, as many never do), that it is not the most reliable age indicator. The chart shown for dental eruption times is based on a Native American population, so be aware that other populations may vary from these time frames.

Bone growth Although dental formation and eruption are more resistant to insults to the body, the growth and development of the skeleton is also important. Consult Chapter 4 to refresh your memory about these processes.

Adults

Adult age estimation is less precise than in subadults because after about 30 years, the morphological changes in the skeleton can be considered primarily degenerative, and different individuals degenerate at different rates. It is tempting to reduce the range of variation to appear more precise, but those wide ranges are reflective of the true nature of human variation.

Ectocranial and endocranial suture closure As was discussed in Chapter 4, the use of ectocranial and endocranial suture closure for age determination is problematic because of the wide age ranges between individuals. However, a review of a sample (144 males and 51 females) of crania from people of various ancestries from the

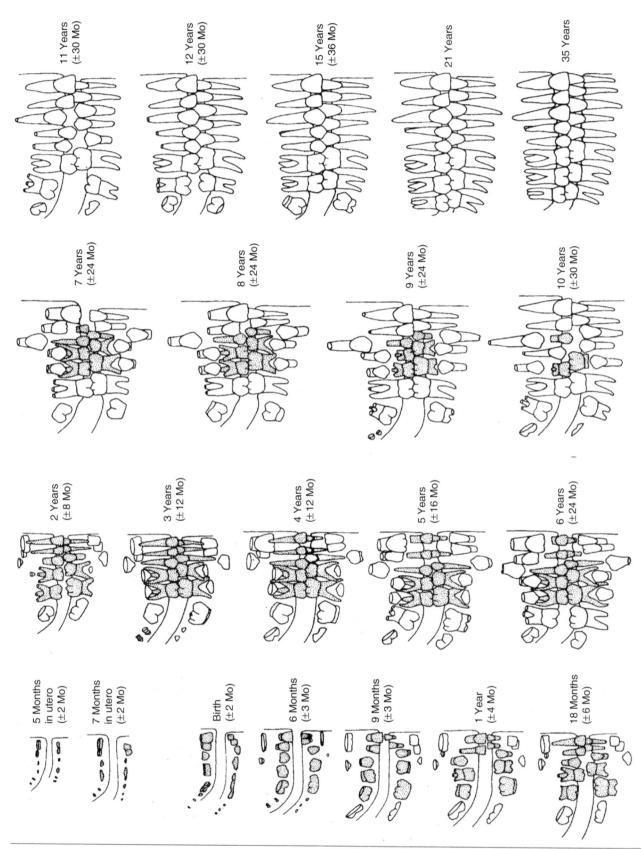

FIGURE 15.20 Dental eruption chart. *Courtesy, D. Ubelaker, Human Skeletal Remains: Excavation, Analysis, Interpretation, Washington: Taraxacum Press*

TABLE 15.3 Skeletal Age (in years): Appearance of Ossification Centers and Epiphyseal Fusion in Various Postcranial Bones (IU = In Utero)

Bone	Element	Appearance	Union	Notes
Clavicle	Diaphysis	Week 5 IU		
	Sternal epiphysis		17–30 for males, 16–33 females (Webb and Suchey 1985)	
	Acromial epiphysis		19–20	
Sternum	Manubrium	Month 5 IU		
	Body sections	1: week 5 IU	All sections to manubrium 15–20 yrs.	
		2 & 3: by week 8 IU	Body section 2 fuses to 3 & 4 at 11–16 yrs.	
		4: after 1 yr.	Body section 3 fuses to 4 at 4–10 yrs.	
Cervical vertebrae	Atlas	Week 7–10 IU	Three major sections 5–6 yrs.	
	Axis	Week approx. 8 IU	Major elements 9–10 yrs.	
	Axis dens tip	Approx. 2 yrs.	To dens approx. 12 yrs.	
	C7–C3 (progressing cranially)	By month 4 IU	Neural arches 2–3 yrs.; arches to centrum 3–4 yrs.	
Thoracic vertebrae	Centrum and both neural arches	By week 10 IU	Fuse from caudally to cranially neural arches 1–3 yrs.; arches to centrum 5–6 yrs.	
Lumbar vertebrae	Centrum and both neural arches (progressing caudally)	By month 4 IU	Progressing caudally, arches 1–5 yrs.; arches to centrum 2–4 yrs.	
Ilium	Primary center	Months 2–3 IU		
	Iliac crest	12–13 yrs. in females; 14–15 yrs. in males	Completed 18–24 yrs. in females, 17–24 in males (Webb and Suchey 1985).	
Ischium	Primary center	Months 3–5 IU	Fuses with pubis 4–8 yrs.	
	Ischial tuberosity	13–16 yrs.	Completed by 21–23 yrs.	
Pubis	Primary center	Months 4–6 IU	Fuses with ischium 4–8 yrs.	
Ossa coxae	All major elements		11–15 yrs. in females, 15–17 yrs. in males	
Sacrum**	Centra (center) for S1–S3	Month 3 IU	S1–3 centra to arches and alae 2–5 yrs.	

TABLE 15.3 (Continued)

Bone	Element	Appearance	Union	Notes
	Neural arches for S1–S3	Months 4–6 IU		
	Alae for S1–S3	Months 6–8 IU		
	Centra for S4, S5	Months 4–5 IU	S4, S5 centra to arches 2–6 yrs.	
	Neural arches for S4, S5	Months 6–8 IU		
	Sacral elements		At spinous processes 7–15, alae and centra approx. 12–20 yrs, years from S5 to S1; S1–S2 in the 20s to sacrum late teens	
	Auricular surface and lateral epiphyses	15–16 yrs.		
Scapula	Body	Week 7–8 IU		
	Coracoid process	Birth–1 yr.	To body 16–17 yrs.	
	Acromion process	13–16 yrs.	18–20 yrs.	
	Inferior angle	15–17 yrs.	20–23 yrs.	
	Vertebral margin	15–17 yrs.	20–23 yrs.	
Humerus	Diaphysis	Week 7 IU		
	Head epiphysis	Birth–6 mos.	To diaphysis: 15–19 in females; 18–22 in males	
	Distal epiphyses	6 mos.–2 yrs.	To diaphysis: 11–15 in females; 12–17 in males	
	Medial epicondyle	After 4 yrs.	To diaphysis: 13–15 in females; 14–16 in males	
Radius	Diaphysis	Week 7 IU		
	Proximal epiphysis	Approx. 5 yrs.	To diaphysis: 11–15 in females; 14–17 in males	
	Distal epiphysis	1–3 yrs.	To diaphysis: 14–17 in females; 16–20 in males	
Ulna	Diaphysis	Week 7 IU		
	Proximal epiphysis	8–10 yrs.	To diaphysis: 12–15 in females; 13–17 in males	
	Distal epiphysis	5–7 yrs.	To diaphysis: 15–17 in females; 17–20 in males	
Hand	Carpals	After birth		
	Metacarpal diaphyses	Week 8–10 IU		
	Metacarpal distal epiphyses 2–5	10 mos.–2.5 yrs.	to diaphysis: 14–15 in females, 16–17 in males*	
	Phalanges vary			

continues

TABLE 15.3 (Continued)

Bone	Element	Appearance	Union	Notes
Femur	Diaphysis	Week 7–8 IU		
	Head	Birth–1 yr.	To diaphysis: 12–16 in females; 14–19 in males	
	Greater trochanter	1–5 yrs.	To diaphysis: 14–16 in females; 16-18 in males	
	Lesser trochanter	7–12 yrs.	To diaphysis: 16–17 yrs.	
	Distal epiphysis	Week 36–40 IU (usually before birth)	To diaphysis: 14–18 in females; 16–20 in males	
Tibia	Diaphysis	Week 8 IU		
	Proximal epiphysis	Near birth	To diaphysis: 13–17 in females; 15–19 in males	
	Distal epiphysis	Approx. 2 yrs.	To diaphysis: 14–16 in females; 15–18 in males	
Fibula	Diaphysis	Week 8 IU		
	Proximal epiphysis	Approx. 4–5 yrs.	To diaphysis: 12–18 in females; 15–20 in males	
	Distal epiphysis	1–2 yrs.	To diaphysis: 12–16 in females; 15-18 in males	
Foot	Calcaneus	Varies: week 3–28 IU		
	Calcaneus posterior epiphysis	4–12 yrs.	Beg. 10–12 in females; 11–14 in males; and completed by 16 in females and 22 in males	

*Scheuer and Black (2000).

**Sacral elements fuse at spinous processes first, then lateral borders, and then centra.

These ages are approximations and are compiled from Scheuer and Black (2000), who often report narrower age ranges than other sources; Baker et al. (2005); Bass (1996); McKern and Stewart (1957); and Webb and Suchey (1985). Also, see hand-wrist radiographs from Greulich and Pyle (1959). Females usually mature more quickly than males by about 1 to 2 years.

Los Angeles Coroner's Office (Baker 1984) suggests the following general guidelines for endocranial suture closure:

1. If all sutures are completely open, the individual is less than 36 years of age, usually less than 27.

2. If all sutures are completely closed, the individual is 26 or older.

Pubic symphysis The pubic symphysis (where the two pubic bones are joined through cartilage in the front of the pelvic girdle) in the young is characterized by an undulating surface that undergoes metamorphosis with advancing age. Several researchers have developed age-determination techniques based on the changing morphology of the symphyseal face. The first was developed by T. W. Todd (1920–21) using dissection-room cadavers. McKern and Stewart (1957) developed a technique using American males killed in the Korean War. Both of the samples from which these systems were derived have limitations in that the dissection-room sample Todd used is based on individuals of uncertain age (Brooks 1985, 1986), and the Korean War dead sample is predominantly young European American males, with few individuals over age 35.

Starting more than 30 years ago, J. M. Suchey, D. Katz, and S. T. Brooks developed a system based on a large sample of individuals for whom legal documentation of age was provided by death certificates. This autopsy-room sample was also more representative of the general population of North America because the majority of the individuals were born throughout the United States and Mexico. At autopsy, bone segments were removed from victims of homicides, suicides, accidents, or unexpected natural deaths. This groundbreaking six-phase system has been used extensively around the world, and has been tested in different populations, which should be expected—remember the scientific method. Within the past few years, several researchers have suggested modifications to the phase descriptions of the Suchey–Brooks system, as well as the addition of a seventh phase to describe older individuals (see Berg 2008; Djuric et al. 2007; Hartnett 2010a; Kimmerle et al. 2008). K. Hartnett and L. Fulginiti (personal communication with K. Hartnett) examined more than 400 male and more than 200 female pubic bones (and ribs that will be discussed in the appropriate section) with known age at death. They developed somewhat different phase descriptions but incorporated many of the descriptions of the Suchey–Brooks research (although the sample sizes are low in some phases in the Hartnett system). The phase descriptions listed here are the descriptions from Brooks and Suchey (1990), although a few comments from Hartnett (2010a) have been added in blue text, and the seventh phase from Hartnett has been included. The original publications should be consulted for exact descriptions of each system (consult Brooks and Suchey 1990; Hartnett 2010a; Suchey et al. 1986; Suchey and Katz 1998; and others). Also, it should be recognized that further testing continues on each of these systems.

The Suchey–Brooks system is illustrated in Figures 15.21 and 15.22. The top and bottom bones of the pairs are from two individuals and are two examples of a phase.

Rib Phases

Iscan et al. (1984, 1985) have selected and illustrated specific phases for age-related changes in the sternal end of the fourth right rib (see Figures 15.23 to 15.28 and Table 15.4). As with all age determination techniques, this system has been tested, and some revisions to the phase descriptions have been suggested. Some believe that the methods

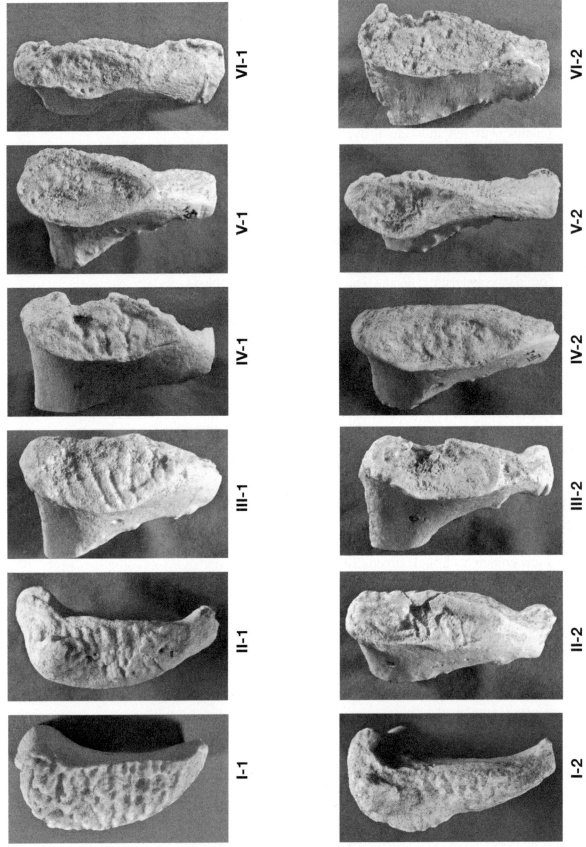

FIGURE 15.21 Male pubic symphyses.

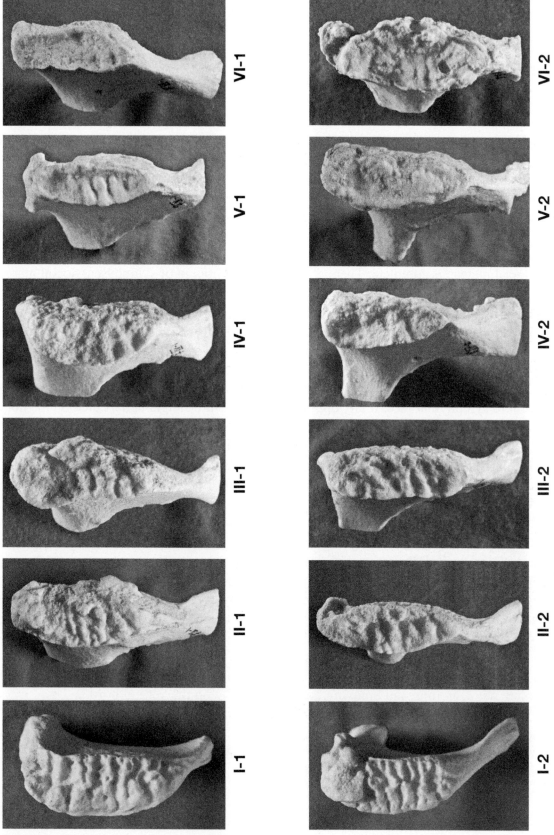

FIGURE 15.22 Female pubic symphyses.

SUCHEY–BROOKS PUBIC AGE PHASE DESCRIPTIONS

Phase I: The symphyseal face has a billowing surface (ridges and furrows) that usually extends to include the pubic tubercle. The horizontal ridges are well marked and ventral beveling may be commencing. Although ossific nodules may occur on the upper extremity, a key to the recognition of this phase is the lack of delimitation of either extremity (upper or lower).

Phase II: The symphyseal face may still show ridge development. The face has commencing delimitation of lower and/or upper extremities occurring with or without ossific nodules. The ventral rampart may be in beginning phases as an extension of the bony activity at either or both extremities.

Phase III: The symphyseal face shows lower extremity and ventral rampart in process of completion. There is a continuation of fusing ossific nodules forming the upper extremity and along the ventral border. The symphyseal face is smooth or can continue to show distinct ridges. The dorsal plateau is complete. There is an absence of lipping of symphyseal dorsal margin and no bony ligamentous outgrowths.

Phase IV: The symphyseal face is generally fine-grained, although remnants of the old ridge and furrow system may still remain. Usually the oval outline is complete at this stage, but a hiatus can occur in the upper ventral rim. The pubic tubercle is fully separated from the symphyseal face by definition of the upper extremity. The symphyseal face may have a distinct rim. Ventrally, bony ligamentous outgrowths may occur on the inferior portion of pubic bone adjacent to symphyseal face. If any lipping occurs, it will be slight and located on the dorsal border. The ventral arc may be large and elaborate in females.

Phase V: The symphyseal face is completely rimmed with some slight depression of the face itself, relative to the rim. Moderate lipping is usually found on the dorsal border, with more prominent ligamentous outgrowths on the ventral border. There is little or no rim erosion. Breakdown may occur on superior ventral border. Ridges and furrows are absent on the face.

Phase VI: Symphyseal face shows ongoing depression as the rim erodes. Ventral ligamentous attachments are marked. In many individuals, the pubic tubercle appears as a separate bony knob. The face may be pitted or porous, giving an appearance of disfigurement with the ongoing process of erratic ossification. Crenulations may occur. The shape of the face is often irregular at this stage. The dorsal surface of the bone is rough and coarse. Projections are present at the medial aspect of the obturator foramen. Bone weight is a major deciding factor between phases 6 and 7.

Phase VII: The face and rim are very irregular in shape and are losing integrity. The rim is complete but is eroding and breaking down, especially on the ventral border. There are no ridges and furrows. The face is porous and macroporous. Distal lipping is pronounced. Bone quality is poor, and the bone is very light and brittle. The dorsal surface of the bone is roughened. The ventral surface of the body is roughened and elaborate. Projections are present at the medial wall of the obturator foramen. The pubic tubercle is elaborate and proliferative.

TABLE 15.4 Comparison of the Statistics of the Pubic Symphysis

Male Comparative Statistics

	Suchey–Brooks*					Hartnett**			
Phase	N	Mean	SD	Range	Phase	N	Mean	SD	Range
1	105	18.5	2.1	15–23	1	14	19.29	1.93	18–22
2	75	23.4	3.6	19–34	2	14	22.14	1.86	20–26
3	51	28.7	6.5	21–46	3	36	29.53	6.63	21–44
4	171	35.2	9.4	23–57	4	69	42.54	8.8	27–61
5	134	45.6	10.4	27–66	5	90	53.87	8.42	37–73
6	203	61.2	12.2	34–86	6	34	63.76	8.06	51–83
7	0	na	na	na	7	96	77.00	9.33	58–97

Female Comparative Statistics

	Suchey–Brooks*					Hartnett**			
Phase	N	Mean	SD	Range	Phase	N	Mean	SD	Range
1	48	19.4	2.6	15–24	1	5	19.80	1.33	18–22
2	47	25	4.9	19–40	2	5	23.20	2.38	20–25
3	44	30.7	8.1	21–53	3	25	31.44	5.12	24–44
4	39	38.2	10.9	26–70	4	35	43.26	6.12	33–58
5	44	48.1	14.6	25–83	5	32	51.47	3.94	44–60
6	51	60	12.4	42–87	6	35	72.34	7.36	56–86
7	0	na	na	na	7	56	82.54	7.41	62–99

*Brooks and Suchey (1990).

**Hartnett (2010a).

Note: SD = standard deviation.

© Cengage

might be applied with some revision to ribs other than the fourth. DiGangi et al. (2009) have also developed a system for the first rib.

K. Hartnett (2010b) and L. Fulginiti also recently completed a test of the Iscan–Loth rib age-determination system on a series of known individuals from Arizona and suggested some slight changes in the phase descriptions, primarily having to do with the weight and overall condition of the bone (it is commonly understood that the skeleton loses bone mass with increasing age in males and females, and particularly in menopausal females; see Table 15.5).

Other Systems for Age Estimation

Although only the pubic symphysis and rib age-determination systems have been covered in detail in this book, many other areas of the dentition and skeleton can be used. The auricular surface of the ilium undergoes a metamorphosis with increasing age (see Buckberry and Chamberlain 2002; Igarashi et al. 2005; Lovejoy et al. 1985). Lamendin et al. (1992) developed a technique for estimating adult age from dentition, which has since been tested on other populations (Martrille et al. 2007; Prince and Ubelaker 2002; and others). Histological methods use thin cross sections of femora, ribs, and other bones to estimate age (Cho et al. 2002; Kerley and Ubelaker 1978; Stout and Paine 1992; and many others).

Phase Descriptions

Male Phase 0 (16 and Younger): The articular surface is flat or billowy with a regular rim and rounded edges. The bone itself is smooth, firm, and very solid (0a, 0b, 0c).

Male Phase 1 (17–19): There is a beginning amorphous indentation in the articular surface, but billowing may also still be present. The rim is rounded and regular. In some cases, scallops may start to appear at the edges. The bone is still firm, smooth, and solid (1a, 1b, 1c).

Male Phase 2 (20–23): The pit is now deeper and has assumed a V-shaped appearance formed by the anterior and posterior walls. The walls are thick and smooth with a scalloped or slightly wavy rim with rounded edges. The bone is firm and solid (2a, 2b, 2c).

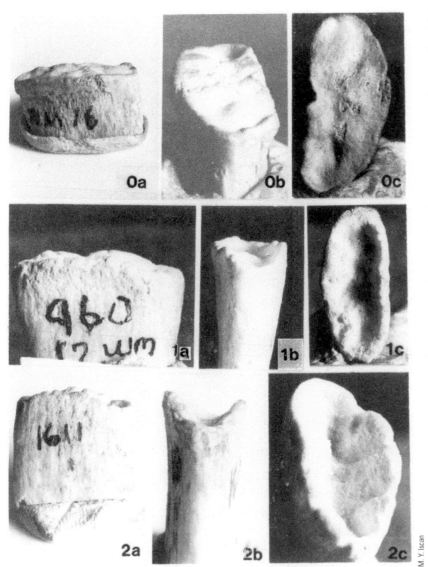

M. Y. Iscan

FIGURE 15.23 Age-related changes at the costochondral junction of the fourth rib in males, phases 0–2.

Male Phase 3 (24–28): The deepening pit has taken on a narrow to moderate U shape. Walls are still fairly thick, with rounded edges. Some scalloping may still be present, but the rim is becoming more irregular. The bone is still quite firm and solid (3a, 3b, 3c).

Male Phase 4 (26–32): Pit depth is increasing, but the shape is still a narrow to moderately wide U. The walls are thinner, but the edges remain rounded. The rim is more irregular with no uniform scalloping pattern remaining. There is some decrease in the weight and firmness of the bone; however, the overall quality of the bone is still good (4a, 4b, 4c).

Male Phase 5 (33–42): There is little change in pit depth, but the shape in this phase is predominantly a moderately wide U. Walls show further thinning, and the edges are becoming sharp. Irregularity is increasing in the rim. The scalloping pattern is completely gone and has been replaced with irregular bony projections. The condition of the bone is fairly good; however, there are some signs of deterioration, with evidence of porosity and loss of density (5a, 5b, 5c).

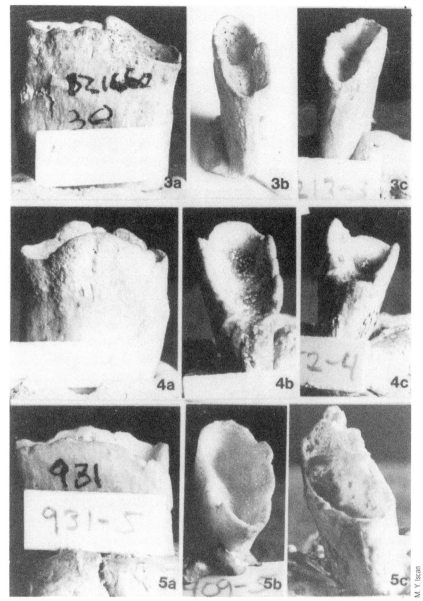

FIGURE 15.24 Age-related changes at the costochondral junction of the fourth rib in males, phases 3–5.

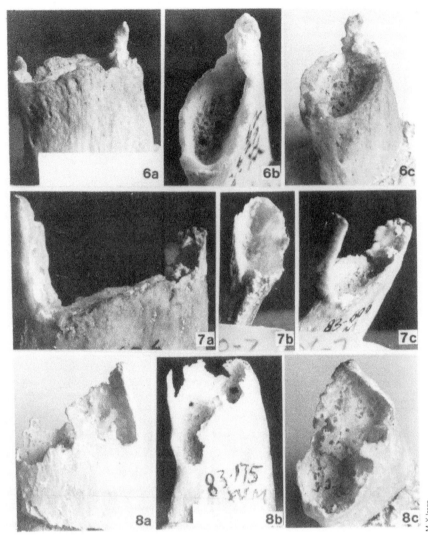

FIGURE 15.25 Age-related changes at the costochondral junction of the fourth rib in males, phases 6–8.

M. Y. Iscan

Male Phase 6 (43–55): The pit is noticeably deep, with a wide U shape. The walls are thin with sharp edges. The rim is irregular and exhibits some rather long bony projections that are frequently more pronounced at the superior and inferior borders. The bone is noticeably lighter in weight, thinner, and more porous, especially inside the pit (6a, 6b, 6c).

Male Phase 7 (54–64): The pit is deep, with a wide to very wide U shape. The walls are thin and fragile with sharp, irregular edges and bony projections. The bone is light in weight and brittle, with significant deterioration in quality and obvious porosity (7a, 7b, 7c).

Male Phase 8 (65 and older): In this final phase, the pit is very deep and widely U-shaped. In some cases, the floor of the pit is absent or filled with bony projections. The walls are extremely thin, fragile, and brittle, with sharp, highly irregular edges and bony projections. The bone is very lightweight, thin, brittle, friable, and porous. "Window" formation is sometimes seen in the walls (8a, 8b, 8c).

Female Phase 0 (13 and younger): The articular surface is nearly flat, with ridges or billowing. The outer surface of the sternal extremity of the rib is bordered by what appears to be an overlay of bone. The rim is regular with rounded edges, and the bone itself is firm, smooth, and very solid (0a, 0b, 0c).

Female Phase 1 (14–15): A beginning, amorphous indentation can be seen in the articular surface. Ridges or billowing may still be present. The rim is rounded and regular, with a little waviness in some cases. The bone remains solid, firm, and smooth (1a, 1b, 1c).

Female Phase 2 (16–19): The pit is considerably deeper and has assumed a V shape between the thick, smooth anterior and posterior walls. Some ridges or billowing may still remain inside the pit. The rim is wavy, with some scallops beginning to form at the rounded edge. The bone itself is firm and solid (2a, 2b, 2c).

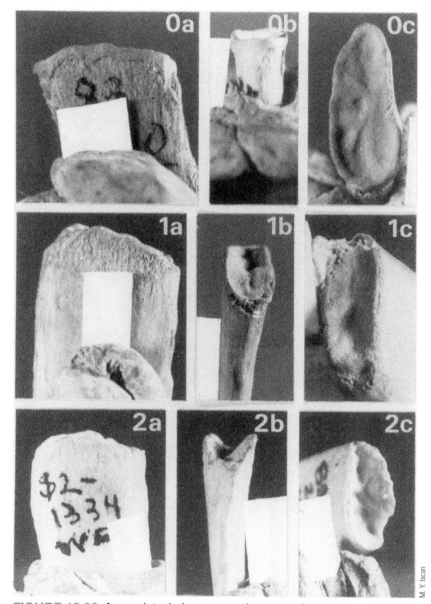

M. Y. İşcan

FIGURE 15.26 Age-related changes at the costochondral junction of the fourth rib in females, phases 0–2.

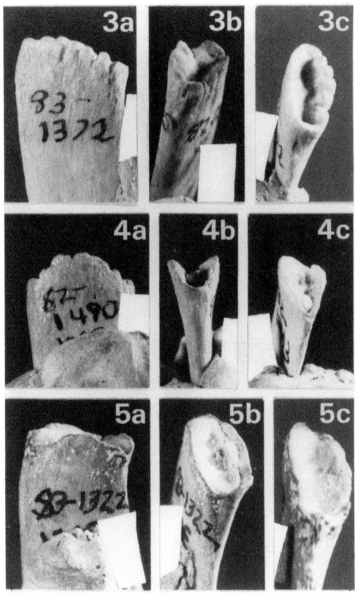

FIGURE 15.27 Age-related changes at the costochondral junction of the fourth rib in females, phases 3–5.

Female Phase 3 (20–24): There is only slight if any increase in pit depth, but the V shape is wider, sometimes approaching a narrow U as the walls become a bit thinner. The still-rounded edges now show a pronounced, regular scalloping pattern. At this stage, the anterior or posterior walls may first start to exhibit a central, semicircular arc of bone. The rib is firm and solid (3a, 3b, 3c).

Female Phase 4 (24–32): There is a noticeable increase in the depth of the pit, which now has a wide V shape or narrow U shape with, at times, flared edges. The walls are thinner, but the rim remains rounded. Some scalloping is still present, along with the central arc; however, the scallops are not as well defined, and the edges look somewhat worn down. The quality of the bone is fairly good, but there is some decrease in density and firmness (4a, 4b, 4c).

Female Phase 5 (33–46): The depth of the pit stays about the same, but the thinning walls are flaring into a wider V shape or U shape. In most cases, a smooth, hard, plaque-like deposit lines at least part of the pit. No regular scalloping pattern remains, and the edge is beginning to sharpen. The rim is becoming more irregular, but the central arc is still the most prominent projection. The bone is noticeably lighter in weight, density, and firmness. The texture is somewhat brittle (5a, 5b, 5c).

Female Phase 6 (43–58): An increase in pit depth is again noted, and its V shape or U shape has widened again because of pronounced flaring at the end. The plaque-like deposit may still appear but is rougher and more porous. The walls are quite thin, with sharp edges and an irregular rim. The central arc is less obvious, and, in many cases, sharp points project from the rim of the sternal extremity. The bone itself is fairly thin and brittle, with some signs of deterioration (6a, 6b, 6c).

Female Phase 7 (59–71): In this phase, the depth of the predominantly flared U-shaped pit not only shows no increase but also actually decreases slightly. Irregular bony growths are often seen extruding from the interior of the pit. The central arc is still present in most cases but is now accompanied by pointed projections, often at the superior and inferior borders, yet may be evidenced anywhere around the rim. The very thin walls have irregular rims with sharp edges. The bone is very light, thin, brittle, and fragile, with deterioration most noticeable inside the pit (7a, 7b, 7c).

Female Phase 8 (70 and older): The floor of the U-shaped pit in this final phase is relatively shallow, badly deteriorated, or completely eroded. Sometimes, it is filled with bony growths. The central arc is barely recognizable. The extremely thin, fragile walls have highly irregular rims with very sharp edges and often fairly long projections of bone at the inferior and superior borders. "Window" formation sometimes occurs in the walls. The bone itself is in poor condition: extremely thin, light in weight, brittle, and fragile (8a, 8b, 8c).

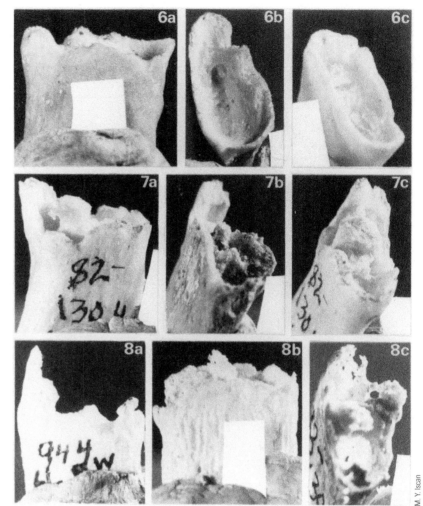

M. Y. İşcan

FIGURE 15.28 Age-related changes at the costochondral junction of the fourth rib in females, phases 6–8.

TABLE 15.5   Descriptive Statistics of Metamorphic Phases of Ribs

	Iscan et al.*				Hartnett**			
Phase	N	Mean	SD	Range	Phase	N	Mean	SD	Range
0	10			<17	0	na	na	na	na
1	4	17.3	0.5	16.5–18.0	1	20	20.00	1.45	18–22
2	15	21.9	2.13	20.8–23.1	2	27	24.63	2	21–28
3	17	25.9	3.5	24.1–27.7	3	27	32.27	3.69	27–37
4	12	28.2	3.83	25.7–30.6	4	47	42.43	2.98	36–48
5	14	38.8	7	34.4–42.3	5	76	52.05	3.5	45–59
6	17	50	11.17	44.3–55.7	6	61	63.13	3.53	57–70
7	17	59.2	9.52	54.3–64.1	7	75	80.91	6.6	70–97
8	12	71.5	10.27	65.0–78.0	8	na	na	na	na

* Modified from Iscan et al. (1984), Table 2, and Iscan et al. (1985).
** Hartnett (2010b).

	Iscan et al.*				Hartnett**			
Phase	N	Mean	SD	Range	Phase	N	Mean	SD	Range
0	10			<14	0	na	na	na	na
1	1	14	na	na	1	7	19.57	1.67	18–22
2	5	17.4	1.52	16–20	2	7	25.14	1.17	24–27
3	5	22.6	1.67	20–24	3	22	32.95	3.17	27–38
4	10	27.7	4.62	24–40	4	21	43.52	3.08	39–49
5	17	40	12.22	29–77	5	32	51.69	3.31	47–58
6	18	50.7	14.93	32–79	6	18	67.17	3.41	60–73
7	16	65.2	11.24	48–83	7	71	81.20	6.95	65–99
8	11	76.4	8.83	62–90	8	na	na	na	na

*Modified from Iscan et al. (1984), Table 2, and Iscan et al. (1985).
**Hartnett (2010b).
Note: SD = standard deviation.

© Cengage

Old Age

The characteristics of older age start by about age 30, at which time the maturation of the skeleton begins to turn to degenerative changes, although this can be exaggerated by mechanical stress. In addition to the morphological changes seen in the pubic bones, ribs, auricular surface and ribs, pathological conditions such as **arthritis** and **osteophytosis** (see Figure 15.29) become more prevalent and pronounced, as does **osteoporosis**, which is increased porosity of the bone, particularly in postmenopausal women (see

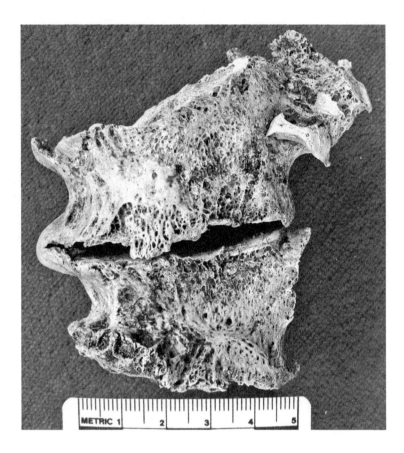

FIGURE 15.29 Osteophyte development in vertebra. Note that in addition to the osteophytes, the vertebral bodies have partially collapsed.

Figures 15.30a, b, and c). These degenerative changes can give corroborative evidence to determinations of older age but are not reliable by themselves, as injury and disease can cause many of these changes even in a younger skeleton.

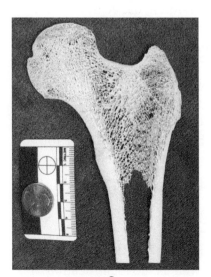
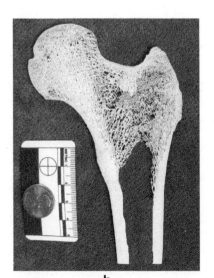
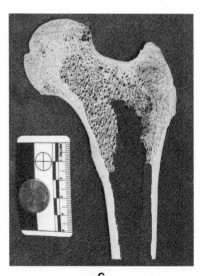

| a | b | c |

FIGURE 15.30a–c Progressive degenerative changes in the trabecular bone in the proximal femur. *Photos, D. L. France; material from the National Museum of Natural History*

FIGURE 15.31a and b
Increased wear on
mandibular dentition.

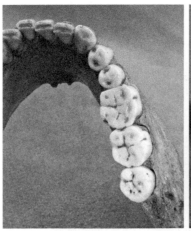 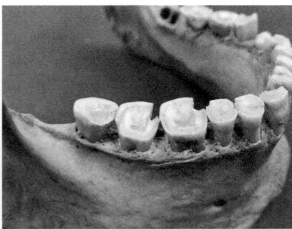

a   b

Dental Wear

The amount of wear on dentition has traditionally been used to determine the relative age of individuals within a population. It should be stressed, however, that humans eat a variety of foods that promote wear at different rates and, consequently, dental wear should not be used to determine the absolute age of an individual, particularly when the dietary and other uses of the teeth in that individual are not known. For examples of teeth with moderate wear and more severe wear, see Figures 15.31a and b. Within a single population in which the diet is fairly similar, however, usually the greater the wear on the teeth, the older the person is.

Seriation is a technique used when determining the relative age of many unidentified individuals within one population. In this technique, the remains are usually placed on a table and repositioned so that the bones and teeth show progression in the degree of morphological and/or degenerative changes from the youngest to the presumed oldest of the individuals. Sometimes a chronological age is assigned to the individuals based on this progression, but this should be done with extreme caution when the ages are to be used in modern populations to aid in personal identification. Some researchers have used seriated samples in the development of techniques of age determination, but these techniques should be used only with caution and with the full knowledge that they were not based on individuals of documented age.

DETERMINATION OF ANCESTRY

Anthropologists use biological clues to determine the social identity of an individual.

There are many good reasons to discontinue the use of racial terminology in science. The terms used (as well as the identification of differences between groups in general) have made it easier in history for one group to attempt to demonstrate that its own individuals are more intelligent, more physically fit, and more deserving of the benefits of society than are individuals who are different. Racism has used these terms as its tools. Racial terms have historically placed people into the four or five regularly named "racial groups," or pigeonholes, even when they do not fit physically. It is generally recognized that there is more variation *within* races as they are usually defined than *between* racial groups. There is a continuum in each characteristic (such as skin color, hair form, and so on) around the world that makes it impossible to categorize every individual in the world into the generally defined racial groups. It is more accurate to investigate traits as **clines** instead of absolute defining characteristics.

Cline: A gradient of frequency of traits in a population.

Forensic physical anthropologists, however, would be derelict in their duty if they ignored the morphological differences that can help to identify individuals. When an anthropologist is asked to help in the identification of a set of remains, part of that identification must include a statement as to probable ancestry because this feature is included in the social identity of that person. This identity was traditionally made in racial terms and was usually made by the person himself or herself. Many government forms still use racial terms for identification. This identification of ancestry is changing, however, in that more of the world's inhabitants are identifying themselves according to the geographic or political location of their ancestors (that is, German, Spanish, or Bosnian, instead of Caucasian).

The question for forensic physical anthropologists then becomes: How closely can we estimate these more refined identities from the physical remains? The answer is that it depends. If a person identifies himself as an African American, it implies that the person's ancestors were from Africa but that he is an American citizen. Of course the forensic anthropologist cannot determine the person's current place of residence by the bones alone, so we would be perhaps misleading the law enforcement official if we say that this is an "African American." It is, however, becoming more feasible to determine, with experience, statistical analysis, and computer programs, the probable ancestral background with more refinement, even to the point at which many forensic anthropologists can determine the regional ancestry of many Native American groups by looking primarily at the facial morphology. Many forensic physical anthropologists are now stating in their reports that, for instance, the remains are from an individual with European ancestry, or African ancestry, or even eastern European ancestry.

One thing must be stated, however. Even as forensic physical anthropologists are becoming more refined in their abilities to detect clues about ancestry in the skeletal morphology, it is important to realize that no matter what terms are used to describe the individuals we study, people will (and should) object to the terms if they are misused. If any term is used maliciously, or with intent to create a hierarchy between recognized groups, its use will increase suspicion and ill will between peoples. Reputable forensic physical anthropologists intend their use of the terms to be clues to the eventual identification of remains and nothing more.

If we agree philosophically that it is important to study population differences, how do we do it? Should we study measurements we take on skeletal material from different populations and statistically evaluate whether or not they are significantly different between populations? Should we study nonmetric or morphoscopic

TABLE 15.6   Features that Can Aid in the Determination of Ancestry Using the Skull

Feature	African Ancestry	Australian Ancestry	European Ancestry	East Asian Ancestry
Central incisors	Blade	Trace	Rarely shoveled	Often shoveled
Cranial shape*	Dolicocranic	Dolicocranic	Mesocranic	Brachycranic
Nasal root (at root of nose)	Wide, rounded	Wide, depressed	Narrow, pinched	Medium, tented
Features that Can Aid in the Determination of Ancestry	Platyrrhiny	Mesorrhiny	Leptorrhiny	Mesorrhiny
Zygomatic bone	Medium	Large	Retreating	Projecting
External auditory meatus (ear opening)	Round	Round	Round	Oval
Facial shape	Prognathic (lower face projects forward)	Prognathic (nonprojecting)	Orthognathic (lower face)	Medium

*The cranial shape is obtained from the cranial index, calculated from

$$\frac{\text{Cranial breadth}}{\text{Cranial length}} \times 100$$
Up to 75 = Dolichocrany (long headed)
75–79.9 = Mesocrany (medium)
80–84.9 = Brachycrany (rounded)
85 and up = Hyperbrachycrany (very rounded) (Bass 1987)

**The nasal aperture shape is obtained from the nasal index:

$$\frac{\text{Nasal breadth}}{\text{Nasal length}} \times 100$$
Up to 47.9 = Leptorrhiny (narrow)
48–52.9 = Mesorrhiny (medium)
53 and up = Platyrrhiny (wide) (Bass 1987)

See also Bass (1996); Brues (1977); Dahlberg (1951); Gill and Rhine (1990); and Krogman (1962).

(a term suggested by Ousley and Hefner 2005) traits that we can see but upon which we cannot necessarily perform a metric analysis? It has been argued for decades within forensic anthropology that professionals who are experienced at looking at traits and who know very well the natural variation within populations are likely as good or better at determining ancestry as those who are less experienced and who rely on metric analysis, but the answer is more likely that one should use both. There have been many metric methods through the years, but the most sophisticated is Fordisc, which is a computer program developed at the University of Tennessee by Richard Jantz and Stephen Ousley in 1993 (now in Fordisc 3: Jantz and Ousley 2005). It incorporates measurements taken by multiple researchers from skeletons around the world and attempts to match a set of measurements taken on an unknown skull with the same measurements representing a population in the world. Although Fordisc is an important tool in forensic anthropology, its application is beyond the scope of this book, so we will now turn to morphoscopic traits.

Most anthropologists use many traits to get a general idea (or the gestalt) of the unknown individual (see Table 15.6). In Figures 15.32 through 15.44, pay close attention to which traits each of the individuals from different populations exhibit, and then look at the overall face and profile. Note the similarities and differences between groups and individuals.

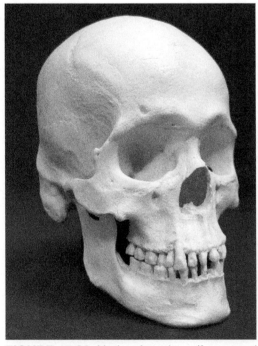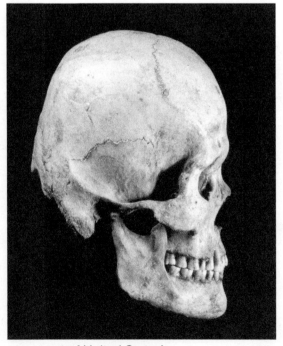

FIGURE 15.32 Native American (from southwestern part of United States).

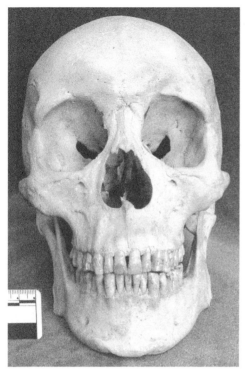
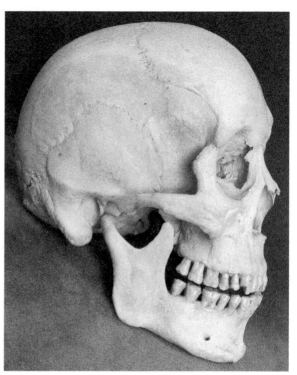

FIGURE 15.33 Mongolian male. *Photos, D. L. France; skull from National Museum of Natural History*

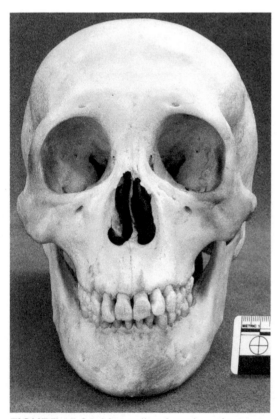
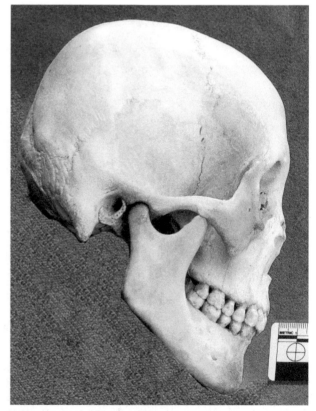

FIGURE 15.34 Mongolian female. *Photos, D. L. France; skull from National Museum of Natural History*

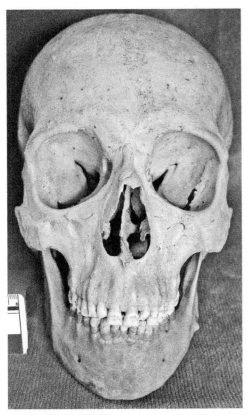
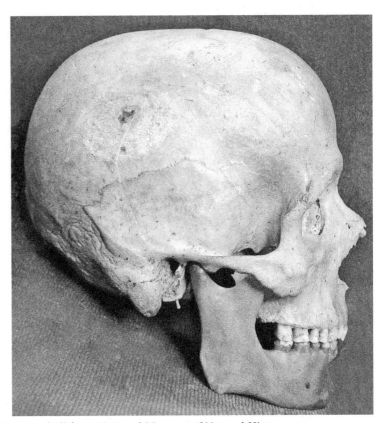

FIGURE 15.35 European male. *Photos, D. L. France; skull from National Museum of Natural History*

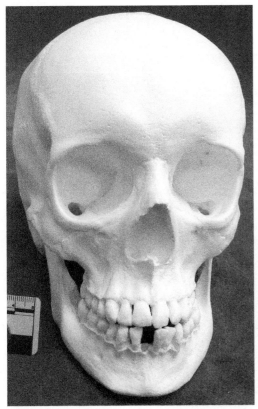
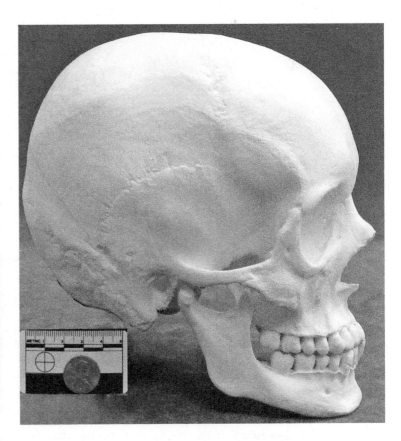

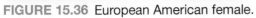

FIGURE 15.36 European American female.

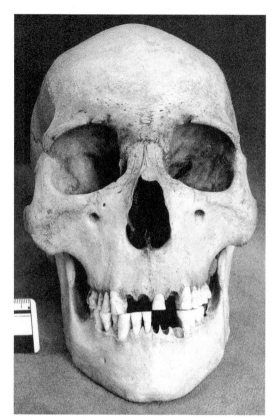
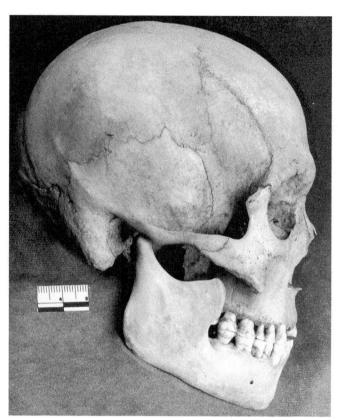

FIGURE 15.37 Eskimo male. *Photos, D. L. France; skull from National Museum of Natural History*

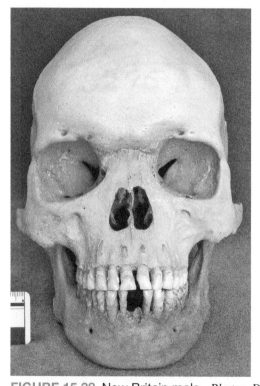
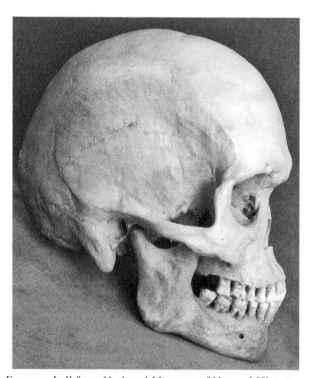

FIGURE 15.38 New Britain male. *Photos, D. L. France; skull from National Museum of Natural History*

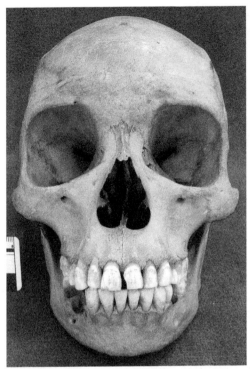
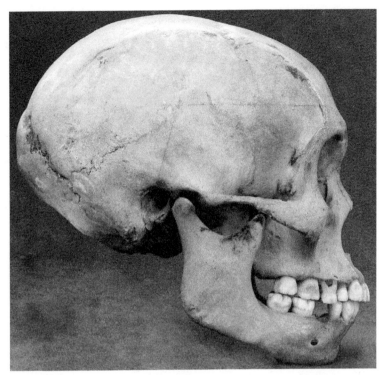

FIGURE 15.39 Australian female. *Photos, D. L. France of material from National Museum of Natural History*

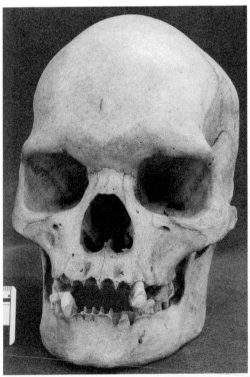
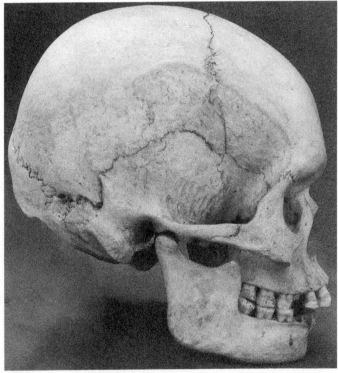

FIGURE 15.40 Australian male. *Photos, D. L. France of material from National Museum of Natural History*

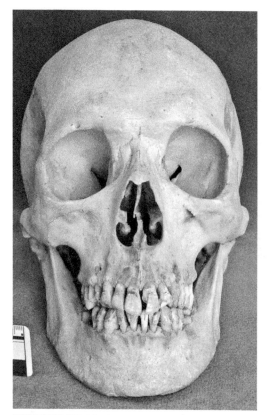

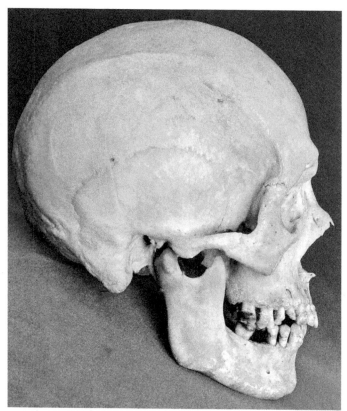

FIGURE 15.41 Japanese male. *Photos, D. L. France; skull from National Museum of Natural History*

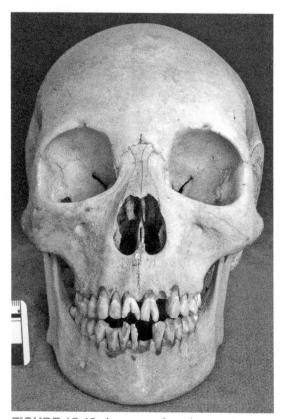

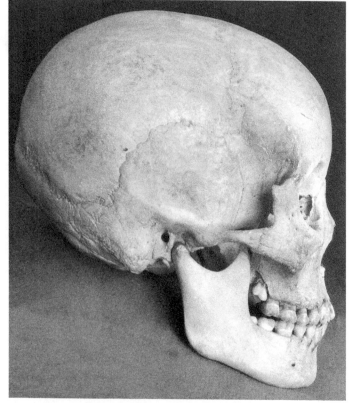

FIGURE 15.42 Japanese female. *Photos, D. L. France; skull from National Museum of Natural History*

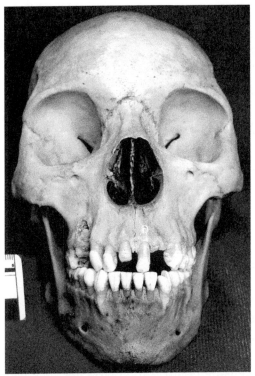

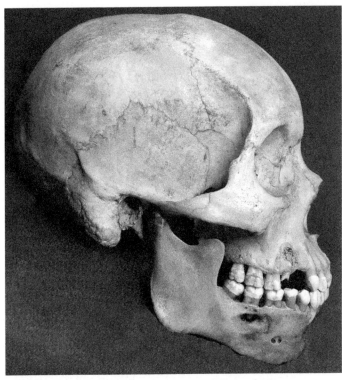

FIGURE 15.43 African American male. *Photos, D. L. France; skull from National Museum of Natural History*

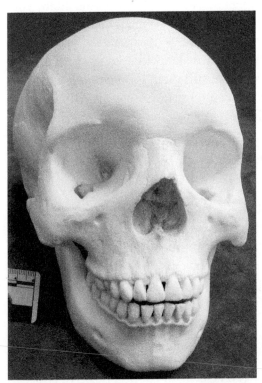

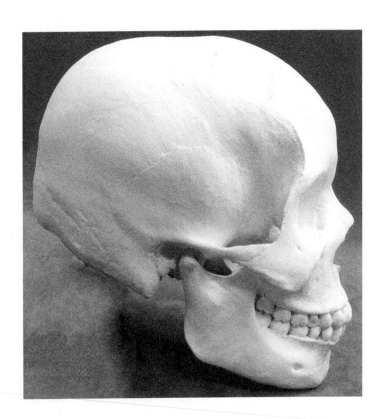

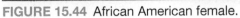

FIGURE 15.44 African American female.

ESTIMATION OF STATURE

The following measurements are lengths, measured in millimeters. The results are in inches; that is, measure the bone in millimeters, multiply that measurement by the "factor," and add the constant. Add the 90 percent prediction interval (PI) number to the result, and then subtract it from the result for the stature range into which 90 percent of the measured individuals will fall. For example, if the femur length for a male of European ancestry is 454 mm, there is a 90 percent chance that his stature is:

$$0.10560 \, (454) + 19.39 = 67.33 \, +/- \, 2.8"$$

FURTHER TRAINING IN FORENSIC ANTHROPOLOGY

If you are interested in a career in forensic anthropology, it is increasingly important to obtain a PhD and then to be certified as an expert by the American Board of Forensic Anthropology (ABFA), currently the only certifying agency for forensic anthropology in this country. The ABFA is not a licensing board, and you do not have to have a license to practice forensic anthropology, but being board certified is important when you are being qualified as an expert in court. Anyone can testify in court if asked (and if you receive a subpoena, you must testify), but to testify as an expert in your field, you must be qualified as an expert in that courtroom. Being board certified in any field means that you are more easily qualified as an expert in court because a certifying board states that you have the knowledge, training, and experience sufficient to make you an expert. For further information, search for the American Board of Forensic Anthropology on the web at www.theABFA.org.

COMPARISON OF ANTEMORTEM TO POSTMORTEM CHARACTERISTICS

There are several ways to obtain a positive identification of remains. A positive identification is what it states: There are enough characteristics in common with the antemortem records that it is so unlikely that the remains could represent someone else that it represents a positive identification. If fingerprints are available, and if enough points of comparison on a latent print (one made before death in, for example, a police fingerprint record) are the same as on the body, a positive identification can be made (see Chapter 13 for examples of how fingerprints are "typed"). Dental comparisons (dental radiographs before and after death) can also, with enough positive comparison points, be considered a positive identification. DNA (nuclear or mitochondrial, depending on the condition of the remains) can be obtained from the soft tissue or bones and can be compared to DNA

TABLE 15.7 Estimating Stature*

Factor	Bone Measurement, in mm	Constant	90% PI	N
Males of European Ancestry				
0.05566	Femur max. L + Tibia L	21.64	+/− 2.5"	62
0.05552	Femur max. L + Fibula L	22.00	+/− 2.6"	54
0.10560	Femur max. L	19.39	+/− 2.8"	69
0.10140	Tibia L	30.38	+/− 2.8"	67
0.15890	Ulna L	26.91	+/− 3.1"	62
0.12740	Humerus L	26.79	+/− 3.3"	66
0.16398	Radius L	28.35	+/− 3.3"	59
Females of European Ancestry				
0.06524	Femur max. L + Fibula L	12.94	+/− 2.3"	38
0.06163	Femur max. L + Tibia L	15.43	+/− 2.4"	42
0.11869	Femur max. L	12.43	+/− 2.4"	48
0.11168	Tibia L	24.65	+/− 3.0"	43
0.11827	Humerus L	28.30	+/− 3.1"	45
0.13353	Ulna L	31.99	+/− 3.1"	40
0.18467	Radius L	22.42	+/− 3.4"	38
Males of African Ancestry				
0.16997	Ulna L	21.20	+/− 3.3"	14
0.10521	Tibia L	26.26	+/− 3.8"	19
0.08388	Femur max. L	28.57	+/− 4.0"	17
0.07824	Humerus L	43.19	+/− 4.4"	20
Females of African Ancestry				
0.11640	Femur max. L	11.98	+/− 2.4"	18

*From Ousley, S., "Should We Estimate Biological or Forensic Stature?" *Journal of Forensic Sciences* 40(5): 768–773 (September 1995).

obtained from antemortem sources (family members, blood sources, hair from hairbrushes, epithelial cells from toothbrushes, and so on). Radiographs from antemortem sources can also be compared to postmortem radiographs (see Figure 15.45).

Medical interventions done before someone died can also be compared to postmortem information. For example, note the surgical plate used to stabilize the wrist in Figure 15.46, and in particular, note the serial number on the plate in Figure 15.47 (part of the number has been smudged because this is a real case and the anonymity must be preserved). Theoretically, one could trace this number through the manufacturer to the hospital, and ultimately to the patient, but sometimes the details of those records are not retained.

There is one complication with all of these techniques: You need to have antemortem information to compare with the postmortem tests.

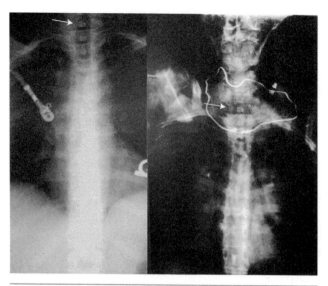

FIGURE 15.45 Comparison of antemortem (left) and postmortem (right) radiographs. Arrows show corresponding vertebrae.

FIGURE 15.46 Surgical intervention at the wrist.

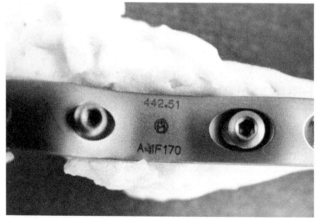

FIGURE 15.47 Wrist plate with serial number.

Except for some information about ancestry, eye color, and some other features that can be obtained now from a genome, postmortem analysis must be compared to some known antemortem records.

That is where the information from the anthropologist can help. The biological profile (age, sex, ancestry, idiosyncrasies) can help to narrow the search in the missing persons database. The popular technique of applying a face to a skull (variously called "facial reconstruction" or "facial approximation") is part science (in that the average tissue depths come from many measurements of tissue depths) and part artistic rendition because the exact shape of the

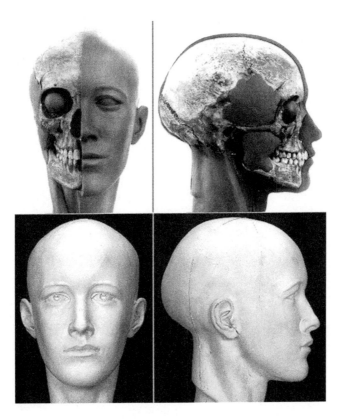

FIGURE 15.48 Facial approximation technique. *Photo, Sergei Nikitin of his work*

nose, the shape of the soft tissue surrounding the eyes, whether or not there are wrinkles on the face, and so on, are not precisely known from the morphology of the skull. The purpose of the facial approximation (see Figure 15.48) is to publish the rendition of the face in newspapers and to show it on television to determine if someone will look at it and say "that looks like Uncle Joe who has been missing for 10 years." It should be used as the last-ditch attempt to narrow the search for a missing person and never as a means of positive identification.

EXERCISE 15.1   NAME _____   SECTION _____   DATE _____

Forensic Anthropology

1. What is the difference between time since death and time since deposition? How might there be a significant difference between those two in how a forensic case is investigated?

2. What are some of the taphonomic influences not mentioned in the text? How might they influence the body (with soft tissue or without soft tissue)?

3. Resolve the unknown individual from the forensic case presented in the first part of this chapter (page 371). What is the age of this individual? The sex? The ancestry? Are there identifiable injuries? Be sure you can justify your responses with appropriate evidence.

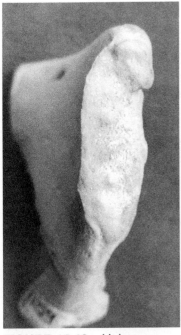

FIGURE 15.49a Unknown pubic symphysis.

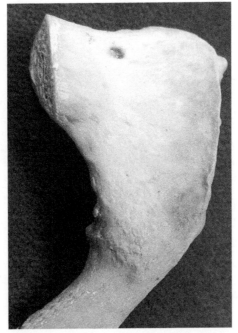

FIGURE 15.49b Unknown pubic bone dorsal surface.

4. Figures 15.49a and b show one pubic bone. Figure 15.49a shows the pubic symphysis, and 15.49b shows the dorsal surface.

a. What is the sex of this individual?

b. Using the Suchey–Brooks age determination system appropriate to the sex you assigned, to what phase did you assign this pubic bone?

c. What is the approximate age of this individual?

FIGURE 15.50 Unknown.

5. What happened to the individual represented in Figure 15.50? Be as specific as possible in your assessment.

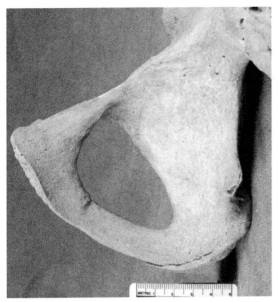

FIGURE 15.51a Unknown.

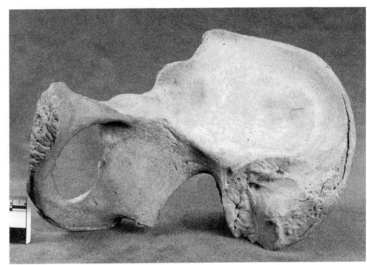

FIGURE 15.51b Unknown.

6. Using Figures 15.51a and b, answer the following:

   a. What is the sex of the individual represented? What did you use to make this determination, and why?

   b. What is the approximate age of this individual? How do you know?

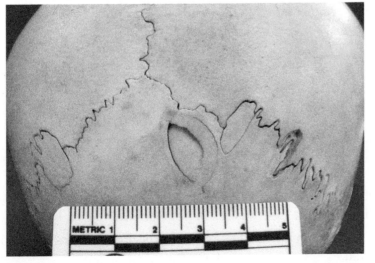

FIGURE 15.52 Unknown.

7. What happened to the individual shown in Figure 15.52? Be as specific as possible.

FIGURE 15.53 Unknown cranium.

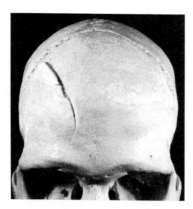

8. Describe what happened to the individual in Figure 15.53. Be as specific as possible.

FIGURE 15.54 Shoveled incisor.

9. Figure 15.54 shows a shoveled central incisor. To what population(s) does this individual possibly belong (only in terms of likelihood)?

10. Should forensic anthropologists determine the ancestry of an individual in a forensic case? Why or why not? What did you learn from comparing the skulls from Figures 15.32 to 15.45?

REEXAMINING THE ISSUES

- Determinations of aspects of the biological profile (age, sex, ancestry, stature, and so on) are based on statistical probabilities derived from studies of populations.
- It is as important to describe skeletal characteristics in a study or in a report as it is to diagnose what those characteristics mean.
- Forensic anthropology (and forensics in general) has exploded in popularity in recent years, but it is as important to demonstrate what cannot be done in forensics as it is to show what can be done (and in this chapter, what is and is not possible in investigations of the skeleton).

Glossary

Abducts Draws away from.

Acetabulum on the ossa coxae, the point of articulation with the head of the femur.

Acheulian tools An early tool type that appears in association with *Homo erectus* remains.

Acromion process Posterior projection on the superior scapula.

Adapids Members of the Eocene family Adapidae, the fossils of which are found in Europe.

Adapoidea One of two Eocene superfamilies of euprimates (the other is Omomyoidea), the first recognizable primates. Adapoidea is thought to be more lemur-like although there are differences from modern lemurs.

Adaptive radiation Relatively rapid increase and spread of an evolving group of organisms that spread into and adapt to new ecological niches.

Adenine One of four chemical bases central to the structure of a DNA nucleotide.

Ad-lib sampling A technique in which primate behavior is recorded by observing any behavior of a group that is interesting and/or readily observable.

Afradapis An adipiform primate from the late Eocene in the Fayum Depression in northern Egypt.

Agglutination Clumping of red blood cells as a result of the destruction of blood antigens by antibodies.

Ala One of the "wings" of the fleshy nose or bony sacrum.

Allele Alternative form of a gene.

Alveolare The apex of the septum between the upper central incisors.

Ameloblasts Cells that secrete enamel.

Amphiarthrosis (plural: amphiarthroses) A joint in which some movement is allowed.

Amphipithecids Members of the Eocene family Amphipithecidae, the fossils of which are found in Asia.

Analogies Characters that are morphological and functionally similar between species but are not shared by common descent.

Anatomical position Body with arms by side, palms forward.

Anencephaly A pathological condition in which the full brain of a fetus does not develop.

Antemortem Before death.

Anterior In front of (*similar to* Ventral).

Anthropoidea Suborder of primates that includes monkeys, apes, and humans.

Antibodies Proteins produced by the body in response to, and in an attempt to neutralize, a foreign antigen.

Antigens As used in this book, proteins that occur on the blood cells of an individual.

Apomorphic Derived characters.

Appendicular The skeleton of the limbs.

Arboreal theory Theory that the characters found on most primates are adaptations that allow primates to pursue an arboreal lifestyle.

Arthritis Inflammation of a joint surface that can cause bony changes at and around the joint.

Articulation In osteology, where two bones move against each other.

Artificial selection Intentional selection of individuals showing desirable traits.

Ascending ramus Of the mandible, the vertical aspect of bone above the gonial angle to the condyles.

Assortative mating Occurs when individuals mate more frequently and more consistently with those similar to themselves or dissimilar to themselves in those traits.

Atlas First cervical vertebra.

Auricular surface Of the ilium, an area that articulates with the sacrum.

Australopithecus Extinct genus of hominins that lived during the Plio-Pleistocene. This genus is usually divided into the gracile species *africanus*, the robust species *robustus, boisei,* and *aethiopicus,* and the very early species *afarensis* (see also *Paranthropus*).

Autosomes Chromosomes that carry DNA for all characteristics except for the sex of the individual.

Axial The skeleton of the head and trunk.

Axis Second cervical vertebra.

Bases Part of a nucleotide held together with a sugar and a phosphate compound. The bases make up the DNA and RNA chains. DNA bases are adenine, guanine, cytosine, and thymine. RNA bases are adenine, guanine, cytosine, and uracil.

Basilar suture *See* Spheno-occipital synchondrosis.

Basion The midpoint of the anterior margin of the foramen magnum.

Bilophodont molars Usually have four cusps situated in two parallel rows.

Binocular vision Vision in which the visual field between the two eyes overlap, creating a greater depth of field.

Binomial In genetics, the mathematical equation consisting of two terms; in classification, a two-word scientific name consisting of a genus name and a species name.

Biological profile Age, sex, ancestry, stature, and other aspects that characterize an individual.

Biped An animal that habitually walks on two legs.

Brachial index Measures the relative lengths of the upper and lower arm.

Brachiator An animal that habitually swings under branches in arm-over-arm locomotion.

Brachycephaly Having a round head (*brachycrany* in the dry cranium).

Bregma The intersection of the coronal and sagittal sutures.

Buccal In the mouth toward the cheek.

Calcaneus The largest bone of the ankle.

Callimiconidae Primitive New World monkey family of Goeldi's marmoset.

Callitrichidae Primitive New World monkey family of tamarins and marmosets.

Canine Single-rooted teeth lateral to the incisors in the anterior mandible and maxilla.

Capitate One of the bones of the wrist.

Carpals The bones of the wrist.

Catarrhini Anthropoid infraorder of Old World monkeys, apes, and humans.

Caudal Toward the tail.

Cavity An open area.

Cebidae New World monkey family including squirrel, spider, capuchin, howler, and other monkey species.

Ceboidea Anthropoid superfamily of New World monkeys.

Centromere The place where two sister chromatids are joined.

Cercopithecidae Old World monkey family that includes baboons, macaques, mangabeys, guenons, and others.

Cercopithecinae Old World monkey subfamily.

Cercopithecoidea Old World monkey superfamily.

Cervical vertebra One of the seven (the number sometimes varies) uppermost vertebrae, in the neck.

Chain of evidence/chain of custody The record of contact with and custody of evidence.

Characters Morphological traits.

Chi-square A measure of the statistical significance of the deviation of a frequency of occurrences from an expected frequency.

Crista galli A ridge of bone in the interior midline of the ethmoid bone.

Chondroblasts Cartilage-forming cells.

Chondroclasts Cartilage-removing cells.

Chromosome A thread-like collection of DNA molecules. Chromosomes carry genes.

Chromatid One of two identical copies of DNA comprising a replicated chromosome.

Clade A group of organisms related through a common ancestor.

Cladistics (cladism) Classification based exclusively on genealogy, such that a group of species is all descended from a common ancestor.

Clavicle The collarbone, maintains a constant distance between the scapula and the sternum.

Cline A gradient of frequency of traits in a population.

Cloaca In osteology, an opening in the bone through which pus drains.

Coccygeal vertebra One of the most inferior vertebrae in the spinal column.

Codominant alleles Alleles that, when paired in an organism, are both expressed (either additively or distinctively).

Codons The three-base code for amino acids on the messenger RNA chain.

Colobidae Old World monkey family that includes langurs and other colobine monkeys.

Comminuted fracture Fracture into many pieces.

Compound fracture Bone fracture in which the broken end(s) of the bone erupt through the skin.

Condylar index Measures the position of the foramen magnum.

Condyle Rounded process at the point of articulation with another bone.

Coracoid process Anterior projection on the superior scapula.

Core In dermatoglyphics, the central-most ridge at the approximate center of a ridge pattern.

Coronal plane The plane through the body parallel to the coronal suture (dividing anterior from posterior).

Coronal suture On the cranium, posterior to the frontal bone, coursing laterally.

Coronoid process The area of the mandible that is the insertion of the masseter muscle (one of the muscles of chewing).

Correlation coefficient A measure of linear dependence or mutual relationship between two random variables.

Costal Referring to a rib.

Costal facets/pits Facets on thoracic vertebrae for the articulation of ribs.

Costochondral Cartilage at the sternal end of the ribs.

Coxa *See* Os coxa.

Cranial Toward the head.

Craniostenosis Premature fusion of the sutures of the cranium.

Cranium The skull minus the mandible.

Crest A projecting ridge.

Cribiform plate A porous structure inside the cranium on the ethmoid bone, which supports the olfactory bulb of the brain.

Crossing over The exchange of genetic information between homologous chromosomes during the first meiotic division.

Crown The part of a tooth above the gum line; covered by enamel.

Crural Referring to the leg or thigh.

Crural index Measures the relative lengths of the thigh and leg bones.

Cuboid One of the bones of the ankle.

Cytoplasm The fluid within the cell.

Cytosine One of four chemical bases central to the structure of a DNA nucleotide.

Deciduous teeth Subadult teeth.

Delta Point in dermatoglyphics where three ridges diverge, or the point nearest the center of divergence of the type lines (also called *triradius*).

Dens *See* Odontoid process.

Dental formula The number and types of teeth in one quadrant, written in shorthand form.

Deoxyribonucleic acid Large molecules composed of four chemical bases: adenine, guanine, cytosine, and thymine, as well as phosphates and sugars. These are the genetic codes for the assembly of amino acids, which are building blocks of proteins.

Dependent variables Variables that can be controlled in the experiment.

Derived characters Evolving from more primitive characters, these are usually acquired by few members of an evolutionary group (they are not found in earlier ancestors).

Dermatoglyphics The study of the ridge patterns on the skin of the hands and feet.

Diaphysis Primary centers of bone growth; the shafts of long bones.

Diastema In general, a gap. In primates this usually refers to a gap in the mandibular teeth that makes room for the maxillary canines.

Distal Away from the center of the body. In the mouth, this term refers to the direction away from the anterior midline.

Diurnal Active during daylight hours.

DNA *See* Deoxyribonucleic acid.

DNA typing A means of identification (in any plant or animal with DNA) using genetic codes.

Dolicocephaly Having a long head (*dolicocrany* in the dry cranium).

Dominant allele An allele that is phenotypically expressed in the heterozygote and that prevents the expression of the recessive allele.

Dorsal In back of (*similar to* Posterior).

Dryopithecus An extinct genus of hominoids from the Miocene.

Eburnation Polishing of bone caused by bone rubbing on bone.

Ectocranium Outside the cranium.

Endochondral bone Bone formed from a cartilage matrix that is derived from specialized mesenchymal cells.

Endocranium Inside the cranium.

Enzyme A protein that accelerates a specific chemical reaction in a living system.

Epiphysis Secondary centers of bone growth at the ends of long bones. These centers eventually unite with the diaphysis, at which time longitudinal growth ceases at that location.

Ethmoid bone Paired bone on the medial eye orbit.

Eukaryotic Cells that have a discrete nucleus and other organelles contained within a plasma membrane.

Euprimates Modern primates.

Evolution Occurs when allele frequency changes from one generation to the next in a population.

Evolutionary classification Classifications based on descent from a common ancestor, as are clades, but also take into account different rates of evolution in different lineages.

External Outside of.

External auditory meatus The bony opening of the ear.

External occipital protuberance A prominence on the external occipital bone approximately in the midline.

Facet A smooth, small point of articulation.

Fayum A primate site in Egypt that has yielded several Oligocene fossil forms.

Femur The bone of the thigh.

Fibula The small bone of the leg, lateral to the tibia.

First cuneiform One of the bones of the ankle.

Focal sampling The researcher records the behavior of a specific animal.

Fontanelle Membranous space between cranial bones in fetal life and infancy.

Foramen A hole or opening.

Foramen magnum "Big hole" on the base of the cranium in the occipital bone. This is where the spinal nerves (cord) enter the cranium.

Foramen ovale Opening on the sphenoid bone (near posterior margin of greater wing.

Forensic physical anthropology Sometimes shortened to forensic anthropology, this is the application of physical/biological methods to answer medicolegal questions.

Forensic science The application of scientific methods to the law.

Fossa A pit, depression, or cavity.

Founder effect A case in which a newly isolated sample from the original population soon diverges genetically from the parent population.

Fovea capitis A pit on the head of the femur that connects the femur to the acetabulum and through which blood is carried to the femur.

Frankfort plane A standard position of reference in which the upper border of the external auditory meatus is on a horizontal plane with the lower border of the eye.

Frontal bone A bone on the anterosuperior portion of the cranium.

Gametes Sex cells (sperm or ova) that contain half of the chromosomes of the adult of that species.

Gender The way in which an individual identifies himself or herself, as opposed to sex, which references the biological features that differentiate males and females.

Gene Section of DNA responsible for the ultimate synthesis of a specific gene product, usually a polypeptide chain of amino acids; portion of DNA with a detectable function.

Gene flow A movement of genes from one population to another.

Gene pool The total complement of genes in a population.

Genetic drift An effect of sampling error and chance fluctuations in gene frequency; a function of population size.

Genome A complete set of chromosomes (and genes) inherited as a unit from one parent.

Genotype The genetic constitution (gene makeup) of an organism.

Gigantopithecus A genus of very large Miocene to Pleistocene hominoids.

Glabella The most forward-projecting point of the forehead in the midline at the level of the supraorbital ridges, and superior to the nasofrontal suture.

Glenoid process (or fossa) On the lateral scapula, this is the point of articulation of the scapula with the head of the humerus.

Gnathion Lowest median point on the lower border of the mandible.

Gonial angle The angle of the mandible at the lowest point on the ascending ramus.

Gradistic classifications Based on gross anatomy and behaviors.

Greater multangular One of the bones of the wrist.

Greater sciatic notch A deep incurve on the posterior ilium.

Guanine One of four chemical bases central to the structure of a DNA nucleotide.

Hamate One of the bones of the wrist.

Haplorhini Primate suborder that includes all higher primates, including tarsiers.

Hardy–Weinberg equilibrium An expression of predicted genetic equilibrium that would occur under ideal conditions.

Harris lines (growth arrest lines) Areas of slowed bone growth resulting in a line of dense bone cells.

Heterodonty An animal with more than one tooth form (incisors, canines, and so on).

Hemizygous Used in reference to males in sex-linked traits, as most of these traits are contained on the X chromosome, and have no corresponding locus on the Y chromosome.

Heterozygote An organism with unlike members of any given pair or series of alleles at a particular locus (for example, AA or BB).

Hominidae Human family.

Hominids Common term to describe humans and other upright bipeds in the fossil record.

Hominin Modern humans and extinct bipedal relatives.

Hominoid Common term to describe lesser apes, great apes, and humans.

Hominoidea Old World superfamily in which apes and humans are classified.

Homo The genus into which humans are categorized.

Homo erectus The hominid species which occurred between *H. habilis* and *H. sapiens*.

Homo habilis The hominid species that occurred between *Australopithecus* and *Homo erectus*.

Homo sapiens The genus and species of modern and archaic humans.

Homologous chromosomes Chromosomes that carry genetic information for the same trait, though not necessarily the same codes for that trait. For instance, one chromosome may carry the dominant code for a trait, the homologous chromosome may carry the recessive code for the same trait, but they both code for the same trait.

Homologies Characters that are morphologically and functionally similar between species resulting from common descent.

Homozygote An organism whose chromosomes carry identical members of a given pair of alleles (for example, AA or BB or aa).

Human Genome Project An international research effort to determine the DNA sequence of the entire human genome.

Humerus The bone of the arm, and the largest bone of the upper limb.

Hylobatidae Hominoid family that includes gibbons and siamangs.

Hyoid bone Small bone suspended below the mandible by many muscles acting on the tongue, pharynx, and neck.

Iliac crest The rounded superior margin of the ilium.

Ilium The upper bone of the os coxa.

Incisor Single-rooted tooth at the anterior of mouth in both maxilla and mandible, central to canines.

Incomplete fracture Fractures in which the bone is not completely broken.

Independent variables The subjects of the hypothesis that, by definition, are not controlled.

Inferior Lower.

Inion An intersection in the midline with a line drawn tangent to the uppermost convexity of the right and left superior nuchal lines.

Insertion The point of attachment of a ligament or tendon on bone.

Intermembral index Measures the relative lengths of the upper and lower limbs.

Interspecies variation Variation between species.

Internal Inside of.

Intramembranous bone Bones that are transformed from mesenchymal tissues, including some bones of the cranial vault, facial bones, mandible, and clavicle.

Intraspecies variation Variation within species.

Introns A section of the DNA or RNA molecule that interrupts the code for genes.

Involucrum A shell surrounding a sequestrum in an infected bone.

Ischial tuberosity A large prominence on the posterior ischium.

Ischium The inferoposterior bone of the os coxa.

Karyotype The summary of the chromosomes within a nucleus often viewed as an image.

Knuckle-walking Locomotor mode of chimpanzees and gorillas in which the animal walks on the knuckles of the front limbs and on the soles of the feet.

Labial In the mouth, toward the lips.

Lacrimal bone On the medial eye orbit.

Lambdoidal suture On the posterior cranium, between the occipital and parietal bones.

Lateral To the side, away from the midline.

Lateral malleolus A downward-projecting process of bone on the lateral fibula.

Leg In popular language, refers to the entire lower limb; in anatomical terms it refers to the area defined by the tibia and fibula.

Lemuroidea Prosimian superfamily of lemurs, found today only on Madagascar.

Leptorrhiny Narrow nasal aperture.

Lesser multangular (trapezoid) One of the bones of the wrist.

Levallois technique A technique of tool manufacture associated with Neanderthal remains.

Ligament Strong connective tissue that holds bones in proximity at a joint.

Ligamentum teres Strong ligament that maintains the close contact between the head of the femur and the acetabulum.

Linea aspera Long raised and roughened line coursing longitudinally on the posterior femur. This is the point of insertion of muscles of the thigh.

Lingual In the mouth, toward the tongue.

Locus Location on a chromosome for a particular trait.

Longitudinal Coursing or placed lengthwise (*opposite of* transverse).

Lorisoidea Prosimian superfamily of lorises found in Africa and southern Asia.

"Lucy" A specimen of *Australopithecus afarensis* found in Hadar, Ethiopia, in 1974.

Lumbar vertebra One of the bones of the spinal column in the lower back.

Lunate bone One of the bones of the wrist.

Mandible Bone of the lower jaw.

Mandibular condyles The articular surfaces of the mandible that articulates with the cranium at the temporomandibular joint.

Mandibular foramen On the medial side of the mandible, a foramen that allows passage of the mental nerve and blood vessels on either side of the midline.

Manubrium The most superior portion of the sternum, usually fused to the rest of the sternum in the adult.

Masseter muscle One of the muscles of chewing.

Mastoid process A downward-projecting process of bone on the temporal bone, onto which the sternocleidomastoid muscle inserts.

Maxilla Bone of the lower face on the cranium.

Mean The average of a set of measurements, calculated by adding the terms and dividing their sum by the number of terms.

Meatus A canal.

Medial Toward the midline.

Medial malleolus A downward-projecting process of bone on the medial tibia.

Meiosis The process of cell division that results in half of the full complement of chromosomes for gametes, or sex cells.

Membranous bone Bone that grows from membranous tissue instead of from a cartilage matrix.

Mendel's principle of segregation See Principle of segregation.

Mental eminence Chin.

Mental foramen Foramen on the mandible (paired) on the lateral aspect.

Mesenchymal cells Unspecialized cells in the embryo that give rise to all connective tissue, including cartilage, bone, and teeth (as well as some other types of cells).

Mesial In the mouth, direction toward the anterior midline.

Mesocephaly Having a medium-shaped head (in between long and round) (*mesocrany* in the dry cranium).

Mesorrhiny Nasal aperture of medium size.

Messenger RNA RNA molecules that take information from the DNA within the nucleus to ribosomes outside of the nucleus.

Metacarpals The five bones of the palm.

Metaphysis Location of bone growth between the diaphysis and epiphysis.

Metastasis The spread of a cancerous growth to areas of the body other than where it originated.

Metatarsals The five bones of the main part of the foot.

Metopic suture Between the two halves of the frontal bone in very young individuals, usually missing or only a remnant in the adult.

Microcephalic Pathologically small brain size, usually resulting in mental retardation.

Mitochondria Organelles within the cytoplasm responsible for manufacturing energy within the cell.

Mitochondrial DNA Deoxyribonucleic acid that occurs outside the nucleus of the cell, in the mitochondria, and is therefore passed from generation to generation only by females.

Mitosis Cell replication and division in which the two resulting cells each have a full complement of genetic information.

Molar Multiple-cusped and multiple-rooted tooth in distal part of mouth.

Molecular clock Calculation from biomolecular data of the time of separation of evolutionary taxa.

Mollison's craniophore An apparatus that places the cranium in the Frankfort plane.

Monosomy The absence of one of a pair of chromosomes in a daughter cell.

Mousterian tool Upper Paleolithic stone tools associated with Archaic *Homo sapiens* and *Homo neandertalensis*.

Mutation An actual alteration in genetic material. This is the basic creative force in evolution and the only way to produce entirely new variation in a population. This is a change in DNA.

Nasal bone Paired bones on the medial aspect of the nose.

Nasion The midline point of intersection of the internasal suture with the nasofrontal suture; the point where the two nasal bones and the frontal bone meet.

Nasospinale The midpoint of a line drawn connecting the two lower margins of the right and left nasal apertures.

Natural selection A process that acts on population variation. Natural selection is differential net reproductive success, in which individuals best adapted to an environment will pass on their genetic information to the next generation.

Navicular One of the bones of the wrist (also called scaphoid), and also one of the bones of the ankle.

Neanderthals Once thought of as a population of archaic *Homo sapiens* in Europe, most paleoanthropologists place Neanderthals in their own species that is transitional from *Homo erectus* to *Homo sapiens*.

Neck Of a tooth, the constricted area just below the crown.

Niche The environment to which a species is adapted, including diet, habitat preference, activity pattern, and other features.

Nocturnal Active during the night.

Nondisjunction Failure of chromosome pairs to separate correctly during cell division.

Nonmetric traits Traits that are not measured but are scored as present or absent (though sometimes scored as small, medium, or large).

Normal distribution A probability distribution depicted graphically by a bell-shaped curve symmetrical about the mean.

Notharctids Members of the Eocene family Notharctidae, the fossils of which are found in North America.

Nuchal Referring to the neck (cervical area of the body).

Nuchal index Measures the area given for the origin of nuchal muscles.

Nucleotide One genetic base (see Deoxyribonucleic acid) attached to a sugar and phosphate group.

Occipital bone Bone of the posterior inferior portion of the cranium.

Occipital condyles Area of articulation between the occipital bone and the atlas (first cervical) vertebra.

Occlusal The chewing surface of the teeth.

Odontoblasts Dentin-forming cells.

Odontoid process A prominence on the second cervical vertebra around which the first cervical vertebra rotates.

Oldowan tool The earliest recognized stone tool.

Omomyoidea One of two Eocene superfamilies of euprimates (the other is Adapoida), the first recognizable primates. Omomyoidea is thought to be more tarsier-like.

Opisthocranion The most posterior point on the cranium not on the external occipital protuberance.

Orale A point on the hard palate where a line drawn tangent to the curves in the alveolar margin in back of the two medial incisor teeth crosses the midline.

Origin of a muscle Area of its attachment to bone that remains relatively fixed during the contraction of that muscle.

Os coxa One of the bones of the hip, consisting of the fused ilium, ischium, and pubis (os pubis) (also called innominate).

Ossification centers The points at which osteoblasts initially invade the cartilage to lay down bone.

Osteoblasts Bone-forming cells.

Osteoclasts Bone-removing cells.

Osteocyte Bone cell.

Osteophyte A bony projection (sometimes called a bone spur) that occurs along a joint surface, often in reference to bony outgrowths along the vertebral borders.

Osteophytosis A condition characterized by multiple osteophytes.

Osteoporosis Increased porosity of bone.

Palatal index Measures the shape of the palate.

Palatal suture Suture that runs from anterior to posterior in the midline of the palate.

Palatine bone Paired bone on the posterior palate.

Parietal bone Paired bone on the laterosuperior portions of the cranium.

Parturition scars Remnants in the female pelvic girdle as a result of having given birth. One example of this is dorsal pitting on the dorsal surface of the pubic bone.

Pascal's triangle A shorthand method of determining coefficients in binomial equations.

Patella Kneecap, a large sesamoid bone.

Pentadactyly Five digits.

Perimortem At or around the time of death.

Periosteum Thin layer of soft tissue that surrounds bone.

Periostitis An inflammation of the periosteum.

Phalanges The bones of the fingers and toes.

Phenotype Characteristics of an individual visually observed or discernable by other means.

Phylogenetic classification scheme A classification scheme based on evolutionary relationships, usually including a time line.

Phylogeny The study of evolutionary lines of descent.

Piezoelectric effect A slight electric charge produced in the bone that may produce more bone.

Pisiform One of the bones of the wrist.

Plasma membrane Outer surface of the cell.

Platyrrhini An infraorder of Anthropoidea of New World monkeys.

Platyrrhiny Wide nasal aperture.

Pleisomorphic Primitive characters.

Plexiform bone Bone cells that are similar to stacked curved bricks when viewed in microscopic cross section.

Polar bodies During oogenesis (production of eggs during meiosis), those nonviable cells that give up their cytoplasm for the one viable gamete produced (also, in another context, a big white bear).

Polymerase chain reaction (PCR) A method for making multiple copies of a particular DNA sequence.

Pongid Common term to describe apes.

Pongidae Hominoid family of apes.

Porion The most anterior point on the upper alveolar process in the midline.

Posterior Behind, toward the back (*similar to* Dorsal).

Postmortem After death.

Prediction interval In stature estimation, a 90 percent prediction interval is the prediction that all individuals with the same measurement will fall within this range.

Premolar Tooth between canine and molar (also called bicuspids). There are no deciduous premolars in humans.

Primates The order of mammals to which prosimians, monkeys, apes, and humans belong.

Primitive characters Found with phylogenetically older organisms, these are usually shared with many organisms in an evolutionary group.

Principle of independent assortment Members of different homologous chromosomes separate independently into gametes. The way in which one set of homologous chromosomes separates into cells has no effect on other homologous chromosome separations.

Principle of segregation Parental traits do not blend in the offspring during meiosis. Homologous chromosomes, carrying the genes for each of those traits, separate into two different cells.

Process Any outgrowth or prominence of bone.

Proconsul An extinct genus of early Miocene hominoid.

Prognathism Projection of the lower face.

Prokaryotic Cells that lack a nucleus and other organelles that are within the plasma membrane.

Pronation Rotation of the hand and forearm so that the palm faces dorsally or toward the body. Some primates can perform the same action with the foot.

Prosimian Common term for Prosimii, the suborder of primates that includes lemurs, lorises, and tarsiers.

Prosthion The most anterior point on the upper alveolar process in the midline.

Proximal Toward the center of the body.

Pseudoarthrosis False joint caused by unreduced dislocation or unstable fracture.

Pubic symphysis The face of the pubic bone at its medial side.

Pubis (or os pubis) The anterior bone of the os coxa.

Punctuated equilibria Slow evolutionary rates of change punctuated by spurts of sudden significant change.

Punnett square A shorthand tool used to calculate offspring genotypes from specific parental genotypes.

Quadruped Animal that habitually walks on four limbs.

Radius The lateral bone of the forearm.

Ramapithecus An extinct genus of hominoid of the Miocene, now considered likely to be a female *Sivapithecus.*

Recessive allele An allele that is not expressed when paired with a dominant allele.

Ribosomes Organelles made of ribosomal RNA (ribonucleic acid) responsible for protein synthesis.

Ridge count The number of ridges transecting a straight line drawn from the core to the delta.

Root Of a tooth, that area below the neck of the tooth that is contained within the tooth socket of the mandible or maxilla.

Sacral vertebra Bone of the spinal column in the lower back, all fused together in the adult to form the sacrum.

Sacrum Fused vertebrae (usually five) between the os coxae.

Sagittal section Any section of the body parallel to the midsagittal plane.

Sagittal suture On the cranial midline, coursing in an anteroposterior direction, separating the parietal bones.

Scan sampling In recording primate behavior, method in which the researcher records the behavior of a group of primates or an individual primate at regular time intervals.

Scapula The shoulder blade, a triangular flat bone on the upper back.

Scapular spine The raised surface on the dorsal scapula that leads to the acromion process.

Scaphoid Another term for navicular in the carpals.

Second cuneiform One of the bones of the ankle.

Sectorial lower first premolar Single-cusped premolar that forms a cutting complex with the upper canine, found in modern pongids and some monkeys.

Sella turcica A fossa in the sphenoid bone that holds the pituitary gland.

Semilunar notch On the proximal ulna, articulates with the distal humerus.

Semiorder Taxonomic classification between suborder and order.

Sequestrum A part of bone that is isolated from the rest of the bone (and body) by an involucrum.

Seriation A technique of placing remains "in series," usually for age determination.

Sesamoid bone A bone encased in tendon. The patella is the largest sesamoid bone in the human body.

Sex The biological features that differentiate males and females, as opposed to gender, which is the way an individual identifies himself or herself.

Sex chromosomes Determine the sex of the individual.

Sex linked Genes that occur on the chromosomes that determine an individual's sex.

Sexual dimorphism Variations in morphology attributed to the two sexes.

Shoveled incisors Incisors shaped like a shovel when viewed from the edge of the tooth toward the gum line.

Sinus Bone cavity lined with mucous membranes.

Sivapithecus An extinct genus of hominoid of the Miocene.

Slow quadrumanos climbing Locomotion found only in orangutans, in which they use their forelimbs and hindlimbs to grasp branches and other supports as they move slowly through the trees.

Slow quadrupedal climbing Locomotion found only in pottos of Africa and lorises of South Asia, in which they move slowly on four limbs.

Sphenoid bone Bone in the interior cranium that is also visible in the lateral eye orbit, and lateral and inferior cranium.

Spheno-occipital synchondrosis This is often called basilar suture, though it is not a suture, located between the occipital and sphenoid bones on the base of the cranium.

Spinous process The sites of attachment on the vertebrae for various muscles and ligaments of the neck and back.

Squamosal suture Between the parietal and the temporal bones.

Standard deviation A gauge of variation or spread within a set of measurements.

Staphylion The midpoint of a line drawn connecting the most forward points on the curves in the posterior margin of the palate.

Stasis Situation in evolutionary history in which there is no morphological change in an organism for long periods of geologic time.

Sternum Breastbone, at the anterior thorax, that consists of the manubrium, body, and xiphoid process.

Strepsirhini Primate suborder that includes lemurs and lorises.

Superciliary arch *See* Supraorbital torus.

Superficial Near the surface.

Superior Above, top.

Superior nuchal line Superior-most point of attachment of the nuchal muscles on the occipital bone. This becomes a raised crest in some animals.

Supination Turning of the palm of the hand upward.

Supraorbital index Measures the height of the skull.

Supraorbital torus Also called superciliary arch or browridges, a rounded process of bone above the eye orbits.

Suture Form of articulation found on a cranium.

Symphyseal face On the pubis, where the two pubic bones are joined through cartilage in the front of the pelvic girdle.

Synapomorphs Derived characters shared among members of an evolutionary group.

Synarthrosis (plural: **synarthroses**) Joints in which the bones are so tightly bound by cartilage that there is virtually no movement between them (such as at the sutures of the cranium).

Synovial fluid Fluid the consistency of egg whites that lubricates some joints.

Talus One of the bones of the ankle.

Taphonomy The events that happen to a body after death. This includes the environment, time, scavengers, and so on.

Tarsals The seven bones of the ankle.

Tarsiioidea Prosimian superfamily of tarsiers, found in southern Asia.

Temporal bone Paired bone on the lateral inferior portions of the cranium.

Temporal line Point of origin of the temporal muscle.

Temporal muscle A major muscle of mastication (chewing), which originates on the temporal line of the temporal bone and inserts on the mandible.

Temporomandibular joint The joint at which the mandible articulates with the cranium.

Tendon Tough fibrous tissue at the end of the insertion of a muscle that attaches that muscle to bone.

Third cuneiform One of the bones of the ankle.

Thoracic vertebra One of the spinal column bones of the thoracic (chest) region.

Thymine One of four chemical bases central to the structure of a DNA nucleotide.

Tibia The largest bone of the leg (in anatomical terms, in which "leg" refers to only the part of the lower limb defined by the tibia and fibula). The tibia is the second largest bone of the leg (in the popular definition of "leg," which includes the upper and lower leg).

Tibial tuberosity Point of insertion of the patellar tendon on the anterior proximal tibia.

Torus An elevation or prominence.

Total ridge count The total number of ridges on all fingers. In prints with whorls, only one ridge count per finger is added to the total.

Trait A distinguishing characteristic or quality of a phenotype (for example, hair color, blood type, tongue rolling, etc.).

Transfer RNA RNA molecules that recognize the DNA code on messenger RNA and transfer amino acids to the appropriate location on the mRNA chain.

Transverse Any crosswise section.

Transverse process Lateral projections of vertebrae. There are costal facets/pits on the transverse processes of the thoracic vertebrae.

Trapezium *See* Greater multangular.

Trapezoid *See* Lesser multangular.

Trephination (or trepination) A surgical technique whereby a section of bone is removed, usually from the cranium. Modern trephination involves drilling a burr hole in the cranium to relieve pressure on the brain.

Triplets The three-base code for amino acids on the DNA chain.

Triquetrum One of the bones of the wrist.

Trisomy An extra chromosome in a daughter cell resulting in three chromosomes instead of two.

Tubercle A small, knob-like projection on bone.

Tuberosity A large, rough eminence or projection on bone.

Type lines The innermost ridges that surround the pattern area in dermatoglyphics.

Ulna The medial bone of the forearm.

Ventral In front (*similar to* Anterior).

Vertebra A bone of the spinal column.

Vertex The uppermost point on the midline of the cranium when it is in the Frankfort plane. In general terms, vertex means top or highest point.

Vertical clinging and leaping Locomotor mode found in some prosimians, in which the animal pushes off of a vertical tree limb with powerful hindlimbs, turns in midair, and lands feet first on another tree limb.

Visual predation theory Theory originally proposed by M. Cartmill, that the first primates developed characteristics that allowed them to prey on insects on the terminal branches of the lower layers of tropical rain forests.

Vomer bone Bone on the inferior cranium, posterior and superior to the palatine bones.

Xiphoid process The most inferior portion of the sternum, often ossified in the adult.

Zygomatic arch Paired arches on the lateral cranium, made up of projections from the zygomatic (malar) bone anteriorly and the temporal bone posteriorly.

Zygomatic bone Paired bones of the lateral face on the cranium.

Bibliography

Alba, D.M., S. Almecija, D. DeMiguel, J. Fortuny, M. Perez de los Rios, et al. 2015 "Miocene Small-Bodied Ape from Eurasia Sheds Light on Hominoid Evolution." *Science* **350**(6260) doi:10.1126/science.aab2625.

Alemseged, Z., F. Spoor, W. H. Kimbel, R. Bobe, D. Geraads, D. Reed, J. G. Wynn 2006 "A Juvenile Early Hominin Skeleton from Dikika, Ethiopia." *Nature* **443**(7109): 296–301.

Alemseged, Z., J. G. Wynn, W. H. Kimbel, D. Reed, D. Geraads, R. Bobe 2005 "New Hominin from the Basal Member of the Hadar Formation, Dikika, Ethiopia, and Its Geological Context." *J Hum Evol* **49**(4): 499–514.

Alexeev, V. P. 1986 *The Origin of the Human Race.* Moscow: Progress.

Andrews, P. J. 1983 "The Natural History of *Sivapithecus.*" Pp. 441–463 in *New Interpretations of Ape and Human Ancestry*, edited by R. Ciochon and R. Corruccini. New York: Plenum.

Andrews, P., L. Martin 1987 "The Phyletic Position of the Ad Dabtiyah Hominoid." *Bull Br Mus Nat Hist* (Geol.) **41**:383–393.

Anemone, R. L. 1990 "The VCL Hypothesis Revisited: Patterns of Femoral Morphology among Quadrupedal and Saltatorial Prosimian Primates." *Am J Phys Anthropol* **83**: 373–393.

Anemone, R. L., H. H. Covert 2000 "New Skeletal Remains of Omomys (Primates, Omomyidae): Functional Morphology of the Hindlimb and Locomotor Behavior of a Middle Eocene Primate." *J Hum Evol* **38**(5): 607–633.

Ankel-Simons, F., J. G. Fleagle, P. S. Chatrath 1998 "Femoral Anatomy of *Aegyptopithecus zeuxis,* an Early Oligocene Anthropoid." *Am J Phys Anthropol* **106**(4): 413–424.

Argue, D., M. J. Morwood, T. Sutikna, et al. 2009 "*Homo floresiensis*: A Cladistic Analysis." *J Hum Evol* **57**(5): 623–639.

Asfaw, B., T. White, O. Lovejoy, B. Latimer, S. Simpson, G. Suwa 1999 "*Australopithecus garhi*: A New Species of Early Hominid from Ethiopia." *Science* **284**: 629–635.

Bacon, A. M., M. Godinot 1998 "Morphological Functional Analysis of the Femora and Tibiae of Quercy 'Adapis': Recognition of Five Morphological Types." *Folia Primatol (Basel)* **69**(1): 1–21.

Baker, B. J., T. L. Dupras, M. W. Tocheri 2005 *The Osteology of Infants and Children.* Texas A&M University Press, College Station.

Baker, R. K. 1984 *The Relationship of Cranial Suture Closure and Age Analyzed in a Modern Multi-Racial Sample of Males and Females.* M.A. thesis, California State University, Fullerton.

Balzeau, A., D. Grimaud-Herve, T. Jacob 2005 "Internal Cranial Features of the Mojokerto Child Fossil (East Java, Indonesia)." *J Hum Evol* **48**(6): 535–553.

Bardai, G., E. Lemyre, P. Moffat, T. Palomo, F. H. Glorieux, J. Tung, et al. 2016 "Osteogenesis Imperfecta Type I Caused by COL1A1 Deletions." *Calcif Tissue Int* **98**(1): 76–84.

Barker, G., H. Barton, et al. 2007 "The Human Revolution in Lowland Tropical Southeast Asia: The Antiquity and Behavior of Anatomically Modern Humans at Niah Cave (Sarawak, Borneo)." *J Hum Evol* **52**: 243–261.

Bass, W. M. 1987 *Human Osteology: A Laboratory and Field Manual* (3rd ed.). Columbia, MO: Missouri Archaeological Society Special Publication No. 2.

Bass, W. M. 1996 *Human Osteology: A Laboratory and Field Manual* (4th ed.). Columbia, MO: Missouri Archaeological Society Special Publication No. 2.

Begun, D. R. 2002 "The Pliopithecoidea." Pp. 221–240 in *The Primate Fossil Record*, edited by W. C. Hartwig. Cambridge, UK: Cambridge University Press.

Begun, D. R. 2010 "Miocene Hominids and the Origins of the African Apes." *Annu Rev Anthropol* **39**: 67–84.

Begun, D. R., M. C. Nargolwalla, L. Kordos 2012 "European Miocene Hominids and the Origin of the African Ape and Human Clade." *Evo Anthropol* **21**: 10–23.

Belmaker, M., E. Tchernov, S. Condemi, O. Bar-Yosef 2002 "New Evidence for Hominid Presence in the Lower Pleistocene of the Southern Levant." *J Hum Evol* **43**(1): 43–56.

Benefit, B. R., M. L. McCrossin 1997 "Earliest Known Old World Monkey Skull." *Nature* **388**: 368–371.

Berg, G. E. 2008 "Pubic Bone Age Estimation in Adult Women." *J Foren Sci* **53**: 569–577.

Berger, L. R., D. J. de Ruiter, S. E. Churchill, et al. 2010 "*Australopithecus sediba*: A New Species of *Homo*-Like Australopith from South Africa." *Science* **328**: 195–204.

Bernor, R. L. 2007 "New Apes Fill the Gap." *Proc Natl Acad Sci USA* **104**(50): 19661–19662.

Birkby, W. H. 1973 *Discontinuous Morphological Traits of the Skull as Population Markers in the Prehistoric Southwest.* PhD dissertation, University of Arizona, Tucson.

Bischoff, J. L., R. W. Williams, R. J. Rosebauer, et al. 2007 "High-Resolution U-Series Dates from the Sima de los Huesos Hominids Yields 600+/-66 kyrs: Implications for the Evolution of the Early Neanderthal Lineage." *J Archaeol Sci* **34**: 763–770.

Bloch, J. I., D. M. Boyer 2002 "Grasping Primate Origins." *Science* November 22; **298**(5598): 1606–1610.

Bloch, J. I., P. D. Gingerich 1998 "Carpolestes simpsoni, New Species (Mammalia, Proprimates) from the Late Paleocene of the Clarks Fork Basin, Wyoming." *Contrib Mus Paleontol Univ Mich* **30**: 131.

Bloch, J. I., M. T. Silcox 2001 "New Basicrania of Paleocene-Eocene *Ignacius*: Re-evaluation of the Plesiadapiform-Dermopteran Link." *Am J Phys Anthropol* **116**(3): 184–198.

Bloch, J. I., M. T. Silcox 2006 "Cranial Anatomy of the Paleocene Plesiadapi Form *Carpolestes simpsoni* (Mammalia, Primates) Using Ultra High-Resolution X-Ray Computed Tomography, and the Relationships of Plesiadapiforms to Euprimates." *J Hum Evol* **50**(1): 1–35.

Blumenschine, R. J., C. R. Peters, F. T. Masao, et al. 2003 "Late Pliocene Homo and Hominid Land Use from Western Olduvai Gorge, Tanzania." *Science* **299**: 1217–1221.

Bocherens, H., D. G. Drucker, D. Billiou, M. Patou-Mathis, B. Vandermeersch 2005 "Isotopic Evidence for Diet and Subsistence Pattern of the Saint-Cesaire I Neanderthal: Review and Use of a Multi-Source Mixing Model." *J Hum Evol* **49**(1): 71–87.

Brooks, S. T. 1985 Personal communication.

Brooks, S. T. 1986 "Comments on 'Known' Age at Death Series." Presented in conjunction with "Skeletal Age Standards Derived from an Extensive Multi-Racial Sample of Modern Americans," by J. Suchey and D. Katz, at the Fifty-Fifth Annual Meeting of the American Association of Physical Anthropologists, Albuquerque, New Mexico.

Brooks, S. T., J. M. Suchey 1990 "Skeletal Age Determination Based on the Os Pubis: A Comparison of the Acsadi-Nemeskeri and Suchey-Brooks Methods." *Hum Evol* **5**(3): 227–238.

Brown, F., J. Harris, R. Leakey, A. Walker 1985 "Early *Homo erectus* Skeleton from West Lake Turkana, Kenya." *Nature* **316**: 788–792.

Brown, P., T. Sutikna, et al. 2004 "A New Small-Bodied Hominin from the Late Pleistocene of Flores, Indonesia." *Nature* **431**(7012): 1055–1061.

Brues, A. M. 1977 *People and Races.* New York: Macmillan.

Brues, A. M. 1990 *People and Races.* Reissued by Waveland Press, Prospect Heights, IL.

Brunet, M., F. Guy, D. Pilbeam, et al. 2002 "A New Hominid from the Upper Miocene of Chad, Central Africa." *Nature* **418**: 145–151.

Brunet, M., F. Guy, D. Pilbeam, et al. 2005 "New Material of the Earliest Hominid from the Upper Miocene of Chad." *Nature* **434**: 752–755.

Buckberry, J. L., A. T. Chamberlain 2002 "Age Estimation from the Auricular Surface of the Ilium: A Revised Method." *Am J Phys Anthropol* **119**: 231–239.

Campbell, B. G. 1976 *Human Evolution: An Introduction to Man's Adaptations* (2nd ed.). New York: Aldine.

Campbell, B. G. 1985 *Human Evolution: An Introduction to Man's Adaptations* (3rd ed.). New York: Aldine.

Carbonell, E., J. M. Bermuda de Castro, et al. 2008 "The First Hominin of Europe." *Nature* **452**: 465–469.

Carlson, B. M. 2004 *Human Embryology and Developmental Biology.* St. Louis: Mosby.

Cartmill, M. 1972 "Arboreal Adaptations and the Origin of the Order Primates." Pp. 97–122 in *Functional and Evolutionary Biology of Primates,* edited by R. Tuttle. Chicago: Aldine.

Cartmill, M. 1974 "Rethinking Primate Origins." *Science* **184**: 436–443.

Cartmill, M. 1992 "New Views on Primate Origins." *Evol Anthropol* **1**: 105–111.

Chaimanee, Y., D. Jolly, M. Benammi, P. Tafforeau, D. Duzer, I. Moussa, J. J. Jaeger 2003 "A Middle Miocene Hominoid from Thailand and Orangutan Origins." *Nature* **422**: 61–65.

Chatterjee, H. J. 2006 "Phylogeny and Biogeography of Gibbons: A Dispersal-Vicariance Analysis." *Int J Primatol* **27**(3): 699–712.

Chester, S. G. B., J. I. Bloch, D. M. Boyer, W. A. Clemens 2014 *Oldest Known Euarchontan Tarsals and Affinities of Paleocene Purgatorius to Primates.* Proc Natl Acad Sci USA **112**(5): 1487–1492.

Cho, J., S. D. Stout, R. W. Madsen, M. A. Streeter 2002 "Population-Specific Histological Age-Estimating Method: A Model for Known African-American and European-American Skeletal Remains." *J Foren Sci* **47**(1): 12–18.

Clark, W. E. Le Gros 1959 *The Antecedents of Man.* New York: Harper & Row.

Cobb, S. N. 2008 "The Facial Skeleton of the Chimpanzee-Human Last Common Ancestor." *J Anat* **212**(4): 469–485.

Conard, N. J., P. M. Grootes, F. H. Smith 2004 "Unexpectedly Recent Dates for Human Remains from Vogelherd." *Nature* **430**: 198–201.

Conroy, G. C. 1990 *Primate Evolution.* New York: Norton.

Conroy, G. C., B. Senut, D. Gommery, M. Pickford, P. Mein 1996 "New Primate Remains from the Miocene of Namibia, Southern Africa." *Am J Phys Anthropol* **99**: 487–492.

Coon, C. S. 1965 *The Living Races.* New York: Alfred A. Knopf.

Cooper, A., C. B. Stringer 2013 "Did the Denisovans Cross Wallace's Line?" *Science* **342**(6156): 321–323.

Corruccini, R. S. 1974 "An Examination of the Meaning of Cranial Discrete Traits for Human Skeletal Biological Studies." *Am J Phys Anthropol* **40**: 425–446.

Crompton, R. H., E. E. Vereecke, S. K. Thorpe 2008 "Locomotion and Posture from the Common Hominoid Ancestor to Fully Modern Hominins, with Special Reference to the Last Common Panin/Hominin Ancestor." *J Anat* **212**(4): 501–543.

Curnoe, D., P. V. Tobias 2006 "Description, New Reconstruction, Comparative Anatomy, and Classification of the Sterkfontein Stw 53 Cranium, with Discussions about the Taxonomy of Other Southern African Early Homo Remains." *J Hum Evol* **50**(1): 36–77.

Dahlberg, A. A. 1951 "The Dentition of the American Indian." Pp. 138–176 in *The Physical Anthropology of the American Indian,* edited by W. S. Laughlin. New York: Viking Fund.

Dart, R. 1925 "*Australopithecus africanus*: The Man Ape of South Africa." *Nature* **115**: 195–199.

Day, M. H., E. H. Wickens 1980 "Laetoli Pliocene Hominid Footprints and Bipedalism." *Nature* **286**: 385–387.

De Bonis, L., G. Bouvrain, D. Geraads, G. Koufos 1990 "New Hominid Skull Material from the Late Miocene of Macedonia in Northern Greece." *Nature* **345**: 712–714.

De Bonis, L., G. D. Koufos 1994 "Our Ancestors' Ancestor: *Ouranopithecus* is a Greek Link in Human Ancestry." *Evol Anthropol* **3**: 75–83.

DeSilva, J. 2011. "A Shift toward Birthing Relatively Large Infants Early in Human Evolution." *Proceedings of the National Academy of Sciences* **108**: 1022–1027.

DiGangi, E. A., J. D. Bethard, E. H. Kimmerle, L. W. Konigsberg 2009 "A New Method for Estimating Age-at-Death from the First Rib." *Am J Phys Anthropol* **138**(2): 164–176.

DiMaggio, E. N., C. J. Campisano, J. Rowan, G. Dupont-Nivet, et al. 2015 "Late Pliocene Fossiliferous Sedimentary Record and the Environmental Context of Early *Homo* from Afar, Ethiopia." *Science* **347**(6228): 1355–1359.

Dittrick, J., J. M. Suchey 1986 "Sex Determination of Prehistoric Central California Skeletal Remains Using Discriminant Analysis of the Femur and Humerus." *Am J Phys Anthropol* **70**: 3–9.

Djuric, M., D. Djonic, S. Nikolic, D. Popovic, J. Marinkovic 2007 "Evaluation of the Suchey-Brooks Method for Aging Skeletons in the Balkans." *J Foren Sci* **52**: 21–23.

Dodo, Y. 1974 "Non-Metrical Cranial Traits in the Hokkaido Ainu and the Northern Japanese of Recent Times." *J Anthropol Soc Nippon* **82**: 31–51.

Dominy, N. J., J. C. Svenning, W. H. Li 2003 "Historical Contingency in the Evolution of Primate Color Vision." *J Hum Evol* **44**(1): 25–45.

Drapeau, M. S., C. V. Ward, W. H. Kimbel, D. C. Johanson, Y. Rak 2005 "Associated Cranial and Forelimb Remains Attributed to *Australopithecus afarensis* from Hadar, Ethiopia." *J Hum Evol* **48**(6): 593–642.

Eldredge, N., S. J. Gould 1972 "Punctuated Equilibria: An Alternative to Phyletic Gradualism." Pp. 82–115 in *Models in Paleobiology,* edited by T. J. M. Schopf. San Francisco: Freeman, Cooper.

Falk, D. 1986 "Evolution of Cranial Blood Drainage in Hominids: Enlarged Occipital/Margina Sinuses and Emissary Foramina." *Am J Phys Anthropol* **70**: 311–324.

Falk, D., C. P. E. Zollikofer, N. Morimoto, M. S. Ponce de Leon 2012 "Metopic Suture of Taung (*Australopithecus africanus*) and its Implications for Hominin Brain Evolution." *Proc Natl Acad Sci USA* **109**(22): 8467–8470.

Falk, D., G. C. Conroy 1983 "The Cranial Venous Sinus System in *Australopithecus afarensis*." *Nature* **306**: 779–781.

Falk, D., C. Hildebolt, K. Smith, et al. 2005a "The Brain of LB1, *Homo floresiensis*." *Science* **308**: 242–245.

Falk, D., C. Hildebolt, K. Smith, et al. 2005b "Response to Comment on the Brain of LB1, *Homo floresiensis*." *Science* **310**: 236.

Finnegan, M. 1972 *Population Definition on the Northwest Coast by Analysis of Discrete Character Variation.* PhD dissertation, University of Colorado, Boulder.

Fleagle, J. G. 1976 "Locomotion and Posture of the Malayan Siamang and Implications for Hominoid Evolution." *Folia Primatol* **26**: 245–269.

Fleagle, J. G. 2013 *Primate Adaptation and Evolution.* New York: Academic Press.

Fleagle, J. G., R. F. Kay 1983 "New Interpretations of the Phyletic Position of Oligocene Hominoids." In *New Interpretations of Ape and Human Ancestry,* edited by R. Ciochon and R. Corruccini. New York: Plenum.

Fleagle, J. G., E. L. Simons 1995 "Limb Skeleton and Locomotor Adaptations of *Apidium phiomense,* an Oligocene Anthropoid from Egypt." *Am J Phys Anthropol* **97**: 235–289.

Fleagle, J. G., E. L. Simons 2005 "*Micropithecus clarki,* A Small Ape from the Miocene of Uganda." *Am J Phys Anthropol* **49**(4): 427–440.

Floud, R., K. Wachter, A. Gregory 1990 *Height, Health and History: Nutritional Status in the United Kingdom 1750–1980.* Cambridge: Cambridge University Press.

France, D. L. 1983 *Sexual Dimorphism in the Human Humerus.* Unpublished PhD dissertation, University of Colorado, Boulder.

France, D. L. 1986 "Osteometry at Muscle Origin and Insertion in Sex Determination." *Am J Phys Anthropol* **76**: 515–526.

France, D. L. 1990 "A Cautionary Note in the Cross-Cultural Use of the Mastoid Process in Sex Determination." *Adli Tip Dergisi J Forens Med Istanbul* **6**(1–2): 149–156.

Franzen, J. L., P. D. Gingerich, J. Habersetzer, J. H. Hurum, W. von Koenigswald, B. Holly Smith 2009 "Complete Primate Skeleton from the Middle Eocene of Messel in Germany: Morphology and Paleobiology" *PLoS ONE* **4**(5): e5723. (Published online May 19, 2009. doi: 10.1371/journal.pone.0005723.)

Gabunia L., A. Vekua 1995 "A Plio-Pleistocene Hominid from Dmanisi, East Georgia, Caucasus." *Nature* **373**: 509–512.

Galbany, J., S. Moya-Sola, A. Perez-Perez 2005 "Dental Microwear Variability on Buccal Tooth Enamel Surfaces of Extant Catarrhini and the Miocene Fossil *Dryopithecus laietanus* (Hominoidea)." *Folia Primatol* (Basel) **76**(6): 325–41.

Galik, K., B. Senut, M. Pickford, et al. 2004 "External and Internal Morphology of the BAR 1002'00 *Orrorin tugenensis* Femur." *Science* **305**: 1450–1453.

Garn, S. M., S. T. Sandusky, N. N. Rosen, F. Trowbridge 1973a "Economic Impact on Postnatal Ossification." *Am J Phys Anthropol* **38**: 1–3.

Garn, S. M., J. M. Nagy, S. T. Sandusky, F. Trowbridge 1973b "Economic Impact on Tooth Emergence." *Am J Phys Anthropol* **39**: 233–238.

Gatesy, J., M. S. Springer 2014 "Phylogenetic Analysis at Deep Timescales: Unreliable Gene Trees, Bypassed Hidden Support, and the Coalescence/Concatalescence Conundrum." *Mol Phylogenet Evol* **80**: 231–266.

Gebo D. L., M. Dagosto, K. C. Beard, X. Ni 2008 "New Primate Hind Limb Elements from the Middle Eocene of China." *J Hum Evol* **55**(6): 999–1014. Epub May 13, 2008.

Gill, G., S. J. Rhine (eds.) 1990 *Skeletal Attribution of Race: Methods for Forensic Anthropology.* Albuquerque: Maxwell Museum of Anthropology, Anthropological Papers No. 4.

Gingerich, P. D., R. D. Martin 1981 "Cranial Morphology and Adaptations in Eocene Adapidae. II. The Cambridge Skull of *Adapis parisiensis.*" *Am J Phys Anthropol* **56**(3): 235–257.

Godinot, M. 1994 "Early North African Primates and Their Significance for the Origin of Simiiformes (=Anthropoidea)." Pp. 235–295 in *Anthropoid Origins.* edited by J. G. Fleagle and R. F. Kay. New York: Plenum.

Godinot, M., M. Mahboubi 1992 "Earliest Known Simian Primate Found in Algeria." *Nature* **357**: 324–326.

Gordon, A. D., L. Nevell, B. Wood 2008 "The *Homo floresiensis* Cranium (LB1): Size, Scaling, and Early *Homo* Affinities." *Proc Natl Acad Sci USA* **105**(12): 4650–4655.

Gould, S. J., N. Eldridge 1977 "Punctuated Equilibria: The Tempo and Mode of Evolution Reconsidered." *Paleobiology* **3**: 115–151.

Grant, P. R. 1999 *Ecology and Evolution of Darwin's Finches.* Princeton, NJ: Princeton University Press.

Grant, P. R., B. R. Grant 2014 *40 Years of Evolution: Darwin's Finches on Daphne Major Island.* Princeton, NJ: Princeton University Press.

Green, D. J., Z. Alemseged 2012 "*Australopithecus afarensis* Scapular Ontogeny, Function and the Role of Climbing in Human Evolution." *Science* **338**(6106): 514–517.

Greulich, W. W., S. I. Pyle 1959 *Radiographic Atlas of Skeletal Development of the Hand and Wrist.* Stanford, CA: Stanford University Press.

Grun, R., C. Stringer, F. McDermott, et al. 2005 "U-Series and ESR Analyses of Bones and Teeth Relating to the Human Burials from Skhul." *J Hum Evol* **49**(3): 316–334.

Gunnell, G. F. 1997 "Wasatchian-Bridgerian (Eocene) Paleoecology of the Western Interior of North America: Changing Paleoenvironments and Taxonomic Composition of Omomyid (Tarsiiformes) Primates." *J Hum Evol* **32**(2–3): 105–132.

Gutierrez, M. 2011 *Taxonomic and Ecological Characterization of a Late Oligocene Mammalian Fauna from Kenya.* Unpublished PhD dissertation, Washington University in St. Louis, *Electronic Theses and Dissertations.* Paper 139.http://openscholarship.wustl.edu/art_sci_etds/21/.

Guy, F., D. E. Lieberman, D. Pilbeam, et al. 2005 "Morphological Affinities of the *Sahelanthropus tchadensis* Late Miocene Hominid from Chad Cranium." *Proc Natl Acad Sci USA* **102**: 18836–18841.

Haeusler, M., H. M. McHenry 2004 "OH62 Leg Length Body Proportions of *Homo habilis* Reviewed." *J Hum Evol* **46**(4): 433–465.

Haile-Selassie, Y. 2001 "Late Miocene Hominids from the Middle Awash, Ethiopia." *Nature* **412**: 178–181.

Haile-Selassie, Y., G. Suwa, T. D. White 2004 "Late Miocene Teeth from Middle Awash, Ethiopia, and Early Hominid Dental Evolution." *Science* **303**(5663): 1503–1505.

Haile-Selassie, Y., L. Gilbert, S. M. Melillo, T. M. Ryan, M. Alene, A. Deino, et al. 2015 "New Species from Ethiopia Further Expands Middle Pliocene Hominin Diversity." *Nature* **521**: 483–488.

Haile-Selassie, Y., B. Z. Saylor, A. Deino, N. E. Levin, M. Alene, B. M. Latimer 2012 "A New Hominin Foot from Ethiopia shows Multiple Pliocene Bipedal Adaptations." *Nature* **483**: 565–569.

Harrison, T. 2010 "Dendropithecoidea, Proconsuloidea and Hominoidea (Catarrhini, Primates)." Pp. 429–469 in *Cenozoic Mammals of Africa*, edited by L. Werdelin and W.J. Sanders. Berkeley: University of California Press.

Harrison, T., X. Ji, et al. 2008 "Renewed Investigations at the Late Miocene Hominoid Locality of Leilao, Yunnan, China." *Am J Phys Anthropol* **135**(S46): 113.

Hartig, G., G. Churakov, et al. 2013 "Retrophylogenomics Place Tarsiers on the Evolutionary Branch of Anthropoids." *Scientific Reports* **3** (1756) doi:10.1038/srep01756.

Hartnett, K. 2010a "Analysis of Age-at-Death Estimation Using Data from a New, Modern Autopsy Sample, Part I: Pubic Bone." *J Foren Sci* **55**(5): 1145–1151.

Hartnett, K. 2010b "Analysis of Age-at-Death Estimation Using Data from a New, Modern Autopsy Sample, Part II: Sternal End of the Fourth Rib." *J Foren Sci*, **55**(5): 1152–1156.

Hauser, G., G. F. De Stefano 1989 *Epigenetic Variants of the Human Skull.* Stuttgart: E. Schweizerbartsche.

Heathcote, G. 2006 Personal communication.

Hillson, S. 2003 *Dental Anthropology.* Cambridge: Cambridge University Press.

Holloway, R. L. 1983 "Cerebral Brain Endocast Pattern of *Australopithecus afarensis* Hominid." *Nature* **303**: 420–422.

Hoppa, R. D., T. N. Garlie 1998 "Secular Trend on the Growth of Toronto Children during the Last Century." *Ann Hum Biol* **25**: 553–561.

Hudjashov, G., T. Kivisild, P. A. Underhill, P. Endicott, J. J. Sanchez, A. A. Lin, et al. 2007 "Revealing the Prehistoric Settlement of Australia by Y Chromosome and mtDNA Analysis." *Proc Natl Acad Sci USA* **104**: 8726–8730.

Igarashi, Y., K. Uesu, T. Wakebe, E. Kanazawa 2005 "New Method for Estimation of Adult Skeletal Age at Death from the Morphology of the Auricular Surface of the Ilium." *Am J Phys Anthropol* **128**: 324–339.

International Human Genome Sequencing Consortium 2004 "Finishing the Euchromatic Sequence of the Human Genome." *Nature* **431**(7011): 931–45.

Iscan, M. Y., S. R. Loth, R. K. Wright 1984 "Age Estimation from the Rib by Phase Analysis: White Males." *J Forens Sci* **29**: 1094–1104.

Iscan, M. Y., S. R. Loth, R. K. Wright 1985 "Age Estimation from the Rib by Phases Analysis: White Females." *J Forens Sci* **30**: 853–863.

Iscan, M. Y., P. Miller-Shaivitz 1986 "Sexual Dimorphism in the Femur and Tibia." Pp. 101–111 in *Forensic Osteology: Advances in the Identification of Human Remains*, edited by K. J. Reichs. Springfield, IL: Charles C. Thomas.

Jameson, N. M., Z. C. Hou, K. N. Sterner, et al. 2011 "Genomic Data Reject the Hypothesis of a Prosimian Primate Clade." *J Hum Evol* **61**: 295–305.

Janecka, J. E., W. Miller, T. H. Pringle, F. Wiens, A. Zitzmann, K. M. Helgen, et al. 2007 "Molecular and Genomic Data Identify the Closest Living Relative of Primates." *Science* **318**(5851): 792–794.

Jantz, R. L., S. D. Ousley 2005 "FORDISC 3.0: Personal Computer Forensic Discriminant Functions." University of Tennessee, Knoxville.

Johanson, D., F. Masao, G. Eck, et al. 1987 "New Partial Skeleton of *Homo habilis* from Olduvai Gorge, Tanzania." *Nature* **327**: 205–209.

Johanson, D. C., T. D. White 1979 "A Systematic Assessment of Early African Hominids." *Science* **203**: 321–330.

Johansson, S. 2013 "The Talking Neanderthals: What do Fossils, Genetics, and Archeology Say?" *Biolinguistics* **7**: 35–74.

Kaifu, Y., H. Baba, F. Aziz, E. Indriati, F. Schrenk, T. Jacob 2005 "Taxonomic Affinities and Evolutionary History of the Early Pleistocene Hominids of Java: Dentognathic Evidence." *Am J Phys Anthropol* **128**(4): 709–726.

Kaminski, R., Y. Chen, T. Fischer, E. Tedaldi, A. Napoli, Y. Zhang, et al. 2016 "Elimination of HIV-1 Genomes from Human T-Lymphoid Cells by CRISPR/Cas9 Gene Editing." *Sci Rep* **6**, Article Number 22555 doi:10.1038/srep22555.

Kang, X., W. He, Y. Huang, Y., Y. Qian, C. Yaoyong, G. Xingcheng, et al. 2016 "Introducing Precise Genetic Modifications into Human 3PN Embryos by CRISPR/Cas-Mediated Genome Editing." *J Assist Reprod Genet* **33**(5): 581–588.

Katz, D., J. M. Suchey 1986 "Age Determination of the Male Os Pubis." *Am J Phys Anthropol* **69**: 427–435.

Kay, R. 1984 "On the Use of Anatomical Features to Infer Foraging Behavior in Extinct Primates." Pp. 21–53 in *Adaptations for Foraging in Nonhuman Primates*, edited by J. Cant and P. Rodman. New York: Columbia University Press.

Kay, R. F., J. G. M. Thewissen, A. D. Yoder 1992 "Cranial Anatomy of *Ignacius graybullianus* and the Affinities of the Plesiadapiformes." *Am J Phys Anthropol* **89**: 477–498.

Kay, R. F., P. S. Ungar 1997 "Dental Evidence for Dietin Some Miocene Catarrhines with Comments on the Effects of Phylogeny on the Interpretation of Adaptation." Pp. 131–151 in *Function, Phylogeny and Fossils: Miocene Hominoids and Great Ape and Human Origins*, edited by D. R. Begun, C. Ward and M. Rose. New York: Plenum.

Kelly, J. 1995 "Evolution of Apes." Pp. 223–230 in *The Cambridge Encyclopedia of Human Evolution*, edited by S. Jones, R. Martin, and D. Pilbeam. Cambridge, UK: Cambridge University Press.

Kelly, J., D. Pilbeam 1986 "The Dryopithecines: Taxonomy, Comparative Anatomy, and Phylogeny of Miocene Large Hominoids." Pp. 361–411 in *Comparative Primate Biology*, Vol. 1, Systematics, Evolution, and Anatomy, edited by D. Swindler and J. Erwin. New York: Alan R. Liss.

Kerley, E. R., D. H. Ubelaker 1978 "Revisions in the Microscopic Method of Estimating Age at Death in Human Cortical Bone." *Am J Phys Anthropol* **49**: 545–546.

Keyser, A. W. 2000 "New Finds in South Africa." *National Geographic* May: 76–83.

Kibii, J. M., S. E. Churchill, P. Schmid, K. J. Carlson, et al. 2011 "A Partial Pelvis of *Australopithecus sediba*." *Science* **333**(6048): 1407–1411.

Kim, U. K., E. Jorgenson, H. Coon, M. Leppert, N. Risch, D. Drayna 2003 "Positional Cloning of the Human Quantitative Trait Locus Underlying Taste Sensitivity to Phenylthiocarbamide." *Science* **299**(5610): 1221–1225.

Kimbel, W. H., G. Suwa, B. Asfaw, Y. Rak, T. D. White 2014 "*Ardipithecus ramidus* and the Evolution of the Human Cranial Base." *Proc Natl Acad Sci USA* **111**(3): 948–953.

Kimmerle, E. H., L. W. Konigsberg, R. L. Jantz, J. P. Baraybar 2008 "Analysis of Age-at-Death Estimation through the Use of Pubic Symphyseal Data." *J Foren Sci* **53**: 558–568.

Kirk, E. C., P. Lemelin, M. W. Hamrick, D. M. Boyer, J. I. Bloch 2008 "Intrinsic Hand Proportions of Euarchontans and Other Mammals: Implications for the Locomotor Behavior of Plesiadapiforms." *J Hum Evol* **55**: 278–299.

Kirk, E. C., E. L. Simons 2001 "Diets of Fossil Primates from the Fayum Depression of Egypt: A Quantitative Analysis of Molar Shearing." *J Hum Evol* **40**(3): 203–229.

Kitchin, F. D., W. H. Evans, C. A. Clarke, R. B. McConnel, P. M. Sheppard 1959 "PTC Taste Response and Thyroid Disease." *BMJ* **1**: 1069–1074.

Kivell, T. L., J. M. Kibii, S. E. Churchill, P. Schmid, L. R. Berger 2011 "*Australopithecus sediba* Hand Demonstrates Mosaic Evolution of Locomotor and Manipulative Abilities." *Science* **333**(6048): 1411–1417.

Klar A. J. 2003 "Human Handedness and Scalp Hair-Whorl Direction Develop from a Common Genetic Mechanism." *Genetics* **165**(1): 269–276.

Kordos, L., D. R. Begun 1997 "A New Reconstruction of RUD77, a Partial Cranium of *Dryopithecus brancoi* from Rudabanya, Hungary." *Am J Phys Anthropol* **103**: 227–294.

Krogman, W. M. 1962 *The Human Skeleton in Forensic Medicine.* Springfield, IL: Charles C. Thomas.

Krogman, W. M., M. Y. Iscan 1986 *The Human Skeleton in Forensic Medicine* (2nd ed.). Springfield, IL: Charles C. Thomas.

Kunimatsu, Y., M. Nakatsukasa, Y. Sawada, T. Sakai, M. Hyodo, H. Hyodo, et al. 2007 "A New Late Miocene Great Ape from Kenya and Its Implications for the Origins of African Great Apes and Humans." *PNAS Proc Natl Acad Sci USA* **104**(49): 19220–19225.

Lalueza-Fox, C., A. Rosas, A. Estalrrich, E. Gigli, P. F. Campos, A. Garcia-Tabernero, et al. 2011 "Genetic Evidence for Patrilocal Mating Behavior among Neandertal Groups." *Proc Natl Acad Sci USA* **108**(1): 250–253.

Lamendin, H., E. Baccino, J. F. Humbert, J. C. Tavernier, R. M. Nossintchouk, A. Zerilli 1992 "A Simple Technique for Age Estimation in Adult Corpses: The Two Criteria Dental Method." *J Foren Sci* **37**: 1373–1379.

Lamichhaney, S., J. Berglund, M. Sallman Almen, K. Maqbool, M. Grabherr, A. Martinez-Barrio, et al. 2015 "Evolution of Darwin's Finches and Their Beaks Revealed by Genome Sequencing." *Nature* **518**: 371–375.

Lartet, E. 1856 "Note Sur la Decouverte Recent d'un Machoire de Singes Superieurs." *C R Acad Sci Paris* 43.

Latimer, B., C. O. Lovejoy 1990a "Hallucal Tarsometatarsal Joint in *Australopithecus afarensis*." *Am J Phys Anthropol* **83**: 135–143.

Latimer, B., C. O. Lovejoy 1990b "Metatarsophalangeal Joints of *Australopithecus afarensis*." *Am J Phys Anthropol* **83**: 13–23.

Leakey, L. S. B., P. V. Tobias, J. R. Napier 1964 "A New Species of the Genus *Homo* from Olduvai Gorge." *Nature* **202**: 7–9.

Leakey, R. E., M. G. Leakey, A. C. Walker 1988 "Morphology of *Afropithecus turkanensis* from Kenya." *Am J Phys Anthropol* **76**: 289–307.

Leakey, M. G., F. Spoor, F. H. Brown, et al. 2001 "New Hominin Genus from Eastern Africa Shows Diverse Middle Pliocene Lineages." *Nature* **410**: 433–440.

Lee, S. H. 2005 "Patterns of Size Sexual Dimorphism in *Australopithecus afarensis*: Another Look." *Homo* **56**(3): 219–232.

Lepre, C. J., D. V. Kent 2010 "New Magnetostratigraphy for the Olduvai Subchron in the Koobi for a Formation, Northwest Kenya, with Implications for Early *Homo*." *Earth Planet. Sci. Lett* **290**: 362–374.

Lordkipanidze, D., M. S. P. de Leon, A. Margvelashvili, et al. 2013 "A Complete Skull from Dmanisi, Georgia and the Evolutionary Biology of early *Homo*." *Science* **342**: 326–331.

Lovejoy, C. O. 2009 "Reexamining Human Origins in Light of *Ardipithecus ramidus*." *Science* **326**(5949): 74, 74e1–74e8.

Lovejoy, C. O., B. Latimer, G. Suwa, B. Asfaw, T. D. White 2009a "Combining the Prehension and Propulsion: The Foot of *Ardipithecus ramidus*." *Science* **326**(5949): 72, 72e1–72e8.

Lovejoy, C. O., R. S. Meindl, T. R. Pryzbeck, R. P. Mensforth 1985 "Chronological Metamorphosis of the Auricular Surface of the Ilium: A New Method for the Determination of Adult Skeletal Age at Death." *Am J Phys Anthropol* **68**: 15–28.

Lovejoy, C. O., S. W. Simpson, T. D. White, B. Asfaw, G. Suwa 2009b "Careful Climbing in the Miocene: The Forelimbs of *Ardipithecus ramidus* and Humans Are Primitive." *Science* **326**(5949): 70, 70e1–70e8.

Lovejoy, C. O., G. Suwa, S. W. Simpson, J. H. Matternes, T. D. White 2009c "The Great Divides: *Ardipithecus Ramidus* Reveals the Postcrania of Our Last Common Ancestors with African Apes." *Science* **326**(73): 100–106.

Lovejoy, C. O., G. Suwa, L. Spurlock, B. Asfaw, T. D. White 2009d "The Pelvis and Femur of *Ardipithecus ramidus*: The Emergence of Upright Walking." *Science* **326**(5949): 71, 71e1–71e6.

Macho, G. A., D. Shimizu, Y. Jiang, I. R. Spears 2005 "*Australopithecus anamensis*: A Finite-Element Approach to Studying the Functional Adaptations of Extinct Hominins." *Anat Rec A Discov Mol Cell Evol Biol* **283** (2): 310–318.

Maiolino, S., D. M. Boyer, J. I. Bloch, C. C. Gilbert, J. Groenke 2012 "Evidence for a Grooming Claw in a North American Adapiform Primate: Implications for Anthropoid Origins." *PLoS ONE* **7**: e29135.

Mangold, J. E., T. J. Payne, J. Z. Ma, G. Chen, M. D. Li 2008 "Bitter Taste Receptor Gene Polymorphisms Are an Important Factor in the Development of Nicotine Dependence in African Americans." *J Med Genet* **45**(9): 578–582.

Martin, N. G. 1975 "No Evidence for a Genetic Basis of Tongue Rolling or Hand Clasping." *J Hered* **66**: 179–180.

Martin, R., K. Saller 1957 *Lehrbuch der Anthropologie*. Stuttgart: Gustav Fischer.

Martrille, L., D. H. Ubelaker, C. Cattaneo, F. Seguret, M. Tremblay, E. Baccino 2007 "Comparison of Four Skeletal Methods for the Estimation of Age at Death on White and Black Adults." *J Foren Sci* **52**: 302–307.

Mayr, E. 1970 *Populations, Species and Evolution*. Cambridge, MA: Harvard University Press.

Mayr, E. 1981 "Biological Classification: Toward a Synthesis of Opposing Methodologies." *Science* **214**: 510–516.

McDougall, I., F. H. Brown, et al. 2005 "Stratigraphic Placement and Age of Modern Humans from Kibish, Ethiopia." *Nature* **433**(7027): 733–736.

McKern, T. W., T. D. Stewart 1957 "Skeletal Age Changes in Young American Males, Technical Report EP-45." Natick, MA: U.S. Army Quartermaster Research and Development Center.

Meyer, M., J-L. Arsuaga, C. de Filippo, S. Nagel, A. Aximu-Petri, B. Nichel, et al. 2016 "Nuclear DNA Sequences from the Middle Pleistocene Sima de los Huesos Hominins." *Nature* **531**: 504–507.

Miller, J. M. 2000 "Craniofacial Variation in *Homo habilis*: An Analysis of the Evidence for Multiple Species." *Am J Phys Anthropol* **112**(1): 103–128.

Moorjani, P., C. E. G. Amorim, P. F. Arndt, M. Przeworski 2016 "Variation in the Molecular Clock of Primates." *Proc Natl Acad Sci USA* **113**(38): 10607–10612.

Morwood, M. J., R. P. Suejono, R. G. Roberts, et al. 2004 "Archaeology and Age of a New Hominin from Flores in Eastern Indonesia." *Nature* **431**: 1087–1091.

Mourant, A. E. 1954 *The Distribution of the Human Blood Groups*. Oxford: Blackwell.

Mourant, A. E., A. C. Kopec, K. Domaniewska-Sobczak 1958 *The ABO Blood Groups*. Springfield, IL: Charles C. Thomas.

Mouri, T. 1976 "A Study of Non-Metrical Cranial Variants of the Modern Japanese in the Kinki District." *J Anthrop Soc Nippon* **84**: 191–203.

Nakatsukasa, M. 2004 "Acquisition of Bipedalism: The Miocene Hominoid Record and Modern Analogues for Bipedal Protohominids." *J Anat* **204** (5): 385–402.

Napier, J. R., A. C. Walker 1967 "Vertical Clinging and Leaping—A Newly Recognized Category of Primate Locomotion." *Folia Primatol* **6**: 204–219.

Olson, S. L., D. T. Rasmussen 1986 "Paleoenvironment of the Earliest Hominoids: New Evidence from the Oligocene Avi of Egypt." *Science* **233**: 1202–1204.

Olson, T. R. 1981 "Basicranial Morphology of Extant Hominoids and Pliocene Hominids: The New Material from the Hadar Formation, Ethiopia, and Its Significance in Early Human Evolution and Taxonomy." Pp. 99–128 in *Aspects of Human Evolution,* edited by C. B. Stringer. London: Taylor and Francis.

Ousley, S. 1995 "Should We Estimate Biological or Forensic Stature?" *J Forens Sci* **40** (6): 768–773.

Ousley, S. D., J. T. Hefner 2005 "The Statistical Determination of Ancestry." Proceedings of the 57th Annual Meeting of the American Academy of Forensic Sciences, February 21–26; New Orleans, LA. Colorado Springs, CO: American Academy of Forensic Sciences.

Partridge, T. C., D. E. Granger, M. W. Caffee, R. J. Clarke 2003 "Lower Pliocene Hominid Remains from Sterkfontein." *Science* 300 (5619): 607–612.

Perelman, P., W. E. Johnson, C. Roos, H. N. Seuanez, J. E. Horvath, M. A. M. Moreira, et al. 2011 "A Molecular Phylogeny of Living Primates." *PLoS Genet* 7(3): e1001342. Doi:10.1371/journal.pgen.1001342.

Pilbeam, D. 1984 "The Descent of Hominoids and Hominids." *Sci Am* 250: 84–96.

Plummer, T. 2004 "Flaked Stones and Old Bones: Biological and Cultural Evolution at the Dawn of Technology." *Am J Phys Anthropol Suppl* 39: 118–164.

Poux, C., O. Madsen, E. Marquard, D. R. Vieites, W. W. de Jong, M. Vences 2005 "Asynchronous Colonization of Madagascar by the Four Endemic Clades of Primates, Tenrecs, Carnivores, and Rodents as Inferred from Nuclear Genes." *Syst Biol* 54 (5): 719–730.

Preuschoft, H. 2004 "Mechanisms for the Acquisition of Habitual Bipedality: Are There Biomechanical Reasons for the Acquisition of Upright Bipedal Posture?" *J Anat* 204 (5): 363–384.

Prince, D. A., D. H. Ubelaker 2002 "Application of Lamendin's Adult Aging Technique to a Diverse Skeletal Sample." *J Foren Sci* 47: 107–116.

Prüfer, K., F. Racimo, N. Patterson, F. Jay, Sankararaman, S. Sawyer et al. 2013 "The Complete Genome Sequence of a Neanderthal from the Altai Mountains." *Nature* 505: 43–49.

Qin, P., M. Stoneking 2015 "Denisovan Ancestry in East Eurasian and Native American Populations." *Mol Biol Evol* 32(10): 2665–2674.

Rae, T. C. 2004 "Miocene Hominoid Craniofacial Morphology and the Emergence of Great Apes." *Ann Anat* 186 (5–6): 417–241.

Rak, Y., A. Ginzburg, E. Geffen 2007 "Gorilla-Like Anatomy on *Australopithecus Afarensis* Mandibles Suggests *Au. Afarensis* Link to Robust Australopiths." *Proc Natl Acad Sci USA* 104(16): 6568–6572.

Rasmussen, D. T., G. C. Conroy, E. L. Simons 1998 "Tarsier-Like Locomotor Specializations in the Oligocene Primate Afrotarsius." *Proc Natl Acad Sci USA* 95(25): 14848–14850.

Reichs, K. J. (ed.) 1997 *Forensic Osteology: Advances in the Identification of Human Remains.* Springfield, IL: Charles C. Thomas.

Richards, M. P., P. B. Pettitt, E. Trinkaus, F. H. Smith, M. Paunovic, I. Karavanic 2000 "Neanderthal Diet at Vindija and Neanderthal Predation: The Evidence from Stable Isotopes." *Proc Natl Acad Sci USA* 97(13): 7663–7666.

Richmond, B. G., W. L. Jungers 2008 "*Orrorin tugenensis* Femoral Morphology and the Evolution of Hominin Bipedalism." *Science* 319(5870): 1662–1665.

Rightmire, G. P. 1998 "Human Evolution in the Middle Pleistocene: The Role of *Homo heidelbergensis.*" *Evol Anthr* 6: 218–227.

Rightmire, G. P. 2004 "Brain Size and Encephalization in Early to Mid-Pleistocene Homo." *Am J Phys Anthropol* 124(2): 109–123.

Rightmire, G. P., D. Lordkipanidze, A. Vekua 2006 "Anatomical Descriptions, Comparative Studies and Evolutionary Significance of the Hominin Skulls from Dmanisi, Republic of Georgia." *J Hum Evol* 50(2): 115–141.

Roede, M. J., J. C. Van Wieringen 1985 "Growth Diagrams 1980—Netherlands Third Nation-Wide Survey." *Tijdschr Soc Geneeskd* 63(Suppl 1): 1–34.

Roos, C., J. Schmitz, H. Zischler 2004 "Primate Jumping Genes Elucidate Strepsirrhine Phylogeny." *Proc Natl Acad Sci USA* 101: 10650–10654.

Rose, M. D. 1983 "Miocene Hominoid Postcranial Morphology: Monkey-like, Ape-Like, Neither or Both?" Pp. 405–417 in *New Interpretations of Ape and Human Ancestry,* edited by R. Ciochon and R. Corruccini. New York: Plenum.

Rosenberg, K. R., L. Zune, C. B. Ruff 2006 "Body Size, Body Proportions, and Encephalization in a Middle Pleistocene Archaic Human from Northern China." *Proc Natl Acad Sci USA* 103(10): 3552–3556.

Ross, C. F. 2000 "Into the Light: The Origin of Anthropoidea." *Ann Rev Anthropol* 29: 147–194.

Rossie, J. D., L. Maclatchy 2006 "A New Pliopithecoid Genus from the Early Miocene of Uganda." *J Hum Evol* 50(5): 568–586.

Rossie, J. B., X. Ni, K. C. Beard 2006 "Cranial Remains of an Eocene Tarsier." *Proc Natl Acad Sci USA* 103(12): 4381–4385.

Ruff, C. 2009 "Relative Limb Strength and Locomotion in *Homo habilis.*" *Am J Phys Anthropol* 138(1): 90–100.

Sanchez-Quinto, F., C. Lalueza-Fox 2015 "Almost 20 Years of Neanderthal Palaeogenetics: Adaptation, Admixture, Diversity, Demography and Extinction." *Philos Trans R Soc Lond B Biol Sci* 370(1660): 20130374.

Sankararaman, S., S. Mallick, N. Patterson, D. Reich 2016 "The Combined Landscape of Denisovan and Neanderthal Ancestry in Present-Day Humans." *Curr Biol* 26(9): 1241–1247.

Sargis, E. J., D. M. Boyer, J. I. Bloch, M. T. Silcox 2007 "Evolution of Pedal Grasping in Primates." *J Hum Evol* 53(1):103–7.

Sarmiento, E. E. 2010 "Comment on the Paleobiology and Classification of *Ardipithecus ramidus.*" *Science* 328(5982): 1105.

Saunders, S. R., M. A. Katzenberg (eds.) 1992 *Skeletal Biology of Past Peoples: Research Methods.* New York: Wiley-Liss.

Schaefer, M., S. Black, L. Scheuer 2009 *Juvenile Osteology: A Laboratory and Field Manual.* London: Elsevier.

Scheuer, L., S. Black 2000 *Developmental Juvenile Osteology.* New York: Academic.

Schultz, A. H. 1937 "Proportions, Variability and Asymmetries of the Long Bones of the Limbs and the Clavicles in Man and Apes." *Hum Biol* 9: 281–328.

Schultz, A. H. 1973 "The Recent Hominoid Primates." In *The Origin and Evolution of Man: Readings in Physical Anthropology,* edited by A. Montagu. New York: Thomas Y. Crowell.

Seiffert, E. R., E. L. Simons, T. M. Ryan, Y. Attia 2005 "Additional Remains of *Wadilemur elegans,* a Primitive Stem Galagid from the Late Eocene of Egypt." *Proc Natl Acad Sci USA* 102(32): 11396–11401.

Seiffert, E. R. J. M. G. Perry, E. L. Simons, D. M. Boyer 2009 "Convergent Evolution of Anthropoid-Like Adaptations in Eocene Adapiform Primates." *Nature* 461: 1118–1121.

Seiffert, E. R., E. L. Simons, D. M. Boyer, et al. 2010 "A Fossil Primate of Uncertain Affinities from the Earliest Late Eocene of Egypt." *Proceedings of the National Academy of Sciences USA* 107: 9712–9717.

Semaw, S., S. W. Simpson, J. Quade, et al. 2005 "Early Pliocene Hominids from Gona, Ethiopia." *Nature* 433(7023): 301–305.

Senut, B. 2002 "From Apes to Humans: Locomotion as a Key Feature for Phylogeny." *Z Morphol Anthropol* 83(2–3): 351–360.

Silcox, M. T. 2003 "New Discoveries on the Middle Ear Anatomy of *Ignacius graybullianus* (Paromomyidae, Primates) from Ultra High Resolution X-Ray Computed Tomography." *J Hum Evol* 44(1): 73–86.

Simons, E. L. 1990 "Discovery of the Oldest Known Anthyropoidean Skull from the Paleogene of Egypt." *Science* 247: 1567–1569.

Simons, E. L. 1995 "The Fossil History of Primates." Pp. 199–208 in *The Cambridge Encyclopedia of Human Evolution,* edited by S. Jones, R. Martin, and D. Pilbeam. Cambridge, UK: Cambridge University Press.

Simons, E. L. 1998 "The Prosimian Fauna of the Fayum Eocene/Oligocene Deposits of Egypt." *Folia Primatol* 69 (Suppl 1): 286–294.

Simons, E. L. 2001 "The Cranium of *Parapithecus grangeri,* an Egyptian Oligocene Anthropoidean Primate." *Proc Natl Acad Sci USA* 98(14): 7892–7897.

Simons, E. L., T. M. Bown 1985 "*Afrotarsius chatrathi,* 1st Tarsiiform Primate (Questionable Tarsiidae) from Africa." *Nature* 313: 475–477.

Simpson, S. W., J. Quade, et al. 2008 "A Female *Homo Erectus erectus* Pelvis from Gona, Ethiopia." *Science* 322: 1089–1092.

Smith, F. H., J. C. M. Ahern, I. Jankovic, I. Karavanic 2016 "The Assimilation Model of Modern Human Origins in Light of Current Genetic and Genomic Knowledge." *Quaternary International* 137(1): 7–19.

Smith, F. H., A. B. Falsetti, et al. 1989 "Modern Human Origins." *Yearbook of Physical Anthropology* 32: 35–68.

Smith, T. M., L. B. Martin, D. J. Reid, L. de Bonis, G. D. Koufos 2004 "An Examination of Dental Development in *Graecopithecus freybergi* (=*Ouranopithecus macedoniensis*)." *J Hum Evol* 46: 551–577.

Spoor, F., P. Gunz, S. Neubauer, S. Stelzer, N. Scott, A. Kwekason, M. C. Dean 2015 "Reconstructed *Homo habilis* Type OH 7 Suggests Deep-Rooted Species Diversity in Early *Homo.*" *Nature* 519: 83–86.

Spoor F., M. G. Leakey, P. N. Gathogo, F. H. Brown, S. C. Antón, I. McDougall, et al. 2007 "Implications of New Early *Homo* Fossils from Ileret, East of Lake Turkana, Kenya." *Nature* 448(7154):688–91.

Springer, M. S., J. Gatesy 2016 "The Gene Tree Delusion" *Mol Phylogenet Evol* 94: 1–33, Part A.

Stedman, H. H., B. W. Kozyak, A. Nelson, D. M. Thesier, et al. 2004 "Myosin Gene Mutation Correlates with Anatomical Changes in the Human Lineage." *Nature* 428: 415–418.

Steiper, M. E., N. M. Young 2006 "Primate Molecular Divergence Dates." *Molecular Phylogenetics and Evolution* 41(2): 384–394.

Steiper, M. E., N. M. Young 2008 "Timing Primate Evolution: Lessons from the Discordance between Molecular and Paleontological Estimates." *Evolutionary Anthropology* 17: 179–188.

Steiper, M. E., N. M. Young, T. Y. Sukarna 2004 "Oligocene Estimate for the Hominoid-Cercopithecoid Divergence." *Proc Natl Acad Sci USA* 101(49): 17021–17026.

Stout, S. D., R. R. Paine 1992 "Histological Age Estimation Using Rib and Clavicle." *Am J Phys Anthropol* **87**: 111–115.

Strachan, T., A. Read 2004 *Human Molecular Genetics* (3rd ed.). New York: Garland Publishing.

Strait, D. S., Grine F. E. 2004 "Inferring Hominoid and Early Hominid Phylogeny Using Craniodental Characters: The Role of Fossil Taxa." *J Hum Evol* **47**(6): 399–452.

Stringer, C. 1995 "Evolution of Early Humans." Pp. 241–251 in *The Cambridge Encyclopedia of Human Evolution,* edited by S. Jones, R. Martin, and D. Pilbeam. Cambridge, UK: Cambridge University Press.

Stringer, C. B., P. Andrews 1988 "Genetic and Fossil Evidence for the Origin of Modern Humans." *Science* **239**(4845): 1263–1268.

Suchey, J. M., S. T. Brooks, R. D. Rawson 1982 "Aging the Female *Os Pubis*." American Academy of Forensic Sciences, Annual Meeting, Orlando, Florida.

Suchey, J. M., D. Katz 1998 "Applications of Pubic Age Determination in a Forensic Setting." Pp. 204–236 in *Forensic Osteology: Advances in the Identification of Human Remains,* edited by K. J. Reichs. Springfield, IL: C. C Thomas.

Suchey, J. M., D. V. Wisely, D. Katz 1986 "Evaluation of the Todd and McKern-Stewart Methods for Aging the Male Os Pubis." Pp. 33–67 in *Forensic Osteology: Advances in the Identification of Human Remains,* edited K. J. Reichs. Springfield, IL: C. C Thomas.

Suchey, J. M., D. V. Wiseley, R. F. Green, T. T. Noguchi 1979 "Analysis of Dorsal Pitting in the Os Pubis in an Extensive Sample of Modern American Females." *Am J Phys Anthropol* **51**(4): 517–540.

Susman, R. L., J. T. Stern, W. L. Jungers 1984 "Arboreality and Bipedality in the Hadar Hominids." *Folia Primatol* **43**: 113–156.

Sussman, R. W. 1991 "Primate Origins and the Evolution of Angiosperms." *Am J Primatol* **23**: 209–223.

Sutherland, L. D., J. M. Suchey 1991 "Use of the Ventral Arc in Pubic Sex Determination." *J Foren Sci* **36**: 501–511.

Sutikna, T., M. W. Tocheri, M. J. Morwood, E. W. Saptomo, Jatmiko, R. Due Awe, et al. 2016 "Revised Stratigraphy and Chronology for *Homo floresiensis* at Lian Bua in Indonesia." *Nature* **532**: 366–369.

Suwa, G., B. Asfaw, R. T. Kono, D. Kubo, C. O. Lovejoy, T. D. White 2009a "The *Ardipithecus ramidus* Skull and Its Implications for Hominid Origins." *Science* **326**(5949): 68e1–68e7.

Suwa, G., R. T. Kono, S. W. Simpson, B. Asfaw, C. O. Lovejoy, T. D. White 2009b "Paleobiological Implications of the *Ardipithecus ramidus* Dentition." *Science* **326**(5949): 94–99.

Szalay, F. S. 2000 "Eosimiidae" in *Encyclopedia of Human Evolution and Prehistory* (2nd ed.), edited by E. Delson, I. Tattersall, J. A. Van Couvering, and A. S. Brooks. New York: Garland.

Szalay, F. S., E. Delson 1979 *Evolutionary History of the Primates.* New York: Academic.

Tabuce, R., L. Marivaux, R. Lebrun, M. Adaci, M. Bensalah, P. Fabre, et al. 2009 "Anthropoid versus Strepsirhine Status of the African Eocene Primates *Algeripithecus* and *Azibius*: Craniodental Evidence." Proceedings of the Royal Society B. December 7, 2009; 276:4087–4094; published online before print September 9, 2009 (doi:10.1098/rspb.2009.133).

Tanner, J. M. 1962 *Growth at Adolescence* (2nd ed.). Oxford: Blackwell Scientific.

Tanner, J. M. 1978 *Foetus into Man—Physical Growth from Conception to Maturity.* London: Open Books.

Tarling, D. 1980 "The Geologic Evolution of South America with Special Reference to the Last 200 Million Years." Pp. 1–41 in *Evolutionary Biology of the New World Monkeys and Continental Drift,* edited by R. Ciochon and A. Chiarelli. New York: Plenum.

Thewissen, J. G., S. T. Hussain, M. Arif 1997 "New Kohatius (Omomyidae) from the Eocene of Pakistan." *J Hum Evol* **32**(5): 473–477.

Tiemel, Chen, Yang Quan, Wu En 1994 "Antiquity of *Homo sapiens* in China." *Nature* **368**: 55–56.

Todd, T. W. 1920–21 "Age Changes in the Pubic Bone." *Am J Phys Anthropol* **3**: 285–334; **4**: 1–70.

Turanov, A. A., A. V. Lobanov, D. E. Fomenko, H. G. Morrison, M. L. Sogin, L. A. Klobutcher, et al. 2009 "Genetic Code Supports Targeted Insertion of Two Amino Acids by One Codon." *Science* **323**(5911): 259–261.

Ubelaker, D. 1999 *Human Skeletal Remains: Excavation, Analysis, Interpretation* (3rd ed.). Taraxacum Press.

Van den Bergh, G. D., Y. Kaifu, I. Kurniawan, R. T. Kono, A. Brumm, E. Setiyabudi, et al. 2016 "*Homo floresiensis*-like Fossils from the Early Middle Pleistocene of Flores." *Nature* **534**: 245–248.

Vekua, A., D. Lordkipanidze, G. P. Rightmire, et al. 2002 "A New Skull of Early *Homo* From Dmanisi, Georgia." *Science* **297**(5578): 85–89.

Vignaud, P., P. Duringer, H. T. Mackaye, et al. 2002 "Geology and Palaeontology of the Upper Miocene Toros-Menalla Hominid Locality, Chad." *Nature* **418**: 152–155.

Villmoare, B., W. H. Kimbel, C. Seyoum, C. J. Campisano, E. N. DiMaggio, J. Rowan, et al. 2015 "Early Homo at 2.8 Ma from Ledi-Geraru, Afar, Ethiopia." *Science* **347** (6228): 1352–1355.

Walker, A., R. E. Leakey, J. M. Harris, F. H. Brown 1986 "2.5-M.yr. *Australopithecus boisei* from West of Lake Turkana, Kenya." *Nature* **322**: 517–522.

Wang, W., R. H. Crompton 2004 "The Role of Load-Carrying in the Evolution of Modern Body Proportions." *J Anat* **204**(5): 417–430.

Wang, W., R. H. Crompton, T. S. Carey, et al. 2004 "Comparison of Inverse-Dynamics Musculo-Skeletal Models of AL 288-1 *Australopithecus afarensis* and KNM-WT 15000 *Homo ergaster* to Modern Humans, with Implications for the Evolution of Bipedalism." *J Hum Evol* **47**(6): 453–478.

Ward, C. V., M. G. Leakey, A. Walker 2001 "Morphology of *Australopithecus anamensis* from Kanapoi and Allia Bay, Kenya." *J Hum Evol* **41**(4): 255–368.

Webb, P. A., J. M. Suchey 1985 "Epiphyseal Union of the Anterior Iliac Crest and Medial Clavicle in a Modern Multiracial Sample of American Males and Females." *Am J Phys Anthropol* **68**(4): 457–466.

Weber, J., A. Czarnetzki, C. M. Pusch 2005 "Comment on the Brain of LB1, *Homo floresiensis*." *Science* **310**(5746): 236.

Weiner, J. 1995 *The Beak of the Finch.* Vintage Books, New York.

White, T. D., B. Asfaw, et al. 2003 "Pleistocene *Homo sapiens* from Middle Awash, Ethiopia." *Nature* **423**(6941): 742–747.

White, T. D. B. Asfaw, Y. Beyene, Y. Haile-Selassie, C. O. Lovejoy, G. Suwa, 2009 "*Ardipithecus ramidus* and the Paleobiology of Early Hominids." *Science* **326**(5949): 64, 75–86.

White, T. D., G. WoldeGrabriel, B. Asfaw, S. Ambrose, Y. Beyene, R. L. Bernor, et al. 2006 "Asa Issie, Aramis and the Origin of *Australopithecus*." *Nature* **440**(7086): 883–889.

Wild, E. M., M. Teschler-Nicola, W. Kutschera, P. Steier, E. Trinkaus, W. Wanek 2005 "Direct Dating of Early Upper Paleolithic Human Remains from Mladec." *Nature* **435**(7040): 332–335.

Wildman, D. E., M. Uddin, G. Liu, L. I. Grossman, M. Goodman 2003 "Implications of Natural Selection in Shaping 99.4% Nonsynonymous DNA Identity between Humans and Chimpanzees: Enlarging Genus *Homo*." *Proc Natl Acad Sci USA* **100**: 7181–7188.

Wolpoff, M. H. 1989 "Multiregional Evolution: The Fossil Alternative to Eden." Pp. 62–108 in *The Human Revolution,* edited by P. Mellars and C. B. Stringer. Princeton, NJ: Princeton University Press.

Wolpoff, M., A. G. Thorne, et al. 1994 "Multiregional Evolutions: A World-Wide Source for Modern Human Populations." Pp. 175–199 in *Origins of Anatomically Modern Humans,* edited by M. H. Nitecki and D. V. Nitecki. New York: Plenum Press.

Wolpoff, M. H., et al. 2001 "Modern Human Ancestry at the Peripheries: A Test of the Replacement Theory." *Science* **291**: 293–297.

Wood, B. 2014 "Human Evolution: Fifty Years after *Homo habilis*." *Nature* **508**(7494): 31–33.

Wood, B. A., P. Constantino 2007 "*Paranthropus boisei*: Fifty Years of Evidence and Analysis." *Yearb Phy Anthropol* **50**: 106–132.

Wu, X., L. A. Schepartz, D. Falk, W. Liu 2006 "Endocranial Cast of Hexian *Homo erectus* from South China." *Am J Phys Anthropol,* January 19 Epub ahead of print.

Xijun Ni, D. L. Gebo, M. Dagosto, et al. 2013 "The Oldest Known Primate Skeleton and Early Haplorhine Evolution." *Nature* **498**: 60–64.

Xu, Q., Q. Lu 2007 *Series Monograph III: Lufengpithecus—An Early Member of Hominidae.* Beijing: Science Press.

Yoshiura, K., A. Kinoshita, T. Ishida, A. Ninokata, T. Ishikawa, T. Kaname, et al. 2006 "A SNP in the ABCC11 Gene Is the Determinant of Human Earwax Type." *Nat Genet* **38**(3): 324–30.

Zalmout, I. S., W. J. Sanders, L. M. MacLatchy, G. F. Gunnell, Y. A. Al-Mufarrreh, et al. 2010 "New Oligocene Primate from Saudi Arabia and the Divergence of Apes and Old World Monkeys." *Nature* **466**: 360–364.

Index

In this index *f* indicates figure and *t* indicates table.

A

A (*see* adenine (A))
ABFA (*See* American Board of Forensic Anthropology (ABFA))
abnormalities in the skeleton, 347–366
  anomalies, 356, 357f
  arthritis, 355f
  blood-supply problems, 351
  blunt trauma, 353
  cancer, 351, 351f
  cranial modifications, 359–360
  cut marks, 356–357
  degenerative joint disease, 354–355
  dental modifications, 360–361, 362f
  developmental problems, 351–352
  dislocations, 355–356, 356f
  fractures, 353–354, 357–358
  gunshot wounds, 357, 357f
  healing of bone, 357–358
  infection, 348–351
  intentional modification, 358–362
  osteophytes, 355, 355f
  osteoporosis, 354, 354f
  postcranial modifications, 360, 361f
  postmortem modifications, 362, 362f
  sharp injury, 356–357
ABO blood group system, 53–54
acetabulum, 108, 108f
Acheulian hand ax, 302, 302f
achilles area, 182f
acquired immunodeficiency syndrome (AIDS), 31
acrocentric, 12f
acromion process, 101, 101f
ad-lib sampling, 235
adapids, 253–254
Adapis, 253–254, 255f, 261f
Adapoidea, 252–254
adaptive radiation, 67
adenine (A), 11, 12f
adolescent growth spurt, 147
Aegyptopithecus, 260, 263f, 276f
Aegyptopithecus mandible, 260, 260f
Afradapis, 254
African American male/female, 405f
Afrotarsius, 258
age determination, 377–396
  auricular surface of ilium, 387–388
  dental eruption chart, 379f
  dental wear, 396

ectocranial and endocranial suture closure, 378, 382
Harnett pubic age determination, 387t
Lamendin technique for estimating age from dentition, 388
old age, 394–395
pubic symphysis, 382–383, 384–387
rib phases, 383, 387, 388–394
seriation, 396
skeletal age (ossification centers/epiphyseal fusion), 380–382t
subadults, 378
Suchey-Brooks pubic age determination, 386, 387t
agglutination, 53
AIDS (*see* acquired immunodeficiency syndrome (AIDS))
alanine, 23t
Algeripithecus, 256
Algeripithecus minutus, 256
allele, 36
allele frequencies, 71
Altiatlasius, 251
alveolare, 330
AM *Homo sapiens* (*see* anatomically modern (AM) *Homo sapiens*)
ameloblasts, 143
American Board of Forensic Anthropology (ABFA), 406
amino acids, 21
amphiarthrosis, 79
amphipithecids, 253
anatomically modern (AM) *Homo sapiens,* 305–308
ancestry, determination of, 396–405
  African American male/female, 405f
  Australian male/female, 403f
  Eskimo male, 402f
  European male/female, 401f
  Japanese male/female, 404f
  Mongolian male/female, 400f
  Native American, 399f
  New Britain male, 402f
  skull, 398t
anemia, 351
anencephaly, 352, 352f
ankle, 112–113, 114f
annealing, 27
anomalies, 356, 357f

Anthropoidea, 154t, 158, 160f
anthropoids, 157, 255–256, 258
anthropometer rod, 318
anthropometry, nonmetric traits, etc.
  (*see* measurements and indices)
antibodies, 53
antigens, 53
Apidium, 259, 259f
arboreal theory, 246
arch, 343, 344f
archaic *Homo sapiens,* 304–306
Archicebus achilles, 255
Ardipithecus kadabba, 274
Ardipithecus ramidus, 274, 280–281
arginine, 23t
arm length, 319, 319f
arthritis, 355f, 394
articulation, 79
artificial selection, 58
ascending ramus, 93f, 94
asparagine, 23t
aspartic acid, 23t
assimilation theory, 306
assortative mating, 67
Atelidae, 160f
Ateloidea, 160f
atlas, 97, 97f
Australian male/female, 403f
Australopithecus, 281, 309f
Australopithecus afarensis, 282–284
Australopithecus afarensis mandible, 283f
Australopithecus afarensis maxilla, 283f
Australopithecus afarensis pedal phalanges, 284f
Australopithecus africanus, 286–287, 288f, 289f, 310f
Australopithecus africanus: Taung, 286f
Australopithecus africanus: Taung mandible, 286f
Australopithecus anamensis, 282, 282f
Australopithecus boisei, maxilla, 286f
Australopithecus deyiremeda, 284
Australopithecus garhi, 285
Australopithecus sediba, 287–288
Australopithecus sediba hand, 287f
australopiths, 281–286
autosomal mutation, 63
autosomes, 11
axis, 97, 97f